COVENANT & CONVERSATION
A WEEKLY READING OF THE JEWISH BIBLE
LEVITICUS: THE BOOK OF HOLINESS

Other works by the author

Rabbi Jonathan Sacks

COVENANT &
CONVERSATION
A Weekly Reading of the Jewish Bible

LEVITICUS: THE BOOK OF HOLINESS

Maggid Books & The Orthodox Union

Covenant & Conversation
Leviticus: The Book of Holiness

First Edition, 2015

Maggid Books
An imprint of Koren Publishers Jerusalem Ltd.

POB 8531, New Milford, CT 06776-8531, USA
& POB 4044, Jerusalem 9104001, Israel
www.korenpub.com

Cover image: The Tribes of Israel Reunited
around the Ark of the Covenant in the Sinai Desert,
after the Exodus from Egypt / Bridgeman Images

The publication of this book was made possible
through the generous support of *Torah Education in Israel*.

ISBN 978-1-59264-022-5, *hardcover*

A CIP catalogue record for this title is
available from the British Library

Printed and bound in the United States

This publication was made possible with the kind support of the
Lee and Cheryl Lasher Family Foundation

Dedicated to our loving parents

Peggy and Philip Zimmerman
Doreen Casella and Howard Lasher

to our dear children

Gabrielle, David, and Jake

*and to all those who taught us Torah in thought and deed,
enriching our lives forever.*

Conversation *and connection inspires,
but it all starts with cherishing the* **Covenant.**

With love,
Cheryl & Lee Lasher
Englewood, NJ, USA

This publication was made possible with the kind support of the
Raphael and Linda Benaroya Foundation

לעילוי נשמת

בננו יקירנו מחמד לבנו
דוד ז״ל **בן רפאל ולינדה (יפה)** הי״ו
נלב״ע י״ג כסלו תשס״ח

מו״ר אבינו
יעקב בן רפאל וז׳ולי ז״ל
נלב״ע י״ז אב תשס״ה

מרת אמנו
רחל בת יום טוב ורוזה ז״ל
נלב״ע כ״ו אדר תשס״ז

In loving memory of

Our beloved Son
David ben Raphael and Linda

Our beloved Father
Yaakov ben Raphael and Julie

Our beloved Mother
Rachel bat Yom Tov and Rosa

Contents

vii

Leviticus: The Democratisation of Holiness

God's Call

Of all the Mosaic books, *Vayikra*, Leviticus, is the one most out of step with contemporary culture. Many find it difficult to relate to its concerns. It opens with an account of sacrifices, something we have not experienced for close to two millennia. Its preoccupation with ritual purity and defilement seems to come from another age, and with the exception of the menstrual cycle, has little contemporary application. The long account of *tzaraat*, usually translated as leprosy, is a good example of the difficulties the text poses. Are we talking about a disease, a defilement, or a punishment, and how, in any case, is it relevant to a spiritual life and our relationship with God?

Little happens in Leviticus. There is not much narrative and the little that does exist is troubling. Two of Aaron's sons, Nadav and Avihu, die on the day of the consecration of the Tabernacle simply, it seems, because of an act of misplaced enthusiasm. Even when Leviticus speaks about ethics, it does so in a perplexing way. The great chapter 19, with its majestic summons – "Be holy, for I the Lord your God am holy" – mixes moral imperatives with ritual and seemingly irrational commands, like the prohibition against wearing clothes of mixed wool and linen, in a way that challenges conventional ideas of logic and coherence. The

1

mindset of Leviticus is far removed from that of secular culture in the West in the twenty-first century.

Yet Leviticus is a – perhaps even the – key text of Judaism. It is here that we read for the first time the command to "Love your neighbour as yourself." It is the source of the even greater moral principle, "You shall love [the stranger] as yourself, for you were strangers in Egypt." It is Leviticus that forbids us to take vengeance or bear a grudge, taking a stand against the psychopathology of hatred and violence. It contains one of the most remarkable of all religious ideas, that we are summoned to be holy because God is holy. Not only are we created in God's image. We are called on to act in God's ways.

At a more practical but no less profound level, Leviticus sets out an entire infrastructure for justice and equity in political and economic life. It is Leviticus that sets out the parameters for employer-employee relationships. It humanises slavery and sets in motion a process that must end in its abolition, however long it takes. It speaks about debt relief and the return of ancestral land in the Jubilee year. This is the text that inspired the modern-day programme of international debt relief known as Jubilee 2000.

When the Americans rang out the message of freedom in 1776 by sounding the Liberty Bell in Philadelphia, they were expressing the mood of the verse engraved on the bell, Leviticus 25:10, in the translation of the King James Bible: "Proclaim liberty throughout all the land unto all the inhabitants thereof."

Leviticus is the central book of the Pentateuch, the Torah. This makes it the most important of the five. Biblical literature often works on the principle of mirror-image symmetry (chiasmus), structured in the form of ABCBA. In any work so patterned, the climax is not at the beginning or the end but in the middle. At the centre of the five Mosaic books, Leviticus is the axis on which they turn.

It is also the purest expression of one of the most important voices in the Torah, the priestly voice, the sensibility the sages call (it is their original name for the book) *Torat Kohanim*, "The Law of the Priests." We hear this voice elsewhere at key points in the Torah. One is the first chapter of Genesis 1 – "In the beginning God created" – which describes creation in the language of the priest. Another is Exodus 19:6, just before the revelation at Mount Sinai, with its mission statement of the Jewish people: "You shall be to Me a kingdom of priests and a holy nation." This is a priestly vocation. Despite the importance of the prophets to the religion of Israel, it is to the role of priest, not prophet, that God summoned our ancestors and summons us. The very name given by tradition to the Mosaic books – Torah – is a priestly word.

Leviticus was the book with which Jewish education traditionally began. For many centuries, as far back as Talmudic times, it was the first text Jewish children studied, their introduction to the word and will of God. "Let the pure come and study purity," say the sages. They want this above others to be the book first engraved on Jewish minds and inscribed in Jewish hearts. Again this is odd when we consider the rabbis' view of their own provenance, the opening line of Mishna Avot: "Moses received the Torah from Sinai and handed it on to Joshua, Joshua to the elders, and the elders to the prophets." The rabbis see themselves as heirs not to the priests but to the prophets. In truth, they were a creative synthesis of both.

It will be my argument that you cannot understand Judaism without the priestly voice. Judaism, from the Torah onward, is a conversation scored for many voices. Why this is so I will explain below, but that it is so is undeniable. It is this internal diversity, this complex harmony and occasional discord, that gives Judaism its dynamism, its ability to defeat entropy, the rule that says that all systems lose energy over time. Among the Torah's voices, the priestly sensibility is the dominant one, despite the fact that Moses, the dominant figure from Exodus to Deuteronomy, was not a priest.

It is this sensibility that communicated the absolute and austere monotheism that made Judaism unique in the ancient world and singular even today. It insists on the total difference between humans and God, but it also knows how to bridge it by aligning our will with His. It is the priestly voice that tells us that human beings are created in the image of God. It speaks of the integrity of difference and the importance of respecting it. It takes abstract ideals and turns them into codes of behaviour that transform lives. The book of Leviticus is a sustained meditation on what holiness is and how it can be translated into life. Indeed it is the priestly voice that identifies God with life and refuses to consecrate death.

Torat Kohanim wrestles with some of the deepest questions of religion. How, in a finite world, can we relate to an infinite God who cannot be identified with any natural phenomenon, who can neither be seen nor visually represented? At a quite different level, how can we take the fire of religious inspiration and turn it into an everlasting flame? How can we recapture "peak experiences" on a regular basis? And how can we take a way of life for the few and make it the possession of the many?

Leviticus is a precisely structured book, divided into three parts. The first is about the holy. Specifically, it is about sacrifices, and more generally, about how to come close to God in the house of God. The second part is set at the boundary between the holy and the world. It is about the things that prevent us from entering sacred space. The third is about taking the holy into the world. The book begins with an elite, the priests, sons of Aaron, a minority within a minority, one specific family within the tribe of Levi. It culminates in a call from God to the entire nation. It begins in the Sanctuary but ends in society. It democratises *kedusha*, holiness, the sign of God's presence, so that it becomes part of the ongoing life of the people as a whole.

Historically, this was taken further still after the destruction of the Second Temple, when prayer replaced sacrifice, repentance substituted for the service of the High Priest on the Day of Atonement, and Torah knowledge, originally a speciality of the priest, became a normative expectation of the people as a whole. *Torat Kohanim*, the Law of the Priests, became what Rabbi Joseph Soloveitchik called *ish hahalakha*, the halakhic personality.

Because of the difficulty we have in relating to Leviticus, I have made the introduction longer than for the other volumes of this series. In the pages that follow, I explain the key concepts of the book: holiness, purity, and sacrifice. I explain the concept of a "voice" within Torah, and why there is more than one. I analyse what makes the priestly voice different from those of kings and prophets. I also explain why the priestly voice, transmuted through time, is essential to Judaism and why without it neither Jews nor Judaism would have survived.

Names matter, and I have for the most part preferred to call the book by its traditional name, *Vayikra*. Leviticus, which means "matters pertaining to the Levites," was the Latin-equivalent translation of *Torat*

Kohanim, "the law of the priests." But tradition eventually came to call it by its first word, *Vayikra,* meaning, "He [God] called." Rashi explains that this is a term of endearment. Many of God's messages in the Torah are prefaced by the words "He said" (*Vayomer*), "He spoke" (*Vayedaber*), or "He commanded" (*Vayetzav*). All three belong to the language of authority. God issues an order that we must obey. But *Vayikra,* "He called, summoned, beckoned," is the language of invitation, friendship, love. In love God called Abraham to follow him. In love God led the way for the wandering Israelites in a pillar of cloud by day, fire by night. In love God calls the people Israel to come close to Him, to be regular visitors at His house, to share His quality of holiness, difference, apartness: to become, as it were, mediators of His presence to the world.

Vayikra is about why love needs law and law needs love. It is about the quotidian acts of devotion that bring two beings close, even when one of them is vaster than the universe and the other is a mortal of flesh and blood. It is about being human, sinning, falling short, always conscious of our fragile hold on life, yet seeking to come close to God and – what is sometimes harder – allowing Him to come close to us.

To understand *Vayikra,* though, we first have to solve a puzzle. Following clues present in the biblical text itself, we will discover, just beneath the surface of the text, an unexpected and quite moving story that emerged in the wake of one of the great crises in Jewish history. That, in the next section, is where we begin.

The Story Beneath the Story

There is an intricate literary device in the Torah, much used but rarely noticed, that I call the *concealed counter-narrative.*[1] The text reads one way on the surface but another way when listened to closely and deeply. The Torah signals this by giving us clues, discrepancies in the text, not obvious enough to be noticed at first glance but sufficient to make the thoughtful reader go back and read the text again and discover that the real story the Torah is telling us is richer and more complex than we first thought.

1.   My book on this subject, not yet published, is *Not in God's Name.*

This is true about the book of *Vayikra* as a whole. Read on the surface it is about ritual: the Sanctuary, the priesthood, sacrifices, purity, and holiness. But if we follow the clues we discover an intense drama, at once human and metaphysical, taking place beneath the surface. To uncover it we need first to find the clues. There are several and they appear only towards the end of the book. The first is the opening verse of Leviticus 25. It looks entirely innocent. It reads, "The Lord said to Moses at Mount Sinai." This is not a sentence that shouts for attention. But on reflection it turns out to be very odd indeed.

The reason is that *the book of Vayikra does not take place at Mount Sinai.* It takes place in the wilderness of Sinai, at the foot of the mountain, not the top. The last time Mount Sinai figured in the narrative was when Moses came down carrying the second set of tablets, the sign that God had re-established His covenant with the people after the sin of the Golden Calf (Ex. 34). From then on, the focus is not on the mountain but in the valley below where the Israelites are constructing the Sanctuary. There is a serious discrepancy here. This passage should have been in the book of Exodus.

If we look at the substance of the chapter we discover the same thing. It is about principles of social justice: the Jubilee year, the release of debts, and the liberation of slaves. Social justice is not a subject we associate with Leviticus, which is about the relationship between humans and God. It is, though, precisely the subject we associate with the book of Exodus. The obvious place for these laws is immediately after the civil legislation contained in Exodus 21–23, which deals with justice in the relationships between humans.

Turning to the next chapter, Leviticus 26, the incongruity continues. This section is about the blessings and curses that come with the covenant: blessings if the people obey, curses if they do not. We now know, thanks to intensive study by scholars of the ancient Near East,[2] that the covenant the Israelites made with God at Sinai was similar in

---

2. George E. Mendenhall, *Law & Covenant in Israel and the Ancient Near East* (Pittsburgh: Presbyterian Board of Colportage, 1955); Delbert R. Hillers, *Covenant: The History of a Biblical Idea* (Baltimore: Johns Hopkins University, 1969); Meredith G. Kline, *Treaty of the Great King* (Grand Rapids: Eerdmans, 1963).

form if not in substance to the suzerainty treaties of the time – peace agreements between two states, one strong, the other weak. These covenants had a highly formalised structure: preamble, historical prologue, then the terms and conditions, first in general terms and then in specific details. Witnesses are named. Provision is made for the deposition of the treaty and for regular public readings.

An essential element of these treaties was the reward for compliance and the punishment that would follow any breach. Even if we did not know this from the historical record we would know it from the book of Deuteronomy, which is structured as a covenant on a massive scale and which, near the end, details the rewards and punishments in a passage parallel to Leviticus 26. So this chapter too should have been in the book of Exodus, just before Exodus 24 which describes the formal acceptance of the covenant by the Israelites.

Even the closing words of *Vayikra*, "These are the commands the Lord gave Moses *at Mount Sinai* for the Israelites," are out of place. *Vayikra* is set not on the mountain but in the Tent of Meeting. Again these words belong at the end of the covenant ceremony in Exodus 24.

What we have, in other words, between Exodus 24 and Leviticus 25 is a massive parenthesis, some forty chapters long, by far the largest of its kind in the Hebrew Bible. This was already noticed by the classical commentators, notably Ibn Ezra and Nahmanides. It is a huge digression. What caused it?

There is only one plausible candidate: the episode of the Golden Calf. Coming so soon after the revelation at Sinai, it marks the single greatest crisis during the wilderness years. So to understand *Vayikra*, we need to go back and examine closely the story of the Golden Calf.

The story in broad outlines is straightforward. Moses ascended Mount Sinai after the great revelation in which God spoke to the entire people. He had been absent for several weeks. The people, unsure of when and if he would return, panicked. Without Moses how would they receive the will and word of God? That, according to many commentators, is what the calf was: not an idol but an oracle, a point at which divine communication was received.[3]

---

3.   Such as was later achieved through the space between the cherubim in the Tabernacle.

The people turned into a mob and crowded around Aaron, the leader in Moses' absence. Unused to such pressure, Aaron made what turned out to be a disastrous decision. He asked the people to give him their gold ornaments, melted them down, and then shaped, "with an engraving tool," a calf. It was a low point in the history of Israel.

Moses was unaware of all this until God told him, "Go down. Your people is destroying itself." He immediately prayed to God to forgive the people. He then went down, saw the scene, smashed the tablets, burned the calf, mixed its ashes with water, had everyone drink it, gathered the Levites, and had them execute punishment against the main wrongdoers. Then he returned to God, asking again for forgiveness. God agreed, but only partially. The guilty would suffer but the people as a whole would survive.

Thus far, the story is clear. What happens next in Exodus 33 is not. This is one of the most obscure passages in the Torah. Its individual episodes are intelligible but the sequence of events is very hard to understand.

It begins with God saying that the people must move on and continue their journey to the Promised Land. In fact, they did so, but not until fifty chapters later, in Numbers 10. God then said that He would not be "in the midst of the people." Instead, He would send "an angel." It would be too dangerous for God to be close to the people, given their tendency to provoke Him to anger. When the people heard this, they were very distressed, despite the fact that God had already said something similar ten chapters earlier (Ex. 23:20). At that time, it occasioned no distress.

Next we read that Moses moved his tent outside the camp. There then follows a bewildering series of conversations between Moses and God. Moses urges God to reconsider His decision not to go with the people: "If Your presence does not go with us, do not let us leave this place" (Ex. 33:15). Then the subject changes to what seem to be metaphysical enquiries about the nature of God. Moses speaks about the "face," the "ways," and the "glory" of God. Then in chapter 34 comes the famous scene in which God places Moses in a crevice in a rock and passes before him, reciting the words that became known as God's Thirteen Attributes of Mercy.

Much is unclear about this passage, two things in particular. What is Moses doing discussing fine points of theology when the people are facing a major crisis in their relationship with God? And why, just before this, did he move his tent *outside the camp*? This seems precisely the wrong thing to do. The entire episode of the Golden Calf happened because Moses was absent. Now was not the time to set a distance between him and the people. In addition, they had just been shocked and grieved to hear that God would no longer be in their midst. For Moses to do likewise would turn an already painful situation into a double blow. That is what I mean by a concealed counter-narrative. It is as if the text were saying: there is a deeper story beneath the surface that needs to be excavated.

What we sense is that once the immediate crisis of the Golden Calf was over, Moses turned to the fundamental problem that had given rise to it in the first place. In this encounter, Moses was praying his most audacious prayer, so audacious that the Torah gives us only fragments, glimpses, forcing us to complete the narrative ourselves. It went something like this:

"Sovereign of the universe, I have moved my tent outside the camp to signal that *it is not my distance from the people that is the problem. It is Yours.* How have the Israelites experienced You thus far? As a terrifying, overwhelming force. They have seen You bring the mightiest empire in the world to its knees. They have witnessed You turn the sea into dry land, send food from heaven and water from a rock. They know that no one can see you and live. But they also fear that no one can *hear* you and live. When You revealed Yourself to them at the mountain, they came to me and said, 'Speak to us yourself and we will listen, but do not have God speak to us or we will die' (Ex. 20:19). When they made the calf, wrongheaded though they were, they were seeking a way of encountering God without terror. They need You to be close."

What Moses was exploring in his questions about the "face," the "ways," and the "glory" of God were the fundamental parameters of the relationship between God and humanity. The God of Abraham was transcendent. Could He also be immanent? Could He relate to humans not only from heaven or the mountain top, but down in the valley in the midst of the camp? Can an infinite God be close to finite human beings? If not, what hope is there for humanity?

Nor was it simply distance that had become problematic. So was predictability. It was as if Moses had said, "We know that sometimes You are angry, and sometimes You are moved by compassion. There are occasions when You execute justice, others when You forgive. Precisely because You are free, we cannot predict which will prevail: punishment or forgiveness. But we are the people who have staked our entire existence on You. How can we live, not knowing when You will next be angry with us, and whether our prayers for forgiveness will succeed?

"You, God, have been gracious to me. You asked me to lead this people and I have striven to do so. I have prayed for Your forgiveness and You have heeded my prayer. But I am mortal. You alone are eternal. What will happen in the future if the people sin and there is no Moses to pray for them? There must be some sustainable order in the life of the spirit. There must be a structure of leadership that does not depend on chance."

If this is what happened in Exodus 33, it is one of the most decisive moments in Judaism. It is difficult at this distance of time to realise how radical a break with the civilisations of the day monotheism was. The God of Abraham differed in two ways from the religions of the ancient world. First, He is transcendent. He is beyond the universe because He created the universe. None of the gods worshipped by the ancients was remotely like this. Even Akhnaton, the pharaoh whom some – most famously Sigmund Freud – identify as the first monotheist, thought that god was the sun. The sun is within the universe, not beyond it. How do you relate to a God who is infinite and unknowable?

Second, God acted in history. That too had never been conceived before. For the ancients, the gods were in nature. They were the rain, the river, the sun, the storm. In nature, time is cyclical. Things are born, grow, reproduce, and die, but nothing really changes. Things are as they are because that is how they were and always will be. With the Exodus, God changed history. More precisely, with the Exodus, God *created* history.

These two facts – creation and history – were profoundly liberating but also deeply alienating. God had now become almost impossibly remote. How can someone within the universe even begin to understand One beyond the universe? And the idea of history as an arena of change is also profoundly destabilising. Cyclical time is reassuring. Yes, there are floods, droughts, famines, natural disasters, but in nature, life eventually returns to normal. It was the anthropologist Mircea Eliade who drew attention to how terrifying the idea of history was at first.[4] What was it like to be the first people to set out on a journey not knowing where it would lead?

At the deepest level, that was what the crisis of the Golden Calf was about. At that moment, Moses was the sole connection between heaven and earth. Absent him, and there was terror. Yet why did the problem surface then and not in the days of Noah or Abraham or the Israelites before now? The answer is that Judaism's fundamental solution to the distance between God and man is *language*. Words alone have the power to cross the abyss between finite humans and the infinite God. God spoke to Adam, Cain, Noah, the patriarchs and matriarchs, and to Moses.

That is a solution that worked for individuals. What happens when the Israelites become a nation? When God spoke to the nation as a whole at Sinai the people found it unbearable and they asked Moses to listen on their behalf. That was why his prolonged absence was devastating. The making of the Golden Calf was a mistake, a sin. But the crisis that led to it was real and enduring. What would become of the people in the absence of Moses or someone like him? How could a nation take the risk of depending entirely on God when God was so distant, overpowering, and unpredictable? That is when God gave the answer that led to the forty-chapter digression in the story of the Israelites' journey from Egypt to the Promised Land.

God answered Moses' request with these words: "Let them make for Me a sanctuary and I will dwell [*veshakhanti*] in their midst" (Ex. 25:8). This is the start of an entirely new relationship between God and the people. The verb "to dwell" had never before been used in relation to God. The root *sh-kh-n* means a neighbour, someone who lives next door. God was about to become not just the force that moves the stars and changes the course of history, but also one who is close, a neighbour. It was from this root that the rabbis coined their name for

4. Mircea Eliade, *Cosmos and History* (New York: Garland Science, 1985).

the divine indwelling, God's presence that was always with the Jewish people, even in exile. They called it the *Shekhina*.

This relationship between God and the people would be mediated by a new kind of religious leader, not Moses the prophet but Aaron the priest. You cannot predict the appearance of a new prophet. There never was another Moses, and after Haggai, Zechariah, and Malachi, prophecy ceased altogether. But the priesthood is predictable. It is dynastic, not charismatic. The priests were the male descendants of Aaron. We still have priests today. The priesthood represents continuity immune to the vicissitudes of time.

Likewise the sense of the Divine Presence: The people could not see God's "face" or understand His "ways," but they could experience His "glory." It was this phenomenon, cloud-like yet radiant, that would dwell in the Sanctuary, the symbolic home of God. There would be a series of regular encounters by bringing "sacrifices," though the Hebrew word *korban* is better translated as "coming close by bringing close." The entire system of *korbanot* and all that went with them was a response to the crisis of the distance of God. That is the story behind the story of *Vayikra*.

The long digression between Exodus 23 and Leviticus 25 is, as Nahmanides saw,[5] entirely taken up with the consequences of the Golden Calf and the new relationship it inaugurated between God and the people. All of it – the construction of the Sanctuary, the offerings to be made there, the special demands of purity for all who entered its precincts, the holiness demanded of a people with God in its midst – is about *bringing God close*, living in the constant presence of the Divine. It is also about bringing cyclical time into Judaism, about *turning the peak experiences of history into daily routines*, the "never again" into the "ever again." This is the choreography of grace, the intricate rituals of sacred space. The King was about to invite His people to enter the palace they had just built for Him out of their gifts of love. This was something altogether new in Jewish experience.

But the risks were obvious. Introducing immanence into Judaism – a God who has a "home" on earth – carried with it the danger that it

5. Nahmanides, Commentary to Leviticus 25:1.

would bring the people close to the other religions of the ancient world. They too had temples, priests, and sacrificial orders. Besides which, how do you introduce infinity into space and eternity into time without blurring the boundaries of reality? It is like bringing particles of matter and antimatter together. If the two collide, the result is annihilation. It becomes very important to keep them apart.

Hence the unique task and mindset of the priest. His role was to protect and maintain boundaries. The fundamental act of the priest is *lehavdil*: "to distinguish, separate, know where things belong and where they don't." The priest knows that this is how God created the world. First, He separated domains: light and dark, upper and lower waters, sea and dry land. Only then could stars, planets, and life emerge. The priest is the guardian of order in a world in which humans are always creating chaos. Only in an ordered universe can holiness survive. Only in an ordered universe can humanity survive. That is the singular message of the priest. It is the basic principle of *Torat Kohanim*.

Leviticus is written almost entirely in the priestly voice. It uses a vocabulary we encounter only rarely in the wisdom or prophetic voices. Alongside *lehavdil*, the other key verb for the priest is *lehorot*, "to teach, instruct, deliver a judgement, make a ruling, guide." It is from this verb that we get the noun *Torah*. The most important adjectives are *kodesh* and *ḥol*, holy and common, and *tahor* and *tamei*, pure and impure, that is to say, a state that allows access to the holy and one that debars it.

These are difficult terms because they belong to areas of existence that stand outside our normal categories for engaging with the world. The idea that God can enter space and time is as paradoxical as relativity, quantum physics, black holes, strange attractors, Higgs bosons, and other counterintuitive phenomena of the very large or very small. The holy is not straightforward or prosaic. Where infinity meets finitude there is danger. Safety comes in the form of law.

In biblical times, the priest was master and teacher of the law. His task was to keep the Divine Presence in the heart of the Israelite camp. The people were to remember constantly that God was in their midst. The priestly universe – Sanctuary, sacrifices, the need for purity – came into being as a result of the sin of the Golden Calf. Moses successfully persuaded God that the people needed to feel Him close, not distant.

This had less to do with God than with the Israelites. God is everywhere at every time but not always are we conscious of Him. Adam and Eve in Eden believed that they could hide. The continuing drama in the Hebrew Bible is of God's attention and human inattention. God is there but we forget that He is there. Holiness is consciousness of the *Shekhina* in the midst of life.

The creation of the priesthood is what Max Weber called "the routinisation of charisma."[6] The priest takes the fire of God, the high drama of sacrificial love, and awe of the Divine Presence – life-changing experiences – and turns them into daily rituals so that they become not rare, exceptional events but routines that shape the character of a nation and transform individual lives. Looked at one way, the priest takes poetry and turns it into prose. Looked at from another perspective, knowing how thin is the veneer of civilisation and how dark the undercurrents of the unconscious mind, the priest takes prose and etches it with poetry. Every day is an encounter with the Divine.

To get inside the mindset of the priest we need to understand the meaning, first of the holy, then of the pure, then of the institution of sacrifice: what they meant then and what they mean now. We need also to see what is distinctive about the priestly conception of the moral life. We will then be able to understand what happened to these institutions when the Temple was destroyed and the sacrificial system came to an end.

Holy: The Space We Make for God

Holiness – *kedusha* – is a key concept of the book of *Vayikra*. The root *k-d-sh* appears 152 times. It appears only once in Genesis, sixteen times in the non-priestly parts of Exodus (chapters 1–24), and fifteen times in Deuteronomy. Its use is overwhelmingly concentrated in those parts of the Mosaic books that speak in the priestly voice. The priest is a holy person performing holy acts in the holy place. But what does the word mean?

At the most prosaic level, *k-d-sh* means "to dedicate, to set aside, to designate for a particular purpose." Thus, for example, a marriage is

6. Max Weber, *Theory of Social and Economic Organization* (London: W. Hodge, 1947).

called *kiddushin* in Hebrew, meaning that a woman has been dedicated to this particular man in an exclusive relationship. When God sanctifies the Jewish people to become "a holy nation" it has the same connotation as in marriage; that is, the people are designated by God to be exclusively His, to worship Him alone. In this sense monotheism is like monogamy, a one-to-one relationship between a people and God.

However, the term clearly means more than this. In his famous book, *The Idea of the Holy*, Rudolf Otto called holiness the *"mysterium tremendans et fascinans,"* the sense at once frightening and enthralling of the great mystery of the infinite.[7] The holy is that in the presence of which one feels awe. By contrast, Eliezer Berkovits argued that in Judaism, the holiness of God means also the closeness of God. God the infinite is also God the intimate.[8]

In an early article, "Sacred and Profane," Rabbi Joseph Soloveitchik spoke of holiness as at-homeness in space and time. The Jew who is at home in sacred space (*kedushat makom*) finds God everywhere. The one who is at home in sacred time (*kedushat zeman*) finds God in all times, in the distant past and dimly glimpsed future.[9] For Rabbi Abraham Isaac Kook, the holy was that dimension within which all things found their unity within the unity of God and His infinite light. The secular is the world of separation, division, and conflict. To ascend to the holy is to see each object, person, discipline, and perspective as a part of the whole, with its own integrity in the scheme of things. Therefore, all things secular can in principle be sanctified once we place them in the service of God, the unity that gives light and life to all.[10]

None of these, however, quite explains the precision and paradox of the concept of holiness as we find it in the Mosaic books. Our starting

7. Rudolf Otto, *The Idea of the Holy: An Inquiry into the Non-Rational Factor in the Idea of the Divine and Its Relation to the Rational* (New York: Oxford University Press, 1958).
8. Eliezer Berkovits, "The Concept of Holiness," in *Essential Essays on Judaism* (Jerusalem: Shalem Press, 2002), 247–314.
9. Joseph Epstein, ed., "Sacred and Profane," in *Shiurei HaRav: A Conspectus of the Public Lectures of Rabbi Joseph B. Soloveitchik* (New York: Ktav, 1994), 4–34.
10. Rabbi Abraham Isaac Kook, *Orot HaKodesh*, 3 vols. (Jerusalem: Mossad HaRav Kook, 1985).

point must be the two focal points of holiness in the Torah. The first is Shabbat, the seventh day of creation:

> Thus the heavens and the earth, and all the host of them, were finished. And on the seventh day God ended His work which He had done, and He rested on the seventh day from all His work which He had done. Then God blessed the seventh day and *made it holy*, because in it He rested from all His work which God had created and made. (Gen. 2:1–3)

The essence of Shabbat is that it is a day of not doing, a cessation, a stopping point, a pause, an absence of activity. In the Exodus version of the Ten Commandments, this is the reason given for the Israelites to do likewise: "Remember the Sabbath day, to keep it holy.... For in six days the Lord made the heavens and the earth, the sea, and all that is in them, and rested on the seventh day. Therefore the Lord blessed the Sabbath day and hallowed it" (Ex. 20:8–11). Shabbat is empty time.

The second key instance of the holy is the *Mikdash*, the Tabernacle or Sanctuary. The primary nature of the *Mikdash* is that it defined a certain space. It was a structure of poles and drapes that marked out certain areas with different degrees of holiness. Although the Tabernacle had furnishings, it was a defined space that contained little, especially the Holy of Holies that contained only the Ark holding the tablets of stone, and the covering, on which were the figures of the cherubim. The Sanctuary was, predominantly, empty space.

Holiness is emptiness: empty space and empty time. What does this mean? By far the most suggestive answer is to be found in Jewish mysticism, specifically the kabbalistic doctrine associated with the school of Rabbi Yitzḥak Luria. For the mystic, the invisible is real, the visible unreal, a mere mask hiding the Divine. The rationalist sees the universe and wonders whether God really exists. The mystic sees God and wonders whether the universe really exists. How are we to reconcile the existence of an infinite, omniscient, and omnipotent God and a finite universe in which humans have physical existence and free will? Surely at every point the Infinite must crowd out the finite. How is it that the universe exists at all?

The answer given by the kabbalists is that it exists because of divine self-effacement, *tzimtzum*. God conceals Himself, as it were, to allow the emergence of a universe in the space left by His self-limitation. "Truly," says Isaiah, "You are a God who hides Himself" (Is. 45:15). And though Jewish mysticism is almost wholly a post-biblical phenomenon, there is a basic insight here that accurately describes what is happening in the Torah's account of creation. Human freedom especially exists because of divine self-limitation. So Adam and Eve found that they were able to sin, and Cain even to commit murder, without God stepping in to intervene. Through voluntary self-restraint, God makes space for man.

But there is a problem here, and it haunts the Bible's narrative. What is the difference between a hidden God and no God? The very existence of the universe testifies to a concealment on the part of God. The word *olam*, "universe," is semantically linked to *ne'elam*, "hidden." That is the divine dilemma. If God were always visible, humans could not exist at all. "No one can see Me and live," says God. "If we continue to hear the voice of God, we will die," say the Israelites at Sinai. But if God is always invisible, hidden, imperceptible, then what difference does His existence make? It will always be as if He were not there.

The answer to this dilemma is holiness. Holiness represents those points in space and time where God becomes vivid, tangible, a felt presence. Holiness is a break in the self-sufficiency of the material world, where infinity enters space and eternity enters time. In relation to time, it is Shabbat. In relation to space, it is the Tabernacle. These, in the Torah, are the epicentres of the sacred.

We can now understand what makes them holy. Shabbat is the time when humans cease, for a day, to be creators and become conscious of themselves as creations. The Tabernacle is the space in which humans cease to be masters – "fill the earth and subdue it" – and become servants. Just as God had to practise self-restraint to make space for the finite, so human beings have to practise self-restraint to make space for the infinite. The holy, in short, is where human beings renounce their independence and self-sufficiency, the very things that are the mark of their humanity, and for a moment acknowledge their utter dependence on He who spoke and brought the universe into being.

The universe is the space God makes for man. The holy is the space man makes for God. The secular is the emptiness created by God to be filled by a finite universe. The holy is the emptiness in time and space vacated by humans so that it can be filled by the infinite presence of God.

In biblical Hebrew, the opposite of *kodesh*, the holy, is *ḥol*. *Ḥol* means "empty." *Ḥillel* means "to violate, desecrate, profane." *Ḥallal* means "hollow, a void, empty space." It also means "dead, slain, bereft of life." Hence the paradox: space or time that is unholy is full of finitude and therefore empty of the Divine. Space or time that is holy is empty of human devices and desires, an emptiness filled with the Divine Presence, the glory of God. We make space for God in the same way that God makes space for us, by *tzimtzum*, self-effacement, self-renunciation.

The most precious thing people can offer to God is their freedom, their will. God does not ask this of everyone, all the time, for were He to do so, He would frustrate the very purpose of the creation of humankind. Instead He asks it of some of the people, some of the time. He asks it of one people, the Israelites; one land, the land of Israel; one day, Shabbat; and one place, the Sanctuary. These constitute breaks in the fabric of finitude, windows through which an infinite light flows into the world.

That light can be dangerous. Stare too long at sunlight and you go blind. The energy pent up in the holy is like antimatter in relation to matter. Without careful guarding it is destructive, as shown by the deaths of Nadav and Avihu on the day the Tabernacle was consecrated. The holy needs to be protected, guarded, insulated, almost like nuclear energy. The priests are the guardians of the sacred, and must themselves be kept as far as possible from the ordinary, the mundane, the mortal – above all, from death.

That is the holy, the point at which humans temporarily renounce their creativity and freedom in order to allow the creativity and freedom of God to be sensed. The holy is where God's glory casts off its cloak of concealment and becomes palpable, tangible. The priests inhabit this liminal space – this boundary between the infinite and finite, the holy and the everyday. They are to Israel what Israel is to humanity, a signal of transcendence, representatives of God to humanity and humanity to God.

The holy, then, is a time or space that in itself testifies to the existence of something beyond itself. Shabbat points to a time beyond time: to creation. The Tabernacle points to a space beyond space. As King Solomon said at the dedication of the Temple: "But will God really dwell on earth? The heavens, even the highest heaven, cannot contain You. How much less this Temple I have built!" (1 Kings 8:27).

The Israelites point, by their very history, to a power more than merely human:

> Ask now about the former days, long before your time, from the day God created human beings on the earth; ask from one end of the heavens to the other. Has anything so great as this ever happened, or has anything like it ever been heard of? ... Has any god ever tried to take for himself one nation out of another nation, by testings, by signs and wonders, by war, by a mighty hand and an outstretched arm, or by great and awesome deeds, like all the things the Lord your God did for you in Egypt before your very eyes? (Deut. 4:32–34)

Israel is the people that in itself testifies to something beyond itself. Otherwise, it would not have survived. It is the tiny nation that out-lived empires.

The holy is where transcendence becomes immanence, where within the universe we encounter the presence of the One beyond the universe. Holiness is the space we make for God.

Sacrifice

It follows that fundamental activity in relation to the holy is *sacrifice*, in the broadest sense. God sacrifices something of Himself to make space for us. We sacrifice something of ourselves to make space for Him.

I have argued that we can only understand *Vayikra* in terms of the spiritual crisis that led to the Golden Calf. In the absence of Moses, the people proved incapable of constituting themselves as a self-disciplined community. They became a mob. Hence the question was not only how could God come close to the people, but also how could the people come close to God? How could they mature, grow, develop, and thus become worthy of the responsibilities of freedom?

What had infantilised the people until now was their total dependency on God. He liberated them from Egypt, led them across the sea, guided them through the desert, gave them food from heaven and water from a rock. They had received. They had not yet given back. The Jewish mystics called the manna *nahama dekisufa*, "the bread of shame," because they had not worked for it. In Judaism, when you enjoy what you have not earned, that is a source of shame.

The one thing God had not yet done for the Israelites was *to give them the chance of giving back something to Him.* The very idea sounds absurd. How can we, God's creations, give back to the God who made us? All we have is His. As David said when initiating the project of the Temple: "Who am I, and who are my people, that we should be able to give as generously as this? Everything comes from You, and we have given You only what comes from Your hand" (1 Chr. 29:14).

God's greatest gift to us is the ability to give to Him. Clearly, from a Judaic perspective, this idea is fraught with risk. The idea that God might be in need of gifts is a hair's breadth from paganism and heresy. Yet, knowing the risk, God allowed Himself to allow the Israelites the opportunity to give something back to God.

Central to sacrifice is what Lewis Hyde in his classic study, *The Gift*,[11] beautifully described as "the labour of gratitude." The construction of the Sanctuary out of the voluntary contributions of the people, together with the sacrificial order it initiated, was important because it gave the Israelites the chance to give back to God. Later, Jewish law recognised giving as an integral part of human dignity when it ruled that *even a poor person completely dependent on charity is still obliged to give charity.*[12] Giving is essential to self-respect. To be in a situation where you can only receive, not give, is to lack human dignity.

---

11. Lewis Hyde, *The Gift: How the Creative Spirit Transforms the World* (Edinburgh: Canongate, 2006).
12. Maimonides, *Mishneh Torah, Hilkhot Shekalim* 1:1; *Mishneh Torah, Matanot Aniyim* 7:5.

During the biblical era, the sacrifices were primarily of animals. There is no doubt that this is connected with two propositions in Genesis. The first is the concession, after the Flood, allowing humans to kill animals for food. Prior to the Flood this had been forbidden. The result was a world "filled with violence," which began with Cain's murder of Abel. Thus the permission to kill animals for food, accompanied by a solemn warning against murder, was intended as a way of channelling violence out of the human condition.

The second is the story of the binding of Isaac, in which God stops Abraham from sacrificing his child, and provides in his place a ram caught by its horns in a thicket. Animal sacrifice is the way in which the Torah directs the Israelites away from human – especially child – sacrifice, which was widely practised in the ancient world. According to the evidence of the prophets and historical books, at times it was even performed in Israel, where it was regarded as the most heinous of sins.

However, the form of the sacrifice is secondary to its essential principle. *The fundamental sacrifice in Judaism is that of the will.* Since freedom of the will is the highest gift of God to man, the way we acknowledge that it is a gift is periodically to give some of it back. That is why the service of God is called *avoda* in Hebrew – the very word that is used to describe the slavery of the Israelites to the Egyptians.

We see here the intimate connection between a religious vision and a political one. Just as it is idolatry to worship human beings rather than God, so it is slavery to sacrifice our freedom to other human beings rather than God. "For the Israelites belong to Me as servants. They are My servants" (Lev. 25:55), says God, which the rabbis interpret to mean, "They are not the servants of other servants [i.e., other human beings]."

The fact that sacrifice in Judaism has nothing intrinsically to do with the offerings of animals on the altar is the reason Judaism was able to survive the loss of the Temple, its rites, and sacrifices with its religious life largely intact. What matters in sacrifice is the act of renunciation. We give up something of ourselves, offering it to God in recognition of the gifts He has given us. It is remarkable how readily the sages found substitutes for sacrifices, most notably in the form of prayer, but also in Torah study (learning about the sacrifices is equivalent to bringing them, say the rabbis), charity, and hospitality.

The Hebrew word for sacrifice – the verb *lehakriv* and the noun *korban* – both mean "bringing close." The meaning is: we are brought close by what we bring close. We come close to the Other by bringing a gift. A gift means I take something of me and dedicate to it you. A gift can be a way of maintaining a relationship. It can be a form of apology and a desire to be forgiven. It can also be a token of thanks. One way or another, a sacrifice in Judaism is always the token of an I-Thou relationship between us and God. It is a gesture of love.

Hence the striking feature of Leviticus and of priestly ritual generally. It always uses the four-letter name of God, *Hashem*, as opposed to the priestly creation narrative which uses the word *Elokim*. *Hashem* is God as person. *Elokim* is God as the force of forces, the totality of powers in the universe. In the moral life, *Hashem* represents compassion, *Elokim* strict justice. A sacrifice to *Elokim* would be a pagan act, an attempt to appease the forces of nature. A sacrifice is always to *Hashem*, an act of turning our face to His, an inherently personal gesture.

The only way of understanding sacrifice in Judaism is to remember that this is a religion built on love. Recall that the two great commands of interpersonal love – love of the neighbour and the stranger – both appear in the book of Leviticus, in the great "holiness code" of chapter 19. Neither abstract reason nor the pursuit of self-interest can make sense of the act of sacrifice. Yet the willingness to sacrifice is essential to families, communities, and the nation. There is no love without the willingness to sacrifice. That is the truth at the heart of Leviticus. When people find the book remote and incomprehensible, that is what they forget: that priestly ritual is the choreography of love.

The logic of the sacrifices has to do with holiness, not morality as such – though, as we will see below, there was a distinctive priestly ethic. Holiness has to do with our relationship with God. Morality has to do with our relationships with human beings. Two of the most striking features of the Torah are that (1) morality is universal whereas holiness is particular, and that (2) morality takes precedence over holiness where the two conflict. Thus holiness is no excuse for a failure of morality.

There are sins for which we bring a sacrifice: *ḥatat, asham, me'ila* and so on. But the sin always represents an offence against God. This may have a moral dimension, but that dimension is not addressed by a sacrifice. That is the theme of the great prophetic denunciations of sacrifice – that people were bringing sacrifices as if they trumped or neutralised moral offences, as if one could bribe God to turn a blind eye to the ways in which he was defrauding or oppressing his fellow human beings. This critique is sustained and devastating. The prophets did not oppose sacrifice but they saw very clearly how the entire structure of temple worship could be misused to anaesthetise consciences that should not be anaesthetised.

Sacrifice is what God allows us to give Him to show our love and gratitude for what He has given us. The converse side of this, as the code of holiness insists, is that we let our love of God be turned into our love of the neighbour and stranger. Just as we give to God, so should we give to them.

Purity

There is a famous midrash in which a Roman challenges Rabban Yoḥanan b. Zakkai on the ritual of the red heifer, one of the laws of purification that does not appear in *Vayikra* but which belongs to the same territory as the laws set out in chapters 11 to 16. The Roman finds the law incomprehensible, irrational, and superstitious. Yoḥanan b. Zakkai asks the Roman whether he believes in exorcism. The Roman says he does. Well then, says Yoḥanan, that is what the rite of the red heifer is, a kind of exorcism. It expels unclean spirits. The Roman, satisfied, leaves.

There then follows a remarkable scene. The students turn to Rabban Yoḥanan and say, "You gave him an answer to satisfy a Roman, but what will you answer us?" Yoḥanan then says, "Know that it is not death that defiles or the ritual that purifies. Rather, God is saying: 'I have established a statute and instituted a decree, and you have no permission to transgress them.'"[13]

The passage is telling us that not only do we find the laws of purity hard to understand. So do the sages, or at least the disciples of the sages. However, we should not misunderstand Rabban Yoḥanan's

13. Numbers Rabba, *Parashat Ḥukkat* 19.

reply to his students. It has often been taken to mean that the laws we call *ḥukkim*, "statutes," have no reason, or at least none we can understand. Rav Saadia Gaon says that statutes are commands given to us by God simply to reward us for obeying them, not because they had any intrinsic logic. The great countervoice is Maimonides, who holds that every command has a reason, even the *ḥukkim*.

What I believe Rabban Yoḥanan was doing was making a sharp distinction – made in our time by philosopher John Rawls[14] – between two kinds of rules: *regulatory and constitutive*. Regulatory rules, as their name implies, regulate something that exists independently of the rules. There were employers and employees before there was employment law. A practice exists and then come the laws to ensure fairness, justice, and so on. In Judaism, *mishpatim*, social legislation, is of this kind.

Constitutive laws *create* a practice. The laws of chess create the game called chess. Without the laws, there is no game. Rabban Yoḥanan was saying that the laws of purity are like this. They are not like medicine because impurity is not like disease, which existed before there were healers, doctors, diagnoses, and cures. Before there were laws of purity, death did not defile and the waters did not purify. The laws created a new reality, but that does not mean that they are irrational or incomprehensible.

Vayikra's purity laws are set out in chapters 11–16 and follow a distinct order. First there is the impurity incurred by contact with repulsive animals, then that brought about by childbirth. Next comes the mysterious phenomenon known as *tzaraat*, often translated as leprosy, but which in fact, as Maimonides pointed out, is a generic name for a series of conditions that have no medical connection: skin disease in humans, discoloration in garments, and mildew on the walls of houses. Then there is the impurity of various flows of bodily fluid – menstrual blood in the case of women, and various discharges that affect men.

These laws are followed by chapter 16, which specifies the rites of the High Priest on the Day of Atonement. The connection between this and the purity laws is that in this chapter, sin is described in terms

---

14. John Rawls, "Two Concepts of Rules," *The Philosophical Review*, vol. 64, no. 1 (Jan. 1955): 3–32.

of *defilement*, and atonement (among other things) is described as a process of purification. Chapters 18 and 20, framing the great "holiness code" of chapter 19, are about forbidden sexual relationships – forbidden specifically to the Israelites because they are a holy people in a holy land.

How are we to understand the laws of purity?

They exist because of the extreme paradox of the Sanctuary. Recall that until the sin of the Golden Calf, God had been transcendent not immanent, distant not close, creator of the universe, shaper of history, and liberator of slaves. Other than this, His connection with human beings had been confined to speech. God speaks and man listens. Man speaks and God listens. The entire world of sanctuary, priesthood, and daily sacrifices did not exist. God was encountered in the exceptional, not the everyday.

The Sanctuary and its service put all this potentially at risk. They were easily mistakable for their pagan counterparts. Other nations had temples, shrines, priests, and sacrifices, but that is because the gods they worshipped were immanent. They lived within the world of nature. They could be appeased, bribed, fed, manipulated. All of this was and is anathema to Judaism. The difference between God and nature, God and *human* nature, is total. To speak of God having a "home" on earth, or of "smelling the sweet savour" of burnt offerings is, from a theological perspective, very dangerous indeed.

Yet God listened to Moses' prayer. He understood that the Israelites needed to feel that God was "in their midst." The answer, therefore, lay in *boundaries*, clearly demarcated lines rigorously supervised by the priests and fastidiously observed by all. If "the holy" is the space we make for God, then purity is what allows us to enter that space and impurity is what prevents us from doing so.

The major common factor in the various forms of impurity is that they have to do with *mortality*, with the fact that we are embodied beings in a physical world, exposed to the "thousand natural shocks that flesh is heir to." To enter sacred space, the space in which we feel close to the presence of infinity and eternity, we must divest ourselves of any consciousness of mortality, disease, and decay.

Hence the supreme source of impurity is death: contact with or proximity to a dead body. Paradoxically, childbirth defiles, even though it represents new life. The reason may be that until quite recently, it was a hazard fraught with the risk of death. Babies were stillborn, many died young, and many mothers died giving birth. The very loss of blood was dangerous. So childbirth may defile because it is an encounter with the risk of death. Alternatively, it may simply be that it defiles because it is a reminder of our mortality and the passing of the generations.

Likewise, the flow of menstrual blood and the reproductive cycle is a sign of human mortality. It may be that the appearance of menstrual blood was a sign that the woman was not pregnant, so it represented a kind of death: the death of the unfertilised egg and of the possibility that month of new life. Seminal and other discharges likewise defiled because they too were a sign of the body functioning in non-normal ways.

Skin disease is the most publicly visible reminder of our physicality. The skin condition called *tzaraat*, leprosy, was regarded as another particularly acute sign of mortality, of disease and decay. "A leprous individual is like one who is dead," say the sages. What connects the different types of *tzaraat* – garments, the walls of houses, and skin – is that they themselves are boundaries between inside and outside, and holiness depends on the health and strength of boundaries.

Holiness and purity depend on the ability to distinguish, separate, and know what belongs where. That is the logic of the dietary laws in chapter 11. Recall that God created the universe in the first chapter of Genesis by bringing order to chaos through the act of separating domains – light and dark, upper and lower waters, sea and dry land. God then filled each with its appropriate objects or life forms. The dietary laws have the same logic. Clean animals, fish, and birds are those that most conspicuously represent order. Lobsters are impure because, though they live in the water, they walk as on land. Amphibians are impure because they lack a definite place. Most fish have fins and scales: therefore those that lack one or the other blur the line that separates fish from other life forms. Ruminants are permitted because they eat what God first ordained animals to eat: "green plants" (Gen. 1:30). By the same token, carnivorous animals and birds of prey are impure because they eat flesh, something forbidden at the dawn of time. And so on. Whatever blurs boundaries is unclean.

The same logic applies to sexual ethics, in a more profound way. Nothing is more disruptive of social order in the long run than sexual anomie. Human offspring have by far the longest period of dependency of any life form and therefore depend on strong and caring families. The relationships within the family – husband and wife, parent and child – are the most common metaphors throughout Tanakh for the relationship between God and the people. This goes to the heart of Judaism as a religion of fidelity, loyalty, and the love that brings new life into being. Judaism is neither hedonistic nor ascetic. It is about the consecration of desire. That is what is at the heart of the two codes of forbidden sexual relations in chapters 18 and 20.

God does not ask of us to sacrifice or devalue our physicality. To the contrary, we are part of the physical world He created, and this is where He wants us to serve Him. Nonetheless, lines have to be drawn and boundaries maintained between God's domain and ours. Failure to observe the boundary between permitted and forbidden caused Adam and Eve to be exiled from Eden. Within a generation the first murder had taken place, and before long "the earth was filled with violence."

This is the Torah's form of chaos theory: as the beating of a butterfly's wing can cause a typhoon on the other side of the earth, so small breaches in boundaries can lead, in time, to anarchy and tyranny. Knowing how rapid the descent can be from civilisation to barbarism, the priestly sensibility is vigilant in maintaining what Wallace Stevens called the "blessed rage for order."[15]

Purity, Rabban Yoḥanan was saying, is not some independent condition that exists in the world independently of Torah. It is the mode of being called for by proximity to the holy. The purity laws exist only because Israel was called on to become a holy nation and only because, through the Tabernacle, God caused His presence to dwell in the midst of the camp. That is why the purity laws are specific to Israel – the people and the land – unlike the moral laws that apply, in broad outline, to everyone. It is always wrong to murder, rob, steal, and commit adultery.

---

15. Wallace Stevens, "The Idea of Order at Key West," in *The Collected Poems of Wallace Stevens* (New York: Alfred A. Knopf, 1971), 128.

The laws of purity are God's special request of the Israelites, the condition of their coming close to eternity in the midst of life.

Ritual

Holiness, sacrifice, purity: these are the subjects of *Vayikra*, the mark of a people that has the Divine Presence in its midst. But *Torat Kohanim*, the priestly sensibility, has other features that make its voice distinctive. It has its own view of what constitutes the religious life, the moral life, and time.

There is an astonishing midrashic passage in which the sages are discussing the question: What is the one sentence that summarises Judaism? The most famous of these passages is the one in the Talmud in which a would-be proselyte asks Hillel to teach him the whole of Torah while he is standing on one leg. Hillel replies, "What is hateful to you do not do to others. That is the Torah. The rest is commentary. Now go and learn." The next passage continues, as it were, where Hillel ends. Other sages offer other opinions:

> Ben Zoma said, "There is a more all-embracing verse, namely, 'Hear O Israel'" (Deut. 6:4). Ben Nannas said, "There is a more all-embracing verse still: 'You shall love your neighbour as yourself'" (Lev. 19:18). Ben Pazzi said, "There is a more embracing verse still: 'Prepare one lamb in the morning and the other towards evening'" (Num. 28:4). A certain rabbi stood up and declared: "The law is in accordance with Ben Pazzi."[16]

Ben Zoma holds that the foundation of Judaism is its faith in the One God. Hence the key text is the declaration of faith, "Hear O Israel." Ben Nannas says that the most distinctive feature of Judaism is its ethics, founded as it is not just on fairness and reciprocity but on love. But Ben Pazzi, whose answer is saved until last, offers a wholly unexpected reply. His quote is the verse in Numbers about the daily sacrifice. What

16. Preface of *HaKotev* to *Ein Yaakov*, by Rabbi Jacob ben Solomon ibn Habib, 6, column b.

is special about Judaism, says Ben Pazzi, is its ritual, its daily acts of dedication, its choreography of small steps and everyday deeds. The passage ends by suggesting that he may have come closer to the heart of Judaism than any of the others.

Judaism, suggests Ben Pazzi, is not just poetry but also prose, not just the fire of romantic love but the daily kindnesses of a successful marriage, not just an exalted faith in the transcendent God but the way it takes faith and translates it into everyday life. Judaism is, in the language of James Joyce, a series of epiphanies of the ordinary. We encounter God not just in the thunder and lightning of Sinai but every morning and evening in ritual and routine. That is what life is and what faith transfigures.

Thoreau said that most people lead lives of quiet desperation. Judaism, argues Ben Pazzi, is a way of living life in quiet celebration. We bring our days to God. Morning and evening, we turn towards Him, offering Him something of ourselves. For that is what faith and love have to become if they are to transform our lives. God is not just a terrifying presence at the top of the mountain. He lives among us in the valley if we place Him at the centre of our lives. God lives not just in drama but in continuity. That is the priestly ethic.

Kings shape history. Prophets capture the moral imagination. But it is the devotion of the priest, the endlessly repeated, precisely prescribed rites, the humble, unspectacular acts of devotion that translate faith into the lives of its followers. We can see the difference it makes in the biblical contrast between Moses and Aaron. Moses is the hero of the Torah. The Pentateuch is made up of the Mosaic books. Aaron is cast in a secondary role. Nor does the Torah paint him in a favourable light. It was Aaron who failed to stop the people from making a golden calf. Yet we hear almost nothing about Moses' children, Gershom and Eliezer, who disappear into obscurity. To this day, by contrast, priests are the descendants of Aaron. The Temple may no longer exist but Aaron's children continue to carry the burden of exemplary holiness. Moses' leadership lasted as long as his lifetime. Aaron's leadership persisted through the generations. Ritual creates continuity. The priests lit an everlasting flame.

Ritual has fared badly in the West, and that is one of the reasons *Vayikra* seems to us so strange and remote a book. Many see ritual as part of the mindset of myth and magic. We now know that you cannot bring rain by a rainmaking ceremony. You cannot bring prosperity by attempting to bribe or placate the gods. Battles are not won by prayer alone. Fate is in our hands, not under the control of mythical forces.

All this is true, but such beliefs are alien to Judaism. Faith is not magic or a pre-technological technology. More than any other group in ancient Israel, the priests envisaged God in the most austere terms, shorn of any anthropomorphic language or anything that might be mistaken for myth. God is wholly other, and it is one of the tasks of the priest to ensure that the worship of God remains wholly other. We serve God not to bring success, but to stay close to Him because He is clarity in a world of confusion, life in a world too often obsessed with death, the enduring presence in the midst of change. Ritual for *Torat Kohanim* has nothing to do with its role in primitive societies.

In Judaism, it is something else entirely. Émile Durkheim, one of the founders of sociology and a man whose father, grandfather, and great-grandfather were all rabbis, showed how ritual creates and sustains the group.[17] It creates a collective identity. It is one thing to worship God and confess our sins in the privacy of the soul, quite another to do so at the Temple in ancient times, or in the synagogue now. We are social animals: "It is not good for man to be alone." The depth and breadth of that sociality depends on our ability to pray together, confess together, and celebrate together. That is why it was needed at that point in the history of Israel. Throughout Genesis, the relationship between God and the patriarchs and matriarchs was I-Thou. Now, predicated of a nation, it had to become We-Thou. That needs the coordinated action of ritual.

When we make the transition from childhood to adulthood, becoming responsible citizens in the community of faith, we enter the world of the commands, participate in its life of worship, and learn to make other people's joy and grief our joy and grief. Ritual binds us to Jews in other places, other times. More than anything else, the shared life of ritual sustained Jews as a nation through two thousand years of

---

17. Émile Durkheim, *The Elementary Forms of the Religious Life* (New York: Free Press, 1965).

exile and dispersion. Ritual turns us from lonely individuals into members of the people of the covenant.

The American anthropologist Roy A. Rappaport went further, arguing that ritual is the enactment of meaning.[18] Human beings are meaning-seeking animals, and one way of achieving meaning is through language. But language also allows us to tell lies. Ritual does not speak; it enacts.[19] It communicates meaning not by saying, but by doing. Ritual inducts us into a world of shared values. We may sometimes betray those values, but by taking part in the ritual we enter the world they define. Rappaport sees this as fundamental:

> In enunciating, accepting, and making conventions moral, ritual contains within itself not simply a symbolic representation of social contract, but tacit social contract itself. As such, ritual, which also establishes, guards, and bridges boundaries between public systems and private processes, is *the* basic social act.[20]

So, without ritual, no community, no continuity, no shared structure of meanings. Judaism gives great prominence to individuals. Its texts do not stereotype. Even rejected figures like Ishmael and Esau, failures like Saul, gentiles like Pharaoh's daughter or the Syrian general Naaman, stand out with an individuality of their own. Even when it comes to revealing God's word, "No two prophets prophesy with the same style," say the sages. But there is a difference between *individuality* and *individualism*. The latter ultimately defeats and destroys community. So a nation of strong individuals needs, all the more, to be held together by ritual.

Torat Kohanim sees the religious life as built on the foundation of its rituals that, barring catastrophe, never change. Even though we no

18. Roy Rappaport, *Ritual and Religion in the Making of Humanity* (Cambridge, UK: Cambridge University Press, 2000).
19. Israel Knohl has argued, as did Yehezkel Kaufmann before him, that what was distinctive about the priestly service in Judaism was that it was a service conducted in silence. The priests made no incantations during their offering of sacrifices. See Yehezkel Kaufmann, *The Religion of Israel*; Israel Knohl, *The Silent Sanctuary* and *The Divine Symphony*.
20. Rappaport, op. cit., 138.

longer have a Temple or sacrifices or a functioning priesthood, Judaism continues to be a religion of rituals and it is this that sustains its continuity through time, etching its days with the charisma of grace, more like a marriage than a romance but no less moving for the quietness of its beauty.

A personal memory: the first time I visited Auschwitz, I was numb with grief and shock. There are no words you can say in the presence of a tragedy so vast, an event so unprecedented. You feel overwhelmed by emotion but have no way of expressing it. Then I entered Block 27 in Stammlager Auschwitz. In the almost empty room a recording was playing of *Kel Malei Raḥamim*, the centuries-old Jewish memorial prayer for the dead, sung in the traditional melody. That is when I broke down in tears.

The words made grief articulate. Precisely because they were a ritual – like blowing the shofar or lighting a memorial candle – they sustained meaning in the face of the most determined effort ever undertaken to destroy it. Because we can still say *Kel Malei Raḥamim*, it means that though Jews died, Judaism did not. And because Judaism did not die, neither will the memories of those who did. Ritual is the defeat of nihilism, the failure of meaning when there is nothing to contain it.

Three Voices: Priest, Prophet, King

Viktor Frankl, the great psychotherapist, once described a thought experiment.[21] You see two shapes, both of them shadows cast by an object on a screen. You can only see the shadow, not the object. One is a rectangle, the other a circle. There is only one object. What is it?

The answer is a cylinder, lit first from the side, then from above. Frankl's point is that in two dimensions, a rectangle cannot be a circle. To say that one thing is both is a contradiction. Add a third dimension, though, and the contradiction vanishes. A cylinder viewed from one perspective looks like a rectangle, and from another a circle. What looks like a contradiction, said Frankl, can sometimes be resolved by

---

21. Viktor Frankl, *The Will to Meaning* (New York: World Publishing Company, 1969).

simply adding a dimension. That applies to Torah, both as a text and as a way of life.

Torah, the five Mosaic books, is unlike any other text in Tanakh. Tanakh, the Hebrew Bible as a whole, contains books of many types and genres. There are historical works, prophetic ones, books of wisdom, liturgical collections like the book of Psalms, short stories like those of Jonah and Ruth, laments, love poems, and so on. Sometimes two books tell the same story from different vantage points in time, like the books of Samuel and Kings on the one hand, Chronicles on the other. But almost all of them are one thing: one book, one subject, one genre, one voice.

Torah is not like that at all. It is the only work in Tanakh that contains law: not only one law, but multiple codes that add up, according to tradition, to 613 commands, a vast legal structure covering all aspects of life, from the structuring of a society to the innermost contours of the emotional and cognitive life. But it is much more than that. It contains cosmology: a story, two stories in fact, of how the universe and humanity came to be. It includes history, poetry, genealogy, and prophecy. No other work is quite like it, and this puzzled many great minds. Most famously, Rashi began his commentary with the question posed by R. Yitzḥak: If the Torah is a book of law, why does it not begin with the first law? Why include an account of creation at all? A book of law should stick to law.

Hence the significance of Frankl's point about circles and squares. What looks like several objects can actually be one. A contradiction in two dimensions can make sense in three. That is precisely what the Torah is: many kinds of text, spoken in several voices, which make sense as a coherent whole only if we add an extra dimension: the infinite eternal we call God. The Torah is God's word to humankind, specifically God's word to the particular people He asked to be His witness to humankind.

Jewish tradition divided the books of the Bible into three categories: Torah; *Neviim*, the prophets; and *Ketuvim*, the writings. What makes them different is not their subject matter but their relative holiness, their relationship to God. To put it at its simplest: Torah is the word of God *to* man. The prophetic books are the words of God *through* man. The other writings are the words of man to God.

Throughout this introduction, we have spoken about *Vayikra* as a book written in the priestly voice. What does that mean, and what are the other voices? It does not mean that *Vayikra* was written by priests or for priests, but rather that it expresses the sensibility, the special mindset, the distinctive mode of consciousness of the priest. There are at least two other major voices in the Torah: the *prophetic* voice and the *wisdom* voice. This does not mean that the Torah is a composite work composed by multiple authors. What it means is that the Torah is a precise literary expression of the fact that there are at least three ways of seeing the world in relation to God.

These voices are as different as rectangles and circles. But as Frankl said, sometimes a contradiction disappears when you add another dimension. That is why the Torah is written the way it is. It forces us to think our way through to a new dimension. The question answered by the literary structure of the Torah is: How do you convey in language intelligible to humans something that is beyond the human? This is of course a philosophical problem, but it is also a literary problem. What kind of text would give humans a sense of the divine?

The Torah's solution is the device of multiple perspectives. God discloses Himself in three ways: creation, redemption, and revelation. *Creation* means the world that is: the wonders of nature, the vicissitudes of history, and the conflict within the human heart between duty and desire. *Redemption* is the world that ought to be: a world of justice, compassion, the dignity of the individual, and the sanctity of life, the world God had in mind when He created humankind and to which we are still travelling. *Revelation* is the word that decodes the world. It is the set of instructions – mitzvot – God has given us for reaching Him. Revelation is what happens when we put the world aside and listen to the will of God. It is the world as seen from the Sanctuary, the Temple, and the synagogue. God is where the three meet and become one.

Each of the three disclosures has its own voice. The one associated with creation is called *ḥokhma,* "wisdom." This is the voice we hear in books like Proverbs, Ecclesiastes, and Job, but we also hear it in the Torah, such as in the story of Joseph. It is the most universal of Judaism's voices and was later associated with kings and their courts.

The voice of redemption is prophetic. The prophet sees God in history and sees history itself as the ongoing drama between God and the people with whom He entered into a covenant. For the prophets, time is not a mere series of events, the random collisions of people in pursuit of power. It is the story of God's love for Abraham and his descendants, and how they often abused and betrayed that love.

The voice of revelation is priestly. Unlike the prophet and the king, the priest does not live in the world of everyday. He is the guardian of sacred space and time, the points at which we withdraw from the world to remind ourselves how small we are and how brief are our lives, microseconds in the history of the cosmos, yet how great they can be when we allow ourselves to be brushed by the wings of eternity.[22]

Put these three voices together and you have a literary expression of the fact that God, as He speaks to us through Torah, cannot be confined to a single perspective or vantage point. He is the One within the many, the unity beneath the diversity, the whole that makes the parts cohere. The God of creation, the God of redemption, and the God of revelation are one and the same. It is we on earth who cannot see all three aspects or hear all three voices simultaneously. By weaving them together in a single work, the Torah points us towards that dimension beyond space and time where the many are one. The Torah is the primal literary expression of the monotheistic mind.

The unity of the Torah is the unity of God. This has huge consequences for the spiritual-political-ethical project we call Judaism. Every civilisation since the dawn of history has been struck by the diversity of the natural world with its multiple life forms and the human world with its multiple cultures. The question has always been how to make sense of that diversity. Polytheism sees it as evidence of multiple gods. Atheism sees it as the play of multiple forces, all of which are blind. Judaism sees it as the creation of a loving God who delights in diversity and asks us to respect that diversity.

---

22. Jeremiah refers to the three when he says, "For the *teaching of the law* by the *priest* will not cease, nor will *counsel* from the *wise,* nor the *word* from the *prophets*" (Jer. 18:18). Likewise, Ezekiel: "They will go searching for a *vision* from the *prophet, priestly* instruction in the *law* will cease, the *counsel* of the *elders* will come to an end" (Ezek. 7:23).

That is why Torah, and Judaism generally, is a conversation scored for many voices. It is also why there was never a single figure in Judaism who embodied the totality of faith. There were prophets, priests, and kings. Sometimes one person held two roles. Moses was a prophet and the functional equivalent of a king. But he was not a priest. For that, he had to turn to Aaron. It is precisely this complexity that makes Judaism the unique faith it is. None of us, even the greatest, is spiritually self-sufficient. We are all God-like – in His image, after His likeness – but none of us is God. The priest may not have been the most dramatic figure in the drama of the Hebrew Bible, but without his rituals and continuities, his daily encounters with the Divine, Judaism would not have survived.

Three Forms of the Moral Life

Not only did kings, priests, and prophets see God differently. They saw the moral life differently as well. This makes Jewish ethics both dynamic and multifaceted. That, surely, is how it should be.

From Plato onward, philosophers have given us elegant simplifications of morality. For Plato, it consisted of knowledge, for Aristotle of virtue. David Hume thought it was about emotions, Kant about duty and reason, Bentham about the greatest happiness for the greatest number. John Stuart Mill spoke of "one very simple principle": never interfere with anyone else unless he is harming others. These are all important insights, but the good life does not reduce to one very simple principle. Judaism gives the subject the complexity it deserves.

There is a wisdom morality, set out in the book of Proverbs. It tells us to be humble: "Pride goes before destruction, and a haughty spirit before a fall" (Prov. 16:18). Be generous: "If your enemy is hungry, give him food to eat, and if he is thirsty, give him water to drink" (25:21). Act with integrity: "The digger of a pit falls into it, and the one rolling a stone, on him it will turn" (26:27). Listen much, speak little: "Whoever watches his mouth, guards his life" (13:3). Be content with what you have: "A heart at peace gives life to the body" (14:30). Learn from experience, keep company with the sages, avoid conflict wherever possible, and be ever mindful of God.

That is the voice of *ḥokhma*, wisdom, as we hear it in Proverbs. Ecclesiastes and Job, two other wisdom works, are more tense and searching. Ecclesiastes is a sustained lament about the pointlessness of life in face of the fact that we are all going to die. Job is a powerful challenge to the entire idea that there is justice on earth. No faith that canonises works as challenging as these could ever be called unquestioning or naïve.

Wisdom is about "creation," that is, the here-and-now, the real, empirical, everyday world in which most people find themselves most of the time. Its ideal type is the *ḥakham*, the wise man, or better still, the wise woman: Proverbs 1–9 sees wisdom as a female attribute, and the book ends with the famous hymn of praise to the *eshet ḥayil*, the woman of moral strength. Its approach to morality, while deeply religious, is also prudential, pragmatic, and experience-based. It is more oriented to virtue than to the rule-based morality we associate with Torah and Halakha. Its basic assumption is that the universe is the work of divine wisdom. Therefore, embedded within it are moral as well as scientific laws. Those who keep them flourish; those who flout them eventually fail. The best way of acquiring a moral sense is to live constantly with *yirat Hashem*, awe in the conscious presence of God.

Judaism's wisdom literature is the closest it comes to other wisdom traditions, like those of ancient Egypt and the philosophical world of ancient Greece. The reason is that wisdom is the universal heritage of humankind, part of what it means to be created in the image of God. We are all born and will all die. Humans face similar conflicts and temptations throughout the world. That is why wisdom is universal and perennial.

The prophet's moral voice is very different. He or she (there were prophetesses as well as prophets) is passionate, visionary, challenging, urgent. The prophet is a disturber of the peace, ready to chide a king, a priest, a fellow prophet, or the people as a whole with their moral failings. Continue to behave as you do, says the prophet, and you will bring destruction. A prophet sees tomorrow implicit in today. He warns of what will happen if we do not change. He also inspires with a vision of the ideal society that we can, with God's help, create. The prophet is often the voice of impending doom, but also of inextinguishable hope. When others see peace, the prophet sees the coming catastrophe. When others are weeping, the prophet sees the consolation. If the voice of wisdom lives in the present, the prophet lives in the future.

The prophet is also bearer of the word. He or she speaks, not as wisdom does, on the basis of observation and experience, but rather on the basis of the word God has planted in his mouth, the message He has charged him with delivering. The prophets were often deeply conflicted people, feeling inadequate to the task they had been given by God, knowing that what they had to say would be unpopular and almost certainly unheeded. Isaiah said he had unclean lips. Jeremiah attempted to be silent. Jonah tried to run away. Yet in the end they delivered God's word, and though at the time people were unresponsive, their wisdom became clear in retrospect and their visions remain among the most powerful ever recorded.

The keywords of the prophet are *tzedek* and *mishpat,* social and legal justice; *ḥesed* and *raḥamim,* kindness and compassion. A prophet thinks in terms of relationships: between rich and poor, powerful and powerless. He or she always sees society with a human face. Politics for the prophet is not about power or interests but about the way we honour human beings, especially those who have less power than we do. Above all, the prophet is always passionately concerned about the relationship between the people and God.

The prophet speaks truth to power, but he or she also speaks truth to the religious establishment, the priesthood, the Temple, and its rituals. The prophets were critical of the sacrificial service, not because they opposed it, but rather, they opposed any dissociation between ritual and ethics. You cannot love God and hate human beings. You cannot bring sacrifices at the Temple and then oppress your fellows. God will not hear your prayers if you fail to hear the cries of those around you. The prophet lives in the cognitive dissonance between the world that is and the world that ought to be. His or hers is the voice summoning us to the work of redemption, making society a place of justice and grace.

The priest has a third approach to morality. His template was the world of Genesis 1 before Adam and Eve committed their sin. It is a place of structure and order, harmony and plenitude, the universe God made and seven times pronounced "good." For the priest, there is a moral ecology in the universe as well as a biological one. Ethics is about respecting the integrity of each person, place, and time. Love is an alignment of the human deed and the divine will. Love your neighbour as yourself because your neighbour too is in the image of God. Love the stranger because we are all ultimately strangers and temporary residents on earth. Never give way to the emotions that disturb the order of society: hate, resentment, revenge.

What the priest understands more profoundly than either the king or the prophet is that there is a *sacred ontology*. Just as the universe has a basic physical and biological structure, so it has a basic moral structure created by the word and will of God. When we obey God's commands, we align ourselves with that structure and the result is blessing. When we disobey the commands, the result is curse. If for the sage, the key virtue is wisdom, and for the prophet justice and compassion, for the priest it is obedience. "Noah did everything just as God commanded him" (Gen. 6:22). "The Israelites had done all the work just as the Lord had commanded Moses" (Ex. 39:42). "So Aaron and his sons did everything the Lord commanded through Moses" (Lev. 8:36). For the priest, these verses tell us how the world should be. When human act coincides with divine will, order is safeguarded against the ever-present threat of chaos.

The keyword of priestly ethics is "holy" and its key text is the remarkable chapter 19 of *Vayikra* with its commands to love the neighbour and the stranger, not to hate one's brother in his heart, and not to harbour vengeance or take revenge, and its prohibitions of sowing seeds of mixed kinds, wearing clothes of mixed wool and linen, eating fruit from a tree in its first three years, and cutting the hair at the sides of one's head. The provisions of Leviticus 19 can seem at first glance like a random assembly of laws that have nothing in common. That is because we fail to understand the idea of holiness, which means honouring the divine order in creation, whether it concerns plant or animal life or the relations between human beings.

The priest is trained to see and protect boundaries. He thinks in terms of polar oppositions: light and dark, day and night, holy and common, pure and impure, permitted and forbidden, neighbour and stranger, kin and non-kin, and the rest. Everything has its place in the scheme of things. An act in place sustains order. An act out of place – a transgression, a sin – creates disorder and calls for a sacrificial act of restoration. There is nothing cold or bloodless about this. The priest cares for order in the universe the way a composer cares about the precise order of notes in a symphony, or an architect the precise arrangement of elements in the design of a building.

For the priest, the moral life is not something we learn by observation (the wisdom ethic) or by empathy and the passion for justice (the prophetic ethic), but by honouring the distinctions God has taught us to see in the structure of reality. There is milk, a sign of life, and meat, a sign of death. There is plant life and there is animal life. There are brothers and others. That is sacred ontology and it creates an ethic of holiness. "Be holy, for I the Lord your God am holy."

The priest knows that there is nothing inevitable about the maintenance of order in the human sphere. He knows the spiritual equivalent of the Second Law of Thermodynamics, the law of entropy that says all systems lose energy over time. In the course of time, for example, inequalities grow between rich and poor. Therefore Leviticus prescribes periodic redistributions: the corner of the field, the forgotten sheaf, the tithe for the poor, the sabbatical and Jubilee years. Over time, the accumulated weight of transgressions grows. So there is the annual rite of the Day of Atonement when the High Priest atones for the sins of the people. The priest never forgets the periodic interventions necessary to avoid national entropy, the growth of chaos and disorder in society.

It is a wonderful system, this threefold approach to the moral life. It has generated an ongoing conversation about the right and the good that has continued from the days of Moses to today. The result has been what Paul Johnson calls "a moral philosophy both solid and subtle, which has changed remarkably little over the millennia."[23] That is what emerges when we combine the wisdom of the sage, the passion of the prophet, and the sense of sacred of the priest.

Crisis and the Return of the Holy

The priestly voice we hear in *Vayikra* does not dominate Tanakh as a whole. For centuries it occupied the background, not the foreground, of Jewish life.

23. Paul Johnson, *A History of the Jews* (London: Weidenfeld and Nicholson, 1987), 582.

The great dramas of the post-Mosaic historical books from Joshua to II Kings are about wars, threats, enemies, alliances, victories, defeats, the distribution of power, and the administration of justice. The key figures were kings and their courts, prophets and their visions. These were the shapers of history. The priest, by virtue of his office, did not live in history. He represented the things that do not change precisely because they are intimations of eternity.

It was in exile, in Babylon, that Torah rose to a prominence in the life of the nation that it rarely had before, because it was now the very basis of the nation's identity. A people in exile have by definition lost all the other things that made them a nation – their land, home, language, landscape, independence, and sovereignty. That is why they almost invariably assimilate to the dominant culture and, whether voluntarily or under pressure, adopt the dominant faith.

It was then that the priestly voice came into its own. For monotheism makes possible something impossible otherwise: *a living relationship with God away from home*. The gods of the ancient world, especially the national ones like Ra for Egypt, Baal for the Canaanites, and Chemosh for the Moabites, were gods of place. Their rule existed within a geographically and politically circumscribed territory. Hence exile meant not only the loss of home but also the loss of potency of the gods of home. That is what the exiles initially felt when they asked, "How can we sing the songs of the Lord in a strange land?" (Ps. 137:4).

But the religion of Israel was different. The God of Israel – the One God, creator of the universe – was the God of everywhere who could be reached anywhere. That was the message of a remarkable man who went with the captives to Babylon. His name was Ezekiel and he was both a prophet and a priest. His message to the exiles was one of hope:

> This is what the Sovereign Lord says: "Although I have removed them far among the nations and scattered them among the countries, yet have I become to them a little sanctuary in the countries where they have gone." (Ezek. 11:16)

You could still pray to God in exile. You could even build "a little sanctuary" there.

In exile, there was no role for Judean kings, nor, other than as voices of hope, was there one for prophets. But ironically, for priests there was. The Temple and its sacrifices were lost, but the faith they represented was still alive and a source of identity. Prayer, study of Torah, and the fulfilment of the commands became a kind of exilic home. That was the first act of the spiritual drama that was to unfold in the coming centuries.

The second came with the return from Babylon, especially in the mid-fifth century BCE with the arrival of two key figures: Ezra and Nehemiah. What they found was that the Jews who had remained in Israel had suffered a massive loss of identity. They desecrated the Sabbath, they had out-married, and many of them could no longer speak Hebrew.[24] That was the situation the two men sought to reverse, beginning with a massive public gathering at the gates of Jerusalem on the New Year, when Ezra (also a priest) read the Torah in public, having stationed Levites throughout the crowd to explain what was being said.[25]

This was a turning point in Jewish history. After the experience of exile, Ezra and Nehemiah understood that the battle for national survival was about to become one less of armies than ideas, a test not of military but of spiritual strength. The prophets had always known this, but only rarely had they won the argument. Now, under the sway of great empires, the terms of Jewish existence had changed.

The third act unfolded in the aftermath of the Maccabean revolt in the second century BCE. The battle we commemorate on Ḥanukka was as much against the Hellenised Jews as the Greeks themselves. When the Maccabees won and began ruling as the Hasmonean kings, they too became Hellenised, at which point a new phase began in the search for a strong religious identity. The fate of the Hasmonean kings showed that you could win a military battle while losing the cultural war.

It is at this point that we begin to hear of new groups like the *perushim* (separatists) and *ḥaverim* (members of fellowships), who had begun voluntarily to adopt new religious stringencies, among them rules that had hitherto applied only to priests. For the time being, these were

24. See Nehemiah 13:15–24.
25. Nehemiah 8:1–12.

small sects, not yet a mass movement. But they were the start of what would eventually become a significant feature of Jewish life: the spread of priestly practices among the people as a whole.

The fourth act was the disastrous rebellion against Rome in 66. Many Jews, among them the historian Josephus and the great political realist among the sages, Rabban Yoḥanan b. Zakkai, sensed that it was doomed to failure and so it was. In 70, the Temple was destroyed and in 73, the last group of rebels committed suicide at Massada rather than be taken captive.

The destruction of the Second Temple – feared, expected, foreseen – was a crisis almost without precedent in the history of Israel. The First Temple had been destroyed six centuries earlier, but the prophets, especially Jeremiah, were sure that the Jews would return and that Babylon's power would come to an end. Few believed this of the Romans. What would Israel do without a Temple, sacrifices, a functioning priesthood, and the great rite of the High Priest on Yom Kippur? How could their spiritual life be continued and their sins atoned? It is out of this historic crisis that rabbinic Judaism was born, carrying to its logical conclusion the work begun centuries before by Ezekiel and then Ezra.

Essentially, the rabbis democratised the priesthood. Without Temple or sacrifices, the entire system of *avoda*, divine service, was translated into the everyday life of ordinary Jews. In prayer, every Jew became a priest offering a sacrifice. In repentance, he became a High Priest, atoning for his sins and those of his people. Every synagogue, in Israel or elsewhere, became a fragment of the Temple in Jerusalem. Every table became an altar, every act of charity or hospitality, a kind of sacrifice.

Torah study, once the speciality of the priesthood, became the right and obligation of everyone. Not everyone could wear the crown of priesthood, but everyone could wear the crown of Torah. A *mamzer talmid ḥakham*, a Torah scholar of illegitimate birth, was higher than an *am haaretz Kohen Gadol*, an ignorant High Priest. In rabbinic Judaism, Jews finally realised the vision intimated more than a thousand years earlier of becoming "a kingdom of priests and a holy nation." It was a remarkable triumph over tragedy.

During this centuries-long process, extraordinary changes took place in Jewish life. The synagogue was born. So was the idea of thrice-daily prayer. Torah study became central to the life of the nation. Holiness, once centred on the Temple, was now diffused into the life of the commandments. Every time someone performed a mitzva, they said, "Blessed are You...who has *made us holy by His commands*." Vast intellectual energy was directed to clarifying the Oral Tradition in relation to every detail of life. Judaism had always been a religion of law, but never so intimately and overwhelmingly.

So in the wake of the destruction of the Second Temple, what had been until then just one of three voices became the dominant one. *Torat Kohanim*, the priestly sensibility that sees Jewish identity in terms of ritual and law, survived. The other two great institutions, kingship and prophecy, did not. Kings are by definition conditional on Israel having independence as a sovereign state. This they had only for a relatively short period, in Second Temple times, between the Maccabean Revolt against the Seleucid Greeks (165–162 BCE), and 63 BCE when Pompey invaded Jerusalem and Israel came under Roman rule.

As for prophecy – the hearing of the divine word within history – that only truly functions when Jews are actors on the historical stage, which they no longer were. The last of the biblical prophets were Haggai, Zechariah, and Malachi in early Second Temple times. In the rabbinic literature we hear only of a *Bat Kol*, a heavenly "echo," as if the voice of heaven had grown faint.

Ezra represented the birth of a new type of leader: the teacher as hero, something the Jewish world had not seen since the days of Moses. Jews still had God's word, but by now it had been canonised. Applying it to the present no longer required revelation – God's word to the prophet – but rather, interpretation.[26] This is part of what the rabbis mean when they say, "A sage is greater than a prophet."

It was those fraught, formative centuries prior to and following the destruction of the Second Temple that posed one of the most

---

26. See Moshe Halbertal, *People of the Book: Canon, Meaning, and Authority* (Cambridge, Mass.: Harvard University Press, 1997).

fundamental questions of all in Judaism: How do you remain in touch with God when you have lost your land, your home, your independence, your freedom, your presence on the historical stage, your kings, prophets, and priests, your Temple, and the entire sacrificial order? When all is lost, what remains?

The answer was *Torat Kohanim*, the world of the priest, democratised, set free from its dependence on the Temple, and transfigured. For sacrifice, read prayer. For revelation, read Torah study. For redemption, read *tzedaka*. In place of the land, read law. Halakha, Jewish law, became the arena in which Jews met God and sanctified their lives, and its scholars became the new priesthood. The very non-historicity of the priestly mind – its image of time as eternity – was ideally suited to the existential condition of Jews in exile, in which nothing truly significant could happen until the redemption, which would be brought about by God, not political action, and which it was forbidden to hasten in any way.

The sage became the functional equivalent of the priest as described by Malachi: "For the lips of a priest should keep knowledge, and people should seek the law from his mouth, for he is the messenger of the Lord of hosts" (Mal. 2:7). The Judaism of law and boundary maintenance, of differentiation between permitted and forbidden, sacred and profane, of study and teaching, and of time experienced as a daily, weekly, and yearly cycle – in short, the mindset of the priests – became what Rabbi Joseph Soloveitchik called *ish hahalakha*, "the halakhic personality." The priestly voice emerged as the dominant one in Jewish life until modern times.

What is the priestly voice? It is a voice of order and harmony. It is timeless, not time-bound. It sees the presence of God in law, physical, moral, and spiritual. It speaks of a world in which everything has its time and place. When people blur boundaries – when cultures become Dionysian, Nietzschean – the priest knows that there is danger ahead. The priest is the one who says, "Good fences make good neighbours." Order and integrity are the essentials of the peaceable kingdom. Hillel summed up the driving force of this vision when he defined the "disciples of Aaron" as those who "seek peace, pursue peace, love people, and bring them close to the Torah."

Leviticus Today

So what is the message of Leviticus to us today?

First, it says that the Jewish people is a nation with God in its midst. That is who we are and why. It is an immense challenge. *Vayikra* does not imply that the Divine Presence is easy to live with. The book reverberates with the tragedy of the deaths of Nadav and Avihu on the day the Tabernacle was consecrated, because they brought an offering God had not commanded. Holiness calls for purity, sacrifice, obedience. But we are called on to be a holy people. The philosopher Ludwig Wittgenstein wrote in his notebook in 1931, "Amongst Jews, 'genius' is found only in the holy man."[27] If the Jewish genius is indeed holiness, then it is because of the vision set forth in *Vayikra*.

It tells us that morality is based at least in part on a sacred ontology, meaning that good and evil are objective facts about the universe, not norms of our own devising. There is an ethic of holiness, and it consists of making distinctions, keeping separate things that are unalike, recognising the integrity of creation and the diversity of life, maintaining boundaries, honouring order and restoring it whenever it is damaged, and seeing sin as something that does real harm in the real world as well as staining the soul. For sin, there must be atonement, collective and individual. Yet despite its apparent austerity, the priestly ethic set out in Leviticus 19 speaks in the language of love.

Moral psychologist Jonathan Haidt has recently shown that the secular West has tended to focus on two dimensions of the moral life: care and the avoidance of harm, and fairness.[28] These are, incidentally, the core of the prophetic ethic: *ḥesed* and *raḥamim*, kindness and compassion, alongside *tzedek* and *mishpat*, fairness and justice. But there are, he argues, three other dimensions and they exist in other cultures: loyalty, respect, and a sense of the sacred. Loyalty runs through the whole of Judaism. It might even be the best way of translating the word

---

27. Ludwig Wittgenstein, *Culture and Value* (Chicago: University of Chicago Press, 1980), 18e.
28. Jonathan Haidt, *The Righteous Mind: Why Good People Are Divided by Politics and Religion* (London: Allen Lane, 2012).

emuna, normally read as "faith." But respect and the sense of the sacred are sustained in the world of the priest. Without priests, it is difficult to maintain a sense of identity, strong institutions, or non-negotiable values. If Haidt is correct, it would go a long way towards explaining why Judaism was so successful a synergy between prophet and priest.

Neuroscience also allows us to reconsider the role of ritual in the life of the mind and its emotions. A whole series of studies in recent years has shown how outstanding achievement in any field depends on many years (the magic number is ten thousand hours) of "deep practice," another name for ritual.[29] Repeated behaviour reconfigures the brain, wrapping neural pathways with myelin, thereby turning reflective behaviour into instinctive response. That is what the thirteenth-century rabbinic work, *Sefer HaḤinukh,* meant by the axiom, "The heart is drawn after the deed."[30] All great creative artists develop rituals.[31] If we want to change, develop willpower, and defeat bad habits, ritual is the most effective way. That is what the priestly mind understands better than any of Judaism's other voices. The soul needs exercise as much as the body, and ritual is what creates habits of the heart.

Vayikra tells us that a sexual ethic is fundamental to the health of the nation as well as to the lives of its citizens. It is difficult to hear this in an age in which the very concept of a sexual ethic and a code of self-restraint are counter-cultural. Yet history has shown this to be true. The ethic of *Vayikra* represents a deep commitment to marriage and the family, to sexual fidelity and respect between parents and children. Today's Dionysiac culture with its sexual free-for-all, far from being modern, is exactly where ancient Greece and Rome were before their decline and fall.

29. There is now a huge popular body of literature on the subject. See Malcolm Gladwell, *Outliers: The Story of Success* (London: Allen Lane, 2008); Matthew Syed, *Bounce: The Myth of Talent and the Power of Practice* (London: Fourth Estate, 2011); David Shenk, *The Genius in All of Us* (London: Icon Books, 2010); Daniel Coyle, *The Talent Code* (New York: Bantam Books, 2009); Geoff Colvin, *Talent is Overrated* (New York: Portfolio, 2008).

30. *Sefer HaḤinukh,* command 216.

31. Mason Currey, *Daily Rituals: How Great Minds Make Time, Find Inspiration, and Get to Work* (London: Picador, 2013).

Perhaps surprisingly, it is *Vayikra*'s code of holiness that is most deeply rooted in economic and social realities. The laws of the sabbatical and Jubilee years still have much to teach us about the periodic adjustments that must be made if we are to free people from the burden of poverty and the indignity of dependence. The free market, as Thomas Piketty has argued in his *Capital in the Twenty-First Century*,[32] is better at creating wealth than distributing it equitably. The priestly solution is not to abandon the free market, but rather to make periodic adjustments to ensure the dignity of all. The laws against crossbreeding of animals, planting mixed seeds in a vineyard, even the law against eating meat and milk together, have suddenly become intelligible in an age when we have discovered how easy it is to destroy the delicate ecology on which life depends.

Even the strange mathematical precision of the priestly mindset, its interest in patterns of three, five, and seven that structure its prose, most clearly in the priestly blessings, have had a recent echo of what scientists call the Anthropic principle: the extreme precision with which the universe is fine-tuned for the emergence of life. The universe has a mathematical structure as the priests in Judaism, and Pythagoras in ancient Greece, knew.

For all this, however, the glory of the Torah is the way it is scored for a multiplicity of voices. The biblical scholar Israel Knohl once made the striking observation that the Temple Scroll, one of the documents of the Dead Sea sect, is what the Torah might have looked like had it been written entirely in the priestly voice. No one can read the Temple Scroll without noting how flat it is, how two-dimensional its imagination and inert its prose. The glory of the Torah is its constant juxtaposition of perspectives, styles, and sensibilities. It is these that give it life and dynamism and richness. It is also this that gives the Torah its unparalleled capacity to represent the complexity of the moral and spiritual life, as well as allow us to sense ever deeper dimensions in its message as we ourselves grow and mature and deepen our understanding.

---

32. Thomas Piketty, *Capital in the Twenty-First Century* (Cambridge, Mass.: Belknap Press, 2014).

Torat Kohanim, the priestly mindset, is an indispensable part of the music of Judaism. If the prophet is Beethoven, the priest is Bach, the sound of order, grace, proportion, balance, and harmony. Never was this more beautifully expressed than in the priestly blessings:

> May God bless you and protect you.
> May God make His face shine on you and be gracious to you.
> May God turn His face towards you and grant you peace.
> (Num. 6:24–26)

Those are the blessings to which the holy life aspires.

So in the end we come back to the beginning and to the word *Vayikra* itself, which Rashi defines as a call uttered in love. In *Vayikra*, God sets out the mystery and majesty of holiness, summoning the people with whom He covenanted to a life driven by its energy, lit by its radiance, transformed by its alignment with the will and word of its Creator. One who lives a life of holiness will – so is the priestly promise – know what it is to feel God's face turned towards him or her, and in that sacred meeting discover the true depth of peace.

Vayikra
ויקרא

Vayikra, the third book of the Torah, is markedly different from the others. It contains no journey. It is set entirely at Sinai. It occupies only a brief section of time: a single month. There is almost no narrative. Yet, set at the centre of the Mosaic books, it is the key to understanding Israel's vocation as "a kingdom of priests and a holy nation," the first collective mission statement in history.

This *parasha*, with which the book opens, details the various kinds of sacrifice the Israelites brought to the Tabernacle. There were five: the burnt offering (*ola*), the grain offering (*minḥa*), the peace offering (*shelamim*), the sin offering (*ḥatat*), and the guilt offering (*asham*).

The first of the essays is about the name of the book itself, *Vayikra*, "And He called." Far from being simply the book's first word, it prepares us for echoes elsewhere and especially at the end, intimating the vast yet almost imperceptible difference between understanding history as God's call, or as mere chance.

The second essay looks at the prophetic critique of the sacrifices, the third at Maimonides' famously controversial analysis. The fourth explores the symbolism of sacrifice in general. The fifth asks what the sin offering tells us about the nature of sin itself. The sixth looks at a nuance in the text that suggests that a leader cannot avoid making mistakes, and explores why this is so.

Between Destiny and Chance

Sometimes in the Torah an entire philosophy is embedded in a single word. That is the case with the word that gives its name not only to the *parasha*, but also to the book as a whole: *Vayikra*, "He called."

This is not a word that seems to promise hidden depths. It is no more than the first word of the book. It seems mere coincidence that it was this word and not another. Yet it turns out that "mere coincidence" is precisely what it is not. Once we uncover the clues and decipher the code, we will find that the beginning and end of *Vayikra* form a meditative essay on the nature of history as coincidence or call, chance or scripted drama. They are an answer to the question: Is there meaning in history?

Vayikra was not the first name the sages gave the book. They called it *Torat Kohanim*, "The Law of the Priests," because much of it is about the Sanctuary and its service, the world of the priests. Hence its English name, Leviticus, from the Greek and Latin meaning "matters concerning the Levites," the tribe from which the priests came.

Yet there was something about this name that was not quite right. Much of the book is indeed about the work of the priests and the Sanctuary. But the book is larger than that. It opens out into broad vistas of personal morality and social justice. The great code in Leviticus 19 tells us that every Jew, not just a priestly elite, is called on to be holy, "because I the Lord your God am holy." So tradition eventually settled on the name *Vayikra*, "He called."

What might lead us to think that there is more to this word than meets the eye? First is the fact that it is seemingly superfluous. Literally translated, the verse reads, "He *called* to Moses; the Lord *spoke* to him from the Tent of Meeting, *saying*...." There are no less than three verbs for speech here: calling, speaking, and saying. Given the terseness of the Torah, especially in legal contexts, the redundancy cries for attention.

Second, the entire phrase, "He called to Moses," is clearly a prelude. Once we get to "the Lord spoke to him, saying," we know we are about to hear substantive details. The opening phrase is a tone-setting one. It creates a mood. God is summoning Moses, and through him the Israelites, but to what?

In English, we use the word "vocation" to describe someone's occupation: their job, their profession, their career. Originally, though, the word meant "a task to which one is called." Though it has now been thoroughly secularised, it was at first a deeply religious idea, derived via Latin and Old French from *Vayikra*, being "called" by God to a sacred task, a mission. So we can already sense in this opening word something quite profound. It is as if God were saying, "What I am about to tell you is not only about what you should *do*. It is also about what you are called on to *be*." We sense already that *Vayikra* is about Israel's vocation as a holy people dedicated to God.

Third, there is something strange and conspicuous about the way the word is written in a Torah scroll. Its last letter, an *aleph*, is written small – almost to the point of invisibility. The standard-size letters spell out the word *vayikar*, meaning, "He encountered, chanced upon." Unlike *vayikra*, which refers to a call, a meeting by request, *vayikar* suggests the opposite: an accidental meeting, a mere happenstance.

The sages, always alert to intertextuality – the way a word or phrase in one place chimes with one in another – immediately recall that *vayikar* is the verb the Torah uses for God's encounter with the pagan prophet Balaam (Num. 23:16). This is how they interpret the contrast:

What is the difference between the prophets of Israel and the prophets of the pagan nations of the world? ... R. Ḥama b. Ḥanina said: "The Holy One, Blessed Be He, reveals Himself to the pagan nations by an incomplete form of address, as it is said, 'And the Lord appeared [*vayikar*] to Balaam,' whereas to the prophets of Israel, He appears in a complete form of address, as it is said, 'And He called [*vayikra*] to Moses.'"[1]

Rashi, more discursively, explains that the verb "to call" denotes something more than mere speech. It implies affection, intimacy, a relationship of love:

All [God's] communications [to Moses], whether they use the words "speak" or "say" or "command," were preceded by a call [*keria*] which is a term of endearment, used by the angels when they address one another, as it is said, "And one called to the other" [*vekara zeh el zeh*, Isaiah 6:3]. However, to the prophets of the nations of the world, His appearance is described by an expression signifying a casual encounter and uncleanness, as it says, "And the Lord appeared to Balaam."[2]

That accounts for the difference between *vayikra* and *vayikar*. What about the small *aleph*? Rabbi Jacob ben Asher (1269–1340) endearingly suggests that it has to do with the character of Moses:

Moses, being both great and humble, wanted only to write *Vayikar*, signifying "chance," as if the Holy One, Blessed Be He, did no more than appear to him in a dream, as in the case of Balaam, to whom God appeared by mere chance. However, God told him to write the word with an *aleph*. Moses then said to Him, because of his extreme humility, that he would only write an *aleph* that was smaller than the other *aleph*s in the Torah, and he did indeed write it small.[3]

---

1. Leviticus Rabba 1:13.
2. Rashi, Commentary to Leviticus 1:1.
3. Baal HaTurim, Commentary to Leviticus 1:1.

This, then, is our point of departure. *Vayikra* is a call uttered in love. It is the opposite of *vayikar*, mere chance, a fortuitous happening. But to grasp the full significance of what is being said, we have to turn to the end of the book.

One of the key literary devices of the Torah is chiasmus, or mirror-image symmetry: a passage that has the form ABCBA. Sometimes the passage is short, as in Genesis 9:6: "He who sheds/the blood/of man/by man/ shall his blood/be shed." But it can sometimes be very long. The end of the book of Exodus parallels the beginning of Genesis. In Genesis, God creates the universe, a cosmos. At the end of Exodus, the Israelites create the Sanctuary, a microcosm. There are clear linguistic parallels between the two texts. So it is in the book of *Vayikra*. The end echoes the beginning. How so?

Just before the end of *Parashat Beḥukkotai*, there is one of the two terrifying passages known as *Tokheḥa*, the "warning" or "rebuke"[4] telling of the curses that will befall the Israelites if they fail to keep their covenant with God:

> As for you who survive, will send faintness into their hearts in the lands of their enemies. The sound of a driven leaf shall put them to flight, and they shall flee as one flees from the sword, and they shall fall though no one is pursuing them.... The land of your enemies will consume you. (Lev. 26:36–38)

These curses contain a recurring motif: the word *keri*. It appears seven times, always a sign of significance in the Torah, and it is used nowhere else in the whole Torah. Here are two occurrences by way of example:

> "If in spite of this, you still do not listen to Me but continue to behave *bekeri* towards Me, then in My anger I will behave towards you *bekeri*, and I Myself will punish you seven times for your sins." (Lev. 26:27–28)

The commentators disagree as to what the word *keri* means. The Targum reads it as "if you harden yourselves," Saadia Gaon as "if you

---

4. The other passage is Deuteronomy 28:15–68.

are rebellious," Rashbam as "if you refuse to follow My way," and Ibn Ezra as "if you are overconfident." Maimonides, however, gives it a quite different interpretation, and does so in a halakhic context, in relation to the command to proclaim a public fast when the Jewish people are in distress:

> It is a positive scriptural command to pray and sound the alarm with trumpets whenever trouble befalls the community.... This is one of the paths to repentance, for when the community cries out in prayer and sounds an alarm when threatened by trouble, everyone realises that evil has come on them as a result of their own wrongdoing... and repentance will cause the trouble to be removed.
>
> If, however, the people do not cry out in prayer and do not sound an alarm but merely say that it is the way of the world for such a thing to happen to them, and that their trouble is a matter of pure chance, they have chosen a cruel path that will cause them to continue in their wrongdoing and thus bring additional troubles on them. For when Scripture says, "If you continue to be *keri* towards Me, then in My anger I will be *keri* towards you" (Lev. 26:27–28), it means: If, when I bring trouble upon you in order to cause you to repent, you say that the trouble is *purely accidental,* then I will add to your trouble the anger of *being left to chance.*[5]

Maimonides understands *keri* to be related to *mikre,* meaning "chance," the way of the world. To regard something as *mikre* means to see it as if it had no larger significance. It just happened. That, says Maimonides, is not how we as Jews should see our fate. It is not mere chance.

This means that for Maimonides, the curses at the end of Leviticus are not divine *retribution* as such. It will not be God who makes Israel suffer; it will be other human beings. What will happen is that God will withdraw His protection. Israel will have to face the world without the sheltering presence of God.

---

5. Maimonides, *Mishneh Torah, Hilkhot Taaniyot* 1:1–3.

This, for Maimonides, is an application of the principle of measure-for-measure (*midda keneged midda*).[6] If Israel believes in divine providence, it will be blessed by divine providence. If it sees history as mere chance – what Joseph Heller, author of *Catch-22*, called "a trash bag of random coincidences blown open by the wind"[7] – then indeed they will be left to chance. And since Israel is a small nation surrounded by large empires, chance will not be kind to them.

We now discern the remarkable idea linking the beginning of *Vayikra* to the end. It is about the difference between *mikra* and *mikre* – between history as God's call and history as mere chance, a sequence of events with no underlying purpose or meaning.

The difference is vast, but in the Hebrew language it is almost imperceptible. The two words sound the same. The only difference is that the former has an *aleph* while the latter does not (*aleph*, the first letter of the Hebrew alphabet, is also the first letter of the Ten Commandments, the *Anokhi*, "I am," of God).

An *aleph* is almost inaudible. Its appearance in the Torah scroll at the beginning of *Vayikra* (the "small *aleph*") is almost invisible. It is as if the Torah were intimating that the presence of God in history will not always be as clear and unambiguous as it was during the Exodus or the division of the Red Sea. For much of the time, it will depend on our own sensitivity. For those who look, it will be visible. For those who listen, it will be audible. But we will need to look and listen. God does not force His presence on us against our will. We have to search Him out.

If we choose *not* to see or hear, then *Vayikra* will become *Vayikar*. God's call will be inaudible. History will seem no more than "a tale/ Told by an idiot, full of sound and fury, /Signifying nothing." There is nothing incoherent about such an idea. It is a self-fulfilling expectation. *If you believe that history is chance, then it will become so.*

But if you believe otherwise, it will be otherwise. So Jewish history has appeared to great minds, among them Pascal, Rousseau, and

6. Shabbat 105b.
7. Joseph Heller, *Good as Gold* (New York: Simon and Schuster, 1979), 74.

Tolstoy.[8] Something about the survival of the Jewish people against all odds seemed to them to testify to the presence of God in their midst. Only thus could such a small, vulnerable, relatively powerless people endure and still be able to say, even after the Holocaust, *Am Yisrael ḥai*, "the Jewish people lives."

Jews were the first people to see meaning in history, to recognise it as something other than a succession of events with no connecting thread. The prophets knew that history is the arena within which God calls us, His covenantal partners, to honour one another by honouring Him. The whole of Jewish history is a commentary on the success or failure of the people to honour that covenant, made at Sinai where the entire book of *Vayikra* is set.[9]

Having come this far, we can now see the Torah's masterstroke. *For it was the prophets, not the priests, who saw God in history.* The prophets lived in the medium of time. They knew the people's past. They foretold its future. They were the map-readers of events. The priests did not live in the midst of history any more than they lived in the midst of society. They inhabited the domain of the holy, where nothing changes. Time for the priest is a cycle, daily, weekly, monthly, yearly, where every offering can be specified in advance. Plato might have been defining the priestly mindset when he called time "the moving image of eternity."[10]

Four of the five books of the Torah are set in history. Genesis is about the pre-history of the Israelites, when they were a family, not yet a nation. Deuteronomy is about their post-history, that is, the time after the wilderness years when they would become a nation in a world of nations. Exodus is about the journey from Egypt to Sinai, Numbers

---

8. See Jonathan Sacks, *A Letter in the Scroll: Understanding Our Jewish Identity and Exploring the Legacy of the World's Oldest Religion* (New York: Free Press, 2000), 35–38.

9. For example, the British historian J.H. Plumb writes: "The concept that within the history of mankind itself a process was at work which would mould his future, and lead man to situations totally different from his past, seems to have found its first expression amongst the Jews. The Greeks had a healthy sense of their own superiority – more, perhaps, than most ancient people – yet they possessed no belief that their history taught them they had a special destiny and a special future." J.H. Plumb, *The Death of the Past* (Harmondsworth: Penguin, 1973), 56.

10. Plato, *Timaeus*, 37.

about the journey from Sinai to the brink of the Promised Land. *Vayikra* is unique. It alone among the five books is not about history. It is about holiness: eternity in the midst of time.

What the word *Vayikra* at the beginning and the sevenfold *keri* at the end do is to enfold the priestly book in prophetic time. They tell us that the priestly and prophetic universes belong to one another. It is Israel's timeless encounters with God that allow it to negotiate safely the currents and rapids of time. Israel's sacred service, mediated by the priest, is the boat in which it travels down the prophet's river of destiny. And the choice is one we must all make. Will we live the life of *vayikra* or *keri*, *mikra* or *mikre*, vocation or accident, destiny or chance?

Just as Jewish history is not mere chance, so it is no mere coincidence that the first word of the Torah's central book is *Vayikra*, "He called." For *Vayikra*, the priestly book, is God's call to Israel to become "a kingdom of priests and a holy nation,"[11] and thereby fulfil the prophetic vision of history as the place where, in the midst of time, we live the truths that are beyond time.

11. Exodus 19:6.

The Gift of Being Able to Give

My late father sold *schmattes*, offcuts of cloth, on Commercial Road, the London equivalent of New York's Lower East Side. He was a proud man, born at the wrong time. Having come to Britain as a child fleeing persecution in Poland, he had to leave school at the age of fourteen to help earn money working with his father to support the family. He was not one of nature's businessmen. He had a fine mind and excellent taste in music, art, and literature, in all of which he was completely self-educated. In another life, he would have been a successful professional. But none of us chooses when to be born, and we are not all equally lucky. Like many of his contemporaries, he dedicated his life to giving his children the opportunities he lacked. That was the blessing he gave us, his four sons.

There was one gift that to me, the eldest, meant more than all the others. From almost as soon as I could walk, we used to go to the synagogue together every Shabbat. On the way back I would ask him questions about what we had done or said during the service. He always gave me the same answer, and it was this that shaped my life. He used to say: "Jonathan, I didn't have an education, so I can't answer your questions. But one day you will have the education I did not have, and when that happens, you will teach me the answers to those questions." If I achieved anything in my life it was because of that reply.

I am not sure that Sigmund Freud had the same kind of father as I did. He surely touched on some element of truth when he formulated the Oedipus complex, the idea that a son at some unconscious level feels he can only make space for himself by displacing his father, and that therefore there is a hidden tension, even a murderous hostility, between the generations. Freud was one of the great minds of the twentieth century, and even when a great mind is wrong, it sheds more light than a hundred lesser intellects that get it right.

What my late father showed me was that there is a way out of this tension, but it needs exceptional humility on the part of the parent. What my father gave me was the opportunity to give back to him. This is very rare. Children know how dependent they are on their parents. They know that when they give their parents a present, it is usually only a token gesture. It is a supremely risky move on the part of parents to genuinely empower a child to give them something of real worth. It is the ultimate act of humility, and it confers on the child a dignity and self-worth like no other.

That, it seems to me, is the ultimate truth about the institution of sacrifices in the Torah, and it is a difficult truth, which is why no other aspect of Judaism proved more internally controversial. About sacrifice in Judaism there is a real and deep cognitive dissonance.

On the one hand, sacrifices occupy a key position in the Mosaic books. Their laws are set out in great detail in *Vayikra*, the middle book of the Torah and the central pillar of its entire edifice. It is no accident that for many centuries, it was customary to make it the first book to be taught to Jewish children when they began their education: "Let the pure [children] come and occupy themselves with the pure [sacrifices]."[1] The sacrifices and the rituals that accompanied them, known generically as *avoda*, "service," are a – perhaps even *the* – core element of Israel's identity. Their importance to the biblical vision cannot be gainsaid.

1. Leviticus Rabba 7:3.

Yet many of Israel's greatest prophets made statements that are, or at least seem to be, devastatingly critical of the whole institution of sacrifices. Amos declares in the name of God:

> I hate, I despise, your religious feasts;
> I cannot stand your assemblies.
> Even though you bring Me burnt offerings and grain offerings,
> I will not accept them.
> Though you bring choice peace offerings,
> I will have no regard for them...
> But let justice roll on like a river, righteousness like a never-failing stream.
> (Amos 5:21–24)

In a similar vein, Isaiah says in the passage we read before Tisha B'Av:

> "The multitude of your sacrifices, what are they to Me?" says the Lord.
> "I have more than enough of burnt offerings...
> Stop bringing meaningless offerings!
> Your incense is detestable to Me...
> Wash and make yourself clean.
> Take your evil deeds out of My sight.
> Stop doing wrong, learn to do right.
> Seek justice.
> Encourage the oppressed.
> Defend the cause of the fatherless.
> Plead the case of the widow." (Is. 1:11–17)

How are we to understand language of this vehemence if sacrifices are a mitzva, a good deed, a commanded act?

One of the most striking features of Judaism is that it makes its appearance as something new in a world already old. Mesopotamia and Egypt, the first two empires, already exist. The land of Canaan is already settled. Judaism is a protest: against empires, hierarchical social structures, and the beliefs that held them in place. The Hebrew Bible is a sustained battle against three things: idolatry (the system), myth (the narrative that justifies the system), and pagan ritual (the acts that sustain the system).

The world against which Judaism is a protest is one that saw the universe as an arena of conflicting powers, seen as gods. They fought among themselves and were at best indifferent, at worst actively hostile, to human beings. The universe of idolatry and myth is one in which chaos and destruction are constant threats, and the human order vulnerable and always at risk. *Sacrifice in pagan society is the way humans placate the gods.* It is how they seek to neutralise the vast forces of nature that seem constantly to threaten the security and stability of human life. They are an expression of fear.

The German scholar of Greek mythology, Walter Burkert, has gone further and argued that sacrificial ritual replays the ancient terror felt by humans *before* the birth of civilisation, when they were the potential prey of wild animals. He invites us to imagine this primal scene:

> A group surrounded by predators: men chased by wolves, or apes in the presence of leopards. The utmost danger is met with excitement and anxiety. Usually there will be but one way of salvation: one member of the group must fall prey to the hungry carnivores, then the rest will be safe for the time being. An outsider, an invalid, or a young animal will be most liable to become the victim. This situation of pursuit by predators must have played a momentous role in the evolution of civilisation, while man, as a hunter, became a predator himself.[2]

Sacrifice, in his view, replays this scene. It represents the victim thrown to the beast so that the rest of the group can escape and survive. Such a view of reality is as far as possible removed from the Judaic view of a transcendent God who created the universe in love, set His image on humankind, granted him dominion over all other forms of life, and whose primary attributes are justice and compassion.

2. Walter Burkert, *Structure and History in Greek Mythology and Ritual* (Berkeley: University of California, 1997), 71.

Sacrifice must have seemed to the prophets, as it did to Maimonides in a later age, as tainted by association with the very doctrines Judaism most opposed: a world in which conflict is endemic and power the ultimate victor. Sacrifice as the attempt to placate the gods by either earning their goodwill or diverting their attention must have seemed both primitive and offensive.

In Judaism, God cannot be bribed.[3] Indeed, the very concept of giving to God something He does not already own is a contradiction in terms. As King David said: "Everything comes from You, and we have given You only what comes from Your hand" (1 Chr. 29:14). Above all – and this is the heart of the prophetic critique – the sacrificial system as practised in the ancient world *dissociated ritual and ethics*. The gods who could be placated by sacrifice had no interest in the good, the right, and the just. They were forces to be appeased, not judges seeking contrition on the part of offenders.

The prophets were not against sacrifice as such, but they were passionate in their opposition to the idea that by offering animals on the altar, people could buy their way into God's good graces, persuading Him to overlook their misdeeds when it came to their conduct towards their fellow humans. This, to them, was sacrilege. To be pious towards heaven while being rapacious on earth seemed to them, as it seems to us, to pervert the very fundamentals of faith.

Why then does the Torah permit, indeed require, sacrifice? God, after all, accepts the sacrifice of Abel (Gen. 4:4), and is moved by the offering of Noah (Gen. 8:21–22) to vow that He would never again "curse the ground because of man."

The answer seems obvious once we take seriously the central image in the Torah of God as father and the Israelites as His children. *The greatest gift a parent can give a child is the dignity of being able to give.* It is not that the parent lacks anything or that the child has genuinely given something he owns. Its significance is that it is a gesture of love – of

---

3. "For the Lord your God is God of gods and Lord of lords, the great God, mighty and awesome, who shows no partiality and accepts no bribes" (Deut. 10:17). "Now let the fear of the Lord be on you. Judge carefully, for with the Lord our God there is no injustice or partiality or bribery" (11 Chr. 19:7).

acknowledgement and thanksgiving and reciprocity. The child knows that he has nothing of his own to give, yet he seeks to answer love with love. For a parent to give a child that possibility is a monumental act of humility. It is this gesture that is at the heart of the biblical institution of sacrifices. God's greatness is His humility, said R. Yoḥanan,[4] and never more so than here.

The radical idea of Abrahamic monotheism is that of a moral universe structured by the twin forces of justice and love. Justice is impersonal, but love, as Judaism understands it, is intensely personal. In the case of sin or guilt offerings, sacrifice represents our acknowledgement of the personal dimension of wrongdoing. We seek not just to put right the moral disorder caused by our sin, but also to restore our damaged relationship with "the judge of all the earth." At other times, sacrifice is a way of expressing thanks of the kind a child feels towards the parents who brought him into being and shelter him from harm.

Love, and its close relation, loyalty, are what structure the human order as conceived by the Torah: marriage, the family, the community, and the nation, the love between husband and wife, parent and child, and between neighbours and strangers. The ethic of the Torah, or as it is sometimes more widely characterised, the Judeo-Christian heritage, is unique in placing interpersonal love as the foundation of human society, thus giving sacrifice a new, transfigured meaning. For we make sacrifices for those we love. Sacrifice is neither the pursuit of personal advantage nor a requirement of justice conceived as an impersonal system of rules. It is the expression of love.

Sacrifice in the Torah is always expressive of an I-Thou relationship between creature and creator. That is why, whenever the Torah speaks about sacrifice, it always uses the Tetragrammaton, the four-letter name of God, *Hashem*, and never the term *Elokim*, which expresses the impersonal idea of "the force of forces," God as creator, or God as justice. Franz Rosenzweig wrote about the difference between *Gesetz*, law, and *Gebot*, command. Law is always impersonal, whereas command is personal. We obey law because of reason or interest. We obey a command because

4. Megilla 31a.

of our relation to the One who commands.[5] Sacrifice in the Torah is precisely a repeated recognition of the personal presence of God at the heart of its collective life. It is a way of paying homage to the lawgiver, not just obeying the law.

Yale law professor Paul W. Kahn has recently argued that it is this dimension of love and sacrifice that makes society coherent in a way not recognised by conventional secular political philosophy:

> Sacrifice is at the heart of both politics and family. Both parent and citizen understand themselves as subject to a demand for sacrifice. They recognise the demand as legitimate because they live in the world of meanings that the sacrificial act affirms. Sacrifice is, accordingly, the way of being in a meaningful world. Sacrifice, we say, is an act of love. In love, we are willing to sacrifice, and through that sacrifice we simultaneously create and discover the subject that we are.[6]

Kahn's point is that social contract theory sees humans as isolated individuals pursuing their collective self-interest. But self-interest cannot explain sacrifice, and thus cannot explain love or loyalty, and it is these that bind people together as a group. "To imagine a family in which sacrifice was not ordinary is to imagine a dysfunctional family; the same is true of the state." Liberalism, he argues, is "speechless in the face of sacrifice." But a political theory that finds sacrifice incomprehensible "has failed to come to grips with the most elementary forms of our experience of meaning. We will never understand sacrifice, however, if we fail to embrace love." In love, "we find salvation from our own finitude."[7]

Lehakriv, the biblical verb meaning "to sacrifice," means "*to bring something close.*" *Korban*, a sacrifice, is "that which is brought close." The entire biblical understanding of sacrifice is that it is an answer to the

---

5. See Franz Rosenzweig and Nahum N. Glatzer, *On Jewish Learning* (Madison, Wis.: University of Wisconsin, 2002).
6. Paul W. Kahn, *Putting Liberalism in its Place* (Princeton, NJ: Princeton University Press, 2005), 224.
7. Ibid.

fundamental existential question of humanity in the face of the infinite: How can we come close to God, who is vaster than the universe and beyond time? From a human perspective, the act of sacrifice is a process of opening ourselves to God by renouncing something of ourselves. We bring a gift of affection, as a child to a parent. We offer something in our possession, our power, our will, our self-sufficiency. We engage in a symbolic act of renunciation. We acknowledge our dependency on God. Sacrifice is the primal act of love.

The result of such "coming close" is that, after it, we return to the world changed. Renouncing our ownership of something (an animal, or part of the harvest), we acknowledge God's ownership of the world. We are not alone in the universe. We are trustees or guardians on behalf of God. For this reason, when the Temple was destroyed, other forms of renunciation could be substituted: of the will (in the case of prayer), or the mind (learning), or of property (*tzedaka* and hospitality to strangers). When we give, we come close to the Soul of Being.

Yet for God to allow such a gesture is a supreme act of *tzimtzum*, self-limitation. If I felt this about my father, who lacked so much, how much more so of the One who lacks nothing and is, in a sense, everything. In merely permitting the act of sacrifice, God was taking, as it were, a momentous risk. Externally, superficially, sacrifices were the point at which the practices of Judaism came closest to those of pagan cults. Their inner meaning was quite different but their outer form was similar.

Hence the sustained critique of sacrifices by the prophets. They were not against the institution, but they recognised that here, more than anywhere else, Jews could lapse into idolatry. They could come to see sacrifices as a way of placating God, leaving them free to act ruthlessly in the world outside the Temple, exercising power over the powerless with neither justice nor mercy. Here more than anywhere else, intention was vital. The wrong intention could turn a holy act into a pagan one.

We cannot begin to understand the sacrificial system in Judaism without seeing it as the way God allowed His people to come close to Him, the space He created for them to be able to offer Him a gift of love, thus overcoming the Oedipal conflict that must otherwise exist between an all-powerful parent and a consciously dependent child. Eventually, of course, prayer took the place of sacrifice, and the offering of *words* became the substitute for an offering of animals or grain. The common factor is the act of *coming close by bringing close.* Like sacrifice, prayer is where we consciously come close to God, offering back in love the gift of our being. We then find ourselves given back to the world purged, cleansed, forgiven, renewed, our love accepted, our worth affirmed.

Maimonides on Sacrifices

The best-known, as well as the most controversial, interpretation of the place of sacrifices in the religious life is that of Moses Maimonides in *The Guide for the Perplexed*.

Maimonides, the greatest rabbi of the Middle Ages, had already written a systematic commentary to the Mishna as well as the *Mishneh Torah*, the greatest of all codes of Jewish law, before writing *The Guide for the Perplexed*. He was internationally recognised as a supreme authority on Jewish law, and was turned to for guidance by Jews from as far afield as Provence, Marseilles, and Lunel in France, to Yemen and Baghdad. He had become a physician in service to the Sultan Saladin in Cairo and was the author of many medical texts. He had long had an interest in philosophy – one of his first published works was a treatise on logic – and he believed, as he wrote in his code, that natural science and philosophy were ways of arriving at the love and fear of God.[1]

These views were not shared by the vast majority of his con-temporaries, who if anything thought that too deep an encounter with "Greek wisdom" could only lead to heresy or at least the dilution and

---

1.   Maimonides, *Mishneh Torah, Hilkhot Yesodei HaTorah* 2:2.

diminution of faith. A chance encounter, however, led Maimonides to set out his views on these subjects at greater length.

Maimonides had been approached by a young Jewish scholar named Joseph ibn Aknin from Morocco. Joseph, who had been educated not only in traditional Jewish studies but also in medicine and philosophy, found his faith challenged until he read Maimonides' *Mishneh Torah*. He sensed that its author was a man to whom he could bring his questions and doubts, so he wrote to Maimonides asking if he could come study with him in Fostat, near Cairo, where the master lived. Maimonides agreed, and starting in 1185, for two years Joseph lived with him, becoming not only a disciple but almost an adopted son. Thereafter he moved, first to Aleppo then to Baghdad, but they continued the relationship in the form of regular letters, always circling around the same topic: how to reconcile the traditional teachings of Judaism with the discipline and doctrines of neo-Platonic and Aristotelian philosophy that had come back into favour through the work of Islamic philosopher-theologians like Averroes (1126–1198).

For the next three years, in what limited spare time was left to Maimonides from his duties as physician, communal leader, and authority on Jewish law, he developed his answers at length in the form of the book known as *The Guide for the Perplexed*. Maimonides knew that his ideas would be controversial and might seem disturbing to those without philosophical training. But as he writes in the introduction: "When I have a difficult subject before me – when I find the road narrow, and can see no other way of teaching a well-established truth except by pleasing one intelligent man and displeasing ten thousand fools – I prefer to address myself to the one man, and to take no notice whatever of the condemnation of the multitude."[2]

So it was when he came to explaining the sacrificial system of the Torah, for it was here that he developed a historical approach to the nature of biblical law. The whole purpose of the Torah, he argued, was to wean people away from idolatry. But this could not happen, as it were, overnight. As in nature, so in human nature, evolution rather than revolution is how change occurs. "It is impossible to go suddenly from one extreme to the other; it is therefore according to the nature of

---

2. Maimonides, *The Guide for the Perplexed*, introduction.

man impossible for him suddenly to discontinue everything to which he has been accustomed."[3]

Proof of this, says Maimonides, is to be found in the Torah itself, when it says: "It came to pass, when Pharaoh let the people go, that God did not lead them by way of the land of the Philistines, although that was near; for God said, 'Lest perhaps the people change their minds when they see war, and return to Egypt'" (Ex. 13:17). To go suddenly from slavery to fighting battles for the possession of the land of Canaan was demanding too much too soon from the Israelites. They needed the experience of hardship in the desert to give them courage. The conquering of Canaan needed a new generation, born in freedom.

If we were to ask why God, who can change nature by way of a miracle, cannot change human nature also, Maimonides replies that that would be to deprive human beings of their freedom. God, precisely because He has given humans freedom, is under, as it were, a self-denying ordinance never to intervene directly in the human heart. If people are slow to change, God exercises patience. So it was that God wanted to wean the people from the various religious practices of those days, but it had to be done gradually:

> The custom which was in those days general among all men, and the general mode of worship in which the Israelites were brought up, consisted of sacrificing animals in those temples which contained certain images, to bow down to those images, and to burn incense before them.[4]

To suddenly discontinue this mode of religious practice would have been impossible: "It would have been contrary to the nature of man, who generally cleaves to that to which he is used."

So instead of banning sacrifices, God restricted them by specifying that they could only be offered in one place, the Sanctuary; they could only be offered by one subsection of the population, the priests; and there was a limit as to which animals could be offered and when. The

---

3. Ibid., III:32.
4. Ibid.

aim was to circumscribe and restrict the practice of sacrifices, while at the same time gradually weaning the people from the idolatrous beliefs they had once held under the influence of the prevailing culture of the time.

That is Maimonides' first point, and the most controversial – introducing a developmental perspective into the commands, by seeming to suggest that what may have been necessary at one time might not be so at a later stage when the Israelites had been fully weaned from their reliance on sacrifice.

This conflicts with Maimonides' categorical statement a mere two chapters later in the *Guide* that Torah law does *not* change over time: "The laws cannot vary... according to the different conditions of persons and times.... It would not be right to make the fundamental principles of the law dependent on a certain time or a certain place."

Nor does it accord with his position in his law code, where he speaks in praise of the *ḥukkim*, "divine decrees" for which the reasons are not known, adding:

> All the laws concerning sacrifices are in the category of decrees. The sages have said that the world stands because of the service of the sacrifices, for from the performance of the decrees and laws, the righteous merit life in the World to Come. Indeed the Torah put the decrees first, as it is said: "Keep My decrees and laws, since it is only by keeping them that a person can [truly] live. I am God (Lev. 18:5)." [5]

As Isadore Twersky notes, the evolutionary explanation Maimonides gives for the sacrifices in the *Guide* is "not easily integrated" with his position in the *Mishneh Torah*, where the sacrifices are seen as virtuous in their own right, and as commands that have no known rational explanation. [6] There is a real tension here which does not admit any simple solution. [7]

---

5. Maimonides, *Mishneh Torah, Hilkhot Me'ila* 8:8.
6. Isadore Twersky, *Introduction to the Code of Maimonides* (New Haven, Conn.: Yale University Press, 1980), 413–15.
7. For an attempt to reconcile the two positions, see David Hartman, *Maimonides: Torah and Philosophic Quest* (Philadelphia: Jewish Publication Society, 1976), 181–83.

In fact, however, Maimonides is making two important observations. One is that the commands do not constitute an undifferentiated set of imperatives and prohibitions, each standing, as it were, alone. For Maimonides, there is an overall logic to the law. The Torah is a system designed to bring about certain fundamental transformations: a society built on justice and compassion, individuals schooled in what is today called "emotional literacy," and a set of true opinions widely diffused within society as to the nature of reality and our place in it. The Torah also takes into account what philosophical systems rarely do, namely the dimension of time in social transformation.

Philosophical systems aim at simplicity: that is both their strength and weakness. It makes them easy to understand but impossible to apply – because life is never as simple as philosophers take it to be. By contrast, the Torah works with the grain of human nature. It recognises that change in human affairs takes a long time – far longer than a single generation. The result is that commandments are ranged across a spectrum. Some are close to an ideal, the endpoint of the journey, while others are closer to existing reality, the starting point of the journey.

Within any sphere of Judaic concern, there are inner and outer dimensions. Thus, for example, there is the leadership of *power* (king-subject), and the leadership of *influence* (teacher-disciple). Power relations are necessary for the maintenance of society, but are not an ideal. Influence relations – as in education – are ideal, but are not sufficient (in pre-messianic times) for the governance of a nation. Kingship is thus an outer dimension of Judaism, while teaching is an inner dimension.

The best way of knowing what is outer and what is inner is to see whether Jewish law seeks to *minimise* or *maximise* the phenomenon in question. When it comes to kings, the Jewish tradition is restrictive (don't multiply horses, wealth, or wives; no arrogance, etc.). When it comes to teachers, it is expansive (honour teachers more than parents and only a little less than God). The phenomena the Torah seeks to minimise, like the power of kings, are outer commands, more like concessions than ideals. Those it seeks to maximise, like the relation of teachers to disciples, are ideals.

Maimonides' argument is that the same applies to *avoda*, the service of God. Prayer is an inner layer, sacrifice an outer one. That is why, he argues, the entire sacrificial structure in Judaism is restrictive rather than expansive. Sacrifices may only be offered up at certain times, and only by the hereditary priesthood, using specified animals, and in a central place. The emphasis is on limitation. Prayer, by contrast, may be offered anywhere, at any time, by anyone (only later, in the days of Ezra, was prayer also structured). It follows that prayer is close to an ideal; sacrifice is more like a concession.

The result of this complex structure is to create a dynamic over time. We can see this in the case of slavery. The Torah permits slavery, though it also restricts it. At the same time, it creates an ideal, a day, Shabbat, in which all relationships of hierarchy and dominance are suspended so that, one day in seven, the slave is as free as his or her owner. Historically, it took several millennia for slavery to be abolished – in America, not until the nineteenth century and not without a civil war. This is one of the glorious paradoxes of Torah, that it is a timeless system which nonetheless operates in and through historical time.[8]

Maimonides helps us to understand the prophetic critique of sacrifices. The prophets, in his view, were saying that sacrifices were not an end in themselves. They were a means of establishing firmly in the minds of the people that God alone was to be served. However, people confused the means with the end, seeing sacrifices as an end in themselves, as if there were no deeper content to the idea of serving God.

It is an understatement to say that Maimonides' view received a mixed reception from Jewish thinkers in subsequent ages. After all, they asked, if sacrifices were only a temporary concession, why do we pray daily for them to be restored? But Maimonides provides a compelling answer to another, no less significant, question: *How, if sacrifices are central to Judaism, was it able to survive the destruction of the Second Temple?* How could Judaism live, as it were, without its heart? His implicit answer is that while sacrifices represent one form of *avoda*, "service" of God, they are only one form, and a relatively peripheral one. Prayer is far closer to Judaism's inner ideal. Thus Judaism was able to survive the destruction of the Temple because although sacrifice was lost, prayer remained.

8. See Nachum Rabinovitch, *Darkah shel Torah* (Jerusalem: Maaliyot, 1998), 3–102.

Are sacrifices a timeless ideal or a way station on the slow journey to pure monotheism? On this, Maimonides the philosopher says one thing; Maimonides the halakhist and author of the *Mishneh Torah* says another. The contradiction may be more apparent than real. Or it may simply be that the tension within the mind of this great thinker mirrors the tension within Judaism itself between the linear time of the prophets, in which the world changes, and the cyclical time of the priests, within which everything stays the same. The important fact remains: Judaism survived the loss of the sacrifices, for as the psalmist had long before declared:

> You do not delight in sacrifice, or I would bring it;
> You do not take pleasure in burnt offerings.
> My sacrifice, O God, is a broken spirit;
> a broken and contrite heart
> You, God, will not despise. (Ps. 51:18–19)

What Do We Sacrifice?

he laws of sacrifices that dominate the early chapters of the book of Leviticus are among the hardest in the Torah to relate to in the present. It has been almost two thousand years since the Temple was destroyed and the sacrificial system came to an end. But Jewish thinkers, especially the more mystical among them, strove to understand the inner significance of the sacrifices and the statement they made about the relationship between humanity and God. They were thus able to rescue their spirit even if their physical enactment was no longer possible.

Among the simplest yet most profound was the comment made by Rabbi Shneur Zalman of Liadi, the first Rebbe of Lubavitch. He noticed a grammatical oddity about the second line of this *parasha*:

> Speak to the Children of Israel and say to them: *"When one of you offers a sacrifice to the Lord, the sacrifice must be taken from the cattle, sheep, or goats."* (Lev. 1:2)

Or so the verse *would* read if it were constructed according to the normal rules of grammar. However, in Hebrew, the word order of the sentence is strange and unexpected. We would expect to read: *adam mikem ki yakriv*, "when one of you offers a sacrifice." Instead, what it says is *adam ki yakriv mikem*, "when one offers a sacrifice *of you*." The essence of sacrifice, said Rabbi Shneur Zalman, is that we offer ourselves. We bring to God our faculties, our energies, our thoughts and emotions. The physical form of sacrifice – an animal offered on the altar – is only an external manifestation of an inner act. The real sacrifice is *mikem*, "of you." We give God something of ourselves.[1]

What exactly is it that we give God when we offer a sacrifice? The Jewish mystics, among them Rabbi Shneur Zalman, spoke about two souls that each of us has – the animal soul (*nefesh habehamit*) and the Godly soul. On the one hand we are physical beings. We are part of nature. We have physical needs: food, drink, shelter. We are born, we live, we die. As Ecclesiastes puts it:

> Man's fate is like that of the animals; the same fate awaits them both: as one dies, so dies the other. Both have the same breath; man has no advantage over the animal. Everything is a mere fleeting breath. (3:19)

Yet we are not simply animals. We have within us immortal longings. We can think, speak, and communicate. We can, by acts of speaking and listening, reach out to others. We are the one life form known to us in the universe that can ask the question "why?" We can formulate ideas and be moved by high ideals. We are not governed by biological drives alone. Psalm 8 is a hymn of wonder on this theme:

> When I consider Your heavens,
> the work of Your fingers,
> the moon and the stars,
> which You have set in place,
> what is man that You are mindful of him,
> the son of man that You care for him?

1. Rabbi Shneur Zalman of Liadi, *Likkutei Torah* (Brooklyn, NY: Kehot, 1984), *Vayikra* 2aff.

Yet You made him a little lower than the angels
and crowned him with glory and honour.
You made him ruler over the works of Your hands;
You put everything under his feet. (Ps. 8:4–7)

Physically, we are almost nothing; spiritually, we are brushed by the wings of eternity. We have a Godly soul. The nature of sacrifice, understood psychologically, is thus clear. What we offer God is (not just an animal but) the *nefesh habehamit*, the animal soul within us.

How does this work out in detail? A hint is given by the three types of animal mentioned in the verse: *behema* (animal), *bakar* (cattle), and *tzon* (flock). Each represents a separate animal-like feature of the human personality.

Behema represents the animal instinct itself. The word refers to domesticated animals. It does not imply the savage instincts of the predator. What it means is something more tame. Animals spend their time searching for food. Their lives are bounded by the struggle to survive. To sacrifice the animal within us is to be moved by something more than mere survival.

Wittgenstein, when asked what was the task of philosophy, answered, "To show the fly the way out of the fly-bottle."[2] The fly, trapped in the bottle, bangs its head against the glass, trying to find a way out. The one thing it fails to do is to look up. The Godly soul within us is the force that makes us look up, beyond the physical world, beyond mere survival, in search of meaning, purpose, goal.

The Hebrew word *bakar*, cattle, reminds us of the word *boker*, "dawn," literally to "break through," as the first rays of sunlight break through the darkness of night. Cattle, stampeding, break through barriers. Unless constrained by fences, cattle are no respecters of boundaries. To sacrifice the *bakar* is to learn to recognise and respect boundaries – between holy and profane, pure and impure, permitted and forbidden. Barriers of the mind can sometimes be stronger than walls.

Finally, the word *tzon*, flocks, represents the herd instinct – the powerful drive to move in a given direction because others are doing

2. Ludwig Wittgenstein, *Philosophical Investigations* (New York: Macmillan, 1953), 309.

likewise.[3] The great figures of Judaism – Abraham, Moses, the prophets – were distinguished precisely by their ability to stand apart from the herd; to be different, to challenge the idols of the age, to refuse to capitulate to the intellectual fashions of the moment. That, ultimately, is the meaning of holiness in Judaism. *Kadosh*, the holy, is something set apart, different, separate, distinctive. Jews were the only minority in history consistently to refuse to assimilate to the dominant culture or convert to the dominant faith.

The noun *korban*, "sacrifice," and the verb *lehakriv*, "to offer something as a sacrifice," actually mean "that which is brought close" and "the act of bringing close." The key element is not so much giving something up (the usual meaning of sacrifice), but rather bringing something close to God. *Lehakriv* is to bring the animal element within us to be transformed through the divine fire that once burned on the altar, and still burns at the heart of prayer if we truly seek closeness to God.

By one of the ironies of history, this ancient idea has become suddenly contemporary. Darwinism, the decoding of the human genome, and scientific materialism (the idea that the material is all there is) have led to the widespread conclusion that we are animals, nothing more, nothing less. We share ninety-eight per cent of our genes with the primates. We are, as Desmond Morris used to put it, "the naked ape."[4] On this view, Homo sapiens exists by mere accident. We are the result of a random series of genetic mutations and just happened to be more adapted to survival than other species. The *nefesh habehamit*, the animal soul, is all there is.

The refutation of this idea – and it is surely among the most reductive ever to be held by intelligent minds – lies in the very act of sacrifice itself as the mystics understood it. We can redirect our animal instincts. We can rise above mere survival. We are capable of honouring boundaries. We can step outside our environment. As Harvard neuroscientist

---

3. The classic works on crowd behaviour and the herd instinct are Charles Mackay, *Extraordinary Popular Delusions and the Madness of Crowds* (London: Richard Bentley, 1841); Gustave le Bon, *The Crowd: A Study of the Popular Mind* (London: T. F. Unwin, 1897); Wilfred Trotter, *Instincts of the Herd in Peace and War* (London: T. F. Unwin, 1916); and Elias Canetti, *Crowds and Power* (New York: Viking Press, 1962).
4. Desmond Morris, *The Naked Ape* (New York: Dell Publishing, 1984).

Steven Pinker put it: "Nature does not dictate what we should accept or how we should live," adding, "and if my genes don't like it they can go jump in the lake."[5] Or as Katharine Hepburn majestically said to Humphrey Bogart in *The African Queen*, "Nature, Mr Allnut, is what we were put on earth to rise above."

We can transcend the *behema*, the *bakar*, and the *tzon*. No animal is capable of self-transformation, but we are. Poetry, music, love, wonder – the things that have no survival value but which speak to our deepest sense of being – all tell us that we are not mere animals, assemblages of selfish genes. By bringing that which is animal within us close to God, we allow the material to be suffused with the spiritual and we become something else: no longer slaves of nature but servants of the living God.

5.   Steven Pinker, *How the Mind Works* (New York: W.W. Norton, 1997), 54.

Dimensions of Sin

This *parasha*, which deals with a variety of sacrifices, devotes an extended section to the *ḥatat*, the sin offering, as brought by different individuals: first the High Priest (4:3–12), then the community as a whole (13–21), then a leader (22–26), and finally, an ordinary individual (27–35).

The whole passage sounds strange to modern ears, not only because sacrifices have not been offered for almost two millennia since the destruction of the Second Temple, but also because it is hard for us to understand the very concepts of sin and atonement as they are dealt with in the Torah.

The puzzle is that the sins for which an offering had to be brought were those committed inadvertently, *beshogeg*. The sinner had forgotten either the law or some relevant fact. To give a contemporary example: suppose the phone rings on Shabbat and you answer it. You would only be liable for a sin offering if either you forgot the law that you may not answer a phone on Shabbat, or you forgot the fact that the day was Shabbat. For a moment you thought it was Friday or Sunday.

It is just this kind of act that we do not tend to see as a sin at all. It was a mistake. You forgot. You did not mean to do anything wrong.

And when you realise that inadvertently you have broken Shabbat, you are more likely to feel regret than remorse. You feel sorry but not guilty.

We think of a sin as something we did intentionally, yielding to temptation perhaps, or in a moment of rebellion. That is what Jewish law calls *bezadon* in biblical Hebrew or *bemezid* in rabbinic Hebrew. That is the kind of act we would have thought calls for a sin offering. In Jewish law, though, such an act cannot be atoned for by an offering at all. So how are we to make sense of the sin offering?

The answer is that there are three dimensions of wrongdoing between us and God. The first is guilt and shame. When we sin deliberately and intentionally, we know inwardly that we have done wrong. Our conscience – the voice of God within the human heart – tells us that we have done wrong. That is what happened to Adam and Eve in the Garden after they sinned. They felt shame. They tried to hide.

For that kind of deliberate, conscious, intentional sin, the only adequate moral response is *teshuva*, repentance. This involves (a) remorse, *ḥarata*, (b) confession, *vidui*, and (c) *kabbalat he'atid*, a resolution never to commit the sin again.[1] The result is *seliḥa umeḥila*: God pardons and forgives us. A mere sacrifice is not enough.

However, there is a second dimension. Regardless of guilt and responsibility, if we commit a sin we have objectively transgressed a boundary. The word *ḥet* means to miss the mark, to stray, to deviate from the proper path. We have committed an act that somehow disturbs the moral balance of the world.

To take a secular example, imagine that your car has a faulty speedometer. You are caught driving at fifty miles per hour in a thirty-miles-per-hour zone. You tell the policeman who stops you that you did not know. Your speedometer was only showing thirty miles per hour. He may sympathise, but you have still broken the law, transgressed the limit, and you will still have to pay the penalty.

That is what a sin offering is. According to Rabbis Samson Raphael Hirsch and David Zvi Hoffman, ignorance, whether of the facts

---

1. Maimonides, *Mishneh Torah, Hilkhot Teshuva* 2:2.

or the law, is a form of negligence.[2] We ought to know the law, especially in the most serious cases. We should also exercise vigilance: we should be mindful about what we are doing. It is not enough to say, "I did not know that today was Shabbat." You should have known. Not knowing whether today is Tuesday or Wednesday may be understandable. Little of significance may turn on that ignorance. But when a fact has significant consequences, there is a duty to pay attention, to be aware. On this view, the sin offering is a penalty for carelessness.

Abrabanel argues that the sin offering was less a punishment for what had been done than a solemn warning against sin in the future. The bringing of a sacrifice, involving considerable effort and expense, was a vivid reminder to the individual to be more careful in the future.[3]

Rabbi Isaac Arama (Spain, fifteenth century) says that the difference between an intentional and an unintentional sin is that in the former case, both body and soul are at fault. In the case of an unintentional sin, only the body is at fault, not the soul. There was physical wrongdoing, but not mental intent. Therefore a physical sacrifice can atone, since it was only the physical act of the body that was in the wrong. Such a sacrifice cannot atone for a deliberate sin, because it cannot rectify a wrong in the soul.[4]

It is also worth noting that what the sacrifice achieves is *kappara*, which means not "forgiveness" but a "covering over" or obliteration of the sin. Noah was told to "cover" (*vekhafarta*) the surface of the ark with pitch (Gen. 6:14). The cover of the Ark in the Tabernacle was called *kapporet* (Ex. 25:17). Once a sin has been symbolically covered, it is forgiven, but as the Malbim points out, in such cases the verb for forgiveness, *s-l-ḥ*, is always in the passive (*venislaḥ*, see Lev. 4:20, 26, 31). The forgiveness is not direct as it is in the case of repentance, but indirect, a consequence of the sacrifice.

A third dimension of sin is that it *defiles*. It leaves a stain on your character. Isaiah, in the presence of God, feels that he has "unclean lips"

---

2. Samson Raphael Hirsch, Commentary to Leviticus 4:2; David Zvi Hoffman, Commentary to Leviticus 4:1–2.
3. Abrabanel, Commentary to Leviticus 4:2.
4. Isaac Arama, *Akedat Yitzḥak* ad loc.

(Is. 6:5). King David says to God, "Wash me thoroughly from my iniquity, and cleanse me from my sin" (Ps. 51:4). About Yom Kippur the Torah says, "On that day atonement will be made for you, to cleanse [*letaher*] you. Then, before the Lord, you will be clean from all your sins" (Lev. 16:30).

Nahmanides says that this is the logic of the sin offering. All sins, even those committed inadvertently, "leave a stain on the soul and constitute a blemish on it, and the soul is only fit to meet its Maker when it has been cleansed from all sin."[5] The result of the sin offering is cleansing, purification.[6]

The late Lubavitcher Rebbe, following midrashic tradition, offered a different, if related, interpretation. Even inadvertent sins testify to something wrong on the part of the person concerned. Bad things do not come about through good people.[7] The sages say that God does not allow even the animals of the righteous to do wrong; how much more so does He protect the righteous themselves from error and mishap.[8] There must therefore have been something wrong with the individual for the mishap to have taken place. Sin may not *leave* a stain on the soul. It may *testify* to a stain on the soul.

This view, characteristic of the Chabad approach, with its emphasis on the psychology of the religious life, shares more than a passing similarity with Sigmund Freud's analysis of the unconscious, which gave rise to the phrase "a Freudian slip."[9] Remarks or acts that seem unintentional often betray unconscious desires or motives. Indeed, we can often glimpse the unconscious more readily at such moments than when the person is acting in full knowledge and deliberation. Inadvertent sins suggest something amiss in the soul of the sinner. It is this fault, which may lie beneath the threshold of consciousness, which is atoned for by the sin offering.

---

5. Nahmanides, Commentary ad loc.
6. On sin as defilement see Paul Ricœur, *The Symbolism of Evil* (New York: Harper & Row, 1967).
7. Taanit 29a.
8. Yevamot 99b; Ketubbot 28b.
9. Freud introduced this idea in his *The Psychopathology of Everyday Life* (1901; reprint, Harmondsworth: Penguin Books, 1987).

So the sin offering is not about guilt but about other dimensions of transgression. It is one of the notable features of Western civilisation, due in part to Pauline Christianity, and partly to the influence of the philosopher Immanuel Kant, that we tend to think about morality and spirituality almost exclusively in terms of the mind and its motives. Only the will, argued Kant, can be good or bad.[10] That, however, turned out to be a dangerous doctrine.[11]

Is it entirely accidental that the culture most influenced by Kant was also the one that gave rise to the Holocaust? It is not – categorically not – that the sage of Konigsberg had anything to do with that tragedy.[12] Yet it remains the case that many good and decent people did nothing to protest the single greatest crime of man against man while it was taking place. Many of them surely thought that it had nothing to do with them. If they bore the Jews no particular ill will, why should they feel guilty? Yet the result of their action or inaction had real consequences in the physical world. A culture that confines morality to the mind is one that lacks an adequate defence against harmful behaviour.

Our acts leave traces in the world. The very fact that unintentional sins require atonement tells us that we cannot dissociate ourselves from our actions by saying, "I didn't mean to do it." Wrong was done – and it was done by us. Therefore we must perform an act that signals our contrition. We cannot just walk away as if the act had nothing to do with us.

The law of the sin offering reminds us that we can do harm unintentionally, and this can have consequences, both physical and psychological. The best way of putting things right is to make a sacrifice: to do something that costs us something. In ancient times, that took the form

10. Immanuel Kant, *Groundwork of the Metaphysics of Morals*, ed. Mary Gregor, Cambridge Texts in the History of Philosophy (Cambridge, UK: Cambridge University Press, 1998), 7.
11. For a critique of Kantian ethics see Bernard Williams, *Morality* (Harmondsworth: Penguin, 1973) and *Ethics and the Limits of Philosophy* (Cambridge, Mass.: Harvard University Press, 1985).
12. However, see Emil L. Fackenheim, *To Mend the World: Foundations of Post-Holocaust Jewish Thought* (Bloomington, Ind.: Indiana University Press, 1994), 271. Fackenheim points out that at his trial, Adolf Eichmann showed himself to be an articulate exponent of Kantian ethics.

of a sacrifice offered on the altar at the Temple. Nowadays, the best way of doing so is to give money to charity (*tzedaka*) or perform an act of kindness to others (*ḥesed*). The prophet said so long ago: "For I desire loving-kindness, not sacrifice" (Hos. 6:6). Charity and kindness are our substitutes for sacrifice and, like the sin offering of old, they help mend what is broken in the world and in our soul.

The sin offering tells us that the wrong we do, or let happen, even if we did not intend it, still requires atonement. Unfashionable though this is, a morality that speaks about action, not just intention – about what happens through us even if we didn't mean to do it – is more compelling, more true to the human situation, than one that speaks of intention alone.

The Sins of a Leader

Sometimes the Torah conveys its most profound ideas by a mere nuance, one that becomes apparent only by attentive listening. *Parashat Vayikra* contains a fascinating example.[1]

It occurs in the context of the laws of the sin offering brought in the case of inadvertent wrongdoing (*shegaga*).[2] The Torah prescribes four different kinds of offering, depending on the offender. One is the High Priest, a second is "the whole community" (understood to mean the great Sanhedrin, the Supreme Court), a third is "the leader" (*nasi*), and the fourth is an ordinary individual. In three of the four cases, the law is introduced by the word *im*, "if" – if such a person commits a sin. In the case of the leader, however, the law is prefaced by the word *asher*, "when." It is *possible* that a High Priest, the Supreme Court, or

---

1. Another example is the way in which, in the long list of instructions about the making of various articles for the Sanctuary, the Torah shifts from the second-person singular ("you shall make") to the third-person plural ("they shall make") in the case of the Ark, thus conveying that everyone has a share in the Ark, in the knowledge and dignity it conveys. See *Covenant and Conversation: Exodus – The Book of Redemption*, 207–215.
2. Leviticus 4:1–35.

an individual may err. But in the case of a leader, the *nasi*, it is probable or even certain.

To understand why, we must first clarify what the word *nasi* signifies. *Nasi* is a generic word for a leader, ruler, king, judge, elder, or prince. It means, in effect, the holder of political power. The *nasi* is not a *Kohen*, a priest, a mediator between God and the people; nor is he a *navi*, the mouthpiece of God to the people and the people to God. Rather, he is one who guides the affairs of the community, settles disputes, and establishes the rule of law.

In Mishnaic times, the *nasi*, the most famous of whom were leaders from the family of Hillel, had a quasi-governmental role as representative of the Jewish people to the Roman government. Rabbi Moses Sofer (Bratislava, 1762–1839) in one of his responsa[3] examines the question of why, when positions of Torah leadership are never dynastic, passed from father to son, the role of *nasi* was an exception. It often did pass from father to son. The answer he gives, and it is historically insightful, is that with the decline of monarchy in the Second Temple period and thereafter, the *nasi* took on many of the roles of a king. His role, internally and externally, was as much political and diplomatic as religious. That in general is what is meant by the word *nasi*.

The Jewish people has experienced many forms of political leadership – elders, judges, kings, community councils, and currently, in the State of Israel, a democratically elected parliament. There may or may not be an ideal form of political leadership in Judaism – depending on the much-debated question as to whether the command in Deuteronomy to appoint a king[4] is an obligation, a permission, or a concession. There are, however, constraints within which any form of Judaic governance must work. One is the overarching sovereignty of the Torah: the priority of right over might. Any command of a ruler which conflicts with Torah law is *ultra vires* and need not, perhaps should not, be obeyed.[5]

---

3. *Responsa Ḥatam Sofer, Oraḥ Ḥayim*, 12.
4. Deuteronomy 17:14–20. Maimonides holds that the appointment of a king is a positive command, Ibn Ezra that it is a permission, Abrabanel that it is a concession.
5. On civil disobedience in Judaism, see the essays in Menachem Kellner, ed., *Contemporary Jewish Ethics* (New York: Sanhedrin Press, 1978), 211–253.

Another is accountability to the people. In the phrase adopted by the American Declaration of Independence (a document which owes much to the biblical faith of the American founding fathers), governmental authority rests on "the consent of the governed."[6]

Why, though, does the Torah consider this type of leadership particularly prone to error? There are three broad avenues of explanation. Rabbi Ovadiah Sforno cites the phrase, "But Yeshurun waxed fat, and kicked" (Deut. 32:15).[7] Those who have advantages over others, whether of wealth or power, tend to find their consciences dulled. Rabbenu Baḥya suggests that rulers tend to become arrogant and haughty. Implicit in these commentators – it is in fact a central theme of Tanakh as a whole – is the idea later stated by Lord Acton in the aphorism, "Power tends to corrupt, and absolute power corrupts absolutely."[8]

Rabbi Elie Munk, citing the Zohar, offers a second explanation. The High Priest and the Sanhedrin were in constant touch with the holy. They lived in a world of ideals. The king or political ruler, by contrast, was involved in secular affairs: war and peace, the administration of government, and international relations. He was more likely to sin because his day to day concerns were not religious but pragmatic.[9]

Rabbi Meir Simcha HaKohen of Dvinsk gives a third account.[10] A king or political leader is especially vulnerable to being led astray by popular sentiment. Neither a priest nor a judge in the Sanhedrin were answerable to the people. The king, however, relied on popular support. Without that he could be deposed. But this is laden with risk. Doing what the people want is not always doing what God wants. That, Rabbi Meir Simcha argues, is what led David to order a census (II Sam. 24), and Zedekiah to ignore the advice of Jeremiah and rebel against the king of Babylon (II Chr. 36). Thus, for a whole series of reasons, a political leader is more exposed to temptation and error than a priest or judge.

6. See Rashi, Commentary to Deuteronomy 1:13.
7. Sforno, Commentary to Leviticus 4:22.
8. This famous phrase comes from a letter written by Lord Acton in 1887. See Martin H. Manser and Rosalind Fergusson, *The Facts on File Dictionary of Proverbs* (New York: Facts on File, 2002), 225.
9. Elie Munk, *The Call of the Torah*, vol. 3 (New York: Mesorah, 1992), 33.
10. *Meshekh Ḥokhma*, Commentary to Leviticus 4:21–22.

There is, however, another reason altogether why political leaders are especially vulnerable to making mistakes.[11] Politics is an arena of conflict. It deals in matters – specifically the pursuit of wealth or power – that are in the short term zero-sum games. The more I have, the less you have. Seeking to maximise the benefits to myself or my group, I come into conflict with others who seek to maximise benefits to themselves or their group. Politics is the mediation of conflict by justice backed with power. Whatever course a politician takes, it will please some and anger others. From this, there is no escape.

Politics also involves difficult judgements. A leader must balance competing claims and will sometimes get it wrong. One particularly striking example involved Solomon's son and successor, Rehoboam:

> Rehoboam went to Shechem, for all the Israelites had gone there to make him king…. [Jeroboam] and the whole assembly of Israel went to Rehoboam and said to him: "Your father put a heavy yoke on us, but now lighten the harsh labour and the heavy yoke he put on us, and we will serve you."
>
> Rehoboam answered, "Go away for three days and then come back to me." So the people went away.
>
> Then King Rehoboam consulted the elders who had served his father Solomon during his lifetime. "How would you advise me to answer these people?" he asked.
>
> They replied, "If today you will be a servant to these people and serve them and give them a favourable answer, they will always be your servants."
>
> But Rehoboam rejected the advice the elders gave him and consulted the young men who had grown up with him and were serving him. He asked them, "What is your advice? How should we answer these people who say to me, 'Lighten the yoke your father put on us'?"

---

11. Note that a sin offering was brought only for a breach of Jewish law, not for a mistake in policy. Nonetheless, I believe the biblical text is at least hinting at the difficulties a leader faces in making the right decisions.

The young men who had grown up with him replied, "Tell these people who have said to you, 'Your father put a heavy yoke on us, but make our yoke lighter' – tell them, 'My little finger is thicker than my father's waist. My father laid on you a heavy yoke; I will make it even heavier. My father scourged you with whips; I will scourge you with scorpions.'"

Three days later Jeroboam and all the people returned to Rehoboam, as the king had said, "Come back to me in three days." The king answered the people harshly. Rejecting the advice given him by the elders, he followed the advice of the young men and said, "My father made your yoke heavy; I will make it even heavier. My father scourged you with whips; I will scourge you with scorpions." So the king did not listen to the people. (1 Kings 12:1–15)

Rehoboam had inherited a fraught political situation. Solomon, his father, had been a wise and successful king, but the people had grown restive. The building of the Temple was hugely demanding. Israel, for a while, resembled a vast labour camp. Besides this, the royal court was expensive and sustained by high taxation. Solomon himself had grown rich while the people groaned under the burden.

Jeroboam, one of Solomon's officials, led a rebellion. Solomon sought to put him to death, but he escaped to Egypt, returning after the king died. Rehoboam now had to make a strategic decision. Should he strengthen his authority by a show of power? Or should he win the people over by loosening and lessening their burdens? The senior advisors counselled the second course. The "young turks" argued the opposite, anticipating Machiavelli's famous rule that it is better for a ruler to be feared than to be loved.[12]

It was the wrong advice, and the result was tragic. The kingdom split in two, the ten northern tribes following Jeroboam, leaving only the southern tribes, generically known as "Judah," loyal to the king. For Israel as a people in its own land, it was the beginning of the end. Always

12. Machiavelli, *The Prince*, ed. Quentin Skinner, Cambridge Texts in the History of Political Thought (Cambridge, UK: Cambridge University Press, 1988), 59.

a small people surrounded by large and powerful empires, it needed unity, high morale, and a strong sense of destiny to survive. Divided, it was only a matter of time before both nations, Israel in the north, Judah in the south, fell to other powers.

Rehoboam and Jeroboam were both actors on the political stage. Yet a not dissimilar rift occurred at a later era, this time not between politicians but between sages. On three occasions, Rabban Gamliel, the *nasi*, and R. Yehoshua, head of the *Beit Din*, disagreed on matters of Halakha. On each occasion Rabban Gamliel asserted his authority at the cost of humiliating R. Yehoshua. The third time was, for the sages, one too many:

> Rabban Gamliel remained sitting and expounding, and R. Yehoshua remained standing, until all the people there began to shout and say to Ḥutzpit the expounder, "Stop!" and he stopped. Then they said, "How long is [Rabban Gamliel] to go on insulting him?... Come, let us depose him.[13]

Rabban Gamliel was then stripped of office until he made an act of apology to R. Yehoshua.

Again the issue was authority versus respect. We do Rabban Gamliel an injustice if we see his high-handed behaviour as simply the mark of an authoritarian personality. The more likely explanation is that he had lived through the last days of the Second Temple period, during which Jewry was fatefully divided between Pharisees and Sadducees and moderates and zealots. The rabbis themselves were divided between the schools of Hillel and Shammai, to the point that it was said that there was a danger of the Torah itself being split into "two Torot." Rabban Gamliel's assertion of authority was an honest attempt to avert further fragmentation. Yet it was the wrong policy. The rabbis resented the attempt to curtail debate, and Rabban Gamliel was removed from office.

There are no universal rules when it comes to leadership. It is an art, not a science. There is no procedure that can guarantee that the

13. Berakhot 27b.

ruler will get it right. Leaders make mistakes. As the Torah signals, it is only a matter of "when," not "if."

Besides the impossibility of knowing in advance the consequences of your decisions, there is another reason why leadership is fraught with risk. This is alluded to by the Mishnaic sage, R. Neḥemya, commenting on the verse, "My son, if you have put up security for your neighbour, if you have struck your hand in pledge for another" (Prov. 6:1):

> So long as a man is an associate [i.e., concerned only with personal piety], he need not be concerned with the community and is not punished on account of it. But once a man has been placed at the head and has donned the cloak of office, he may not say: "I have to look after my welfare, I am not concerned with the community." Instead, the whole burden of communal affairs rests on him. If he sees a man doing violence to his fellow, or committing a transgression, and does not seek to prevent him, he is punished on account of him, and the Holy Spirit cries out: "My son, if you have put up security for your neighbour" – meaning, you are responsible for him.... You have entered the gladiatorial arena, and he who enters the arena is either conquered or conquers.[14]

A private individual is responsible only for his own sins. A leader is held responsible for the sins of those he leads, at least those he might have prevented. The Talmud puts it simply:

> Whoever can prevent the members of his household from sinning, and does not, is seized for the sins of his household. If he can prevent his fellow citizens and does not, he is seized for the sins of his fellow citizens. If he can prevent the whole world from sinning, and does not, he is seized for the sins of the whole world.[15]

With power comes responsibility, and the greater the power, the greater the responsibility.

14. Exodus Rabba 27:9.
15. Shabbat 54b.

There is no textbook for leadership. Every situation is different and each age brings its own challenges. A ruler, in the best interests of his or her people, may sometimes have to make decisions that a conscientious individual would shrink from in private life. He may have to decide to wage a war, knowing that some will die. He may have to levy taxes, knowing that this will leave some impoverished. In many cases, only after the event will the leader know whether the decision was justified, and it may depend on factors beyond his control.

The Jewish approach to leadership is thus an unusual combination of realism and idealism – realistic in its acknowledgement that leaders inevitably make mistakes, idealistic in its constant subjection of politics to ethics, power to responsibility, pragmatism to the demands of conscience. What matters is not that leaders never get it wrong – that is inevitable, given the nature of leadership – but that they are always exposed to prophetic critique and that they constantly study Torah to remind themselves of transcendent standards and ultimate aims. The most important thing from a Torah perspective is that a leader is sufficiently honest to admit his mistakes. Hence the significance of the sin offering.

Rabban Yoḥanan b. Zakkai sums it up with a brilliant double entendre on the word *asher*, "*When* a leader sins." He relates it to the word *ashrei*, "happy," and says:

> Happy is the generation whose leader is willing to bring a sin offering for his mistakes.[16]

Leadership demands two kinds of courage: the strength to take a risk, and the humility to admit when a risk fails.

---

16. Tosefta, Bava Kamma 7:5.

Tzav

צַו

Parashat Tzav continues the laws of sacrifices begun in the previous *parasha*, this time from the perspective of the priests performing the ritual. Rules are set out for burnt and grain offerings, sin and guilt offerings, and peace offerings, each with its own specific procedures. Details are then set out for the induction of Aaron and his sons into office, prior to the inauguration of the service of the Sanctuary.

In the essays that follow, the first looks at the place of sacrifices in human civilisation and the connection between religion and violence. The second is about the thanksgiving offering and the role of gratitude in the emotional life. The third asks why the Torah is so emphatic in its prohibition against eating blood. The fourth concerns the transformation of Jewish life after the destruction of the Temple. How was it that Judaism survived the loss of its most central institutions: the Temple, the priesthood, and the sacrificial service? The fifth is about a difficult passage in the *haftara* where Jeremiah says that God did *not* originally command the Israelites to offer sacrifices. What might this mean?

Violence and the Sacred

J udaism is less a philosophical system than a field of tensions –
between universalism and particularism, exile and redemption, priests
and prophets, cyclical and linear time, and so on through a long list of
polarities. Rarely is this more in evidence than in the conflicting statements within Judaism about sacrifices.

On the one hand, reading the book of Psalms, it is impossible to
miss the sense of excitement and joy with which people came to Jerusalem to worship at the Temple and offer sacrifices to God:

> I will sacrifice a thanksgiving offering to You and call on the
> name of the Lord.
> I will fulfil my vows to the Lord in the presence of all His
> people.
> In the courts of the house of the Lord – in your midst,
> Jerusalem. Hallelujah. (Ps. 116:17–19)

To give back to God, to thank Him for the gift of life, to atone for
your sins, to join your people as they come together to pay homage
to their heavenly king, to be in the place that more than any other

was the home of the Divine Presence: this is what the sacrificial system was about. It was vivid, emotional, sometimes penitential, often joyous: the tryst, the lovers' meeting, between God and His covenanted people. The dry prose of *Vayikra* and its sacrificial laws should not blind us to the fact that there was a profoundly affective dimension to the service. It spoke to the heart, its hopes and fears. It was high religious drama.

Despite this, time and again reading the prophets we are struck by how impassioned their critique of the sacrificial system was. We hear it in Amos and Hosea, Isaiah and Jeremiah. Micah gave it one of its most famous expressions:

> With what shall I come before the Lord
> And bow down before the exalted God?…
> Will the Lord be pleased with thousands of rams,
> With ten thousand rivers of oil?…
> He has shown you, O man, what is good.
> What does the Lord require of you?
> To act justly and to love mercy,
> And to walk humbly with your God. (Mic. 6:6–8)

The conflict runs deep, but it is a tension, not a contradiction. What the prophets were saying is that Judaism is a monotheism, not a dualism. There is one world, not two. If we love God then we must love our fellow human beings, the neighbour and the stranger. If we seek God's justice, we must practise justice. If we call for God's forgiveness, we too must be forgiving. To compartmentalise our relationships with God and with our fellow humans, caring about one while neglecting the other, is just such a dualism. The priest reminded people of their duties to God. The prophet reminded them of their duties to humankind. One without the other is unsustainable and indefensible.

Yet anyone who thinks deeply about the religious life must ask: why sacrifices? Why *this* way of serving God? Maimonides says that this is how other nations served the gods in those days. To command the Israelites to behave otherwise would have been asking too much, too soon, of a human nature that is slow to change.[1] Yet God did not hesitate to forbid them from making idols and icons despite the fact that this too was ubiquitous in ancient times. So even on Maimonides' theory, there is still a question. Why did God permit a form of service shared by other nations in the ancient world and that was in some ways less than ideal? Many answers have been offered in the history of Jewish thought. One of the most intriguing is given by the early fifteenth-century Jewish thinker, Rabbi Joseph Albo (Spain, 1380–1444), in his *Sefer HaIkkarim* (*The Book of Principles*, 1425).[2]

Albo's theory took as its starting point not sacrifices but two other questions. The first: Why after the Flood did God permit human beings to eat meat? (Gen. 9:3–5). Initially, neither human beings nor animals had been meat eaters (Gen. 1:29–30). What caused God, as it were, to change His mind? The second: What was wrong with the first act of sacrifice, Cain's offering of "some of the fruits of the soil" (Gen. 4:3–5)? God's rejection of that offering led directly to the first murder, when Cain killed Abel. What was at stake in the difference between the offerings Cain and Abel brought to God?

Albo's theory is that killing animals for food is inherently wrong. It involves taking the life of a sentient being to satisfy our needs. Cain knew this. He believed there was a strong kinship between man and the animals. That is why he offered not an animal sacrifice, but a vegetable one (his error, according to Albo, is that he should have brought fruit, not vegetables – the highest, not the lowest, of non-meat produce). Abel, by contrast, believed that there was a qualitative difference between man and the animals. Had God not told the first humans: "Rule over the fish of the sea and the birds of the air and over every living creature that moves in the ground"? That is why he brought an animal sacrifice.

Once Cain saw that Abel's sacrifice had been accepted while his own was not, he reasoned thus: if God, who forbids us to kill animals for food, permits and even favours killing an animal as a sacrifice, and if, as Cain believed, there is no ultimate difference between human beings

1. Maimonides, *The Guide for the Perplexed*, III:32.
2. Rabbi Joseph Albo, *Sefer HaIkkarim* III:15.

and animals, then I shall offer the highest living being as a sacrifice to God, namely my brother Abel. *Cain killed Abel as a human sacrifice.*

That is why God permitted meat-eating after the Flood. Before the Flood, the world had been "filled with violence." Perhaps violence is an inherent part of human nature. If humanity were to be allowed to exist at all, God would have to lower His demands. *Let humans kill animals,* He said, *rather than kill human beings* – the one form of life that is not only God's creation but also God's image. Hence the otherwise almost unintelligible sequence of verses after Noah and his family emerge on dry land:

> Then Noah built an altar to the Lord and, taking some of all the clean animals and clean birds, he sacrificed burnt offerings on it. The Lord smelled the pleasing aroma and said in His heart, "Never again will I curse the ground because of man, even though every inclination of his heart is evil from childhood..."
>
> Then God blessed Noah and his sons, saying to them...
>
> "Everything that lives and moves will be food for you. Just as I gave you the green plants, I now give you everything...
>
> Whoever sheds the blood of man, by man shall his blood be shed; for in the image of God, has God made man." (Gen. 8:29–9:6)

According to Albo the logic of the passage is clear. Noah offers an animal sacrifice in thanksgiving for having survived the Flood. God sees that human beings need this way of expressing themselves. They are genetically predisposed to violence ("every inclination of his heart is evil from childhood"). If society were to survive, humans would need to be able to direct their violence towards non-human animals, whether as food or sacrificial offerings. The crucial line to be drawn is between human and non-human. The permission to kill animals is accompanied by an absolute prohibition against killing human beings, "for in the image of God, has God made man."

It is not that God approves of killing animals, whether for sacrifice or food, but that to forbid this to human beings, given their genetic predisposition to bloodshed, is utopian. It is not for now but for the end of days. Until then, the least bad solution is to let people kill animals rather than murder their fellow humans. Animal sacrifices are a concession to human nature.[3] *Sacrifices are a substitute for violence directed against mankind.*

The contemporary thinker who has done most to revive this understanding is French-American literary critic and philosophical anthropologist René Girard, in such books as *Violence and the Sacred*, *The Scapegoat*, and *Things Hidden Since the Foundation of the World*. The common denominator in sacrifices, he argues, is

> ... internal violence – all the dissensions, rivalries, jealousies, and quarrels within the community that the sacrifices are designed to suppress. The purpose of the sacrifice is to restore harmony to the community, to reinforce the social fabric. Everything else derives from that.[4]

The worst form of violence within and between societies is *vengeance*, "an interminable, infinitely repetitive process." This is in line with Hillel's saying, on seeing a human skull floating on water, "Because you drowned others, they drowned you, and those who drowned you will in the end themselves be drowned" (Mishna Avot 2:7).

There is no natural end to the cycle of retaliation and revenge. The Montagues keep killing and being killed by the Capulets. So do the Tattaglias and the Corleones and the other feuding groups in fiction and history. It is a destructive cycle that has devastated whole communities. According to Girard this was the problem that religious ritual was developed to resolve. The primary religious act, he says, is the sacrifice, and the primary sacrifice is the scapegoat. If tribes A and B who have been fighting can sacrifice a member of tribe C, then both will have sated their desire for bloodshed without inviting revenge, especially if tribe C is in no position to retaliate. Sacrifices divert the destructive energy of violent reciprocity.

---

3. On why God never chooses to *change* human nature, see Maimonides, *The Guide for the Perplexed*, III:32.
4. René Girard, *Violence and the Sacred* (Baltimore: Johns Hopkins University Press, 1977), 8.

Why then, if violence is embedded in human nature, are sacrifices a feature of ancient rather than modern societies? Because, argues Girard, there is another and more effective way of ending vengeance:

> Vengeance is a vicious circle whose effect on primitive societies can only be surmised. For us the circle has been broken. We owe our good fortune to one of our social institutions above all: our judicial system, which serves to deflect the menace of vengeance. The system does not suppress vengeance; rather, it effectively limits itself to a single act of reprisal, enacted by a sovereign authority specialising in this particular function. The decisions of the judiciary are invariably presented as the final word on vengeance.[5]

Girard's terminology here is not one to which we can subscribe. Justice is not vengeance. Retribution is not revenge. Revenge is inherently I-Thou, or We-Them. It is personal. Retribution is impersonal. It is no longer the Montagues versus the Capulets, but both under the impartial judgement of the law. But Girard's substantive point is correct and essential. The only effective antidote to violence is the rule of law.

Girard's theory confirms the view of Albo. Sacrifice (as with meat-eating) entered Judaism as a substitute for violence. It also helps us understand the profound insight of the prophets that *sacrifices are not ends in themselves, but part of the Torah's programme to create a world redeemed from the otherwise interminable cycle of revenge. The other part of that programme, and God's greatest desire, is a world governed by justice.* That, we recall, was His first charge to Abraham, to "instruct his children and his household after him to keep the way of the Lord by *doing what is right and just*" (Gen. 18:19).

Have we therefore moved beyond that stage in human history in which animal sacrifices have a point? Has justice become a powerful enough reality that we no longer need religious rituals to divert the

5.   Ibid., 15.

violence between human beings? Sadly, the answer is no. The collapse of the Soviet Union, the fall of the Berlin Wall, and the end of the Cold War led some thinkers to argue that we had reached "the end of history." There would be no more ideologically driven wars. Instead the world would turn to the market economy and liberal democracy.[6]

The reality was radically different. There were waves of ethnic conflict and violence in Bosnia, Kosovo, Chechnya, and Rwanda, followed by even bloodier conflicts throughout the Middle East, sub-Saharan Africa, and parts of Asia. In his book *The Warrior's Honour*, Michael Ignatieff offered the following explanation of why this happened:

> The chief moral obstacle in the path of reconciliation is the desire for revenge. Now, revenge is commonly regarded as a low and unworthy emotion, and because it is regarded as such, its deep moral hold on people is rarely understood. But revenge – morally considered – is a desire to keep faith with the dead, to honour their memory by taking up their cause where they left off. Revenge keeps faith between generations...
>
> This cycle of intergenerational recrimination has no logical end.... But it is the very impossibility of intergenerational vengeance that locks communities into the compulsion to repeat...
>
> Reconciliation has no chance against vengeance unless it respects the emotions that sustain vengeance, unless it can replace the respect entailed in vengeance with rituals in which communities once at war learn to mourn their dead together.[7]

Far from speaking to an age long gone and forgotten, the laws of sacrifice tell us three things as important now as then:

First, violence is still part of human nature, never more dangerous than when combined with an ethic of revenge.

6. Francis Fukuyama, *The End of History and the Last Man* (New York: Free Press, 1992).
7. Michael Ignatieff, *The Warrior's Honor: Ethnic War and the Modern Conscience* (Toronto: Penguin, 2006), 188–190.

Second, rather than denying its existence, we must find ways of redirecting it so that it does not claim yet more human sacrifices.

Third, the only ultimate alternative to sacrifices, animal or human, is the one first propounded millennia ago by the prophets of ancient Israel, few more powerfully than Amos:

> Even though you bring Me burnt offerings and offerings of grain,
> I will not accept them...
> But let justice roll down like a river,
> And righteousness like a never-failing stream. (Amos 5:23–24)

Giving Thanks

Elaine and I were on our honeymoon. We had arrived at a little town on the Italian coast called Paestum. It had a long and ancient history and you can still see the well-preserved ruins of several Greek temples. What drew us, though, was the sea. The sun was dazzling, the beach glorious, the sea inviting. There was just one problem. I could not swim. My parents did not know that the Talmud mentions teaching your child to swim as a parental duty, and somehow I never learned. But as I looked at the people in the sea, I noticed that the water was very shallow indeed. There were people standing several hundred yards from the beach, yet the sea only came up to their knees. What could be safer, I thought, than to walk out into the water and stop before I was out of my depth?

I did. I walked out several hundred yards and indeed the sea only came up to my knees. I turned and started walking back. To my surprise and shock, I found myself suddenly out of my depth. I had walked into a deep depression in the sea bed. I struggled to swim, and failed. There was no one nearby. The swimmers were far away. As I went under for the fifth time, I knew I was drowning. My life was about to end. As I recall, I had two thoughts: "What a way to start a honeymoon," and "What is the Italian for 'Help'?"

Of course someone did save me, otherwise I would not be writing these lines. To this day I do not know who it was. By then I was more or less unconscious. Someone must have seen me struggling, swam over, took hold of me, and brought me to safety. Since then, the words we say on waking every day have had a deep meaning for me: "I thank You, living and enduring God, for You have restored my life to me: great is Your faithfulness." Anyone who has survived great danger knows what it is to feel deep gratitude, to know existentially, not just abstractly, that life is a gift of God. Every day is a reason to give thanks.

It is this feeling that underlies one of the sacrifices detailed in *Parashat Tzav*: the *korban toda*, the thanksgiving offering: "If he offers it [the sacrifice] as a thanksgiving offering, then along with this thanksgiving offering he is to offer unleavened loaves mixed with oil, unleavened wafers spread with oil, and loaves of fine flour, well-kneaded and mixed with oil" (Lev. 7:12).

Though we have been without sacrifices for almost two millennia, a trace of the thanksgiving offering survives to this day in the form of the blessing known as *HaGomel*: "Who bestows good things on the unworthy," said in the synagogue at the time of the reading of the Torah by one who has survived a hazardous situation.

The sages define a hazardous situation as surviving one of the four dangers mentioned in Psalm 107, a song on the theme of giving thanks, beginning with the best-known words of religious gratitude in Judaism: "Give thanks to the Lord for His loving-kindness is forever."[1] They are:

1. *Crossing the sea*: "Some went out on the sea in ships; they were merchants on the mighty waters…. They mounted up to the heavens and went down to the depths; in their peril, their courage melted away. Then they cried out to the Lord in their trouble, and He brought them out of their distress. He stilled the storm to a whisper; the waves of the sea were hushed."

2. *Crossing a desert*: "Some wandered in desert wastelands, finding no way to a city where they could settle. They were hungry and

1. Berakhot 54b.

thirsty, and their lives ebbed away. Then they cried out to the Lord in their trouble, and He delivered them from their distress."

3. *Recovery from serious illness*: "They loathed all food and drew near the gates of death. Then they cried to the Lord in their trouble, and He saved them from their distress. He sent forth His word and healed them; He rescued them from the grave."

4. *Release from captivity*: "Some sat in darkness and the deepest gloom, prisoners suffering in iron chains…. Then they cried to the Lord in their trouble, and He saved them from their distress. He brought them out of darkness and the deepest gloom and broke away their chains."

These are still the situations of hazard on which we say *HaGomel* when we come through them safely. Some nowadays include air travel.

In his book *A Rumor of Angels*, the American sociologist Peter Berger describes what he calls "signals of transcendence" – phenomena within the human situation that point to something beyond.[2] Among them he includes *humour* and *hope*. There is nothing in nature that explains our ability to reframe painful situations in such a way that we can laugh at them, nor is there anything that can explain the human capacity to find meaning even in the depths of suffering.

These are not, in the classic sense, proofs of the existence of God, but they are experiential intimations. They tell us that we are not random concatenations of selfish genes, blindly reproducing themselves. Our bodies may be products of nature ("dust you are, and to dust you will return"), but our minds, thoughts, and emotions – all that is meant by the word "soul" – are not. There is something within us that reaches out to something beyond us: the soul of the universe, the beating heart of existence, the divine "You" to whom we speak in prayer and to whom our ancestors, when the Temple stood, made their offerings.

Though Berger does not include it, one of the "signals of transcendence" is surely the instinctive human wish to give thanks. Often this is merely human. Someone has done us a favour, given us a gift,

---

2. Peter Berger, *A Rumor of Angels: Modern Society and the Rediscovery of the Supernatural* (Garden City, NY: Doubleday, 1969).

comforted us in the midst of grief, or rescued us from danger. We feel we owe them something. That something is *toda*, the Hebrew word that means both "acknowledgement" and "thanks."

But often we feel something more. It is not just the pilot we want to thank when we land safely after a hazardous flight, or the surgeon when we survive an operation. It is as if some larger force was operative, as if there we sensed the presence of what Adam Smith called an "invisible hand" moving the pieces on the human chessboard. We feel as if heaven itself had reached down and come to our aid. As John Milton is believed to have said: "Gratitude bestows reverence, allowing us to encounter everyday epiphanies, those transcendent moments of awe that change forever how we experience life and the world."

Insurance companies tend to describe natural catastrophes as "acts of God," but we do the opposite. God, we sense, is in the good news, the miraculous survival, the escape from catastrophe. That instinct – to offer thanks to a force, a protective presence, over and above natural circumstance and human intervention – is itself a signal of transcendence. That is what was once expressed in the thanksgiving offering, and still is in the *HaGomel* prayer.

It is not just the feeling of gratitude that seeks religious expression. Sometimes the causality is in the opposite direction. It is religious expression that trains us to feel grateful. Prayer can be a form of cognitive transformation.

Reading or watching the daily news, it is easy to feel that life is a succession of dangers and disasters, since it is these that command attention. We are genetically conditioned to notice the things that are a potential threat. The safety of our ancestors depended on it. The result is that good news is seldom newsworthy. The plane that crashes captures the headlines, not the ten thousand that did not.

There is a simple experiment to show how this works. Draw a black dot on a piece of paper, hold it up in front of a crowd, and ask them what they see. Almost all will reply, "A black dot." You then point out to them that the dot occupies less than one per cent of the surface of the paper. They simply do not notice the other ninety-nine per cent. It is "background."

Our morning prayers open with the Dawn Blessings in which we give thanks to God for giving us back our consciousness after sleep, for the human body and our restored soul, the earth we stand on and the freedom with which we rise, and so on through a whole litany of thanks. What this does is to *foreground the background*, focusing our attention on the things we normally take for granted. It is a cognitive shift designed to make us attentive to the myriad blessings with which we are surrounded. And as a famous experiment has shown, those who have an attitude of gratitude tend to live longer and healthier.[3] To give thanks for what we have is, as Ben Zoma taught, a better way of living than to be driven by a sense of what we lack,[4] the default cognitive mode of a consumer society.

So it is with profound wisdom that Jewish tradition teaches us to make our first words on waking the prayer I learned to say with such passion after I was rescued from drowning: "I thank You, living and enduring God, for You have restored my life to me: great is Your faithfulness." The first word of this prayer, *Modeh*, not only comes from the same Hebrew root as *toda*, "thanksgiving," it is also the root of the word *Yehudi*, "Jew." We acquired the name from Jacob's fourth son, Judah, who was given it by his mother Leah, who said when he was born: "This time I will thank God" (Gen. 29:35). *To be a Jew is to offer thanks.* This, the first word we should say each morning, is the meaning of our name and the constitutive gesture of our faith.

There were Jews who, after the Holocaust, sought to define Jewish identity in terms of suffering, victimhood, and survival. One theologian spoke of a 614th commandment: You shall not give Hitler a posthumous victory. The historian Salo Baron called this the "lachrymose" reading of history: a story written in tears. To be sure, there is Jewish suffering. Yet had this been all, Jews would not have handed on their identity to their children as their most precious legacy. To be a Jew is to feel a sense of gratitude, to see life itself as a gift, to be able to live through suffering without being defined by it and thus to give hope the victory over fear. To be a Jew is to offer thanks.

---

3. Deborah D. Danner, David A. Snowdon, and Wallace V. Friesen, "Positive Emotions in Early Life and Longevity: Findings from the Nun Study," *Journal of Personality and Social Psychology*, vol. 80, no. 5 (2001): 804–813. For a general survey of the health impact of thanksgiving, see Robert A. Emmons, *Thanks!: How the New Science of Gratitude Can Make You Happier* (Boston: Houghton Mifflin, 2007).
4. Mishna Avot 4:1.

Blood, Idolatry, and War

This *sedra*, speaking about sacrifices, prohibits the eating of blood:

> Wherever you live, you must not eat the blood of any bird or animal. If anyone eats blood, that person must be cut off from his people. (Lev. 7:26–27)

This is not just one prohibition among others. The ban on eating blood is fundamental to the Torah. For example, it occupies a central place in the covenant God makes with Noah – and through him, all humanity – after the Flood: "But you must not eat meat that has its lifeblood still in it" (Gen. 9:4). So too, Moses returns to the subject in his great closing addresses in the book of Deuteronomy:

> But be sure you do not eat the blood, because the blood is the life, and you must not eat the life with the meat. You must not eat the blood; pour it out on the ground like water. Do not eat it, so that it may go well with you and your children after you,

because you will be doing what is right in the eyes of the Lord.
(Deut. 12:23–25)

What is so wrong about eating blood? Maimonides and Nahmanides
offer conflicting interpretations. For Maimonides – consistent with his
programme throughout *The Guide for the Perplexed* – it is part of the
Torah's extended battle against idolatry. He notes that the Torah uses
identical language about idolatry and eating blood:

> I will *set My face against* that person who eats blood and will cut
> him off from his people. (Lev. 17:10)

> I will *set My face against* that man [who engages in Moloch worship]
> and his family and will cut him off from his people. (Lev. 20:5)

In no context other than blood and idolatry is the expression "set My
face against" used. Idolators, says Maimonides, believed that blood was
the food of the spirits, and that by eating it, they would have "something
in common with the spirits." Eating blood is forbidden because of its
association with idolatry.[1]

Nahmanides says, contrariwise, that the ban has to do with human
nature. We are affected by what we eat:

> If one were to eat the life of all flesh, and it would then attach
> itself to one's own blood, and they would become united in one's
> heart, and the result would be a thickening and coarseness of the
> human soul so that it would closely approach the nature of the
> animal soul which resided in what he ate…

Eating blood, implies Nahmanides, makes us cruel, bestial, animal-like.[2]

Which explanation is correct? We now have copious evidence,
through archaeology and anthropology, that both are. Maimonides was
quite right to see the eating of blood as an idolatrous rite. Human sacrifice

1.   Maimonides, *The Guide for the Perplexed*, III:46.
2.   Nahmanides, Commentary to Leviticus 17:13.

was widespread in the ancient world. Among the Greeks, for example, the god Kronos required human victims. The Maenads, female worshippers of Dionysus, were said to tear living victims apart with their hands and eat them. The Aztecs of South America practised human sacrifice on a vast scale, believing that without its meals of human blood, the sun would die: "Convinced that in order to avoid the final cataclysm it was necessary to fortify the sun, they undertook for themselves the mission of furnishing it with the vital energy found only in the precious liquid which keeps man alive."

Barbara Ehrenreich, from whose book *Blood Rites: Origins and History of the Passions of War*,[3] these facts come, argues that one of the most formative experiences of the first human beings must have been the terror of being attacked by an animal predator. They knew that the likely outcome was that one of the group, usually an outsider, an invalid, a child, or perhaps an animal, would fall as prey, giving the others a chance to escape. It was this embedded memory that became the basis of subsequent sacrificial rites.

Ehrenreich' thesis is that "the sacrificial ritual in many ways mimics the crisis of a predator's attack. An animal or perhaps a human member of the group is singled out for slaughter, often in a spectacularly bloody manner." The eating of the victim and his or its blood temporarily occupies the predator, allowing the rest of the group to escape in safety. That is why blood is offered to the gods. As Mircea Eliade noted, "the divine beings who play a part in initiation ceremonies are usually imagined as beasts of prey – lions and leopards (initiatory animals par excellence) in Africa, jaguars in South America, crocodiles and marine monsters in Oceania."[4] Blood sacrifice appears when human beings are sufficiently well organised in groups to make the transition from prey to predator. They then relive their fears of being attacked and eaten.

Ehrenreich does not end there, however. Her view is that this emotional reaction – fear and guilt – survives to the present as part

---

3. Barbara Ehrenreich, *Blood Rites: Origins and History of the Passions of War* (New York: Metropolitan, 1997).
4. Mircea Eliade, *Rites and Symbols of Initiation: The Mysteries of Birth and Rebirth* (Dallas: Spring Publications, 1994).

of our genetic endowment from earlier times. It leaves two legacies: one, the human tendency to band together in the face of an external threat; the other, the willingness to risk self-sacrifice for the sake of the group. These emotions appear at times of war. They are not the *cause* of war, but they invest it with "the profound feelings – dread, awe, and the willingness to sacrifice – that make it 'sacred' to us." They help explain why it is so easy to mobilise people by conjuring up the spectre of an external enemy.

War is a destructive and self-destructive activity. Why then does it persist? Ehrenreich's insight suggests an answer. It is the dysfunctional survival of instincts, profoundly necessary in an age of hunter-gatherers, into an era in which such responses are no longer necessary. Human beings still thrill at the prospect of shedding blood.

Maimonides was right to see in the blood sacrifice a central idolatrous practice. Nahmanides was equally correct to see it as a symptom of human cruelty. We now sense the profound wisdom of the law forbidding the eating of blood. Only thus could human beings be gradually cured of the deeply ingrained instinct, deriving from a world of predators and prey, in which the key choice is to kill or be killed.

Evolutionary psychology has taught us about these genetic residues from earlier times which – because they are not rational – cannot be cured by reason alone, but only by ritual, strict prohibition, and habituation. The contemporary world continues to be scarred by violence and terror. Sadly, the ban against blood sacrifice is still relevant. The instinct against which it is a protest – sacrificing life to exorcise fear – still lives on.

Why Civilisations Die

In her book *The Watchman's Rattle*, subtitled "Thinking Our Way Out of Extinction," Rebecca Costa delivers a fascinating account of how civilisations die. They do so, she argues, because their problems become too complex.[1] Societies reach what she calls a cognitive threshold. They simply cannot chart a path from the present to the future.

The example she gives is the Mayans. For a period of 3,500 years, between 2600 BCE and 900 CE, they developed an extraordinary civilisation, spreading over what is today Mexico, Guatemala, Honduras, El Salvador, and Belize with an estimated population of fifteen million people.

Not only were they master potters, weavers, architects, and farmers. They developed an intricate cylindrical calendar system, with celestial charts to track the movements of the stars and predict weather patterns. They had their own unique form of writing as well as an advanced mathematical system. Most impressively, they developed a water-supply infrastructure involving a complex network of reservoirs, canals, dams, and levees.

1. Rebecca D. Costa, *The Watchman's Rattle: Thinking Our Way Out of Extinction* (New York: Vanguard, 2010).

Then suddenly, for reasons we still do not fully understand, the entire system collapsed. Sometime between the middle of the eighth and ninth centuries, the majority of the Mayan people simply disappeared. There have been many theories as to why it happened. It may have been prolonged drought, overpopulation, internecine wars, a devastating epidemic, food shortages, or a combination of these and other factors. One way or another, having survived for thirty-five centuries, Mayan civilisation failed and became extinct.

Rebecca Costa's argument is that whatever the causes, the Mayan collapse, like the fall of the Roman Empire and the Khmer Empire of thirteenth-century Cambodia, occurred because problems became too many and complicated for the people of that time and place to solve. There was cognitive overload and systems broke down.

It can happen to any civilisation. It may, she says, be happening to ours. The first sign of breakdown is gridlock. Instead of dealing with what everyone can see are major problems, people continue as usual and simply pass their problems on to the next generation. The second sign is a retreat into irrationality. Since people can no longer cope with the facts, they take refuge in religious consolations. The Mayans took to offering sacrifices.

Archaeologists have uncovered gruesome evidence of human sacrifice on a vast scale. It seems that, unable to solve their problems rationally, the Mayans focused on placating the gods by manically making offerings to them. So, apparently, did the Khmer.

Which makes the case of Jews and Judaism unusual, perhaps unique. They faced two centuries of crisis under Roman rule between Pompey's conquest in 63 BCE and the collapse of the Bar Kokhba rebellion in 135 CE. They were hopelessly factionalised. Long before the Great Rebellion against Rome and the destruction of the Second Temple, Jews were expecting some major cataclysm.

Some groups, like the Qumran sectarians known to us from the Dead Sea Scrolls, did indeed withdraw into apocalyptic visions and desert retreats. Others, like the Sadducees, seem to have carried on as if nothing were about to change. But the Pharisees and their heirs, the rabbis, did precisely the opposite of the Mayans and the Khmer. Instead of focusing obsessively on sacrifices, they dedicated their energies to finding *substitutes* for sacrifice.

One was *gemillat ḥasadim*, acts of kindness. Rabban Yoḥanan b. Zakkai comforted R. Yehoshua, who wondered how Israel would atone for its sins without sacrifices, with the words, "My son, we have another atonement as effective as this: acts of kindness, as it is written [Hos. 6:6], 'I desire kindness and not sacrifice'" (*Avot DeRabbi Natan* 8).

Another was Torah study. The sages interpret Malachi's words (1:11), "In every place offerings are presented to My name," to refer to scholars who study the laws of sacrifice (Menaḥot 100a). "One who recites the order of sacrifices is as if he had brought them" (Taanit 27b).

Another was prayer. Hosea said, "Take words with you and return to the Lord.... We will offer our lips as sacrifices of bulls" (Hos. 14:3), implying that words could take the place of sacrifice. "He who prays in the house of prayer is as if he brought a pure oblation" (Y. Berakhot 8d).

Yet another was *teshuva*. The Psalm (51:19) says "the sacrifices of God are a contrite spirit." From this the sages infer that "if a person repents, it is accounted to him as if he had gone up to Jerusalem and built the Temple and the altar and offered on it all the sacrifices ordained in the Torah" (Leviticus Rabba 7:2).

A fifth was fasting. Since going without food diminished a person's fat and blood, it counted as a substitute for the fat and blood of a sacrifice (Berakhot 17a). A sixth was hospitality. "As long as the Temple stood, the altar atoned for Israel, but now a person's table atones for him" (Berakhot 55a). And so on.

What is striking in hindsight is how, rather than clinging to the past, sages like Rabban Yoḥanan b. Zakkai thought forwards to a worst-case-scenario future. The great question raised by *Parashat Tzav* and its subject matter, the different kinds of sacrifice, is less "Why were sacrifices commanded in the first place?" than, "Given how central they were to the religious life of Israel in Temple times, how did Judaism survive without them?"

The short answer is that overwhelmingly, the prophets, the sages, and the Jewish thinkers of the Middle Ages realised that sacrifices were symbolic enactments of processes of mind, heart, and deed that could be expressed in other ways as well. We can encounter the will of God by Torah study, engage in the service of God by prayer, make financial sacrifice by charity, create sacred fellowship by hospitality, and so on.

Jews did not abandon the past. We still refer constantly to the sacrifices in our prayers. But they did not cling to the past. Nor did they take refuge in irrationality. They thought through to the future and created institutions like the synagogue and house of study and school that could be built anywhere and sustain Jewish identity even in the most adverse conditions.

That is no small achievement. The world's greatest civilisations have all, in time, become extinct while Judaism survived. In one sense that was surely divine providence. But in another, it was the foresight of people like Rabban Yoḥanan b. Zakkai who resisted cognitive breakdown. They created solutions today for the problems of tomorrow. They did not seek refuge in the irrational. Instead they quietly built the Jewish future.

Judaism is the civilisation that did not die because, despite its respect for and loyalty to the past, it is a fundamentally future-oriented faith. We see this in the Torah in a very pointed way in its description of the death of Sarah. Abraham was then 137 years old. He had just lost the woman who had shared his life's journey and who had twice saved his life. He might have been paralysed by grief. Yet this is what we read: "Abraham came to mourn for Sarah and weep for her. Then Abraham rose from beside his dead wife" (Gen. 23:2–3): a mere ten words in Hebrew.

We then read how Abraham bought the first plot of land in Israel and arranged for a wife for his son. Long before, God had promised him children and a land. By the time Sarah died he owned no land, and had one unmarried child. Instead of complaining to God that He had not fulfilled His promises, he understood that he had to take the first step. First he had to build the future. That was how he honoured the past.

What the sages did after the destruction of the Second Temple is one of the great religious achievements of all time: creating a form of faith that would hold Jews to their identity, linking them to God and to one another through the longest exile ever endured by a people, despite an unparalleled history of dispersion and persecution. Finding substitutes for sacrifice, they showed how a civilisation inspired by eternity can defeat death itself.

Jeremiah on Sacrifices

The rabbis had an extraordinary gift for the unexpected. Take as an example the *haftara* they chose for Yom Kippur. It is a day marked by fasting and other afflictions. It atones only for sins against God, not those against our fellow humans. Yet the sages chose to read the passage in Isaiah where the prophet says:

> Is this the kind of fast I have chosen,
> a day when a man will oppress himself?
> When he bows his head like a rush in the wind,
> when he lays his bed with sackcloth and ashes?
> Is this what you call a fast,
> a day for the Lord's favour?
> No; this is the fast I choose:
> to loose the chains of injustice
> and untie the cords of the yoke,
> to set the oppressed free
> and break every yoke.
> Share your food with the hungry
> and provide the poor wanderer with shelter –

when you see the naked, clothe them,
and do not turn away from your own flesh and blood. (Is. 58:5–7)

This is a stunningly counterintuitive choice, and yet it is clearly the right one. The rabbis saw themselves as heirs to the prophets,[1] and this is exactly what a prophet would have said on Yom Kippur. Do not think that you can win God's forgiveness by abasing yourself before Him while ignoring the suffering of human beings. God wants us to honour Him by honouring His image, humankind.

More remarkable still is the *haftara* of *Parashat Tzav*. The *parasha* is about sacrifices: sin, guilt, and peace offerings, sacrifices that were to be burnt and others parts of which were to be eaten. It is about the induction of the priests who were to officiate at the sacrificial rites. It is a text that assumes the centrality of the sacrificial system in the ongoing relationship between the Israelites and God. Yet tradition took as the *haftara* Jeremiah's denunciation of the sacrifices in God's name. It also contains one of the most surprising passages in the whole of Tanakh, in which the prophet seems to deny that sacrifices were part of the original divine plan for His relationship with Israel:

> For when I brought your forefathers out of Egypt, *I neither spoke to them nor commanded them about burnt offerings and sacrifices,* but I gave them this command: Obey Me, and I will be your God and you will be My people. Walk in all the way I command you, that it may go well with you. (Jer. 7:22–23)

How could Jeremiah say that God "neither spoke to them nor commanded them about burnt offerings and sacrifices" when the Torah is full of commands about sacrifice? This is a very difficult text. Most of the commentators assumed that it was not to be taken literally. According to Rabbi David Kimḥi (Radak), the meaning is that the first commands given to the Israelites, at Mara prior to their arrival at Sinai, related to Shabbat and civil legislation, not sacrifice.[2] Maimonides adds

1. Mishna Avot 1:1.
2. Commentary to Jeremiah 7:22.

that Jeremiah was saying that God commanded the sacrifices only as a means to an end, the knowledge of and closeness to God. The people, however, erred in seeing them as an end in themselves.[3] That is not what God commanded.

However there were commentators, among them Abrabanel, who believed that Jeremiah meant what he said. The entire sacrificial system was not part of the original divine intention. It became so only after the sin of the Golden Calf. To understand this, it is necessary to go back and re-read that episode. The clue lies in Exodus 33, another difficult passage.

Recall that Exodus 32 sets out the entire narrative of the Golden Calf. The Israelites, not knowing what has happened to Moses on Mount Sinai, panic. They gather round Aaron, demanding a substitute through which they can access the word of God. Aaron makes a calf out of their gold ornaments. God tells Moses what has happened and orders him to go down. Moses prays for forgiveness, goes down, destroys the calf, punishes the people, and returns up the mountain to pray again for their forgiveness. God does not destroy the people as He had originally threatened to do but insists that the wrongdoers must be punished.

It is the next chapter that is almost incomprehensible. Events happen, but the sequence is hard to fathom. In some cases, they seem to happen backwards. God tells the Israelites to remove their ornaments. But according to the text they have already removed them. God says, "My 'face' will go with you," then Moses says, "If Your face does not go with us, don't make us leave this place." But God has just said that His face *would* go with them. Then God says something that undercuts this completely: "You cannot see My face, for no one may see Me and live." So God's 'face' will and won't go with them. No one, not even Moses, can see it. But just a few verses earlier, the Torah said, "The Lord would speak to Moses face to face, as one speaks to a friend." The chapter seems to be saying all manner of contradictory things at once.

The entire dialogue between Moses and God is obscure. Moses asks God to teach him His "ways," show him His "glory," and other requests that have nothing to do with the aftermath of the Golden Calf but seem instead to be a search for theological understanding. What was

3. Maimonides, *The Guide for the Perplexed*, III:32.

Moses doing asking abstract questions about the nature of God when his people felt traumatised, abandoned, and confused?

The most puzzling incident in the chapter is the statement that, immediately prior to his dialogue with God, *Moses removed his tent from the camp*. Of all the things Moses might have done at that time, this was surely the most inexplicable. The people needed him close, not distant, especially when, immediately beforehand, God had said that He Himself would not be present in the camp.

The most compelling explanation is that this was one of the extremely bold acts that Moses performed at that time. In the previous chapter we saw him smash the first set of tablets. We heard him issue one of the most audacious prayers in the Bible: "Please forgive their sin – but if not, then blot me out of the book You have written." The act of removing his tent from the camp should be understood in the same light. It was what the sages call an act of audacity towards Heaven itself.[4]

Moses was declaring in effect that he would not accept the role of being God's representative within the camp. If God Himself would not be there, neither would he. The dialogue that followed is one of the most consequential in the history of faith. It was to change forever the structure of Judaism. It is the reason the book of *Vayikra* exists.

Schopenhauer called it the problem of porcupines in winter.[5] What do porcupines do in the bitter cold? If they huddle too close, they injure one another with their spines. If they keep too much of a distance from one another, they freeze. That problem, transposed to the relationship between God and humanity, is what dominates the whole Torah.

In the early chapters of Genesis, God is close to human beings. He speaks to Adam and Eve and to Cain like a close friend. He lets Adam name the animals. He acts, literally, as his matchmaker. He warns Cain of the danger of losing control of his anger. But it does not help. All three sin. In an obscure verse in Genesis 6, shortly before the Flood, we read that "the sons of God saw that the daughters of humans were beautiful, and they married any of them they chose." It is not entirely clear what

---

4. The sages call this *ḥutzpah kelapei Shemaya*, Sanhedrin 105a.
5. Schopenhauer, *Parerga und Paralipomena*, vol. 2, chap. XXXI, section 396.

this means, but it tells us that heaven and earth were too close, and the denizens of both committed sins.

For the rest of Genesis, God intervenes occasionally: in the tower of Babel and in Sodom and Gomorrah. Otherwise He is a personal presence in the lives of the patriarchs. Something new emerges at the beginning of Exodus: divine intervention with elemental force, liberating the Israelites and bringing the great empire of Egypt to its knees. This is God the supernatural, performing miracles, bringing plagues, turning sea into dry land, sending manna from heaven and water from a rock.

God's presence is terrifying. Even His voice is unbearably intense. At Mount Sinai, the Israelites begged for it to cease. "If we continue to hear His voice we will die." Instead they asked Moses to be their intermediary. But their total reliance on Moses as the mouthpiece of God led to the people's panic after he had been absent up the mountain for forty days.

Moses now begins a difficult dialogue with God. He asks for God's "face" to go with the people. He asks God to help him understand His "ways." He then asks to see God's glory, *kavod*. God says He will cause "all His goodness" to pass before him. None of these terms is simple. One in particular, the concept of "face," seems to be ambiguous. God "speaks to Moses face to face," but a few verses later He says, "You cannot see My face, for no man can see Me and live." There seems to be a difference between speaking and seeing face to face. Much of this is obscure, but what is clear is that all these terms have to do with the different modes through which God manifests Himself to human beings.

One thing shines through the entire passage: Moses' passionate and persistent plea that God should stay close to the people. "If Your face does not go with us, do not send us up from here. For by what shall it be known that I and Your people have found favour in Your sight? Is it not in Your going with us so that we are distinguished, I and Your people, from all the other people upon the face of the earth?" What makes us different, says Moses, is that You are close, not distant. This is Your people, he insists, not just my people. You cannot abandon them. It is not enough that You send an angel or emissary before them. You have to be there in their midst.

Until then, Moses had been the people's sole intermediary with God. But it was this very fact, Moses seems to imply, that led to the making of the Golden Calf. So dependent were the people on me that my absence frightened them into rash and regrettable behaviour. They need another way of relating to You, one that is constant, regular, predictable, that does not depend on chance or circumstance. They need some way of understanding You, for as of now they simply do not know when You will be angry with them and when You will be forgiving.

God had already made it clear at the beginning of the chapter that direct personal closeness could be too dangerous. If the people sin and there is no intermediary between them and Him, there will be no way of avoiding divine wrath capable of destroying them. Now He explains further. In language strikingly similar to the words in which He explained His identity to Moses at the burning bush – "I will be what I will be" – He now says: "I will have mercy on whom I will have mercy, and I will have compassion on whom I will have compassion."

God is free. It is only because God is free that human beings too are free. Therefore God cannot be predicted or constrained. Justice and compassion are matters of ultimate choice. Judges must practise justice. Parents may exercise compassion. But God is both a judge and a parent ("My child, my firstborn, Israel"). There is no way of knowing, therefore, which way God will choose. So there is no way of excluding uncertainty from the Divine-human encounter.

Besides which, adds God, even you, Moses, with whom I *speak* face to face, cannot *see* My face. You want My "face" to go with the people. But they cannot even hear My voice directly without fearing that they will die. This is a very poignant moment. God admits, as it were, that He is simply too overwhelming a presence for the people to encounter directly. Moses acknowledges the point but then changes his request. He says, "Please show me Your glory." "Glory" is less blinding than "face." The Israelites had seen God's glory before, when they ate the manna (Ex. 16). There then follows the great theophany at which Moses, hidden in the cleft of a rock, sees God's "back" and hears Him declare, "The Lord, the Lord..." Then God tells Moses to prepare a second set of tablets and the covenant is renewed.

There can be little doubt that despite – perhaps even because of – the obscurity of the passage, we are in the presence of one of the turning points in Jewish history. It bears a striking resemblance to the episode in which Jacob wrestles with the angel alone at night. They have a number of features in common. They share a keyword, "face." It occurs multiple times in both passages. Jacob, after the encounter, calls the place where it occurred Peniel, saying, "I have seen God face to face and I survived." Both men bear the physical mark of the encounter. Jacob limps. Moses' face shines. And out of both encounters something radically new is born. In Jacob's case, he has a new name. In Moses' case there is a new covenant, concretised in the form of the second set of tablets. Both encounters represent supreme crises in the life of faith, and afterwards each emerges with new strength.

What emerges from the great encounter in Exodus 33 is not forgiveness. That is the theme of Exodus 32 and 34. Rather, there is now to be a new relationship between God and the Israelites, one that would satisfy Moses' request that God be "in the midst" of the people, while at the same time not exposing them to the risk of an overpowering presence they would find unbearable. God will have to "screen" His presence the way Moses had to "veil" his face once it shone with the light of God. Technically, what would go with the people would be God's "glory," not His "face." Something new would enter the religious life of Israel. The transcendent God would now become immanent. The God beyond the heavens would become the God who dwells in the midst of the camp.

A new word enters the relationship between God and the people: the verb *shakhen*, "to dwell among." Hitherto, this had been a word used exclusively of humans. Now it is given a local habitation and name. "Let them make for Me a sanctuary [*mikdash*] and I will dwell [*veshakhanti*] among them." An entire choreography is set out for the Divine-human encounter. Sacrifices, until now offered spontaneously by Cain and Abel, Noah and Abraham, would be offered at set times in specific ways. An entirely new form of religious leadership would be introduced into the life of the Israelites: a priesthood. We have encountered priests before, but until now they have been non-Israelites: Malkizedek of Shalem, Yitro the Midianite, and the priests of Egypt whose land Joseph did not nationalise.

A rigorous set of rules would be established for those who enter the Sanctuary's sacred space. They would be differential: some for the

High Priest, others for ordinary priests, yet others for the people as a whole. The result would be a form of Divine Presence, known in rabbinic Hebrew as the *Shekhina*, very different from the God of creation who makes universes and the God of redemption who overthrows empires. This is the God who is close, who can be met in fixed places at predictable times, who travels with the people in the desert and will later be with them even in exile. This is God as *shakhen*, as "neighbour," and also as *kavod*, "glory." This is God as He gives a specific kind of dignity to man.

We can define the nature of this dignity, for it is the single most striking difference between the chapters that follow the Golden Calf and those that preceded it. Until now God has given and humans have received. God has acted, while humans have been the objects of Divine action. Now for the first time the people become active. They build the Tabernacle. They contribute to its upkeep. They are able to bring sacrifices. They support a priesthood that in turn acts as guardians of the holy for the sake of the people.

There is order and routine in the religious life. In place of the unique intercession of Moses in dialogue with God, there is now to be an annual day of atonement, at which the High Priest will confess and atone for the sins of the people. The religious life has been rescued from the vagaries of chance to the predictability of order and structure.[6] The fear the Israelites felt at the absence of Moses has been acknowledged and a decision taken that it should not happen again. The sin of the Golden Calf remains a sin, but care has been taken that this too should not happen again.

This entire sequence of events is what Jeremiah meant when he said in God's name, "For when I brought your forefathers out of Egypt, *I neither spoke to them nor commanded them about burnt offerings and sacrifices*, but I gave them this command: Obey Me, and I will be your God and you will be My people." God's original intent on bringing the people out of Egypt was to be their king: their legislator, their ruler, their protector, their judge. Israel would be a nation under the sovereignty of

---

6. The role of the sacrificial system in protecting the people against the anxiety of rejection is emphasised in Moshe Halbertal, *On Sacrifice* (Princeton, NJ: Princeton University Press, 2012).

God alone. That is what Gideon meant in the era of the judges when he told the people who wanted to appoint him as their king, "I will not rule over you, nor will my son rule over you. God will rule over you" (Judges 8:23). That is how Isaiah saw God in his great vision: as a king in heaven seated on a throne, surrounded by ministering angels.

But the Israelites needed more. Such was the essence of Moses' request. Yes, they knew that God, Sovereign of the universe, was their king. But they needed to experience Him also as a *shakhen*, a neighbour. They needed to feel Him close, but in such a way that they were not blinded by His light, deafened by His voice, overwhelmed by His infinity. They also needed specific times and places where they could come close, not just on never-to-be-repeated occasions like the division of the Red Sea or the theophany at Mount Sinai.

Hence the Sanctuary and sacrifices, and later, the synagogue, study, and prayer. This was not God's original intention – if we have read Exodus 33 and Jeremiah 7 rightly as two texts that explain one another. But it was a request to which God acceded. This was a dazzling reversal. It meant that Moses, having agreed that the Golden Calf was a sin, understood that beneath it was a genuine yearning on the part of the people for an encounter with God that they could relate to without anxiety and terror.[7]

And so, in a sense, it has remained. Nowhere do we see this more vividly than by comparing the great cathedrals of Europe with synagogues like the Altneuschul in Prague and those of the Ari and Rabbi Joseph Karo in Safed. The cathedrals were built to express the vastness of God and the smallness of mankind. The synagogues, small and simple, convey the closeness of God and the potential greatness of mankind.

After God's anger at the Golden Calf came His love, and out of the call in love – the meaning of *Vayikra* – came the choreography of devotion: once in the service of sacrifices, and now in the offering of words and minds.

---

7. This is also the reading given by Judah Halevi in *The Kuzari*, 1:97. According to Halevi, the people wanted some visible sign of God's presence as they had had in the pillar of cloud and fire while they were travelling. Their sin lay in not waiting for divine instruction as to what exactly the sign should be.

Shemini
שְׁמִינִי

The *parasha* represents the climax of the long narrative begun in Exodus 25 with the command to construct the Sanctuary. It celebrates the day its service was begun. What should have been a joyous occasion turns into tragedy when two of Aaron's sons die after having brought "strange fire." The *parasha* continues with an account of the dietary laws, specifically what animals, fish, and birds may be eaten.

In the essays that follow, the first looks at the opening phrase of the *parasha*, "on the eighth day," and suggests that it is part of a large pattern in the Torah in which the eighth day represents human creativity following the divine creation of the universe. The second and third are about the tragedy of the deaths of Nadav and Avihu, Aaron's sons, on the day the service of the Sanctuary was consecrated. The fourth is about the poignant scene between Moses and Aaron after Nadav and Avihu die, a moment that encapsulates the tension between the public face and the private grief of a leader.

The fifth is about the dietary laws. What is their logic? The essay suggests that the existence of restrictions on what we may eat and what we may kill for food has to do with the integrity of nature and the fact that we, as humans, are not owners but guardians of the universe. The dietary laws are thus part of the ecological dimension of the Torah, rediscovered in our time.

The Eighth Day

The great moment had come. For seven days, beginning on the twenty-third of Adar, Moses had consecrated Aaron and the priests. Now, on Rosh Ḥodesh Nisan, the time had arrived for Aaron to begin his service, ministering to the people on behalf of God:

> It came to pass *on the eighth day* that Moses called to Aaron and his sons and the elders of Israel, and he said to Aaron, "Take a young bull for a sin offering, and a ram for a burnt offering, without blemish, and offer them before the Lord." (Lev. 9:1)

What is the significance of the "eighth day," the phrase that gives this *parasha* its name? To understand the profound symbolism of the number eight, we have to go back to creation itself.

In the beginning, when all was "waste and void," God created the universe. Day by day, the world unfolded. First, there were the domains: light and dark, the upper and lower waters, sea and dry land. Then there were the objects that filled the domains: the sun, moon, and stars, then the fish and birds, and finally the land animals, culminating in mankind. Then came Shabbat, the seventh day, the day of limits and of holiness, on which first God, then His covenantal people, rested in order to show that there are *boundaries* to creation ("Why is God's name *Shaddai*? Because He said to the universe, 'Enough' [*dai*].")[1] There is integrity to nature. Everything has its proper place, its ecological niche, its function and dignity in the totality of being. *Holiness consists of respecting boundaries and honouring the natural order.*

Thus, the seven days. But what of the eighth day – the day *after* creation? For this, we have to turn to *Torah Shebe'al Peh*, the oral tradition.

On the sixth day, God made His most fateful decision: to create a being who, like Himself, had the capacity to create. To be sure, there is a fundamental distinction between human creativity ("something from something") and divine creativity ("something from nothing"). That is why human beings are "the *image* of God" but not gods themselves.

Yet the ability to create goes hand in hand with the ability to destroy. There cannot be one without the other. Every new technology can be used to heal or harm. Every power can be turned to good or evil. That is why, unlike all other elements of creation, the Torah prefaces the making of man with a reflective statement – "Let us make..." – as if to signal the risk implicit in creating a being with the power of speech, imagination, and free will: the one life form capable of disobeying God and threatening the order and orderliness of nature.

The danger immediately becomes clear. God tells the first man not to eat of the fruit of one tree. The nature of the tree is irrelevant; what matters is its symbolic function. It represents the fact that *creation has boundaries* – the most important being the boundary between the permitted and forbidden. That is why there had to be, even in paradise, something that was forbidden. When the first two human beings ate of the forbidden fruit, the essential harmony between man and nature was broken. Humanity lost its innocence. For the first time, *nature* (the world we find) and *culture* (the world we make) came into conflict. The result was paradise lost.

The sages were intrigued by the chronology of the narrative. According to them, the entire drama of the creation and disobedience of Adam and Eve took place on the sixth day. On that day, they were

1. Ḥagiga 12a.

made, they were commanded about the tree, they transgressed the command, and were sentenced to exile. Not only were they condemned to leave the garden. Also, as the day reached its close and night began to fall, they experienced darkness for the first time.[2]

In compassion, God allowed them a stay of sentence. They were given an extra day in Eden – namely Shabbat. For the whole of that day, the sun did not set. As it too came to a close, *God showed the first human beings how to make light*:

> With the going out of the Sabbath, the celestial light began to fade. Adam was afraid that the serpent would attack him in the dark. Therefore God illuminated his understanding, and he learned to rub two stones against each other and produce light for his needs.[3]

This, according to the sages, is the reason we light a Havdala candle at the end of Shabbat to inaugurate the new week.

There is, in other words, a fundamental difference between the light of the first day ("And God said, 'Let there be light'") and that of the eighth day. The light of the first day is the illumination God makes. The light of the eighth day is the illumination God teaches *us* to make. It symbolises our "partnership with God in the work of creation."[4] There is no more beautiful image than this of how God empowers us to join Him in bringing light to the world. On Shabbat we remember God's creation. On the eighth day (Motza'ei Shabbat) we celebrate *our* creativity as the image and partner of God.

To understand the full depth of what the sages are saying, it is necessary to go back to one of the great myths of the ancient world: the story of Prometheus. To the Greeks, the gods were essentially hostile to mankind. Zeus wanted to keep the art of making fire secret, but Prometheus stole a spark and taught men how to make it. Once the theft was discovered, Zeus punished him by having him chained to a rock, with an eagle pecking at his liver.

2. *Avot DeRabbi Natan* 42; Deuteronomy Rabba 13.
3. *Pesiḳta Rabbati* 23; *Pirkei DeRabbi Eliezer* 20.
4. Shabbat 10a, 119b.

Against this background we see the revolutionary character of Jewish faith. We believe that God *wants* human beings to exercise power: responsibly, creatively, and within limits set by the integrity of nature. The rabbinic account of how God taught Adam and Eve the secret of making fire is the precise opposite of the story of Prometheus. God seeks to confer dignity on the beings He made in His image as an act of love. He does not hide the secrets of the universe from us. He does not seek to keep mankind in a state of ignorance or dependence. The creative God empowers us to be creative and begins by teaching us how. He wants us to be guardians of the world He has entrusted to our care. That is the significance of the eighth day. It is *the human counterpart of the first day of creation.*

We now understand the symbolic significance of the eighth day in relation to the Tabernacle. As we have noted elsewhere, the linguistic parallels in the Torah show that the construction of the Tabernacle in the wilderness mirrors the divine creation of the world. The Tabernacle was intended to be a miniature universe, constructed by human beings. Just as God made the earth as a home for mankind, so the Israelites in the wilderness built the Tabernacle as a symbolic home for God. It was *their* act of creation.

Thus it had to begin on the eighth day, just as Adam and Eve began their creative endeavour on the eighth day. Just as God showed them how to make light, many centuries later, He taught the Israelites how to make a space for the Divine Presence so that they too would be accompanied by light – God's light, in the form of the fire that consumed the sacrifices and the light of the Menora. If the first day represents divine creation, the eighth day signifies human creation under the tutelage and sovereignty of God.

We can now also understand the significance of the other major theme of *Parashat Shemini*, namely the list of permitted and forbidden foods.

Many explanations have been given of the dietary laws. Some see them as rules of hygiene. Potentially disease-ridden animals are to be avoided. Others see them as a discipline of self-restraint. In the words of Rav: "the commandments were given to refine human beings."[5] Yet others see in them a set of laws that have no logic other than the fact

---

5.   Genesis Rabba 44:1.

that they were given by God. On this view, the holy – our glimpse of the Infinite – inevitably transcends our understanding.

However, the simplest and most profound explanation is the one given in *Parashat Shemini* by the Torah itself:

> I am the Lord your God; *hallow* yourselves and be *holy*, because I am *holy*.... I am the Lord who brought you up out of Egypt to be your God; therefore be *holy*, because I am *holy*.... You must distinguish [*lehavdil*] between the unclean and the clean, between living creatures that may be eaten and those that may not be eaten. (Lev. 11:44–47)

A similar statement appears later, in Leviticus 20:24–26:

> I am the Lord your God, who has set you apart [*hivdalti*] from the nations. You must therefore make a distinction [*vehivdaltem*] between clean and unclean animals and between unclean and clean birds. Do not defile yourselves by any animal or bird or anything that moves along the ground – those which I have set apart [*hivdalti*] as unclean for you. You are to be *holy* to Me because I, the Lord, am *holy*, and I have set you apart [*vaavdil*] from the nations to be My own.

The keywords are "holy" (which appears seven times in these two passages) and *lehavdil*, "to distinguish" (which appears five times).

To be holy is to make distinctions, to recognise and honour the divine order of creation. Originally, according to the Torah, human beings (and animals) were to be vegetarians ("I give you every seed-bearing plant on the face of the earth and every tree that has fruit with seed in it; they will be yours for food," [Gen. 1:29]). After the Flood, humanity was permitted to eat meat, with the exception of blood (which represents the sanctity of life itself). A concession was made to the human tendency to violence. It is as if God had said: If you must kill, then kill animals, not human beings.

However, the people of Israel were to serve as role models of a higher ideal. They were permitted to kill animals for food, but only those that best exemplified divine order. Amphibians were forbidden because they lack a definite place. Others were forbidden because they lack clear form – sea creatures that lack a shape defined by fins and scales; land animals that are not ruminants with clearly defined cloven hoofs. Creatures that prey on others are also forbidden. The overall logic of the dietary laws – the laws of a people called on to be holy – is to permit only those animals that are paradigm cases, clear examples, of order. On this I cannot do better than quote the insightful words of Leon Kass:

> The Levitical dietary laws fit the human animal in his distinctive uprightness: Celebrating the principle of rational separation, they celebrate not only man's share in rationality but also his openness to the mystery of intelligible yet embodied form…. The low is made high – or at least higher – through acknowledgement of its dependence on the high; the high is "brought down," democratised and given concrete expression in the forms that govern ordinary daily life. The humdrum of existence and the passage of time are sanctified when the hallowed separateness of the Seventh Day is brought into human life when it is commemorated as the Sabbath. Likewise the commonness of eating is sanctified through observance of divine commandments, whose main principles remind the mindful eaters of the supreme rule of the Holy One.[6]

Human beings become holy when they become distinction-making animals, when they recognise and act so as to honour the boundaries of nature.

We now see an extraordinary and intimate connection between five themes:

1. the creation of the universe;
2. the building of the Sanctuary;
3. the dietary laws;
4. the Havdala ceremony at the end of Shabbat;
5. the number eight.

6. Leon Kass, *The Hungry Soul* (Chicago: University of Chicago Press, 1999), 222.

The story of creation tells us that nature is not a blind struggle between contending forces in which the strongest wins and power is the most important gift. To the contrary: the universe is fundamentally good. It is a place of ordered harmony, the intelligible design of a single creator. That harmony is constantly threatened by mankind. In the covenant with Noah, God establishes a minimum threshold for human civilisation. In the covenant with Israel, He establishes a higher code of holiness. The principle of holiness, as of creation itself, is the maintenance of boundaries, within which every form of life receives its due.

The Sanctuary, with its partitions, represents *boundary-making in space*. The dietary laws, with their divisions of permitted and forbidden, represent *boundary-making in life*, in the act of eating, the most natural of human activities. The priest – the person who most exemplifies holiness – is the maintainer and defender of boundaries. His specific mission is to make distinctions ("to distinguish [*lehavdil*] between the *holy* and the profane, between the unclean and the clean" – note again the keywords *holy* and *lehavdil*).

In the ceremony of Havdala, we mark the boundary between sacred and secular time as Shabbat ends and the eighth day begins. That is when, at the start of the working week, we become again God's partners in the ongoing task of creation. Like Him, we begin by *creating light* and proceed to *make distinctions* ("Blessed are You...who makes a distinction between sacred and profane, light and darkness..."). The eighth day thus becomes the great moment at which God entrusts His creative work to the people He has taken as His covenantal partners. So it was with the Tabernacle, and so it is with us.

This vision epitomises the priestly voice within Judaism. It is a vision of great beauty. It sees the world as a place of order in which everything has its place and dignity within the richly differentiated tapestry of creation. To be holy is to be a guardian of that order, a task delegated to us by God. That is both an intellectual and ethical challenge: intellectually, to be able to recognise the boundaries and limits of nature; ethically, to have the humility to preserve and conserve the world for the sake of generations yet to come.

Fire: Holy and Unholy

The shock is immense. For several weeks and many chapters – the longest prelude in the Torah – we have read of the preparations for the moment at which God would bring His presence to rest in the midst of the people. Five *parashot* (*Teruma, Tetzaveh, Ki Tissa, Vayak'hel,* and *Pekudei*) describe the instructions for building the Sanctuary. Two (*Vayikra, Tzav*) detail the sacrificial offerings to be brought there. All is now ready. For seven days the priests (Aaron and his sons) are consecrated into office. Now comes the eighth day, when the service of the Tabernacle will begin.

The entire people have played their part in constructing what will become the visible home of the Divine Presence on earth. With a simple, moving verse the drama reaches its climax: "Moses and Aaron went into the Tent of Meeting and when they came out, they blessed the people. God's glory was then revealed to all the people" (Lev. 9:23).

Just as we think the narrative has reached closure, a terrifying scene takes place:

> Aaron's sons, Nadav and Avihu, took their censers, put fire into them, and added incense; and they offered unauthorised fire

before God, which He had not instructed them to offer. Fire came forth from before God, and it consumed them so that they died before God. Moses then said to Aaron: "This is what God spoke of when He said: 'Among those who approach Me, I will show Myself holy; in the sight of all the people I will be honoured.'" (10:1–3)

Celebration turned to tragedy. The two eldest sons of Aaron die. The sages and commentators offer many explanations. Nadav and Avihu died because: they entered the holy of holies;[1] they were not wearing the requisite clothes;[2] they took fire from the kitchen, not the altar;[3] they did not consult Moses and Aaron;[4] nor did they consult one another.[5] According to some they were guilty of hubris. They were impatient to assume leadership roles themselves;[6] and they did not marry, considering themselves above such things.[7] Yet others see their deaths as delayed punishment for an earlier sin, when at Mount Sinai they "ate and drank" in the presence of God (Ex. 24:9–11).

These interpretations represent close readings of the four places in the Torah which mention the deaths of Nadav and Avihu (Lev. 10:2, 16:1, Num. 3:4, 26:61), as well as the reference to their presence on Mount Sinai. Each is a profound meditation on the dangers of over-enthusiasm in the religious life. However, the simplest explanation is the one explicit in the Torah itself. Nadav and Avihu died because they offered unauthorised – literally, "strange" – fire, meaning "that which was not commanded." To understand the significance of this, we must go back to first principles and remind ourselves of the meaning of *kadosh*, "holy," and thus of *mikdash* as the home of the holy.

The holy is that segment of time and space God has reserved for · His presence. *Creation involves concealment.* The word *olam*, universe,

1. *Midrash Tanḥuma* (Buber), *Parashat Aḥarei Mot* 7.
2. Leviticus Rabba 20:9.
3. *Midrash Tanḥuma*, ad loc.
4. *Yalkut Shimoni*, 1:524.
5. *Midrash Tanḥuma*, ad loc.
6. Aggada (Buber), *Vayikra* 10.
7. Leviticus Rabba 20:10.

is semantically linked to the word *ne'elam*, "hidden." To give mankind some of his own creative powers – the use of language to think, communicate, understand, imagine alternative futures, and choose between them – God must do more than create Homo sapiens. He must efface Himself (what the kabbalists called *tzimtzum*) to create space for human action. No single act more profoundly indicates the love and generosity implicit in creation. God as we encounter Him in the Torah is like a parent who knows He must hold back, let go, refrain from intervening, if His children are to become responsible and mature.

But there is a limit. To efface Himself entirely would be equivalent to abandoning the world, deserting his own children. That, God may not and will not do. How then does God leave a trace of His presence on earth?

The biblical answer is not philosophical. A philosophical answer (I am thinking here of the mainstream of Western philosophy, beginning in antiquity with Plato, in modernity with Descartes) would be one that applies universally – i.e., at all times, in all places. But there *is* no answer that applies to all times and places. *That is why philosophy cannot and never will understand the apparent contradiction between divine creation and human free will, or between Divine Presence and the empirical world in which we reflect, choose, and act.*

Jewish thought is counter-philosophical. It insists that truths are embodied precisely *in* particular times and places. There are holy times (the seventh day, seventh month, seventh year, and the end of seven septennial cycles, the Jubilee). There are holy people (the Children of Israel as a whole; within them, the Levites, and within them, the priests). And there is holy space (eventually, Israel; within that, Jerusalem; within that, the Temple; in the desert, they were the Tabernacle, the Holy, and the Holy of Holies).

The holy is that point of time and space in which the presence of God is encountered by *tzimtzum* – self-renunciation – on the part of mankind. *Just as God makes space for man by an act of self-limitation, so man makes space for God by an act of self-limitation.* The holy is where God is experienced as absolute presence. Not accidentally but essentially, this can only take place through the total renunciation of human will and initiative. That is not because God does not value human will and initiative. To the contrary: God has empowered mankind to use them to become His "partners in the work of creation."

However, to be true to God's purposes, there must be times and places at which humanity experiences the reality of the divine. Those times and places require absolute obedience. The most fundamental mistake – the mistake of Nadav and Avihu – is to take the powers that belong to man's encounter with the world, and apply them to man's encounter with the Divine. Had Nadav and Avihu used their own initiative to fight evil and injustice they would have been heroes. Because they used their own initiative in the arena of the holy, they erred. They asserted their own presence in the absolute presence of God. That is a contradiction in terms. That is why they died.

We err if we think of God as capricious, jealous, angry: a myth spread by early Christianity in an attempt to define itself as the religion of love, superseding the cruel/harsh/retributive God of the "Old Testament." When the Torah itself uses such language it "speaks in the language of humanity"[8] – that is to say, in terms people will understand.

In truth, Tanakh is a love story through and through – the passionate love of the creator for His creatures that survives all the disappointments and betrayals of human history. God needs us to encounter Him, not because He needs mankind but because we need Him. If civilisation is to be guided by love, justice, and respect for the integrity of creation, there must be moments in which we leave the "I" behind and encounter the fullness of being in all its glory.

That is the function of the holy – the point at which "I am" is silent in the overwhelming presence of "There is." That is what Nadav and Avihu forgot – that to enter holy space or time requires ontological humility, the total renunciation of human initiative and desire.

The significance of this fact cannot be over-estimated. When we confuse God's will with our will, we turn the holy – the source of life – into something unholy and a source of death. The classic example of this is "holy war," jihad, Crusade – investing imperialism (the desire to rule

8. Berakhot 31a.

over other people) with the cloak of sanctity as if conquest and forced conversion were God's will.

The story of Nadav and Avihu reminds us yet again of the warning first spelled out in the days of Cain and Abel. *The first act of worship led to the first murder.* Like nuclear fission, worship generates power, which can be benign but can also be profoundly dangerous.

The episode of Nadav and Avihu is written in three kinds of fire. First there is the fire from heaven:

> Fire came forth from before God and consumed the burnt offering. (Lev. 9:24)

This was the fire of favour, consummating the service of the Sanctuary. Then came the "unauthorised fire" offered by the two sons.

> Aaron's sons Nadav and Avihu took their censers, put fire in them, and added incense; and they offered unauthorised fire before the Lord, which He had not instructed them [to offer]. (Lev. 10:1)

Then there was the counter-fire from heaven:

> Fire came forth from before the Lord, and it consumed them so that they died before the Lord. (Lev. 10:2)

The message is simple and intensely serious: Religion is not what the European Enlightenment thought it would become: mute, marginal, and mild. It is fire – and like fire, it warms but it also burns. And we are the guardians of the flame.

Spontaneity: Good or Bad?

P arashat Shemini tells the tragic story of how the inauguration of the Tabernacle, a day about which the sages say that God rejoiced as much as He had at the creation of the universe,[1] was overshadowed by the deaths of two of Aaron's sons, Nadav and Avihu:

> Aaron's sons Nadav and Avihu took their censers, put fire in them, and added incense; and they offered unauthorised fire before the Lord, which He had not instructed them [to offer]. Fire came forth from before the Lord, and it consumed them so that they died before the Lord. (Lev. 10:1–2)

In the previous essay we noted the many explanations given by the sages and later commentators as to what Nadav and Avihu's sin was. But the simplest answer, given by the Torah itself here and elsewhere (Num. 3:4, 26:61), is that *they acted on their own initiative*. They did what they had not been commanded. They behaved spontaneously, evidently out of sheer enthusiasm in the mood of the moment, offering

---

1. Megilla 10b.

"unauthorised fire." Evidently it is dangerous to act spontaneously in matters of the spirit.

But is it? Moses acted spontaneously in far more fraught circumstances when he shattered the tablets of stone on seeing the Israelites cavorting around the Golden Calf. The tablets – hewn and engraved by God Himself – were perhaps the holiest objects there have ever been. Yet Moses was not punished for his act. The sages say that though he acted of his own accord without first consulting God, God assented to his act.[2] Rashi refers to this moment in his very last comment on the Torah, whose final verse speaks about "all the strong hand, and all the great awe, which Moses performed before the eyes of all Israel":

> [This refers to when Moses] took the liberty of shattering the tablets before their eyes, as it is said, "I shattered them before your eyes." The Holy One, Blessed Be He, consented to his opinion, as it is said, "which you shattered" – "*Yishar Ko'aḥ* for shattering them!"[3]

Why then was spontaneity wrong for Nadav and Avihu, yet right for Moses? The answer is that Nadav and Avihu were priests. Moses was a *navi*, a prophet. These are two different forms of religious leadership. They involve different tasks, different sensibilities, indeed, different approaches to time itself.

The priest serves God in a way that never changes over time (except, of course, when the Temple was destroyed and its service, presided over by the priests, came to an end). The prophet serves God in a way that is constantly changing over time. When people are at ease, the prophet warns of forthcoming catastrophe. When they suffer catastrophe and are in the depths of despair, the prophet brings consolation and hope.

The words said by the priest are always the same. The priestly blessing uses the same words today as it did in the days of Moses and Aaron. But the words used by a prophet are never the same. "No two

---

2. Shabbat 87a.
3. Rashi, Commentary to Deuteronomy 34:12.

prophets use the same style."[4] So for a prophet, spontaneity is of the essence. But for the priest engaged in divine service, it is completely out of place.

Why the difference? After all, the priest and the prophet were serving the same God. The Torah uses a kind of device we have only recently re-invented in a somewhat different form. Stereophonic sound – sound coming from two different speakers – was developed in the 1930s to give the impression of audible perspective. In the 1950s, 3D film was developed to do for sight what stereo had done for sound.

From the pioneering work of Pierre Broca in the 1860s to today, using MRI and PET scans, neuroscientists have striven to understand how our bicameral brain allows us to respond more intelligently to our environment than would otherwise have been possible. Twin perspectives are needed to fully experience reality.

The twin perspectives of the priest and prophet correspond to the twin perspectives on creation represented respectively by Genesis 1:1–2:3, spoken in the priestly voice, with an emphasis on order, structure, divisions and boundaries, and Genesis 2:4–3:24, spoken in the prophetic voice, with an emphasis on the nuances and dynamics of interpersonal relationships.

There is another area in which there was an ongoing argument between structure and spontaneity, namely *tefilla*, prayer, specifically the *Amida*. After the destruction of the Temple, Rabban Gamliel and his court at Yavneh established a standard text for the weekday *Amida*, comprising eighteen (or later, nineteen) blessings in a precise order.[5] Not everyone, however, agreed. R. Yehoshua held that individuals could say an abridged form of the *Amida*. According to some interpretations, R. Eliezer was opposed to a fixed text altogether and held that one should, each day, say something new.[6]

This disagreement is precisely parallel to another one about the source of the daily prayers:

4. Sanhedrin 89a.
5. Mishna Berakhot 4:3.
6. Y. Berakhot 4.

It has been stated: R. Yose son of R. Ḥanina said: The prayers were instituted by the patriarchs. R. Yehoshua b. Levi said: The prayers were instituted to replace the daily sacrifices.[7]

According to R. Yose son of R. Ḥanina, Shaḥarit was established by Abraham, Minḥa by Isaac, and Maariv by Jacob. According to R. Yehoshua b. Levi, Shaḥarit corresponds to the daily morning sacrifice, Minḥa to the afternoon sacrifice. On the face of it, the disagreement has no practical consequences, but in fact, it does.

If the prayers were instituted by the patriarchs, then their origin is prophetic. If they were established to replace the sacrifices, then their provenance is priestly. Priests were forbidden to act spontaneously, but prophets did so as a matter of course. Someone who saw prayer as priestly would, like Rabban Gamliel, emphasise the importance of a precise text. One who saw it as prophetic would, like R. Eliezer as understood by the Talmud Yerushalmi, value spontaneity and each day try to say something new.

Tradition eventually resolved the matter in a most remarkable way. We say each *Amida* twice, once privately and silently in the tradition of the prophets, then a second time publicly and collectively by the *sheliaḥ tzibbur*, the "reader's repetition," in the tradition of a priest offering a sacrifice at the Temple. (There is no reader's repetition in the Maariv service because there was no sacrifice at nighttime). During the silent *Amida* we are permitted to add extra words of our own. During the repetition we are not. That is because prophets acted spontaneously, but priests did not.

The tragedy of Nadav and Avihu is that they made the mistake of acting like prophets when they were, in fact, priests. But we have inherited both traditions. For without structure, Judaism would have no continuity, but without spontaneity, it would have no fresh life. The challenge is to maintain the balance without ever confusing the place of each.

7. Berakhot 26b.

Between Hope and Humanity

It should have been the great day of celebration. The Tabernacle, Israel's first collective house of worship, was complete. All preparations had been made. For seven days, Moses had performed the inauguration. Now, the eighth day, the first of Nisan, had arrived. The priests, led by Aaron, were ready to begin their service.

It was then that tragedy occurred. Two of Aaron's sons, Nadav and Avihu, brought "strange fire, which [God] had not commanded them." Fire "came forth from the Lord" and they died. There then follow two scenes between Moses and Aaron. The first:

> Moses then said to Aaron, "This is what the Lord spoke of when He said, 'Among those who are near to Me I will show Myself holy; in the sight of all the people I will be honoured.'" Aaron remained silent. (Lev. 10:3)

Moses then commanded their bodies to be removed, and forbade Aaron and his remaining sons to engage in rituals of mourning. He gave them further instructions to prevent such tragedies from occurring in the future, and then proceeded to check whether the sacrifices of the day had been performed. He discovered that Aaron and his sons had burned the sin offering, instead of eating it as prescribed:

> When Moses inquired about the goat of the sin offering and found that it had been burned up, he was angry with Eleazar and Itamar, Aaron's remaining sons, and asked, "Why didn't you eat the sin offering in the Sanctuary area? It is most holy; it was given to you to take away the guilt of the community by making atonement for them before the Lord. Since its blood was not taken into the Holy Place, you should have eaten the goat in the Sanctuary area, as I commanded."
>
> Aaron replied to Moses, "Today they sacrificed their sin offering and their burnt offering before the Lord, but such things as this have happened to me. Would the Lord have been pleased if I had eaten the sin offering today?" When Moses heard this, he approved. (Lev. 10:16–20)

Without going into the details of these exchanges, their psychology is enthralling. Moses tries to comfort his brother, who has lost two of his sons. He tells him that God has said, "Among those who are near to Me, I will show Myself holy." According to Rashi, he said, "Now I see that they [Nadav and Avihu] were greater than you and me." The holier the person, the more God demands of them.

It is as if Moses said to Aaron: "My brother, do not give up now. We have come so far. We have climbed so high. I know your heart is broken. So is mine. Did we not think – you and I – that our troubles were behind us, that after all we suffered in Egypt, and at the Red Sea, and in the battle against Amalek, and in the sin of the Golden Calf, we were finally safe and free? And now this has happened. Aaron, don't give up, don't lose faith, don't despair. Your children died not because they were evil but because they were holy. Though their act was wrong, their intentions were good. They merely tried too hard." But despite Moses' words of consolation, "Aaron remained silent," lost in a grief too deep for words.

In the second exchange, Moses is concerned with something else – the community, whose sins should have been atoned for by the sin offering. It is as if he had said to Aaron: "My brother, I know you are in a state of grief. But you are not just a private person. You are also the High Priest. The people need you to perform your duties, whatever your inner feelings." Aaron replies: "Would the Lord have been pleased if I had eaten the sin offering today?" We can only guess at the precise import of these words. Perhaps they mean this: "I know that in general, a High Priest is forbidden to mourn as if he were an ordinary individual. That is the law, and I accept it. But had I acted on this inaugural day as if nothing had happened, as if my sons had not died, would this not seem to the people as if I were heartless, as if human life and death meant nothing, as if the service of God meant a renunciation of my humanity?" This time, Moses is silent. Aaron is right, and Moses knows it.

In this exchange between two brothers, a momentous courage is born: the courage of an Aaron who has the strength to grieve and not accept any easy consolation, and the courage of a Moses who has the strength to keep going in spite of grief. It is almost as if we are present at the birth of an emotional configuration that will characterise the Jewish people in centuries to come. Jews are a people who have had more than their share of suffering. Like Aaron, they did not lose their humanity. They did not allow their sense of grief to be dulled, deadened, desensitised. But neither did they lose their capacity to continue, to carry on, to hope. Like Moses, they never lost faith in God. But like Aaron, they never allowed that faith to anaesthetise their feelings, their human vulnerability.

That, it seems to me, is what happened to the Jewish people after the Holocaust. There were, and are, no words to silence the grief or end the tears. We may say – as Moses said to Aaron – that the victims were innocent, holy, that they died *al kiddush Hashem*, "in sanctification of God's name." Surely that is true. Yet nonetheless, "Aaron remained silent." When all the explanations and consolations have been given, grief remains, unassuaged. We would not be human were it otherwise. That, surely, is the message of the book of Job. Job's comforters were pious in their intentions, but God preferred Job's grief to their vindication of tragedy.

Yet, like Moses, the Jewish people found the strength to continue, to reaffirm hope in the face of despair, life in the presence of death. A mere three years after coming eye to eye with the Angel of Death, the Jewish people, by establishing the State of Israel, made the single most powerful affirmation in two thousand years that *Am Yisrael ḥai,* the Jewish people lives.

Moses and Aaron were like the two hemispheres of the Jewish brain: human emotion on the one hand, faith in God, the covenant, and the future on the other. Without the second, we would have lost our hope. Without the first, we would have lost our humanity. It is not easy to keep that balance, that tension. Yet it is essential. Faith does not render us invulnerable to tragedy but it gives us the strength to mourn and then, despite everything, to carry on.

The Integrity of Nature

The second half of Exodus and the first part of Leviticus form a carefully structured narrative. The Israelites were commanded to construct a sanctuary. They carried out the command. This is followed by an account of sacrifices to be offered there. Then, in the first part of this *parasha*, the priests are inducted into office.

What happens next, though, is unexpected: the dietary laws, a list of permitted and forbidden species, animals, fish, and birds. What is the logic of these laws? Why are they placed here? What is their connection with the Sanctuary?

The late Rabbi Elie Munk offered a fascinating suggestion.[1] As we have mentioned before, the Sanctuary was a human counterpart of the cosmos. Several keywords in the biblical account of its construction are also keywords in the narrative of creation at the beginning of Genesis. The Talmud compares God's joy on seeing the Sanctuary completed to His joy when heaven and earth were made.[2] The two are parallel: the

1. Elie Munk, *The Call of the Torah*, vol. 2 (New York: Mesorah, 2004), 99.
2. Megilla 10b.

universe is the home God made for man. The Sanctuary was the home human beings made for God.

Rabbi Munk reminds us that the first command God gave the first human was a dietary law. "You are free to eat from any tree in the garden; but you must not eat from the tree of the knowledge of good and evil, for when you eat of it you will surely die" (Gen. 2:16–17). The dietary laws in *Parashat Shemini* parallel the prohibition given to Adam. As then, so now, a new era in the spiritual history of humankind, preceded by an act of creation, is marked by laws about what one may and may not eat.

Why? As with sex, so with eating: these are the most primal activities, shared with most other forms of life. Without sex there is no continuation of the species. Without food, even the individual cannot survive. These, therefore, have been the focus of radically different cultures.

On the one hand, there are hedonistic cultures in which food and sex are seen as pleasures and pursued as such. On the other are ascetic cultures – marked by monastic seclusion – in which sex is avoided and eating kept to a minimum. The former emphasise the body, the latter the soul.

Judaism, by contrast, sees the human situation in terms of integration and balance. We are body *and* soul. Hence the Judaic imperative, neither hedonistic nor ascetic, but transformative: we are commanded to *sanctify* the activities of eating and sex. From this flow the dietary laws and the laws of family purity (*nidda* and *mikve*), two key elements of *kedusha*, the life of holiness.

We can go further. Genesis 1 is not the only account of creation in Tanakh, the Hebrew Bible. There are several others. One is contained in the last chapters of the book of Job. It is this that deserves close attention.

Job is the paradigm of the righteous individual who suffers. He loses all he has, for no apparent reason. His companions tell him that he must have sinned. Only this can reconcile his fate with justice. Job maintains his innocence and demands a hearing in the heavenly tribunal. For some thirty-seven chapters the argument rages, then in chapter 38 God addresses Job "out of the whirlwind." God offers no answers. Instead, for four chapters, He asks questions of His own, rhetorical questions that have no answer: "Where were you when I laid the earth's

foundation? ... Have you journeyed to the springs of the sea or walked in
the recesses of the deep? ... Does the rain have a father? ... From whose
womb comes the ice?"

God shows Job the whole panoply of creation, but it is a very
different view of the universe than that set out in Genesis 1–2. There
the centre of the narrative is the human person. Man and woman were
created last, made in God's image, given dominion over all that lives. In
Job 38–41 we see not an anthropocentric, but a *theocentric*, universe. It is
as if we were not on earth but in heaven. Job is the only person in Tanakh
who sees the world, as it were, from God's point of view.

Particularly striking is the way these chapters deal with the animal
kingdom. What Job sees are not domestic animals, but wild, untameable
creatures, magnificent in their strength and beauty, living far from and
utterly indifferent to humankind:

> Do you give the horse his strength or clothe his neck with a
> flowing mane?
> Do you make him leap like a locust, striking terror with
> his proud snorting? ...
> Does the hawk take flight by your wisdom and spread his
> wings towards the south?
> Does the eagle soar at your command and build his nest
> on high? ...
> Can you pull in the Leviathan with a fishhook or tie down
> his tongue with a rope?
> Can you put a cord through his nose or pierce his jaw
> with a hook? ...
> Nothing on earth is his equal – a creature without fear.
> He looks down on all that are haughty;
> he is king over all that are proud. (Job 39:19–41:34)

This is the most radically non-anthropocentric passage in the Hebrew
Bible. It tells us that man is not the centre of the universe, nor are we
the measure of all things. Some of the most glorious aspects of nature
have nothing to do with human needs, and everything to do with the

divine creation of diversity. One of the few Jewish thinkers to state this clearly was Maimonides:

> I consider the following opinion as most correct according to the teaching of the Bible and the results of philosophy, namely that the universe does not exist for man's sake, but that each being exists for its own sake, and not because of some other thing. Thus we believe in creation, and yet need not inquire what purpose is served by each species of existing things, because we assume that God created all parts of the universe by His will; some for their own sake, and some for the sake of other beings.[3]

And again:

> Consider how vast are the dimensions and how great the number of these corporeal beings. If the whole of the earth would not constitute even the smallest part of the sphere of the fixed stars, what is the relation of the human species to all these created things, and how can any of us imagine that they exist for his sake and that they are instruments for his benefit?[4]

We now understand what is at stake in the prohibition of eating certain species of animals, birds, and fish, many of them predators like the creatures described in Job 38–41. They exist for their own sake, not for the sake of humankind. The vast universe, and earth itself with the myriad species it contains, has an integrity of its own. Yes, after the Flood, God gave humans permission to eat meat, but this was a concession, as if to say: Kill if you must, but let it be animals, not other humans, that you kill.

With His covenant with the Israelites, God invited humanity to begin a new chapter in history. This was not yet the Garden of Eden, paradise regained. But, with the construction of the Sanctuary – a symbolic home for the Divine Presence on earth – something new had begun. One sign of this is the fact that the Israelites were not permitted

3. Maimonides, *The Guide for the Perplexed*, III:13.
4. Ibid., III:14.

to kill any and every life form for food. Some species must be protected, given their freedom, granted their integrity, left unsubjected to human devices and desires.

The new creation – the Sanctuary – marks a new dignity for the old creation, especially its wild, untamed creatures. Not everything in the universe was made for human consumption. In the face of nature there must be reverence and restraint.

Tazria
תזריע

Parashat Tazria continues the laws of purity and impurity begun in *Parashat Shemini*. One of the key roles of the priest was to be able to distinguish *tahor* from *tamei*, pure from impure, the latter debarring an individual from entering the sacred space of the Sanctuary.

These categories flow from the contrast between God and human beings. God is immortal, humans are mortal. God is spiritual, humans are also physical, and whatever is physical is subject to disease and decay. Conditions that render a person *tamei* are those that testify to our mortality and physicality. People who had a reminder of mortality in ways specified by the Torah may not enter holy space until they are healed and purified.

The *parasha* begins with the laws relating to childbirth – the impurity it brings, and also the command to circumcise a male child on the eighth day. It continues with laws relating to a still-unidentified condition, *tzaraat*, often translated as leprosy, but which refers to something larger than a disease, because it affects not only people but also clothes and houses. The *parasha* describes some of the symptoms, which may appear following a skin inflammation, or a burn, on part of the skin covered by hair, or a bald spot, as well as on garments. It was the task of the priest to examine such symptoms, declaring the person clean or unclean or to be quarantined until a clearer diagnosis could be made. The sages see *tzaraat* as a punishment for the sin of evil speech.

The first essay is an attempt to place *brit mila*, circumcision, in the larger context of sexuality and violence. The second is about

Judaism's radical replacement of power with love. The third is about the laws of childbirth. The fourth is about *tzaraat* and why the rabbis understand it as they did. The fifth is about the *haftara* and the fascinating encounter between the prophet Elisha and Naaman, commander of the Syrian army.

Circumcision, Sex, and Violence

P*arashat Tazria* opens with the command that, for males, is the distinguishing mark of Jewish identity: circumcision.

> On the eighth day, the flesh of the foreskin [of the child] shall be circumcised. (Lev. 12:3)

The traditional name for this is *brit mila*, literally "the covenant of circumcision." It is the *only* command to bear this explicit association with the divine-human partnership between God and Israel. For Jewish males it is the sign of identity, the mark they carry for the rest of their lives. It is an ontological sign – a state of being rather than a state of doing – testifying to membership in the people of the covenant, the "kingdom of priests and a holy nation."

The point is made powerfully in a Talmudic passage. It says that when King David entered the bathhouse and found himself standing naked, he said, "Woe is me, for I stand naked without a single commandment to my merit." But as soon as he remembered the covenant of circumcision in his flesh, he was comforted.[1] *Mila* is the command Jewish men carry with them for the whole of their lives.

Already in the days of Abraham at the dawn of Jewish history it had this significance. It was the first command given specifically to a Jew.[2] It first appears in the great passage in Genesis 17 where God outlines the covenant He is about to make with Abraham and his descendants:

> Abram fell face down, and God said to him, "As for Me, this is My covenant with you: You will be the father of many nations…" Then God said to Abraham, "As for you, you must keep My covenant, you and your descendants after you for the generations to come. This is My covenant with you and your descendants after you, the covenant you are to keep: Every male among you shall be circumcised…. For the generations to come every male among you who is eight days old must be circumcised." (Gen. 17: 3, 9–12)

To this day we call circumcision, "the covenant of Abraham our father."

As to why the command is repeated here, Maimonides gives the answer in his commentary to the Mishna.[3] Although Abraham was given the command of circumcision as the sign of God's covenant with him, the covenant God made with the Israelites at Mount Sinai superseded all previous commands. Therefore, the fact that we perform circumcision today is not because of the command to Abraham, but because it was repeated as part of the covenant at Sinai. The command is *historically* linked with Abraham but *legislatively* with the revelation to Moses.

Spinoza, the child of the Enlightenment who abandoned Judaism and was excommunicated by the Jewish community of Amsterdam, wrote in his *Tractatus Theologico-Politicus* a remarkable sentence: "The sign of circumcision is, as I think, so important, that I could persuade myself that it alone would preserve the [Jewish] nation for ever."[4] As a

---

1. Menahot 43b.
2. This way of putting it is, of course, an anachronism. The word "Jew" was not used until many centuries later. Abraham was described as an *Ivri*, a Hebrew.
3. Maimonides, Commentary to the Mishna, Hullin 7:6.
4. Baruch Spinoza, "On the Vocation of the Hebrews," in *Tractatus Theologico-Politicus*.

permanent mark of difference and singularity, *brit mila* was a guarantor of Jewish identity through the generations.

The obvious question, though, is: Why *this* command more than any other? Why did circumcision become the mark of Jewish difference, the sign of the covenant, and the symbol of Jewish identity? Why a mark in the flesh, and why this part of the flesh? There is no explicit statement in the Torah, but there must surely be a reason, and it must go to the heart of what makes Jews and Judaism different.

The commentators offer several explanations:

1. According to *Midrash Sekhel Tov*[5] and *Sefer HaHinukh*,[6] it exists to serve as an outward sign to differentiate Jews from gentiles. It is like the other signs such as tzitzit, *tefillin*, and mezuza, different only in that it is actually a part of one's body.
2. According to one explanation given by Maimonides,[7] it is a unifying mark that identifies Jews as part of a people, linking them together as a nation in the most ultimate, existential way.
3. Nahmanides sees it as a way of conferring *kedusha*, sanctity, on the act of procreation.[8] Abrabanel gives a similar explanation.
4. Rabbi Joseph Albo in *Sefer HaIkkarim*[9] takes it as a sign of continuity and perseverance across the generations.
5. In *The Kuzari*,[10] Judah HaLevi says that it was given to help people control their bodily lusts. Maimonides offers a similar explanation:

    > Similarly, with regard to *circumcision*, one of the reasons for it is, in my opinion, the wish to bring about a decrease in sexual intercourse and a weakening of the organ in question, so that this activity be diminished and the organ be in as quiet a state as possible.... None of the activities necessary

---

5. To Genesis 17:11.
6. Command 2.
7. Maimonides, *The Guide for the Perplexed*, III:49.
8. Commentary to Genesis 17:4.
9. Rabbi Joseph Albo, *Sefer HaIkkarim* 4:45.
10. Judah Halevi, *The Kuzari*, I:115.

for the preservation of the individual is harmed thereby, nor is procreation rendered impossible, but violent concupiscence and lust that go beyond what is needed are diminished. It is indubitable that circumcision weakens the faculty of sexual excitement and sometimes perhaps diminishes the pleasure.... In my opinion, this is the strongest of the reasons for circumcision.[11]

Each of these is part of the answer, but there may be a way of seeing the command in the wider context of the Torah as a whole.

To see what this might be, we have first to ask a question about the first book of the Torah, Genesis. What makes the patriarchs different? How does Abraham mark a new beginning? What is it that he brings to the world that was not there before?

Genesis, the book of beginnings, tells the story of God's disappointment with humankind. Having given them freedom, He finds that they abuse it. Adam and Eve sin. Cain kills Abel. Within a short time the world is "full of violence." God brings a flood, saves Noah and his family, and begins again.

This time, God vows never again to bring a flood to destroy the world. He limits His demand to Noah to several simple commands, chief of which is the prohibition against murder (Gen. 9:6). Human beings are for the first time permitted to kill animals for food so long as they do not exercise needless cruelty (the stated example is a prohibition against eating a limb from a living animal). Again, humanity disappoints, this time by attempting to build a tower that will blur the boundaries between heaven and earth. God divides humanity into many languages and cultures and scatters them across the face of the earth, and begins again with Abraham.

But what is the religion of Abraham? Other than circumcision, Abraham was given no commands.[12] Nor do we find him challenging his contemporaries about idolatry. He does not speak as a prophet. He

---

11. Maimonides, *Guide for the Perplexed*, III:49.
12. The sages attribute to Abraham the institution of the morning prayer; see Berakhot 26b and Maimonides, *Mishneh Torah, Hilkhot Melakhim UMilḥamot* 9:1. But this was not commanded of him.

does not deliver a critique of polytheism. He does not call all human-kind to worship the One God. Only in midrashic tradition is Abraham the breaker of idols and the maker of converts. These things are not explicit in the text itself.[13] What then is distinctive about the way of life Abraham represents?

The book gives us one inescapable clue. Wherever and whenever a member of the covenantal family finds him- or herself entering another society or group, there is always a moment of danger – and *the danger is always rooted in an absence of sexual ethics.* There are six such episodes.[14]

Twice Abraham and Sarah are forced to leave home because of famine. Once (Gen. 12) they travel to Egypt. The second time they go to Gerar (Gen. 20). Isaac and Rebecca are forced into almost exactly the same situation in Genesis 26, when they too travel to Gerar.

On all three occasions, the men fear that they will be killed so that their wives can be taken into the royal harem. On the first occasion Abram says to Sarai, "When the Egyptians see you, they will say, 'This is his wife.' Then they will kill me but will let you live" (Gen. 12:12). On the second he says, "I said to myself, 'There is surely no fear of God in this place, and they will kill me because of my wife'" (Gen. 20:11). On the third, Isaac says, "The men of this place might kill me on account of Rebecca, because she is beautiful" (Gen. 26:7).

On all three occasions, Abraham and Isaac are forced to pass off their wives as their sisters, something they would only do in the face of a real and present danger of being killed.

The fourth episode takes place when two visitors (angels in human form) come to Lot in Sodom (Gen. 19). The local populace sur-rounds the house, demanding of Lot that he bring them out "so that we can have sex with them" (19:5) – intended homosexual rape.

The fifth happens when Dinah "went out to visit the women of the land" and was abducted and raped by the local prince, Shechem.

13. Joshua 24 refers to Terah, Abraham's father, as an idol worshipper, but again there is no mention of this in Genesis.
14. There is a seventh: Judah's casual relationship with a woman he takes to be a pros-titute, but who is in fact his daughter-in-law Tamar. This case has certain unique features that differentiate it from the other six, so I have not included it among the examples.

Dinah's brothers Simeon and Levi have to execute a bloody reprisal in order to rescue their sister (Gen. 34).

The sixth occurs when Joseph is left alone with Potiphar's wife, who attempts to seduce him, and when she fails, brings against him a false accusation of rape. There is no violence in this case, but Joseph is thrown into prison, ostensibly for life, for a crime he did not commit (Gen. 39:6–20).

So we have six episodes, in five of which there is actual or potential violence and in the sixth a flagrant miscarriage of justice – and all are about sexual desire. Hence the unexpected conclusion that *what makes the difference between the patriarchs and matriarchs of Genesis and their neighbours is less religious belief than sexual ethics.* Why is this so significant?

The answer lies in violence, not sexuality itself. Judaism is not critical of the sexual urge as such. It did not tend to give a sexual reading of the sin of Adam and Eve. Abraham calls Sarah a beautiful woman. We see Isaac and Rebecca embracing. There is nothing puritanical or ascetic about Judaism's approach to sexual desire.

What is being hinted at is a proposition stated in terms of evolutionary biology by David Buss in *The Murderer Next Door*.[15] What is it, he asks, that leads humans to murder one another? His answer is sexual desire.

In primate societies, alpha males, those who are stronger than the others, have the greatest freedom in their choice of mates. It is sexual desire that causes them to seek dominance, and this in turn leads them to acts of violence against other males in their own or other groups.

Neo-Darwinians like Buss believe that the primary driver of behaviour is reproduction: the act of passing on one's genes to the next generation. There is, though, a marked difference between males and females in this respect. The female investment in childbirth is far greater than that of the male. The female carries the young during pregnancy and cares for them during childhood. The interest of the female is therefore in the male best able to protect her and provide her with food and shelter while she is carrying or feeding the next generation.

15. David Buss, *The Murderer Next Door: Why the Mind Is Designed to Kill* (New York: Penguin, 2005).

The male has no such interest. His contribution ends with ejaculation. What interests him, therefore, is impregnating as many females as possible, thus ensuring the largest possible number of those who will carry his genes. The only interest the male has in fidelity is not in his own but in that of the female. Males will not willingly make sacrifices for children not carrying their own genes. Even today, children are seventy times more likely to be murdered by a stepfather than by their biological father.[16]

The argument has recently been restated by William Tucker in *Marriage and Civilization: How Monogamy Made Us Human.* He sums up his argument in these words:

> In almost all species, males spend most of their time fighting among themselves for access to females. The unique social contract of monogamy – a male for every female, a female for every male – lowers the temperature of sexual competition and frees its members to work together in co-operation. It is at this juncture that human societies – even human civilisations – are born.[17]

The Torah's story remains compelling in the light of all we know about the history of sexuality. It suggests that in the earliest (hunter-gatherer) societies, pair-bonding was the norm. Hence the statement of monogamy in Genesis 2:24, "For this reason a man will leave his father and mother and be united to his wife, and they will become one flesh."

However, with the development of agriculture, cities, and economic surplus, some humans became richer and more powerful than others. We then find a regression to more primitive, even prehuman,

---

16. Martin Daly and Margo I. Wilson, "Some Differential Attributes of Lethal Assaults on Small Children by Stepfathers Versus Genetic Fathers," McMaster University, Hamilton, Ontario, Canada, http://anthro.vancouver.wsu.edu/media/Course_ files/anth-395-nicole-hess/daly-and-wilson-some-attributes-of-lethal-assaults-on-small-children-ethology-and-sociobiology.pdf.
17. William Tucker, *Marriage and Civilization: How Monogamy Made Us Human* (Washington, DC: Regnery, 2014), 5.

forms of behaviour. Kings, rulers, and pharaohs – human alpha males – could command an almost open-ended gratification of sexual desire. Polygamy became possible for a minority of males. Harems made their appearance: hence Abraham and Isaac's fears that they would be killed so that their wives could be taken into the harem. Well into medieval Europe, the phenomenon *jus primae noctis,* the right of a feudal overlord to deflower the bride of any of his tenants on the first night of marriage, persisted.

The Torah describes this phenomenon in an enigmatic passage:

> Man began to increase on the face of the earth, and daughters were born to them. The sons of God saw that the daughters of man were beautiful, and they married any of them they chose. Then the Lord said, "My spirit will not continue to judge man forever, since he is nothing but flesh. His days shall be 120 years." The titans were on the earth in those days and also later. The sons of God had come to the daughters of man and had fathered them. [The titans] were the mighty ones of old, men of renown. The Lord saw that man's wickedness on earth was increasing. Every impulse of his innermost thought was only for evil, all day long. God regretted that He had made man on earth, and He was pained to His very core. (Gen. 6:1–6)

Who were the "sons of God" and the titans (*nefilim*)? Most commentators translate the first phrase as "sons of rulers, judges." They were people in positions of power. Saadia Gaon and Maimonides understand the phrase "daughters of man" as girls or women of the lower classes, commoners, serfs, or slaves. "Titans" is as graphic a word as we could want for alpha males. In short, the Torah is telling us what we know now from other sources, that in the evolution from hunter-gatherer to settled populations and the growth of civilisation, there was a breakdown in sexual ethics.

According to the Torah, this was the prelude to the statement:

> Now the earth was corrupt in God's sight and was full of violence. (Gen. 6:11)

The central message of Genesis is that sexual anomie – the unfettered play of Darwinian forces and alpha males – leads to a society marked by widespread violence. William Tucker, in the book cited above, presents compelling historical evidence for precisely this equation. The Torah views this whole cluster of behaviour with distinct abhorrence.[18] Such behaviour privileges some people against others. It turns women into instruments of male desire. It places power, not love, at the heart of human relationships. It treats women as objects rather than as subjects with equal dignity and integrity. It divorces sex from compassion and concern. It dishonours the most intimate human bond, the one in which we are most like God Himself: the love that brings new life into the world.

Above all, though, it leads to violence, and the Torah regards violence – the cause of the Flood – as the single greatest threat to humanity. Murder, the supreme prohibition of the Noahide code, is not merely a crime but a sin since the human person is the image of God, and murder is therefore a form of sacrilege.

Hence circumcision as the sign of the covenant. The purpose of circumcision, as all the commentators note in one way or another, is to mitigate sexual pleasure, control sexual desire, and consecrate the fundamental biological imperative of reproduction. Given the evolutionary and genetic asymmetry between males and females – with females placing a premium on fidelity, males on adultery and promiscuity – it becomes obvious why this should be a constraint of male rather than female desire. For it is males who overwhelmingly throughout history have committed crimes of violence. Eighty-seven per cent of murders are committed by men.[19] And the primary driver of violence is sexual desire.

The meaning of *brit mila* should now be clear. It counteracts a set of drives to which the human male is prone, which are socially dysfunctional and sometimes dangerous. Most significant is the connection

18. It should be noted as well that this is also what leads King David, and then King Solomon, into sin. The Tanakh is telling us that even the greatest are neither immune from the temptation nor capable of resisting it.
19. Buss, op. cit., 22.

between violence and male sexual desire. A second is the male tendency to promiscuity, adultery, multiple and serial relationships, and the relative lack of male interest in the continuing responsibilities of parenthood. In Britain in 2012, around ninety-two per cent of single-parent families were headed by a woman; only eight per cent by men.[20] As Margaret Mead is reported to have said, the primary challenge of any civilisation is how to socialise males into becoming fathers.[21]

Covenant is about faithfulness in human relations, especially in the bond between male and female. That bond must be consecrated. It should be exclusive. Though the Torah does not legislate monogamy – it was not to become obligatory until the edict of Rabbenu Gershom in the tenth century – it is clearly implied by Genesis 2, as well as by the stories of tension between Sarah and Hagar, Rachel and Leah.

Sigmund Freud, a Jew though not a believing one, placed sexuality at the heart of his analysis of the human personality and of civilisation itself. Libido was one of the primary human instincts. On the one hand, it was a desire for life as opposed to *thanatos*, the death instinct. On the other, unchecked, it led to conflict and chaos. Civilisation, for Freud, depended on the ability to defer instinctual gratification.

This is the key to understanding *brit mila*. It is the consecration of sexual desire. Judaism takes a balanced view of the human personality. Our instincts are not evil in themselves. The religious life is not a matter of self-denial and renunciation. But neither is it hedonism, the unrestrained pursuit of pleasure. Instinct has its darker side, which culminates in violence. The good life involves education of the passions and the acquisition of habits of self-restraint. The holy life involves the sanctification of instinct. Only thus can we create a gracious society in which love, not power, rules the affairs of humankind.

20. *Lone Parents with Dependent Children*, January 2012, UK Office for National Statistics.
21. Quoted in Jerry Jensen and Larry Cyril Jensen, *Families: The Key to a Prosperous and Compassionate Society for the 21st Century* (Lewiston, NY: Edward Mellen, 1999), 91.

The Circumcision of Desire

I n the previous essay, we suggested that the underlying logic behind circumcision, *brit mila*, is the connection between male sexuality and violence. In this essay, I want to take the idea a stage further.

It is hard to trace with any precision the moment when a new idea makes its first appearance on the human scene, especially one as amorphous as that of love. But love has a history.[1] There is the contrast we find in Greek, and then Christian, thought between *eros* and *agape*: sexual desire and a highly abstract love for humanity in general.

There is the concept of chivalry that makes its appearance in the age of the Crusades, the code of conduct that prized gallantry and feats of bravery to "win the heart of a lady." There is the romantic love that makes its appearance in the novels of Jane Austen, hedged with the proviso that the young or not-so-young man destined for the heroine must have the right income and country estate, so as to exemplify the "truth universally acknowledged, that a single man in possession of a good

---

1. See, for example, C. S. Lewis, *The Four Loves* (New York: Harcourt, Brace, 1960); Simon May, *Love: A History* (New Haven, Conn.: Yale University Press, 2011).

fortune, must be in want of a wife."[2] And there is the moment in *Fiddler on the Roof* where, exposed by their children to the new ideas in pre-revolutionary Russia, Tevye turns to his wife Golde, and the following conversation ensues:

> Tevye: Do you love me?
> Golde: I'm your wife!
> Tevye: I know! But do you love me?
> Golde: Do I love him? For twenty-five years I've lived with him, fought with him, starved with him. Twenty-five years, my bed is his…
> Tevye: Shh!
> Golde: If that's not love, what is?
> Tevye: Then you love me!
> Golde: I suppose I do!

The inner history of humanity is in part the history of the idea of love. And at some stage a new idea makes its appearance in biblical Israel. We can trace it best in a highly suggestive passage in the book of one of the great prophets of the Bible, Hosea.

Hosea lived in the eighth century BCE. The kingdom had been divided since the death of Solomon. The northern kingdom in particular, where Hosea lived, had lapsed after a period of peace and prosperity into lawlessness, idolatry, and chaos. Between 747 and 732 BCE there were no less than five kings, the result of a series of intrigues and bloody struggles for power. The people, too, had become lax: "There is no faithfulness or kindness, and no knowledge of God in the land; there is swearing, lying, killing, stealing, and committing adultery; they break all bounds and murder follows murder" (Hos. 4:1–2).

Like other prophets, Hosea knew that Israel's destiny depended on its sense of mission. Faithful to God, it was able to do extraordinary things: survive in the face of empires and generate a society unique in the ancient world, with the equal dignity of all as fellow citizens under the sovereignty of the creator of heaven and earth.

2. The famous first line of Jane Austen's *Pride and Prejudice*.

Faithless, however, it was just one more minor power in the ancient
Near East, whose chances of survival against larger political predators were minimal.

What makes the book of Hosea remarkable is the episode with
which it begins. God tells the prophet to marry a prostitute, and see
what it feels like to have a love betrayed. Only then will Hosea have a
glimpse into God's sense of betrayal by the people of Israel. Having liberated them from slavery and brought them into their land, God saw them
forget the past, forsake the covenant, and worship strange gods. Yet He
cannot abandon them despite the fact that they have abandoned Him.
It is a powerful passage, conveying the astonishing assertion that *more
than the Jewish people love God, God loves the Jewish people.* The history
of Israel is a love story between the faithful God and His often faithless
people. Though God is sometimes angry, He cannot but forgive. He
will take them on a kind of second honeymoon, and they will renew
their marriage vows:

> Therefore I am now going to allure her;
> I will lead her into the desert
> and speak tenderly to her...
> I will betroth you to Me forever;
> I will betroth you in righteousness and justice,
> in love and compassion.
> I will betroth you in faithfulness,
> and you will know the Lord. (Hos. 2:16–22)

It is this last sentence – with its explicit comparison between the covenant and a marriage – that Jewish men say when they put on the hand-
tefillin, winding its strap around the finger like a wedding ring.

One verse in the midst of this prophecy deserves the closest
scrutiny. It contains two complex metaphors that must be unravelled
strand by strand:

> "On that day," declares the Lord,
> "you will call Me 'my husband' [*ishi*];
> you will no longer call Me 'my master' [*baali*]." (Hos. 2:18)

This is a double pun. *Baal*, in biblical Hebrew, means "a husband," but in a highly specific sense – namely, "master, owner, possessor, controller." It signalled physical, legal, and economic dominance. It was also the name of the Canaanite god – whose prophets Elijah challenged in the famous confrontation at Mount Carmel. Baal (often portrayed as a bull) was the god of the storm, who defeated Mot, the god of sterility and death. Baal was the rain that impregnated the earth and made it fertile. The religion of Baal is the worship of *god as power.*

Hosea contrasts this kind of relationship with the other Hebrew word for husband, *ish.* Here he is recalling the words of the first man to the first woman:

> This is now bone of my bones
> and flesh of my flesh;
> She shall be called "woman" [*isha*],
> because she was taken from man [*ish*]. (Gen. 2:23)

Here the male-female relationship is predicated on something quite other than power and dominance, ownership and control. Man and woman confront one another in sameness and difference. Each is an image of the other, yet each is separate and distinct. The only relationship able to bind them together without the use of force is marriage as covenant – a bond of mutual loyalty and love in which each makes a pledge to the other to serve one another.

Not only is this a radical way of reconceptualising the relationship between man and woman. It is also, implies Hosea, the way we should think of the relationship between human beings and God. God reaches out to humanity not as power – the storm, the thunder, the rain – but as love, and not an abstract, philosophical love, but a deep and abiding passion that survives all the disappointments and betrayals. Israel may not always behave lovingly towards God, says Hosea, but God loves Israel and will never cease to do so.

How we relate to God affects how we relate to other people. That is Hosea's message – and vice versa: *how we relate to other people affects the way we think of God.* Israel's political chaos in the eighth century BCE was intimately connected to its religious waywardness. A society built on corruption and exploitation is one where might prevails over right. That is not Judaism but idolatry, Baal-worship.

Now we understand why the sign of the covenant is circumcision. For faith to be more than the worship of power, it must affect the most intimate relationship between men and women. In a society founded on covenant, male-female relationships are built on something other and gentler than male dominance, masculine power, sexual desire, and the drive to own, control, and possess. *Baal* must become *ish*. The alpha male must become the caring husband. Sex must be sanctified and tempered by mutual respect. The sexual drive must be circumcised and circumscribed so that it no longer seeks to possess and is instead content to love.

There is thus more than an accidental connection between *monotheism* and *monogamy*. Although biblical law does not command monogamy, it nonetheless depicts it as the normative state from the start of the human story: Adam and Eve, one man, one woman. Whenever in Genesis a patriarch marries more than one woman, there is tension and anguish. The commitment to one God is mirrored in the commitment to one person.

The Hebrew word *emuna*, often translated as "faith," in fact means faithfulness, fidelity, precisely the commitment one undertakes in making a marriage. Conversely, for the prophets there is a connection between idolatry and adultery. That is how God describes Israel to Hosea. God married the Israelites but they, in serving idols, acted the part of a promiscuous woman (Hos. 1–2).

The love of husband and wife – a love at once personal and moral, passionate and responsible – is as close as we come to understanding God's love for us and our ideal love for Him. When Hosea says, "You will know the Lord," he does not mean knowledge in an abstract sense. He means the knowledge of intimacy and relationship, the touch of two selves across the metaphysical abyss that separates one consciousness from another. That is the theme of *Song of Songs*, that deeply human yet deeply mystical expression of *eros*, the love between humanity and God. It is also the meaning of one of the definitive sentences in Judaism: "You shall love the Lord your God with all your heart and with all your soul and with all your strength" (Deut. 6:5).

Judaism from the beginning made a connection between sexuality and violence on the one hand, marital faithfulness and social order on the other. Not by chance is marriage called *kiddushin*, "sanctification." Like covenant itself, marriage is a pledge of loyalty between two parties, each recognising the other's integrity, honouring their differences even as they come together to bring new life into being. Marriage is to society what covenant is to religious faith: a decision to make love – not power, wealth, or *force majeure* – the generative principle of life.

Just as spirituality is the most intimate relationship between us and God, so sex is the most intimate relationship between us and another person. Circumcision is the eternal sign of Jewish faith because it unites the life of the soul with the passions of the body, reminding us that both must be governed by humility, self-restraint, and love.

Brit mila helps transform the male from *baal* to *ish*, from dominant partner to loving husband, just as God tells Hosea that this is what He seeks in His relationship with the people of the covenant. Circumcision turns biology into spirituality. The instinctive male urge to reproduce becomes instead a covenantal act of partnership and mutual affirmation. It was thus as decisive a turn in human civilisation as Abrahamic monotheism itself. Both are about abandoning power as the basis of relationship, and instead aligning ourselves with what Dante called "the love that moves the sun and other stars."[3] Circumcision is the physical expression of the faith that lives in love.

3. *The Divine Comedy*, 30:143–45.

The Sacrifices of Childbirth

At the start of this *parasha* is a cluster of laws that challenged and puzzled the commentators. They concern a woman who has just given birth. If she gives birth to a son, she is "unclean for seven days, just as she is unclean during her monthly period." She must then wait for a further thirty-three days before coming into contact with holy objects or appearing at the Temple. If she gives birth to a girl, both time periods are doubled: she is unclean for two weeks and must wait a further sixty-six days. She then has to bring two offerings:

> When her purification period for a son or a daughter is complete, she shall bring to the priest, to the Communion Tent entrance, a yearling sheep for a burnt offering, and a young common dove, or a turtle dove for a sin offering. [The priest] shall offer [the sacrifice] before God and atone for [the woman], thus cleansing her of the blood coming from her womb. This law applies whether a woman gives birth to a boy or to a girl. (Lev. 12:6–7)

The problems are obvious. Why does she need to bring a sacrifice? We could understand if she had to bring a thanksgiving offering, giving thanks for her recovery and for her child. But that is not what she is commanded. Instead she must bring a burnt offering – normally brought for a serious offence – together with a sin offering. What, though, is her offence? What is her sin? She has just fulfilled the first command in the Torah, to "be fruitful and multiply" (Gen. 1:28). She has done nothing wrong. Why does she need atonement?

Here are some of the suggestions of the commentators:

1. Rabbenu Baḥya and Rabbi Shlomo Ephraim ben Aaron Luntschitz (*Kli Yakar*, 1550–1619) both suggest that the offerings recall the sin of Eve in Eden and her punishment that "I will make your pain in childbearing very severe; with pain you will give birth to children" (Gen. 3:16).[1]

2. Ibn Ezra, following a suggestion in the Talmud, says that the woman during the anguish of labour may have thought or expressed ideas that were sinful or that she now regrets (such as vowing not to have future relations with her husband).[2]

3. Nahmanides says that the sacrifices are a kind of "ransom" or relief offering for having survived the dangers of childbirth, as well as a form of prayer for a full recovery.[3]

4. Sforno says that the woman has been intensely focused on the physical processes accompanying childbirth. She needs both time and the bringing of an offering to rededicate her thoughts to God and matters of the spirit.[4]

5. Rabbi Meir Simcha of Dvinsk says that the burnt offering is like an *olat re'iya*, an offering brought when appearing at the Temple on festivals, following the injunction, "Do not appear before Me empty-handed" (Ex. 23:15). The woman celebrates her ability to appear before God at the Temple.[5]

1. Rabbenu Baḥya and *Kli Yakar*, Commentary to Leviticus 12:6.
2. Nidda 31b; Ibn Ezra, Commentary to Leviticus 12:6.
3. Nahmanides, Commentary to Leviticus 12:7.
4. Sforno, Commentary to Leviticus 12:8.
5. *Meshekh Ḥokhma*, Commentary to Leviticus 12:6.

Without displacing any of these ideas, we might however suggest another set of perspectives. The first is about the fundamental concepts that dominate this section of Leviticus, the words *tamei* and *tahor*, normally translated as (ritually) "unclean/clean," or "defiled/pure." It is important to note that these words do not have the kind of resonance they bear in English. *Tamei* does not mean impure or defiled. It is a technical term meaning that one is in a condition that prevents him from entering the Tabernacle or Temple. *Tahor* means the opposite, that he may enter.

How are we to understand this? The Tabernacle, and at a later date, the Temple, were symbols of the presence of God within the human domain – at the heart of the camp during the wilderness years and at the centre of the nation during the years of the monarchy.

But they were only symbols, because in monotheism God is everywhere equally. The very concepts of place and time in relation to God are metaphorical. It is not that God is here rather than elsewhere but that we, as humans, feel His presence here rather than elsewhere. It was essential therefore that, from a human perspective, the experience of being in the domain of the holy was an experience of pure transcendence.

God is eternal. God is spiritual. We and the universe are physical and whatever is physical is subject to birth, growth, decline, decay, and death. It is these things that must be excluded from the Sanctuary if we are to have the experience of standing in the presence of eternity.

What therefore bars us from entering the holy is anything that reminds us or others of our mortality: the fact that we are born and will one day die. Contact with death *or even birth* has this effect. Both therefore debar the person who has had such contact from the domain of the holy. Special, though different, processes of purification had to be undergone both by those who had come into contact with the dead (Num. 19:1–22) and by a mother who had given birth.

The same is true of anything that draws attention to our physicality. That is why, for example, people who suffered from the skin disease called *tzaraat* ("leprosy"), or the flow of menstrual blood or a seminal discharge, also had to undergo a rite of purification. Likewise, a priest with a physical blemish was disqualified from serving in the priesthood (Lev. 21:16–23) and was precluded from approaching the altar to offer the fire-offerings.[6]

The woman who had just given birth was therefore *teme'a*, not because of the sin of Eve but because birth, like death, is a signal of mortality, which has no place in the Temple, the space set aside for consciousness of eternity and spirituality.

As for the burnt offering, this is a reminder of the binding of Isaac, and of the animal sacrificed as a burnt offering in his place (Gen. 22:13).

I have argued elsewhere[7] that the binding of Isaac was intended as a protest against the absolute power parents had over children in the ancient world – *patria potestas*, as it was called in Roman law. Essentially, the child was regarded as the property of his parents. A father had total legal power over a child, even to the extent of life and death. That was one reason why child sacrifice was so widely practised in the ancient world.[8]

The Torah makes an implicit comment on this in its account of the name given to the first human child. Eve called him Cain – from the Hebrew meaning "ownership" – saying, "I have *acquired* a child through God" (Gen. 4:1). Treat your child as a possession and you may turn him into a murderer: that is what the text implies.

The narrative of the binding of Isaac is a statement for all time that *parents do not own their children*. The whole story of the birth of Isaac points in that direction. He was born when Sarah was already postmenopausal (Gen. 18:11), incapable of having a child naturally. Isaac was clearly the special gift of God. As the first Jewish child, he became the

---

6. Maimonides makes the interesting observation that the prohibition against a priest with a physical blemish serving in the Temple had nothing to do with holiness per se, but was due to popular perception: "For the multitude does not estimate man by his true form but by the perfection of his bodily limbs and the beauty of his garments, and the Temple was to be held in great reverence by all." *The Guide for the Perplexed*, 111:45.

7. Jonathan Sacks, *The Great Partnership: God, Science and the Search for Meaning* (London: Hodder, 2011), 177–181.

8. On child sacrifice, see Jon D. Levenson, *The Death and Resurrection of the Beloved Son: The Transformation of Child Sacrifice in Judaism and Christianity* (New Haven, Conn.: Yale University Press, 1995).

precedent for all subsequent generations. The binding was intended to establish that children belong to God. Parents are merely their guardians.

That, in relation to the firstborn, was also the message of the tenth plague in Egypt. All firstborn were to have been priests in the service of God. Only after the sin of the Golden Calf did this role devolve on the tribe of Levi. The same idea lies behind the ritual of the redemption of the firstborn. Hannah dedicated her child, Samuel, to God, as did the wife of Manoah, mother of Samson. A mother brought a burnt offering, as did Abraham, in lieu of the child. By so doing she acknowledged that she was not the owner of the child, merely its guardian. In bringing the offering it was as if she had said: "God, I know I should dedicate this child entirely to Your service. Please accept this offering in his place."

As for the sin offering, there is a fascinating rabbinic passage that sheds light on it. It describes a conversation between God and the angels prior to the creation of man:

> When the Holy One, Blessed Be He, came to create man, He created a group of ministering angels and asked them, "Do you agree that we should make man in Our image?"
>
> They replied, "Sovereign of the universe, what will be his deeds?"
>
> God showed them the history of mankind.
>
> The angels replied, "What is man that You are mindful of him?" [Let man not be created].
>
> God destroyed the angels.
>
> He created a second group, and asked them the same question, and they gave the same answer.
>
> God destroyed them.
>
> He created a third group of angels, and they replied, "Sovereign of the universe, the first and second group of angels told You not to create man, and it did not avail them. You did not listen. What then can we say but this: The universe is Yours. Do with it as You wish."
>
> And God created man.
>
> But when it came to the generation of the Flood, and then to the generation of those who built the Tower of Babel,

the angels said to God, "Were not the first angels right? See how great is the corruption of mankind."

And God replied [Is. 46:4], "Even to old age I will not change, and even to grey hair, I will still be patient."[9]

The angels were opposed to the creation of man because they knew in advance that of all life forms, humans alone were capable of sinning and thus threatening the work of the Creator. The passage implies that God knew that humans would sin and yet persisted in creating humanity. This may explain the sin offering brought on the birth of a child.

The child will one day sin: "There is none on earth so righteous as to do only good and never sin," says Ecclesiastes (7:20). So a mother brings a sin offering in advance to atone, as it were, for any sin the child may commit while still a child, as if to say: "God, you knew humans would sin, yet still You created them and commanded us to bring new lives into the world. Therefore, please accept this sin offering in advance for any wrong my child may do."

Parents are responsible in Jewish law for sins their children commit. That is why, when a child becomes bar or bat mitzva, a parent makes the blessing thanking God "for making me exempt from the punishment that might have accrued to me through this one."[10]

Thus the sacrifices a woman brings on the birth of a child, and the period during which she is unable to enter the Temple, have nothing to do with any sin she may have committed or any "defilement" she may have undergone. They are, rather, to do with the basic fact of human mortality, together with the responsibility a parent undertakes for the conduct of a child, and an acknowledgement that every new life is the gift of God.

9. Sanhedrin 38b.
10. Genesis Rabba 63:10.

Of Skin Disease, Mildew, and Evil Speech

Much of *Parashat Tazria* and the following *parasha*, *Parashat Metzora*, are about the condition known as *tzaraat*. It was the Septuagint, the early Greek translation of the Hebrew Bible, that translated it as *lepra*, giving rise to a long tradition identifying it with leprosy.

Some such disease, involving skin discoloration and sores, is certainly implied in the stories of Miriam and Naaman, both of whom were smitten by *tzaraat*. However, this cannot be the whole meaning of the term, at least in the present context, because as Maimonides and Sforno – both of whom were doctors – point out, the symptoms described in the Torah correspond neither to leprosy nor to any other known disease.[1]

Tzaraat as described in *Parashot Tazria* and *Metzora* refers not only to various skin conditions but also to mildew on clothes and the walls of houses. Maimonides emphasises this when he writes: "*Tzaraat* is a comprehensive term covering a number of dissimilar conditions. So, whiteness in a person's skin is called *tzaraat*. The falling off of some of his hair on the head or the chin is called *tzaraat*. A change of colour in

---

1. See Sforno, Commentary to Leviticus 13:2; Maimonides, *Mishneh Torah, Hilkhot Tumat Tzaraat* 16:10 and *The Guide for the Perplexed*, III:47.

garments or in houses is called *tzaraat*."[2] There is no disease that affects not only people but also clothes and walls.

In any case, the Torah is not a book of medicine. Occasionally it refers to medicine. Someone who injures another must pay, among other things, for his medical expenses until he is cured (Ex. 21:19). But a priest is not a doctor, and it was the priests who supervised cases of *tzaraat*. The language of *tuma* and *tahara*, impurity and purity, in which this entire section is couched, is quite different from the concepts of sickness and health, being ill and being cured.

All this raises a fundamental question: What are we to make of a phenomenon that does not correspond to anything in our experience? How could there be a condition that made sense to Moses and the Israelites but not to us?

A fascinating study undertaken by a nineteenth-century British prime minister, William Ewart Gladstone, provides us with a clue. Guy Deutscher tells the story in his book, *Through the Language Glass*.

Gladstone was in his spare time a formidable classicist who, according to *The Times*, treated Homer "with an almost rabbinical veneration." He was puzzled by a phrase used by Homer, "the wine-dark sea." Whichever way you look at it, the sea does not look like wine. It can look blue or green or grey, but not the red or purple of Greek wine. The only other thing that Homer describes as wine-dark is oxen. But oxen can be black, bay, or brown. They do not look like red wine.

Equally puzzling is his use of the word *chlôros*, meaning "green." Homer applies it to fresh twigs, the olive-wood club of the Cyclops, and honey. By a stretch of the imagination one can imagine twigs and olive wood looking green, but not honey. [3]

Gladstone came to a radical conclusion. Homer was not using these words to refer to colour at all. His argument was that sensitivity to colour evolved only later. The Greeks of Homer's era saw the world in terms of shadings of black and white with a dash of red, but no more. Thus "wine-dark" did not mean "red" as opposed to blue or green or

---

2. Maimonides, *Mishneh Torah, Hilkhot Tumat Tzaraat* 16:10.
3. Guy Deutscher, *Through the Language Glass: How Words Colour Your World* (London: Heinemann, 2010), 25–40.

yellow or grey, but simply "dark." *Chlôros* in Homer's day did not mean "green" but "pale, light, fresh, and young-looking."

It may be, in other words, that we completely misunderstand the way Homer used certain words because we are projecting onto them sensitivities and sensibilities that did not exist in Homer's day. What for us are words describing colour, for Homer were about shading: not red and green but light and dark.

Another set of examples that have to do not with time but place are given by Richard E. Nisbett in his *The Geography of Thought*. He documents the surprising differences in the ways Westerners and Easterners like the Chinese perceive the world. Westerners are far more likely to think in terms of isolated objects and abstract ideas. Easterners think in terms of dynamic relationships. So for example, when shown three pictures, one of a chicken, one of a cow, and one of grass, and asked, "Which two go together?" Western children are more likely to say, "The cow and the chicken," because they are both animals. They both belong to the same category or concept. Chinese children are more likely to say, "The cow and the grass," because where there are cows, there is grass.[4]

This is a very striking insight. What we see is not simply determined by what is there. Perception is shaped by the words we use and the concepts available to us at any given time in the civilisation of which we are a part. When we in the scientific West come across, in the Torah, a condition like *tzaraat*, we are likely to assume that it is speaking the language of medicine and we are puzzled at the linkage between skin disease and discoloration of clothes and walls.

However, it is far more likely that what we have here is a phenomenon like Homer's use of the word "wine-dark" or the way Chinese children relate cows to grass; that is, a way of thinking that is quite unlike our own and has nothing to do with medicine. The ancient Israelites were certainly capable of thinking of *tzaraat* as a skin disease. Elisha tells Naaman how to cure his condition by bathing in the Jordan in a way completely unrelated to the procedures set out here in *Vayikra*, which deal not with healing but with purification.

4. Richard E. Nisbett, *The Geography of Thought: How Asians and Westerners Think Differently – and Why* (New York: Free Press, 2003), 140.

What then links human skin, garments, and walls of houses? The answer is that *they all mark a boundary between inside and outside.* They are the outer surfaces covering something whose essential significance is within.

Priests, and the sensibility they embodied, were intensely concerned with boundaries: between sacred and secular, pure and impure, permitted and forbidden. That is the logic of the prohibitions against eating meat and milk together, wearing clothes of mixed wool and linen, sowing a field with mixed seeds, or crossbreeding animals. Decay in a boundary, whether it be skin, clothes, or walls, is to the priestly mind a sign of disorder within.

What might this be? The sages are guided here by the principle that "the words of Torah may be poor in one place but rich in another,"[5] meaning that an obscure text can sometimes be understood by considering other passages elsewhere. The most obvious clue is Moses' warning in the book of Deuteronomy:

> Take care with regard to the plague of *tzaraat,* so that you observe [the laws] diligently, and do according to all that the priests the Levites shall teach you, as I commanded them, so you shall observe to do. *Remember what the Lord your God did to Miriam* along the way after you came out of Egypt. (Deut. 24:8–9)

The connection between *tzaraat* and "what the Lord your God did to Miriam" lies in an episode in the book of Numbers, when Miriam and Aaron spoke disparagingly about Moses:

> Miriam and Aaron began to talk against Moses because of his Cushite wife, for he had married a Cushite. "Has the Lord spoken only through Moses?" they asked. "Hasn't He also spoken through us?" And the Lord heard this. (Num. 12:1–2)

What precisely their complaint was is not explicit in the text. Moses, however, made no response, because he was "the humblest man on the

5. Y. Rosh HaShana 3:5.

face of the earth." God then avenged Moses' honour. He told Miriam and Aaron that Moses was unique and that they were wrong to speak against him. His "anger burned against them." We then read:

> When the cloud lifted from above the tent, Miriam's skin was *metzoraat* – it became as white as snow. (Num. 12:10)

Thus Miriam was punished by *tzaraat* because she spoke disparagingly about her brother. (Why Aaron was not also afflicted is a question we will not pursue here.) Hence the sages' conclusion that *tzaraat* is a punishment for *lashon hara*, evil or derogatory speech.

The sages offer a similar explanation for a curious detail in the encounter between God and Moses at the burning bush. At one point Moses says, "But they [the Israelites] will not believe in me" (Ex. 4:1). God then gave him three signs: a staff that turned into a snake, Moses' hand that became as leprous (*metzoraat*) as snow, and water that turned into blood. Two of these signs, the snake and the blood, recur later in the story, when Moses, accompanied by Aaron, confronts Pharaoh and his magicians. But the leprous hand does not recur.

The sages conclude that the hand that turned leprous was not a *sign* but a *punishment*. They say in reference to this episode that, "One who casts aspersions on the innocent is physically afflicted." How had Moses cast aspersions on the innocent? The Talmud explains as follows:

> Moses said, "They will not believe in me." But the Holy One, Blessed Be He, knew that they would believe. He said to Moses: "They are believers, the children of believers, but in the end, you yourself will not believe, as is written, 'because you did not believe in Me'" (Num. 20:12).[6]

Moses spoke ill of the Israelites and because of that was punished by his hand turning white – another connection between *tzaraat* and *lashon hara*, evil speech.

6. Shabbat 97a.

Why, though, this punishment for that sin? The answer seems to lie in the nature of *tzaraat*. It is a condition that is hard to hide. Skin disease is not an internal symptom of which others may be unaware. It draws attention to itself. And the fact that garments and even the walls of a house could be affected made it seem as if the very objects surrounding a person were marking him out as the centre of unwanted attention.

The nature of the punishment testified to the kind of sin that provoked it. It was a sin that sought to hide – therefore it was made public. It was a sin that sought to make someone else a pariah – therefore the one who committed it was made a pariah: "As long as he has the disease he remains unclean. He must live alone; he must live outside the camp" (Lev. 11:46).

This is the nature of malicious gossip. It is the kind of thing that people speak with hushed voices and often deny when accused of it. It sows suspicion and dissension. It wrecks communities. It can destroy reputations and careers. It damages relationships, undermining the respect and trust on which families and communities depend. It is secretive and devastating.

Nothing could do more to damage the kind of nation God was inviting the Israelites to become through their collective experience in Egypt and in the wilderness: a community built on shared memories, hopes, and expectations, and a sense, given by covenant, of collective responsibility.

In his commentary to Deuteronomy, Rashi quotes a midrash that says that Moses was often the subject of *lashon hara*. If he left his tent early, people said he had had a row with his wife. If he left his tent late, they said, "He has been plotting against us."[7] Moses himself, as we saw in relation to his own sister and brother, was humble enough not to be affected by this, but it was harmful nonetheless. Gossip of this kind destroys the fabric of community and the authority on which leadership depends.

So *tzaraat* represents a kind of poetic justice. This is how Maimonides describes it:

7. Rashi, Commentary to Deuteronomy 1:12, based on Sifre ad loc.

All agree that leprosy is a punishment for slander. The disease begins in the walls of houses. If the sinner repents, the object is attained. If he remains in his disobedience, the disease affects his bed and house furniture. If he still continues to sin, the leprosy attacks his own garments, and then his body.[8]

Even as a practitioner of gossip was denying that he had said anything negative at all, his walls, his garments, and eventually his very skin were testifying against him. It was as if God were saying: if you sin in private I will advertise your guilt in public. I will demonstrate your guilt and malice to the world.

Thus a seemingly uninspiring, even unintelligible passage of the Bible dealing ostensibly with an obscure disease became, as understood by the Oral Tradition, a compelling lesson in morality whose relevance would never fade.

It is fundamental to *Torat Kohanim*, the mindset of the priest, that there is a moral law at work in the universe just as there are physical, scientific laws. In the long run, sins do not go unpunished, especially those that people believe they can commit without anyone finding out. Those who sin in private will eventually be exposed in public.

Words hurt. Words harm. Verbal injuries may cut deeper even than physical injuries. They tear the fabric of society. They damage relationships and destroy trust – and without trust, no society can survive. It was the fate of the slanderer, who sought to undermine relationships of trust, to be condemned to live outside the camp as a moral outcast. The power of that message remains.

---

8. Maimonides, *The Guide for the Perplexed*, III:47.

The General and the Prophet

The main theme of the *haftara* of *Parashat Tazria*, taken from the second book of Kings, is a fascinating story about two utterly different individuals brought together by circumstance: Naaman, commander of the Syrian army and thus an enemy of Israel, and the prophet Elisha, Elijah's successor, a man of God, visionary, and worker of miracles.

The connection between the *haftara* and the *parasha* is the subject of *tzaraat*, the skin disease usually translated as leprosy. The narrative begins with a pointed description of Naaman. He is "a great man," "highly regarded," a "valiant soldier." These three phrases, cumulatively painting a picture of the conventional military hero, are followed by a single word, piercing in its unexpectedness: *metzora*. He is a leper.

Whatever interpretation we give of this condition in the *parasha* itself, where the sages take it to be something more and other than a conventional disease of the skin, here it is clear that it is to be understood in its plain sense. The hero is disfigured.

The story is set in motion by a small detail. A group of Syrian soldiers had been engaged in border raids against Israel and had taken captive an Israeli girl, who was employed as a servant to Naaman's wife. The girl tells the woman that if only her husband would visit the prophet, whom she does not name, in Samaria, she is sure that he would be able to cure his leprosy.

Naaman hears this and tells his master, the king of Syria, who gives his approval to the visit and sends a letter to the king of Israel, together with a large gift of silver, gold, and clothing, requesting the king to see to it that Naaman is cured. In an amusing scene, the Israelite king, unaware of Elisha's powers of cure, takes the letter as a provocation and a pretext for war. "Am I God? Can I kill and bring back to life?" He trembles and tears his clothes, fearing a Syrian attack.

Elisha hears about it, realises that it is he whom the soldier seeks, and sends a message to the king telling him to direct Naaman to him. Naaman travels with his considerable entourage of horses and chariots to the home of the prophet. The prophet, who does not appear in person, sends out a messenger with a simple instruction. "Bathe seven times in the Jordan and your skin will be healed."

At this, Naaman is furious. He is expecting a conventional faith healer to come out, express appropriately flattering words to this important visitor, utter some magical formula, "wave his hand over the spot and cure me of my leprosy." Not only is he offended that the prophet does not come out to greet him and perform the appropriate gestures. He even proposed that the cure be effected by waters of the river Jordan. Does he not know, says Naaman, that we have better rivers in Damascus than in the whole of Israel?

He is about to storm off in a fury when his servants urge him not to be so hasty. After all, they reason, if he had ordered you to perform some arduous task, would you not have undertaken it? Since he is only suggesting that you bathe seven times in a river, what do you lose by obeying his words?

The general does so and is cured. "Then his flesh was restored and became clean like that of a young boy." With touching simplicity, awestruck by the sudden lifting of his disfigurement, Naaman returns and this time meets the prophet. He declares, "Now I know that there is no God in all the world except in Israel." He urges the prophet to accept the gift that he has brought, but Elisha refuses.

Naaman now makes a request. He asks for two donkey-loads of earth from the land of Israel so that he can worship the God of Israel on his return to Syria. He asks forgiveness of the prophet that he may still have to accompany his master, the king of Syria, when he worships at the temple to Rimmon, the god of Syria, and asks him not to consider it idol worship when he bows there alongside the king. The prophet gently replies, "Go in peace."

Naaman, a key enemy of Israel, now believes in the God of Israel but has still not understood the difference between monotheism and the local gods of place. Hence his request for soil from the land of Israel so that he can worship its God.

The story is full of charm. It is notable for the way wisdom is distributed among the story's minor characters. It is the Israeli girl prisoner who suggests going to Israel in the first place, and Naaman's servants who persuade their master to follow the prophet's instructions. The conventionally important characters lack understanding. The king of Israel completely misinterprets the situation. And Naaman himself fails to realise what a true prophet is like. He is incensed by Elisha's failure to act as a standard miracle worker, with genuflections, gestures, and an expectation of rich reward.

No less significant is the way it shows how a gentile can become convinced of the truth of Israel's God. There is no suggestion, either on Naaman's part or Elisha's, that this should lead to some form of conversion – leaving Syria, perhaps, to live in Israel, or adopting any of Israel's customs. It is enough that he now knows that there is one true God.

The central values of Tanakh are strongly in evidence in this story. Healing comes not through any magical performance but through a simple act of obedience. The dignity given to the minor characters, and the irony that attaches to the major ones, confirm the proposition we encountered earlier, in the first book of Samuel: "The Lord does not look at the things man looks at. Man looks at the outward appearance, but the Lord looks at the heart" (1 Sam. 16:7).

There is a touching simplicity in many of the narratives associated with Elisha. To be sure, the world in which these stories are set is one of wars, power, and political intrigue. But there is, they suggest, a different reality, in which virtue is unrelated to office, in which goodness is rewarded, and evil, though it may hold sway in the short term, is defeated in the end. Stories like these, so different from the epics of other ancient cultures, still speak to us today and their message still rings true. Naaman's cure may be miraculous, but somehow that is not the point of the story.

Simple obedience to the word of the Lord, without fuss or fanfare, equivocation or excuse: that is the value that drives the prophets, cutting through the often cruel and Machiavellian politics of the ancient world.

Metzora
מְצוֹרָע

Parashat *Metzora* continues with the process of purification for the phenomenon known as *tzaraat*, the decay that causes skin disease in humans and discoloration in garments and the walls of houses. It continues with the purification procedure for bodily discharges in men and women.

In *Parashat Tazria* we noted the connection, already hinted at in the Torah, between *tzaraat* and *lashon hara*, evil speech. So the first essay is about speech in Judaism, and the second about why evil speech is so disruptive of relationships. The third is about the price Jews have historically paid for speaking badly of one another. The fourth asks if Judaism has a concept of good speech as opposed to evil speech. The fifth is about the purity laws in general, while the sixth looks at the *haftara* and how outsiders sometimes see the good news that those within cannot yet see.

The Power of Speech

As we saw in *Parashat Tazria*, the sages identify *tzaraat* – the condition that affects human skin, the fabric of garments, and the walls of a house – not as an illness but as a punishment, and not for any sin but for one specific sin, that of *lashon hara*, evil speech.

This prompts the obvious question: Why evil speech and not some other sin? Why should speaking be worse than, say, physical violence? There is an old English saying: "Sticks and stones may break my bones/but words will never harm me." It is unpleasant to hear bad things said about you, but surely no more than that.

There is not even a direct prohibition against evil speech in the Torah. There is a prohibition against gossip: "Do not go around as a gossiper among your people" (Lev. 19:16). *Lashon hara* is a subset of this larger command. Here is how Maimonides defines it: "There is a far greater sin that falls under this prohibition [of gossip]. It is 'the evil tongue,' which refers to whoever speaks disparagingly of his fellow, even though he speaks the truth."[1]

---

1. Maimonides, *Mishneh Torah, Hilkhot Deot* 7:2.

The sages go to remarkable lengths to emphasise its seriousness. It is, they say, as bad as all three cardinal sins together – idol worship, bloodshed, and illicit sexual relations.[2] Whoever speaks with an evil tongue, they say, is as if he denied God.[3] They also say: it is forbidden to dwell in the vicinity of any of those with an evil tongue, and all the more to sit with them and to listen to their words.[4] Why are mere words treated with such seriousness in Judaism?

The answer touches on one of the most basic principles of Jewish belief. The ancients worshipped the gods because they saw them as powers: lightning, thunder, the rain and sun, the sea and ocean that epitomised the forces of chaos, and sometimes wild animals that represented danger and fear. Judaism was not a religion that worshipped power, despite the fact that God is more powerful than any pagan deity.

Judaism, like other religions, has holy places, holy people, sacred times, and consecrated rituals. What made Judaism different, however, is that it is supremely *a religion of holy words*. With words God created the universe: "And God said, Let there be…and there was." Through words He communicated with humankind. In Judaism, language itself is holy. That is why *lashon hara*, the use of language to harm, is not merely a minor offence. It involves taking something that is holy and using it for purposes that are unholy. It is a kind of desecration.

After creating the universe, God's first gift to the first man was the power to use words to name the animals, and thus to use language to classify. This was the start of the intellectual process that is the distinguishing mark of Homo sapiens. The Targum translates the phrase, "And man became *a living creature*" (Gen. 2:7) as "a speaking spirit." Evolutionary biologists nowadays take the view that it was the demands of language and the advantage this gave humans over every other life form that led to the massive expansion of the human brain.[5]

2. Arakhin 15b.
3. Ibid.
4. Arakhin 15a.
5. See Steven Pinker, *The Language Instinct* (New York: William Morrow, 1994); Robin Dunbar, *Grooming, Gossip and the Evolution of Language* (Cambridge, Mass.: Harvard University Press, 1996); Guy Deutscher, *Through the Looking Glass: Why the World Looks Different in Other Languages* (New York: Metropolitan/Henry Holt, 2010).

When God sought to halt the plan of the people of Babel to build a tower that would reach heaven, He merely "confused their language" so they were unable to communicate. Language remains basic to the existence of human groups. It was the rise of nationalism in the nineteenth century that led to the gradual downplaying of regional dialects in favour of a single shared language across the territory over which a political authority had sovereignty. To this day, differences of language, where they exist within a single nation, are the source of ongoing political and social friction, for example between English and French speakers in Canada; Dutch, French, German, and Walloon speakers in Belgium; and the Spanish and Basque (also known as Euskara) languages in Spain. *God created the natural universe with words. We create – and sometimes destroy – the social universe with words.*

So the first principle of language in Judaism is that it is creative. We create worlds with words. The second principle is no less fundamental. Abrahamic monotheism introduced into the world the idea of a God who transcends the universe, and who therefore cannot be identified with any phenomenon within the universe. God is invisible. Hence in Judaism all religious images and icons are a sign of idolatry.

How then does an invisible God reveal Himself? Revelation was not a problem for polytheism. The pagans saw gods in the panoply of nature that surrounds us, making us feel small in its vastness and powerless in the face of its fury. A God who cannot be seen or even represented in images demands an altogether different kind of religious sensibility. Where can such a God be found?

The answer again is: in words. God spoke. He spoke to Adam, Noah, Abraham, Moses. At the revelation at Mount Sinai, as Moses reminded the Israelites, "The Lord spoke to you out of the fire. You heard the sound of words but saw no form; there was only a voice" (Deut. 4:12). In Judaism, words are the vehicle of revelation. The prophet is the man or woman who hears and speaks the word of God.

That was the phenomenon that neither Spinoza nor Einstein could understand. They could accept the idea of a God who created heaven and earth, the force of forces and cause of causes, the originator of, as we call it nowadays, the Big Bang, the God who was the architect of matter and the composer of order. God, Einstein famously said, "does not play dice with the universe." Indeed, it is ultimately faith in the universe as the product of a single creative intelligence that underlies the scientific mindset from the outset.

Judaism calls this aspect of God *Elokim*. But we believe in another aspect of God also, which we call *Hashem*, the God of relationship – and relationship exists by virtue of speech. For it is speech that allows us to communicate with others and share with them our fears, hopes, loves, plans, feelings, and intentions. Speech allows us to convey our inwardness to others. It is at the very heart of the human bond. A God who could create universes but not speak or listen would be an impersonal god – a god incapable of understanding what makes us human. Worshipping such a god would be like bowing down to the sun or to a giant computer. We might care about it but it could not care about us. That is not the God of Abraham.

Words are remarkable in another way as well. We can use language not just to describe or assert. We can use it to create new moral facts. The Oxford philosopher J. L. Austin called this special use of language "performative utterance."[6] The classic example is making a promise. When I make a promise, I create an obligation that did not exist before. Nietzsche believed that the ability to make a promise was the birth of morality and human responsibility.[7]

Hence the idea at the heart of Judaism: *brit*, covenant, which is nothing other than *a mutually binding promise between God and human beings.* What defines the special relationship between the Jewish people and God is not that He brought them from slavery to freedom. He did that, says the prophet Amos, to other people as well: "Did I not bring Israel up from Egypt, the Philistines from Caphtor, and the Arameans from Kir?" (Amos 9:7). It is the fact that at Sinai God and Israel entered into a mutual pledge that linked them in an everlasting bond.

Covenant is the word that joins heaven and earth, the word spoken, the word heard, the word affirmed and honoured in trust. For that reason,

6. J. L. Austin, *How to Do Things with Words* (Cambridge, Mass.: Harvard University Press, 1962).
7. Friedrich Nietzsche, essay 2 in *On the Genealogy of Morality*, ed. Keith Ansell-Pearson, trans. Carol Diethe (Cambridge, UK: Cambridge University Press, 1994).

Jews were able to survive exile. They may have lost their home, their land, their power, their freedom, but they still had God's word, the word He said He would never break or rescind. The Torah, in the most profound sense, is the word of God, and Judaism is the religion of holy words.

It follows that to misuse or abuse language to sow suspicion and dissension is not just destructive. It is sacrilege. It takes something holy, the human ability to communicate and thus join soul to soul, and use it for the lowest of purposes, to divide soul from soul and destroy the trust on which non-coercive relationships depend.

That, according to the sages, is why the speaker of *lashon hara* was smitten by leprosy and forced to live as a pariah outside the camp. The punishment was measure for measure:

> What is special about the person afflicted with *tzaraat* that the Torah says, "He shall live alone; he must live outside the camp" (Lev. 13:46)? The Holy One, Blessed Be He, said, "Since this person sought to create division between man and wife, or a person and his neighbour, [he is punished by being divided from the community], which is why it says, 'Let him live alone, outside the camp.'"[8]

Language, in Judaism, is the basis of creation, revelation, and the moral life. It is the air we breathe as social beings. Hence the statement in Proverbs (18:21), "Death and life are in the power of the tongue." Likewise, the verse in Psalms, "Whoever of you loves life and desires to see many good days, keep your tongue from evil and your lips from telling lies" (Ps. 34:13–14).

Judaism emerged as an answer to a series of questions: How can finite human beings be connected to an infinite God? How can they be connected to one another? How can there be co-operation, collaboration, collective action, families, communities, and a nation, without the coercive use of power? How can we form relationships of trust? How can we redeem the human person from his or her solitude? How can we create collective liberty such that my freedom is not bought at the cost of yours?

8. *Yalkut Shimoni* 1:552.

The answer is: through words, words that communicate, words that bind, words that honour the Divine Other and the human other. *Lashon hara*, "evil speech," by poisoning language, destroys the very basis of the Judaic vision. When we speak disparagingly of others, we diminish them, we diminish ourselves, and we damage the very ecology of freedom.

That is why the sages take *lashon hara* so seriously, why they regard it as the gravest of sins, and why they believe that the entire phenomenon of *tzaraat*, leprosy in people, mildew in clothes and houses, was God's way of making it public and stigmatised.

Never take language lightly, implies the Torah. For it was through language that God created the natural world, and through language that we create and sustain our social world. It is as essential to our survival as the air we breathe.

Language and Relationship

One of the more surprising things about *lashon hara*, evil speech, in Judaism, is that *it refers to speech that is true*. False speech, libel, or slander, are something else and fall under a different prohibition. Here is Maimonides, explaining the distinction:

> There is a far greater sin that falls under this prohibition [of gossip]. It is *the evil tongue*, which refers to one who speaks disparagingly of his fellow, *even though he speaks the truth*. But whoever tells a lie is called "one who gives his fellow a bad name" [*motsi shem ra*]. However, the one who possesses an evil tongue is one who sits and says, "A certain individual did such and such. His ancestors were so and so. I heard such and such about him." Scripture says of those who speak disparagingly of others, "May the Lord cut off all smooth lips, the tongue that speaks proud things." (Ps. 12:4)[1]

This definition, though, is quite strange. Why should it be a sin to tell the truth, even if it casts a negative light over the one about whom you say

1. Maimonides, *Mishneh Torah, Hilkhot Deot* 7:2.

it? Is truth always pleasant or positive? We all have failings. We all sin. Judaism accepts this. It has never idealised the human situation. Surely honesty requires that we tell the truth, however harsh it is.

This paradox suggests that Judaism has a different understanding of language than the one that prevails in the West and had its origins in ancient Greece. The philosophers, heirs to the Greeks, tended to think of language as conveying information. What matters is whether it is true or false. If the factual assertion contained within a sentence corresponds with the way things are, it is true. If not, it is false. We use language to share information. That is its role in the human situation. Hence the only thing that matters is truth.

Judaism sees things differently. One way of approaching this is through a discovery made by the anthropologist Bronislaw Malinowski. During the First World War, the young Malinowski was engaged in fieldwork among the Trobriand islanders of New Guinea. Attempting to enter into the lifeworld of the people he was studying, he developed an interest in how social structures answer to basic human needs.

One phenomenon that captured his attention was the fact that Trobriand islanders spent a great deal of their time conversing, but relatively little in exchanging information. The islanders did not talk in order to inform others of what they did not know. They did so just to be together, to cement their bonds of friendship. Malinowski concluded that their conversation "serves to establish bonds of personal union between people brought together by the mere need of companionship."[2]

He called this "phatic communion," and it is what we do, for example, when we say to someone, "How are you?" or "Have a good day." The question is not a request for information; the wish is not a command. These are acts of communication whose content is almost irrelevant. They take place simply to affirm the social bond. Indeed, deep conversations between friends can sometimes involve an almost tangible

2. Bronislaw Malinowski, "The Problem of Meaning in Primitive Languages," in *The Meaning of Meaning: A Study of the Influence of Language upon Thought and of the Science of Symbolism* by C. K. Ogden and I. A. Richards (London: K. Paul, Trench, Trubner, 1923).

sense of the presence of an other. We call communication "staying in touch" as if it were a kind of embrace.

Phatic communion is the connection formed when two people talk, regardless of what they say. It is the encounter of two persons in which each recognises in the other an answering presence. It says that someone else is there, attending to us, listening and responding to our being, confirming our existence. Speech is intimately related to the social, to our need to belong to something larger than the self.

The evolutionary psychologist Robin Dunbar has gone further and argued that speech emerged among humans to fulfil the same function as grooming in primates.[3] All social animals need to find ways of keeping the group together, managing disputes, appeasing frayed emotions, helping individuals within the group recover their poise after a bruising encounter. Primates do this by grooming, stroking one another. But this degree of intimacy is possible only in a relatively small group. Humans, by using language as a substitute for embrace, can manage more relationships and thus build larger groups.

What Malinowski and Dunbar have done in their different ways is to remind us that language is not just about conveying information. Hence truth is not the only consideration. Conversation is about creating and sustaining relationships so that the group (the family, the village, the tribe, ultimately the nation as a whole) can function smoothly and cohesively without splitting apart whenever there is a conflict between two strong personalities.

If this is so, it explains why *lashon hara* is regarded so seriously by the sages. Jews have always been a nation of strong individuals. They stand out starkly in the pages of Tanakh and the debates that make up the Midrash and the Talmud. The Lord may be our shepherd, but no Jew was ever a sheep. Every Jew has his or her opinion. Every Jew needs to feel valued, important, significant in the scheme of things, listened to, heard.

In such a group, the maintenance of cohesion is difficult but essential. That is one reason why speech was seen in Judaism not simply as a means of conveying information, though it is that as well, but also and essentially as a means of holding the group together without coercive

3.   Dunbar, op. cit.

force. That is why a statement can still be *lashon hara* despite the fact that it is true. For what matters is not just the information it conveys but the effect it has on relationships within the group. If it divides the group, poisons relationships, and sets one person against another, then it is destructive of relationships and of the group itself.

We see this clearly in the Torah, most obviously in the case of Joseph and his brothers. We read at the beginning of the story that Joseph "brought an evil report" about some of his brothers to his father (Gen. 37:2). This and other factors led to a complete breakdown of communication between them: "When his brothers saw that their father loved him more than any of them, they hated him and could not speak a kind word to him" (literally: "they could not speak him to peace," 37:4). Eventually, they plotted to kill him and sold him as a slave. Where relationships are damaged by evil speech, communication breaks down, and violence is often waiting in the wings.

The most compelling literary illustration of *motsi shem ra*, slander, and *lashon hara*, evil speech, is Shakespeare's tragedy *Othello*. Iago, a high-ranking soldier, is bitterly resentful of Othello, a Moorish general in the army of Venice. Othello has promoted a younger man, Cassio, over the more experienced Iago, who is determined to take revenge. He does so in a prolonged and vicious campaign, which involves, among other things, tricking Othello into the suspicion that his wife, Desdemona, is having an adulterous affair with Cassio. Othello asks Iago to kill Cassio, and he himself kills Desdemona, smothering her in her bed. Emilia, Iago's wife and Desdemona's attendant, discovers her mistress dead and as Othello explains why he has killed her, realises the nature of her husband's plot and exposes it. Othello, in guilt and grief, commits suicide, while Iago is arrested and taken to be tortured and possibly executed.

It is a play entirely about the evil of slander and suspicion, and portrays literally what the sages say figuratively, that "Evil speech kills three people: the one who says it, the one who listens to it, and the one about whom it is said."[4]

Shakespeare's tragedy makes it painfully clear how much evil speech lives and thrives in the dark corners of suspicion. Had the others

4. Arakhin 15b.

known what Iago was saying to stir up fear and distrust, the facts might have become known and the tragedy averted. As it was, he was able to mislead the various characters, playing on their emotional weaknesses and envy, getting each to believe the worst about one another. It ends in serial bloodshed and disaster.

The age of computers, smartphones, and social networking sites has added another dimension to the destructive possibilities of evil speech. To take one example from Britain: Hannah Smith was a fourteen-year-old schoolgirl living in Lutterworth, Leicestershire. Bright and outgoing, she enjoyed an active social life and seemed to have an exciting future ahead of her. On the morning of August 2, 2013, Hannah was found hanged in her bedroom. She had committed suicide.

Seeking to unravel what had happened, her family soon discovered that she had been the target of anonymous abusive posts on a social networking website. Hannah was a victim of the latest variant of the oldest story in human history: the use of words as weapons by those seeking to inflict pain. The new version is called cyberbullying.

Hannah was not the only victim. There have been many others. Another highly publicised case, this time in the United States, was that of fifteen-year-old Amanda Todd, who committed suicide on October 10, 2012, after being exploited, blackmailed, and subjected to a tormenting profile on a well-known social networking site. Michael Harris tells her story in his book on the impact of online relationships, *The End of Absence*.[5] Online abuse has become one of the great hazards of virtual relationships.

Cyberbullying is *lashon hara* for the twenty-first century. In general, the Internet has what is called a disinhibition effect.[6] It allows people to say what they would not say under normal conventions of face-to-face encounter. Greek myth told the story of Gyges' ring that had the magical property of making whoever wore it invisible, so that he or she could get away with anything.[7] Social media that enable people to post

5. Michael Harris, *The End of Absence* (New York: Current, 2014), 49–72.
6. John Suler, "The Online Disinhibition Effect," *CyberPsychology & Behavior* 7(3), 2004: 321–326.
7. See Plato, *The Republic*, book 2, 359a–360d.

anonymous comments or adopt false identities are as near as anyone has yet come to inventing a Gyges' ring. That is what is so dangerous about it.

Hence the renewed relevance of the idea implicit in the connection between evil speech and *tzaraat*, the condition that affected not only human beings but also garments and walls. Here is Maimonides' account:

> It [*tzaraat*] was a sign and wonder among the Israelites to warn them against slanderous speaking. For if a man uttered slander, the walls of his house would suffer a change. If he repented, the house would again become clean. But if he continued in his wickedness until the house was torn down, leather objects in his house on which he sat or lay would suffer a change. If he repented they would again become clean. But if he continued in his wickedness until they were burned, the garments which he wore would suffer a change. If he repented they would again become clean. But if he continued in his wickedness until they were burned, his skin would suffer a change and he would become infected by *tzaraat* and be set apart and alone until he no more engaged in the conversation of the wicked which is scoffing and slander.[8]

Evil speech is subversive: it is a sin that seeks to conceal itself. People who speak badly about others do so in private, in hushed, conspiratorial tones, and often deny that they have done so. Iago keeps his intentions hidden. Social media gives people the opportunity to hide behind a cloak of anonymity or false identities. But the effect is deeply destructive. That is because speech is much more than the conveying of information. It is the substance of relationship, and when this is poisoned, trust and the social bond are undermined. We use the phrase "character assassination" precisely because some form of violence is being committed, even if it is verbal rather than physical.

That is why, as long as the condition of *tzaraat* existed, what had been done in private was broadcast in public, first by the walls of the offender's house, then by his clothes, and finally by his skin. It was not just a punishment. It was a public shaming. There is poetic justice

8.   Maimonides, *Mishneh Torah, Hilkhot Tumat Tzaraat* 16:10.

in this idea and though *tzaraat* no longer exists in its biblical form, still the moral remains.

The stories of victims of evil speech, from the fictitious Othello to the real-life tragedies of Hannah Smith and Amanda Todd, are a painful reminder of how right the sages are to reject the idea that "words can never harm me," and insist to the contrary that evil speech kills. Free speech is not speech that costs nothing. It is speech that respects the freedom and dignity of others. Forget this and free speech becomes very expensive indeed.

The Self-Inflicted Wound

There was, as we have seen in the previous essays, no sin about which the sages are so emphatic in their denunciation as evil speech. They linked the word *metzora*, a leper, to the phrase *motzi shem ra*, one who speaks negatively of his fellow. Not only is it deeply wrong in itself; it leads eventually to a complete loss of faith:

> This is the progress of the scorners and the wicked. First they indulge in idle talk…. Then they speak ill of the righteous…. This leads them to speak against the prophets and their message…. From this they come to speak against God and deny His existence.[1]

The fact that the *metzora* had to live outside the camp as a pariah was, say the sages, a punishment measure for measure. By his bad speech he sought to divide society, so he is condemned temporarily to live outside society.[2]

1. Maimonides, *Mishneh Torah, Hilkhot Tumat Tzaraat* 16:10.
2. *Yalkut Shimoni* I:552.

Nonetheless, it is a fault we can trace throughout Jewish history. Joseph brought a bad report about some of his brothers to their father. Moses, say the sages, was guilty when he said about the Israelites, "They will not believe in me." As was Miriam when she spoke against her brother, and as were the spies when they brought back an evil report about the land. And so on.

During the periods of both Greek and Roman rule, there were Jews who acted as informants against their own people. It was Hellenised Jews in the second century BCE who invited the Seleucid ruler Antiochus IV to impose forced Hellenisation on the Jewish population of Israel – a process that led to the rebellion we recall each year on Ḥanukka. Less than a war between Jews and Greeks, the Maccabean revolt was a *kulturkampf*, a war of cultures, between Jew and Jew.

There were similar defections to Rome two centuries later. Tiberius Julius Alexander, chief of staff of Titus, the Roman general who conquered Jerusalem and destroyed the Second Temple, was a Jew who had renounced his Jewishness – a nephew of the Alexandrian Jewish philosopher Philo.

So deep was the problem that the sages introduced a special paragraph into the weekly prayers, "For the slanderers let there be no hope."[3] Sadly, it continued.

In the Middle Ages, many public denunciations of Jews and Judaism were led by converted Jews. Nicholas Donin, a former student of Rabbi Yechiel ben Yosef of Paris, compiled a list of thirty-five accusations against the Talmud, which led to the Paris Disputation of 1240 and the burning of twenty-four cartloads of Talmuds in 1242.

Another Jew-turned-Christian, Pablo Christiani, was responsible for the Barcelona Disputation of 1263, in which he debated with Nahmanides (Ramban). Failing to defeat him in argument, he turned to other methods and was responsible for Nahmanides' enforced exile two years later. It was Christiani who persuaded Louis IX of France to make Jews wear a distinctive badge that made them recognisable as Jews in public.

---

3.   There were various versions of this prayer in early rabbinic times, some referring to "heretics" and "sectarians." Nonetheless, the word "slanderers" suggests those who brought evil reports about Jews to the Roman or other non-Jewish authorities.

It was a Jewish convert to Christianity, Joseph (later Johannes) Pfefferkorn who in the early sixteenth century wrote a series of anti-Jewish tracts calling for the expulsion of Jews from major German cities, and persuaded Emperor Maximilian to seize Jewish books, especially copies of the Talmud. The great humanist Erasmus called Pfefferkorn "a criminal Jew [before his conversion, he had been found guilty of burglary and theft] who had become a most criminal Christian."

Internal arguments within the Jewish community also brought disaster. In the early thirteenth century, for example, a bitter dispute broke out between devotees and critics of Maimonides. For the former, he was one of the greatest Jewish minds of all time. For the latter, he was a dangerous thinker whose works contained heresy and whose influence led people to abandon the commandments.

There were ferocious exchanges. Each side issued condemnations and excommunications against the other. There were pamphlets and counter-pamphlets, sermons and counter-sermons, and for awhile, French and Spanish Jewry were convulsed by the controversy. Then, in 1232, Maimonides' books were burned by the Dominicans. The shock brought a brief respite; then extremists desecrated Maimonides' tomb in Tiberias. In the early 1240s, following the Disputation of Paris, Christians burned all the copies of the Talmud they could find. It was one of the great tragedies of the Middle Ages.

Did the Dominicans take advantage of Jewish accusations of heresy against Maimonides to level their own charges? Was it simply that they were able to take advantage of the internal split within Jewry, to proceed with their own persecutions without fear of concerted Jewish reprisals? One way or another, throughout the Middle Ages, many of the worst Christian persecutions of Jews were either incited by converted Jews, or exploited internal weaknesses of the Jewish community.

Moving to the modern age, one of the most brilliant exponents of Orthodoxy was Rabbi Meir Loeb ben Yechiel Michal Malbim (1809–1879), chief rabbi of Rumania. An outstanding scholar whose commentary to Tanakh is one of the glories of the nineteenth century, he was at first welcomed by all groups in the Jewish community as a man of learning and religious integrity. Soon, however, the more "enlightened" Jews discovered, to their dismay, that he was a vigorous traditionalist, and they began to incite the civil authorities against him. In posters and pamphlets they portrayed him as a benighted relic of the Middle Ages, a man opposed to progress and the spirit of the age.

One Purim, they sent him a gift of a parcel of food that included pork and crabs, with an accompanying message: "We, the local progressives, are honoured to present these delicacies and tasty dishes from our table as a gift to our luminary." Eventually, in response to the campaign, the government withdrew its official recognition of the Jewish community, and of Malbim as its chief rabbi, and banned him from delivering sermons in the Great Synagogue. On Friday, March 18, 1864, policemen surrounded his house early in the morning, arrested him, and imprisoned him. After Shabbat, he was placed on a ship and taken to the Bulgarian border, where he was released on condition that he never return to Rumania. This is how the *Encyclopaedia Judaica* describes the campaign:

> M. Rosen has published various documents which disclose the false accusations and calumnies Malbim's Jewish-assimilationist enemies wrote against him to the Rumanian government. They accused him of disloyalty and of impeding social assimilation between Jews and non-Jews by insisting on adherence to the dietary laws, and said, "This rabbi by his conduct and prohibitions wishes to impede our progress." As a result of this, the prime minister of Rumania issued a proclamation against the "ignorant and insolent" rabbi.... In consequence the minister refused to grant rights to the Jews of Bucharest, on the grounds that the rabbi of the community was "the sworn enemy of progress."[4]

Similar stories could be told about several other outstanding scholars – among them, Rabbi Zvi Hirsch Chajes, Rabbi Azriel Hildesheimer, Rabbi Yitzhak Reines, and even the late Rabbi Joseph Soloveitchik of blessed memory, who was brought to court in Boston in 1941 to face trumped-up charges by the local Jewish community. Even these shameful

4. Gershom Scholem, *Encyclopaedia Judaica*, 11:822.

episodes were only a continuation of the vicious war waged against the Hasidic movement by their opponents, the *mitnagdim*, which saw many Hasidic leaders (among them the first Rebbe of Chabad, Rabbi Shneur Zalman of Liadi) imprisoned on false testimony given to the local authorities by other Jews.

A not dissimilar phenomenon occurred in Russia during the rise of communism. Its prophet, Karl Marx, was descended from a line of rabbis; his father had him converted to Christianity when he was six years old. Marx was savage in his disdain for Jews. His 1843 essay "On the Jewish Question" drew heavily on the anti-Semitic theories of Bruno Bauer. Jews epitomised the capitalist order he sought to overthrow.[5] Many Jews were drawn to the revolutionary cause, and they too were attracted to its messianic universalism, which led them to oppose not only Judaism, but also Zionism and Jewish socialism (Bundism), which they saw as particularistic and parochial.

For example, Rosa Luxemburg, the Marxist theorist, resolutely refused to identify as a Jew. To followers of Marx, she wrote, "The Jewish question as such does not exist." When a Jew wrote to her claiming her attention for the atrocities being committed against her people, she wrote back, "Why do you come with your special Jewish sorrows?" She felt, she said, every people's pain, none more than others. "I cannot find a special corner in my heart for the ghetto." Eventually she was murdered.[6]

The Talmud contains a striking passage about prophets who speak badly about their own people:

> The Holy One, Blessed Be He, said to [the prophet] Hosea, "Your children have sinned," to which he should have replied, "They are Your children, the children of Your favoured ones, children of Abraham, Isaac, and Jacob. Extend Your mercy to them." Not only he did not say this, but he said to Him: "Sovereign of the universe, the whole world is Yours: exchange them for a different

5. Sander Gilman, *Jewish Self-Hatred* (Baltimore: Johns Hopkins University Press, 1986), 188–208.
6. J. L. Talmon, *Israel Among the Nations* (London: Weidenfeld and Nicolson, 1970), 43–45.

nation." Said the Holy One, Blessed Be He, "What shall I do with this old man? I will order him: Go and marry a promiscuous woman and have children born of promiscuity. Then I will order him: Send her away from thy presence. If he can send her away, then I too send Israel away."[7]

This is a remarkable text that needs unpacking. The book of Hosea begins with God commanding the prophet to marry an unfaithful woman. He does. She then has children. God orders the prophet to call two of them Lo-ruhama, "unloved," and Lo-ami, "not My people." The Talmud, puzzled by these events, suggests that the prophet himself was being tested for speaking badly about his own people, telling them that God no longer loved them or considered them as His people. God was showing him that it is hard to disown those you once loved even if they have been unfaithful to you.

The prophets were social critics. It was their task to admonish the people. But *you cannot be a prophet unless you love, and show that you love, the people whom you are criticising.* That is the point the Talmud is making.[8] There may be a fine line between the constructive criticism of a friend and the destructive criticism of an enemy, but we can usually tell the difference. The prophets often said harsh things to their contemporaries, but they identified with them and always carried an underlying message of hope.

The divisiveness of Jewry through the ages, and the willingness of Jews to slander their opponents to the non-Jewish authorities, represents a profound moral and spiritual failure, one for which they eventually paid a heavy price. The sages know what they are saying when they speak of evil speech and slander as destructive of community. It is as if they understand God as saying: *If you wish Me to love you, then you must love one another.* Love does not mean being uncritical, but it does mean being loyal. If you criticise me, but I know that you care for me, I can

7. Pesahim 87a.
8. The political philosopher Michael Walzer has two fine books on this subject: *Interpretation and Social Criticism* (Cambridge, Mass.: Harvard University Press, 1987) and *The Company of Critics* (New York: Basic Books, 1988).

accept the criticism and grow thereby. But if you criticise me to a third party, then I know you intend harm, and I can no longer distinguish between valid criticism and malicious defamation.

We no longer know the condition known to the Torah as *tzaraat*, but we still understand what the sages have to say about Jews who denounce their fellow Jews to others.

Is There Such a Thing as Lashon Tov?

Judaism, especially in its approach to *lashon hara*, evil speech, involves a sustained meditation on the power of words to heal or harm, mend or destroy. Just as God created the world with words, so we create and can destroy relationships with words.

What is strange, though, is that the sages spoke little about the corollary, *lashon tov*, "good speech." The phrase does not appear in either the Babylonian Talmud or the Talmud Yerushalmi. It figures only in two midrashic passages, where it refers to praising God. But *lashon hara* does not mean speaking badly about God. It means speaking badly about human beings. If it is a sin to speak badly about people, is it a mitzva to speak well about them? My argument will be that it is.

In *Ethics of the Fathers* we read the following:

Rabban Yoḥanan b. Zakkai had five [pre-eminent] disciples, namely R. Eliezer b. Hyrcanus, R. Yehoshua b. Ḥananya, R. Yose the Priest, R. Shimon b. Netanel, and R. Elazar b. Arakh. He used to recount their praise: Eliezer b. Hyrcanus: a plastered well that never loses a drop. Yehoshua b. Ḥananya: happy is the one who gave birth to him. Yose the Priest: a pious man.

> Shimon b. Netanel: a man who fears sin. Elazar b. Arakh: an ever-flowing spring.[1]

However, the practice of Rabban Yoḥanan in praising his disciples seems to stand in contradiction to a Talmudic principle:

> Rav Dimi, brother of Rav Safra, said: Let no one ever talk in praise of his neighbour, for praise will lead to criticism.[2]

Rashi[3] gives two explanations of this statement. Having delivered excessive praise (*yoter midai*), the speaker himself will come to qualify his remarks, admitting for the sake of balance that the person of whom he speaks also has faults. Alternatively, others will point out his faults. For Rashi, the crucial consideration is whether the praise is judicious, accurate, true, or overstated. If the former, it is permitted; if the latter, it is forbidden. Evidently Rabban Yoḥanan was careful not to exaggerate.

Maimonides, however, sees matters differently. He writes: "Whoever speaks well about his neighbour *in the presence of his enemies* is guilty of a secondary form of evil speech [*avak lashon hara*], since he will provoke them to speak badly about him."[4] For Maimonides, the issue is not whether the praise is moderate or excessive, but the context in which it is delivered. If it is done in the presence of friends of the person about whom you are speaking, it is permitted. It is forbidden only when you are among his enemies and detractors. Praise then becomes a provocation, with bad consequences.

Are these merely two opinions or is there something deeper at stake? There is a famous passage in the Talmud which discusses how one should sing the praises of a bride at her wedding:

> Our Rabbis taught: How should you dance before the bride [i.e., what should one sing]?

1. Mishna Avot 2:10–11.
2. Arakhin 16a.
3. To Arakhin ad loc.
4. Maimonides, *Mishneh Torah, Hilkhot Deot* 7:4.

> The School of Shammai says: [Sing,] "The bride is as she is."
> The School of Hillel says: [Sing,] "The bride is beautiful and graceful."
> The School of Shammai said to the School of Hillel, "If she were lame or blind, would you sing that the bride is beautiful and graceful? Does the Torah not say, 'Keep far from falsehood'?"
> The School of Hillel answered the School of Shammai: "According to your view, if someone has made a bad purchase in the market, should you praise it in his eyes or depreciate it? Surely, one should praise it in his eyes."[5]

The disciples of Hillel hold that at a wedding, one should sing that the bride is beautiful, whether she is or not. Shammai's disciples disagree. Whatever the occasion, it is wrong to tell a lie. "Do you call that a lie?" the Hillelites respond. In the eyes of the groom at least, the bride is beautiful, just as in the eyes of someone who has just made a purchase, he has made a good deal, even if in your opinion, he hasn't.

What's really at stake here is not just temperament – puritanical Shammaites versus good-natured Hillelites – but two views about the nature of language. The Shammaites think of language as a way of making statements, which are either true or false. The Hillelites understand that language is about more than making statements. We can use language to encourage, empathise, motivate, and inspire. Or we can use it to discourage, disparage, criticise, and depress. Language does more than convey information. It conveys emotion. It creates or disrupts a mood. The sensitive use of speech involves social and emotional intelligence. Language, in J. L. Austin's famous account, can be performative as well as informative.

The argument between Hillel and Shammai is similar to that between Maimonides and Rashi. For Rashi, as for Shammai, the key question about praise is: Is it true, or is it excessive? For Maimonides as for Hillel, the question is: What is the context? Is it being said among enemies or friends? Will it create warmth and esteem or envy and resentment?

5. Ketubbot 16b–17a.

We can go one further, for the disagreement between Rashi and Maimonides about praise may be related to a more fundamental disagreement about the nature of the command, "You shall love your neighbour as yourself" (Lev. 19:18). Rashi interprets the command to mean: do not do to your neighbour what you would not wish him to do to you.[6] Maimonides, however, says that the command includes the duty "to speak in his praise."[7] Rashi evidently sees praise of one's neighbour as optional, while Maimonides sees it as falling within the command of love.

We can now answer a question we might have asked at the outset about the teaching in Avot that speaks of Yoḥanan b. Zakkai's disciples. Avot is about ethics, not history or biography. Why then does it tell us that Rabban Yoḥanan had disciples? Surely, that is a fact, not a value, an item of information, not a guide as to how to live.

However, we can now see that the Mishna is telling us something profound. The first statement in Avot includes the principle: "Raise up many disciples." How, though, do you create disciples? How do you inspire people to reach the full measure of their potential? The answer suggested by the Mishna is: by acting as did Rabban Yoḥanan b. Zakkai when he praised his students, showing them their individual strengths.

He did not flatter them. He guided them to see their specific talents. Eliezer b. Hyrcanus, the "plastered well that never loses a drop," was not creative, but he had a remarkable memory – not unimportant in the days before the Oral Torah was written in books. Elazar b. Arakh, the "ever-flowing spring," was creative, but needed to be fed by mountain waters (years later, he separated from his colleagues and forgot all he had learned).

Rabban Yoḥanan b. Zakkai took a Hillel-Maimonides view of praise. He used it not so much to describe as to motivate. And that is *lashon tov*. Evil speech diminishes us, good speech helps us grow. Evil speech puts people down, good speech lifts them up. Focused, targeted praise, informed by considered judgement of individual strengths, and sustained by faith in people and their potentiality, is what makes teachers

---

6. Rashi, Commentary to Sanhedrin 84a.
7. Maimonides, *Mishneh Torah, Hilkhot Deot* 6:3.

great and their disciples greater than they would otherwise have been. That is what we learn from Rabban Yoḥanan b. Zakkai.

So there is such a thing as *lashon tov*. According to Maimonides, it falls within the command of "Love your neighbour as yourself." According to Avot, it is one way of "raising up many disciples." It is as creative as *lashon hara* is destructive. Seeing the good in people and telling them so is a way of helping it become real, becoming a midwife to their personal growth. If so, then not only must we praise God. We must praise people, too.

The Laws of Purity

The sequence of passages beginning with chapter 11 of Leviticus (towards the end of *Parashat Shemini*), occupying the whole of *Parashot Tazria* and *Metzora*, and culminating in chapter 16 (the opening of *Parashat Aḥarei Mot*) is a tightly organised sequence of laws revolving around the keywords *tamei* and *tahor*, "impure" and "pure."

The word *tamei* in one or other of its forms appears no less than 106 times, while the root *tahor* appears sixty-two times. This is an extraordinary density. The root *tamei* appears only 285 times in Tanakh as a whole, and *tahor* 207 times, so that Leviticus accounts for around one-third of the occurrences of these words in the Hebrew Bible's thirty-nine books. The only rival in this respect is the book of Ezekiel. Ezekiel was both a prophet and a priest, and his is the most identifiably priestly voice in the non-Mosaic books.

The "purity" sequence is preceded by a general statement about the role of the priests: "to distinguish between the holy [*kodesh*] and the common [*ḥol*], and between the ritually unclean [*tamei*] and the clean [*tahor*]" (Lev. 10:10). That was one of the fundamental priestly duties, to "distinguish," differentiate and maintain the boundaries between different states and conditions, especially those that had to do with the strict demands of holy space, the Tabernacle, and later, the Temple.

Priestly passages are often marked by mathematical precision and linguistic symmetry, and that is very much in evidence here. The laws are clustered into seven groups:

1. impurity from eating or touching the carcasses of animals classified as repulsive to eat (11:1–47);
2. impurity from childbirth (12:1–8);
3. impurity from leprosy on skin and garments (13:1–59);
4. rectification of impurity from leprosy on skin (14:1–32);
5. impurity from leprosy on the walls of houses (14:33–57);
6. impurity from bodily discharges (15:1–33);
7. impurity from sin, rectified on the Day of Atonement (16:1–34).

All seven passages begin with the words, "The Lord spoke [*vayedaber*] to Moses," and they all contain, near or at the end, the phrase, "This is the law of… [*zot torat*]," with the sole exception of the last, the law of Yom Kippur, which ends with a similar phrase, "This will be an everlasting statute for you" (16:34).

The seventh, the impurity of sin, is different from the others since the purity concerned is more metaphorical than literal. Unlike the others, it has no physical symptoms or physical causes, such as contact. There is, as it happens, a seventh literal form of impurity, the most fundamental of all, that caused by contact with or proximity to a dead body, but that is dealt with elsewhere in the Torah, in Numbers 19:1–22. The reason it is placed there rather than here is almost certainly because it is linked with the death of two of Israel's leaders, Miriam and Aaron, and the announcement of the death of Moses. The law of the High Priest and the Day of Atonement may, conversely, appear here rather than elsewhere (in one or other of the passages dealing with holy days) in order to preserve the sevenfold structure, reminiscent of another passage written in the priestly voice, the seven-day scheme of creation in Genesis 1:1–2:3.

How are we to understand the concepts of purity and impurity?

First and foremost, these are concepts that have their main application in relation to the holy space of the Sanctuary. To enter its precincts one has to be pure, or purified. The chief exception is a woman's issue of menstrual blood, from which she had to be purified not in order to enter the Temple, but rather to resume physical relations with her husband. In general, "pure" and "impure" are not categories applying to life as a whole. They are not ethical terms like good and bad, right and wrong, permitted and forbidden, which apply to secular as well as sacred space and time.

They have, rather, to do with Israel's vocation as "a kingdom of priests and a holy nation," with the camp of the Israelites in the wilderness as a space in the centre of which was the Tabernacle, and with the land of Israel, especially at those sacred times of the year where people were expected to appear at the Temple.

The second thing to note, and it is subtle and easily misunderstood, is best conveyed by the well-known story about Rabban Yoḥanan b. Zakkai and the Roman who asked him about the rite of the red heifer (Num. 19) which purified people who had come in contact with the dead. This involved sprinkling those affected with special water in which had been dissolved the ashes of the heifer, together with those of the cedar wood, hyssop, and scarlet that had been burned with it. The Roman told Rabban Yoḥanan that this looked to him like a superstitious ritual. Rabban Yoḥanan replied with an answer designed to appeal to a Roman. He told him, in effect, that it was a form of exorcism for unclean spirits. The Roman was satisfied with this answer, but the rabbi's disciples were not.

He then replied with a very radical statement: "The dead does not defile, nor do the waters purify. The truth is that the rite of the red heifer is a divine decree. The Holy One, Blessed Be He, said: I have ordained a statute, I have issued a decree, and you are not permitted to transgress My decree."[1]

On the face of it, Rabban Yoḥanan was saying that the rite of the Red Heifer transcends human understanding, and that it represents the unfathomable will of God. However, I believe that the point Rabban Yoḥanan is making is different. There are two types of law: regulative and constitutive. Regulative law controls and sets limits to an activity

---

1. Numbers Rabba 19:1; *Pesikta DeRav Kahana* 4:7; *Pesikta Rabbati* 14:14.

that exists independently of the law. Law did not create employment, for example, or slavery, or violence. Instead it sought and seeks to regulate them: to ban them in some cases, and in others, to set out clear rules and limits.

It is quite different, for instance, in relation to the laws of chess. The laws created the game, and without them there is no chess. Constitutive law creates a phenomenon, it does not merely regulate one. That is what Rabban Yoḥanan was saying about the laws of *tuma* and *tahara*. They do not refer to some states of being that exist independently of the Tabernacle, the laws of the Torah, and the divine command. They only exist because God has stipulated that they exist, just as, for example, Shabbat only exists because God so ordered it. There is nothing in physical reality that makes Shabbat different from all other days, so that you could tell that a certain day was Shabbat because, say, of the quality of the light or the air or the temperature. The laws of purity, like the laws of holiness, are constitutive, not regulative. So the concept of impurity is not like the idea of uncleanliness, which could have physical manifestations. *Tuma* and *tahara* are spiritual categories brought into being by God's command.

What then do they represent? Recall that they exist primarily in connection with holy space such as the Temple. Remember also that the Temple is the "home" of God only in the most metaphorical sense. God is everywhere, in the Temple and outside, in the holy land and outside. It is only from a human point of view that one place is different from another, in that in the Temple, one is peculiarly conscious of being in the direct, unmediated presence of God.

The concepts of holiness and purity, the two organising principles of the priestly mind, represent the sensed presence of eternity, infinity, and pure spirituality. They are the polar opposites of what makes humans mortal, finite, and physical. God is radically Other. He is that which is not mortal, finite, and physical. Therefore, whatever inescapably reminds us of our physicality and mortality – whether it be birth or death, or a skin disease, or the flow of menstrual blood, or the unusual discharge of some bodily fluid, or contact with the carcass of a repulsive animal – conveys *tuma*, that is, a state from which we must be cleansed before entering the domain of the holy.

There is nothing intrinsically defiling about our physicality. To the contrary, the Torah asks us to seek God within the physical world, to sanctify rather than foreswear physical pleasures such as eating and drinking and the marital bond. There is nothing ascetic or otherworldly about the Torah's ethic. Some of the rabbis went so far as to say that a Nazirite, who foreswore wine and grape products, had to bring a sin offering because he had deprived himself of a legitimate pleasure. One of the key principles of the book of Deuteronomy, about life in the Promised Land, is "You shall rejoice in all the good things the Lord your God has given to you and your household" (Deut. 26:11). There is no sense of opposition within Tanakh, as we find, for example, in certain Greek and early Christian texts, between the soul and the body, such that we have to afflict the latter in order to enjoy the former. That is not what *tuma* and *tahara* are about.

They are about the intense and vigilant preparation we must make before entering, as it were, God's space. We have to ensure that we have divested ourselves of all lingering traces of that which reminds us of our mortality and physicality, our vulnerability to disease, decay, and death, not because we can escape them, nor that we should deny them, but simply to remind ourselves that God utterly transcends all such accidents and attributes of materiality. In the Temple we are in the presence of radical transcendence.

It is not that God needs us to be pure if He is to be with us. On the phrase about the Tent of Meeting "which remains with the [Israelites] even when they are unclean" (Lev. 16:16), the sages say: "Even though they [the Jews] are unclean, the Divine Presence is among them."[2] It is rather that *we* need to be pure if we are to open ourselves to the Divine Presence. The act of purification is an act of preparation for coming into contact with the Divine.

We no longer have a Temple, so many of these laws are inapplicable nowadays, other than the law of purification after the menstrual flow of blood and the special rules observed by *Kohanim*, members of the priestly lineage. Yet, if only metaphorically, we can still be moved by the words of the psalm:

2. Sifra, *Parashat Aḥarei Mot* 16:5.

Wash away all my iniquity
and cleanse me from my sin.
Cleanse me with hyssop, and I will be clean;
wash me, and I will be whiter than snow.
Hide Your face from my sins
and blot out all my iniquity.
Create in me a pure heart, O God,
and renew a steadfast spirit within me.
Do not cast me from Your presence
or take Your Holy Spirit from me. (Ps. 51:4–13)

There remains a psychological sense in which we seek purity as we come into the presence of God.

The Outsider

The *haftara* of *Parashat Metzora* tells a remarkably vivid story of individuals and a nation in crisis. The reading begins with Act 2 of the drama. Act 1 sets the scene. Israel, the northern kingdom, is nearing the end of its endurance. Samaria, the capital, is under siege. Surrounding it is the army of Syria under Ben Hadad. Food within the city has almost run out. Prices have gone sky-high. A donkey's head sells for eighty shekels of silver. Women are killing their children. A woman appeals to the king for help. He replies, "If God does not help you, where can I get help for you?"

The king, at the end of his tether, is furious with Elisha, apparently believing that if the prophet had prayed hard enough, God would have sent rescue. He threatens to cut off his head. He sends a messenger to the prophet, who calmly assures him that the siege will be lifted the next day, and food will be so readily available that a measure of flour will sell for a mere shekel. The messenger mocks him, saying that this is impossible. The prophet replies, "You will see it with your own eyes but you will not eat of it." With that, the *haftara* begins.

The scene has shifted. We now find ourselves in the company of four lepers – hence the link with the *parasha* which is about leprosy – outside the city, since lepers were condemned to live "outside the camp." To a modern eye and ear they are like characters from a Samuel Beckett play. The world is coming to an end, and the outsiders are watching it with an air of detachment.

They consider their options. If they go into the city, they will die because there is no food. If they stay where they are, they will die, because they too have no food. They decide to go over to the Syrian camp and surrender. Almost certainly they will be put to death, but what have they to lose?

They arrive at the camp at dusk and an astonishing sight meets their eyes. There is no one there. The Syrian army has fled, leaving behind all their food, clothing, gold, and silver. The lepers do not waste time wondering what has happened. They eat and drink and take some of the silver and gold for themselves. Suddenly they stop. They remember the people starving in Samaria. They say they must immediately go and share the good tidings with them. "This is a day of good news and we are keeping it to ourselves. If we wait until daylight, punishment will overtake us. Let's go immediately and report this to the royal palace."

They go and tell their story. The king is suspicious. He thinks it is a trap. The Syrians are lying in wait, knowing that the people are starving. As soon as they go into the camp to get food, the army will attack. On the other hand, they cannot simply stay and do nothing, for if they do so they will all die. The king sends out some scouts to check on the situation. They return, confirming what the lepers have said.

The people rush out to collect the abandoned food with the result that, as the prophet had foretold, the next day a measure of flour sold for a shekel. The king's officer who had scoffed at the prophecy has been put in charge of the city gate, but is trampled to death in the rush. Again the prophet's words proved true. The officer saw the food but did not live to eat it.

What had happened that made the Syrian army flee? The biblical text says they heard "the sound of chariots and horses and a great army." They believed that they belonged to the Hittites and Egyptians who had come to Israel's aid, and they fled, abandoning the camp and everything in it.

Stephen Rosenberg[1] conjectures that the episode took place during the reign of Ben Hadad III who reigned from 810 BCE. During that time, the Assyrians under Adad-Niri III attacked Syria and took tribute from it. In 805 BCE, they sent a military expedition to the borders of Syria, and this may have been what the Syrians thought was the Hittite army. As for the Egyptian army, coming up from the southwest, Rosenberg suggests this may have been the Philistines, intent on revenge for the Syrian attack on Gath some years earlier. Hearing of armies approaching from both sides, the Syrian king would certainly have abandoned the siege of Samaria to return home and defend his own territory.

What is fascinating is the way this momentous sequence of events is seen through the eyes not only of the king, his officer, and the prophet, but also of four complete outsiders, the lepers. It is they who are the first on the scene, the first to realise what has happened, and the first to bring the good news to the people. They are not heroes in the conventional sense, but they do serve to exemplify one important truth: that sometimes outsiders see what insiders do not.

The classic example is Moses himself. He was a double outsider, an Israelite who had grown up in the palace of Pharaoh – even more so because he spent many of his formative years away from both in Midian with his wife Zipporah and father-in-law Yitro, a pagan priest. Not surprisingly, he called his first son Gershom, saying, "I have been a stranger in a strange land." To the Egyptians he was an Israelite, to the Israelites initially he seemed like an Egyptian. Outsiders are often agents of change who can see what others cannot, hear what they cannot.

So too was Abraham. The sages interpret his description as *HaIvri*, "the Hebrew," to mean, "The whole world was on one side (*ever*) and he was on the other."[2] He was in, but not of, his world. He fought for his neighbours and prayed for them, but kept to himself and to his faith.

Jews have been cast as the outsiders for much of their history. They were regarded in Christian Europe as pariahs, said the classic

1. Stephen Rosenberg, *The Haphtara Cycle* (Northvale, NJ: Jason Aronson, 2000), 115–118.
2. Genesis Rabba 41.

sociologist Max Weber.[3] Jewish intellectuals in the modern age were doubly alienated, outsiders to their societies because they were Jews, outsiders to the Jewish community because they had abandoned their faith and much of their identity.

Thorstein Veblen said in an essay on "the intellectual pre-eminence of Jews" that the Jew becomes "a disturber of the intellectual peace ... a wanderer in the intellectuals' no-man's-land, seeking another place to rest, farther along the road, somewhere over the horizon."[4]

It took four almost complete outsiders to Judaism – Moses Hess, Leon Pinsker, Max Nordau, and Theodor Herzl – to mobilise the movement that eventually became known as Zionism. To be sure, two rabbis, Zvi Hirsch Kalischer and Yehuda Alkalai, had already written the first proto-Zionist texts, but even they were far from the rabbinic mainstream. Kalischer served as a rabbi in Thorn, now Torun, in Poland. Alkalai was the rabbi of Semlin (Zemun), today part of Belgrade, then on the border of Ottoman-occupied Serbia. Neither was the recognised leader of any major movement.

There is no equating these figures. They were utterly different and none was an outcast. What makes the *haftara* so fascinating, however, is the image it gives us of the four lepers, lowest of the low, becoming the harbingers of the good news that only they, because of their outcast state, were in a position to see.

Sometimes outsiders do see what the rest of the world misses, and sometimes it is good news.

3. Max Weber, *Ancient Judaism* (New York: Free Press, 1967), 336–55.
4. Thorstein Veblen, "The Intellectual Pre-eminence of Jews in Modern Europe," *Political Science Quarterly* (March 1990): 1919.

Aharei Mot
אחרי מות

Parashat Aharei Mot describes the service of the High Priest on the Day of Atonement. It was a dramatic and highly charged ritual during which he cast lots on two identical goats, one of which was offered as a sacrifice while the other was sent into the wilderness to die, the so-called "scapegoat." The entry of the High Priest into the Holy of Holies marked the spiritual high-point of the Jewish year.

The *parasha* also outlines the prohibition against eating blood, and the laws of forbidden sexual relations, both of them aspects of the life of purity God asks of the Jewish people.

The first of the following essays looks at the transformation of atonement from the pleas of Moses after the sin of the Golden Calf and the subsequent service of the High Priest. The second, third, and fourth look at different aspects of the ritual of the scapegoat. One is about the difference between the two key processes of Yom Kippur: atonement and purification. The next is about the "scapegoat" in other cultures. It turns out to be not the same idea as in Judaism, but rather its opposite. The fourth is about the two goats and the idea that they symbolise twins, in particular, Jacob and Esau. What is the connection between the two brothers and Yom Kippur?

The fifth essay is about the remarkable transformation of Yom Kippur after the destruction of the Second Temple and the role of R. Akiva in rescuing hope from tragedy. The last is about Nahmanides' understanding of *Vayikra* 18 and the centrality of the land of Israel to the life and faith of Judaism.

From Never Again to Ever Again

Consider two events in the Torah that on the surface could not be less alike. The first is one of the most dramatic moments in Jewish history. The Israelites had just witnessed the revelation of God at Mount Sinai. For the first and last time in history, an entire people received a theophany and made a covenant with the Creator of heaven and earth. Moses then ascended the mountain and for forty days and nights received the Torah, the details of the covenantal code. Then, with a shock undiminished across the millennia, God tells Moses to stop and go down the mountain, "for the people whom you brought out of Egypt have become corrupt." From the heights, the Israelites descended to the depths. They made a golden calf.

What follows is a fast-paced drama. Immediately, Moses prays to God to hold back His anger. His prayer is urgent and abrupt. He makes no defence of the Israelites. He has not yet seen what they did. Instead, he tells God that for His own sake He must not destroy the people, otherwise the Egyptians will say that He took the Israelites out of Egypt not to free them but to kill them. Besides which, he says, You already promised the patriarchs that You would give their children the land. For Your sake, then, if not for the sake of the people, reconsider. God agrees.

Moses then descends the mountain, hears the commotion, and sees the people cavorting around the calf. Without delay, he smashes the tablets of stone that God Himself had engraved as the record of the covenant. He burns the calf, grinds it to powder, mixes it with water, and makes the people drink it. He summons his brother Aaron to hear his account of what has happened. He then asks the people, "Who is on the side of the Lord?" The Levites gather round him, and they execute punishment on the makers and instigators of the calf. Three thousand people die that day. The next day, Moses entreats God again, this time staking his very life on the outcome: If, he says to God, You will not forgive them, then "blot me out now from this book You have written."

Moses continues to plead with God for forty days and forty nights, begging Him not to remove His presence from the camp. In a remarkable scene, God passes before Moses who, He says, will "see My back, since My face cannot be seen," and utters the words that have become known as the Thirteen Attributes of Mercy, "The Lord, the Lord, the compassionate and gracious God, slow to anger, abounding in love and faithfulness…" (Ex. 34:6–7). This subsequently became the basis for all *Seliḥot*, penitential prayers. Moses himself understood this, and used these words later during the sin of the spies (Num. 14:17–20).

God then instructs Moses to carve a second set of tablets to replace the first that were broken. After a further forty days, Moses descends with the new tablets, a visible symbol of the fact that God had forgiven the people and still held to His covenant with them. That is the first story.

The second event occupies the opening chapter of *Parashat Aḥarei Mot*. Once a year, the High Priest was to enter the Holy of Holies and seek atonement, first for himself, then for his "house" (his family, or his fellow priests), and then for the entire people. The ceremony was elaborate and unusual. At the heart of it was a unique ritual. Two goats identical in appearance were to be taken and lots cast over them, one "for the Lord," the other "for Azazel." The first was offered as a sin offering. Over the second, the High Priest confessed "all the iniquities of the Children of Israel and all their transgressions and sins," laying his hands on the animal. The goat "bearing all their iniquities" was taken into the wilderness where it eventually died, cast down a precipice.

Immense care had to be taken over all the details of the ritual. The Torah dramatises this by opening its account of the service of the High Priest with a reminder that two sons of Aaron had died on the day of the inauguration of the Sanctuary by doing an act they had not been commanded. There is no room in the Sanctuary service for improvisation, innovation, or alteration. No less powerful was the visual symbolism of the day. The High Priest, normally dressed in splendid robes of gold, had to wear only the simplest linen garments when he entered the Holy of Holies, and he was to be utterly alone while making his atonement.

The two narratives are utterly dissimilar. The first is full of passion and emotion: God's anger, Moses' powerful pleas, his own anger on seeing the calf and the people's dissolution, Aaron's helplessness in the face of the mob, the bloody scenes of reprisal. You could write a novel or make a film about it. It is the stuff of drama.

The second is pure ritual. The subject happens to be Aaron, because he was the High Priest in Moses' time, but the same acts, offerings, confessions, and sprinklings of blood, the same casting of lots over the goats and the taking of one into the desert, occurred year after year until the destruction of the Temple. There is no emotion, no subjectivity, no variation, no dialogue between priest and God. Yes, there was drama and a sense of occasion. We know from post-biblical sources, Jewish and non-Jewish, how spectacular the scene was at the Temple on Yom Kippur. But there is nothing unpredictable about it, at least as far as human action is concerned. Nothing is spontaneous as it was when Moses prayed or when he broke the tablets. The two events belong to different worlds.

Yet they are, in a deep sense, two versions of the same thing. Both were about human contrition and divine forgiveness. Both were aimed at the restoration of relationship between God and the people, despite the people's sins. Both were focused on the same day. It was the tenth of Tishrei when Moses descended the mountain with the second tablets, the last scene in the first drama. It was the tenth of Tishrei on which, in all subsequent years, the High Priest performed the rites of atonement on Yom Kippur.

What we see in these two scenes is a process, the logic of which is vital if we are to understand the complex nature of Judaism as a living tradition.

The thinker in modern times who gave the phenomenon its name was the German sociologist Max Weber. Weber noted that a particular type of personality is usually to be found at the birth of a new order of society. He called such a type *charismatic*.[1] In the case of Judaism, this was Moses – though, precisely because Judaism is unusual, contrarian, often a protest against existing practices, Moses is the most unlikely of all charismatic leaders. He was not a natural speaker. He was – especially after the Golden Calf – deliberately distant from the people. Far from attracting a following of devotees, he was often opposed by the people, sometimes even by his own brother and sister. But he was charismatic in the sense that he, as the mouthpiece and emissary of God, set his seal on the people, defining its mission and way of life for all time. There was only one Moses.

But what happens after the charismatic leader is gone? What becomes of a people after its initial exhilaration of freedom has evaporated? What is the fate of a religion after the epiphany? How do you recapture the one time for all time? That is the challenge that Weber defined in a somewhat ungainly phrase as "the routinisation of charisma."

The supreme example of this is Yom Kippur as it appears in this *parasha*. As the Israelites move from Exodus to Leviticus, from the first year of their journey to the second, so the task of securing atonement moves from Moses to Aaron, from prophet to priest, from unpredictable drama to rule-governed ritual – *and it must be so*. Not every generation has a Moses. Not every age lends itself to high religious drama. Life would be unbearable if we never knew in advance what we had to do to be forgiven.

That is the difference between *Torat Neviim* and *Torat Kohanim*, the worlds respectively of the prophet and the priest. It is the difference

---

1. Max Weber, "The Nature of Charismatic Authority and its Routinization," in *Theory of Social and Economic Organization*, trans. Talcott Parsons (New York: Free Press, 1964).

between the unique and the universal, the "never again" and the "ever again," the epoch-making event and enduring, endlessly repeated rituals that give a nation its character and continuity. Judaism lives, breathes, and stays young because it never fully resolves the tension between these two modes of the religious life: between Aggada and Halakha, prophetic passion and priestly consistency, the ever-changing yet never-changing. It takes a prophet to argue with God, but it takes a priest to transform a people through the deep routines that reconfigure human nature into habits of holiness.

The Scapegoat: Shame and Guilt

The strangest and most dramatic element of the service on Yom Kippur, set out in *Parashat Aḥarei Mot* (Lev. 16:7–22), was the ritual of the two goats, one offered as a sacrifice, the other sent away into the desert "to Azazel." They were, to all intents and purposes, indistinguishable from one another: they were chosen to be as similar as possible in size and appearance. They were brought before the High Priest and lots were drawn, one bearing the words "To the Lord," the other, "To Azazel." The one on which the lot "To the Lord" fell was offered as a sacrifice. Over the other, the High Priest confessed the sins of the nation, and it was then taken away into the desert hills outside Jerusalem where it plunged to its death. Tradition tells us that a red thread would be attached to its horns, half of which was removed before the animal was sent away. If the rite had been effective, the red thread would turn to white.

Much is puzzling about the ritual. First, what is the meaning of "to Azazel," to which the second goat was sent? It appears nowhere else in Scripture. Three major theories emerged as to its meaning. According to the sages and Rashi, it means "a steep, rocky, or hard place," in other words, a description of its destination. According to the Torah, the goat was sent "to a desolate area" (*el eretz gezera*, Lev. 16:22). According to the sages, it was taken to a steep ravine where it fell to its death. That, according to the first explanation, is the meaning of Azazel.

The second, suggested cryptically by Ibn Ezra and explicitly by Nahmanides, is that Azazel was the name of a spirit or demon, one of the fallen angels referred to in Genesis 6:2, similar to the goat-spirit called Pan in Greek mythology, Faunus in Latin. This is a difficult idea, which is why Ibn Ezra alluded to it, as he did in similar cases, by way of a riddle, a puzzle, that only the wise would be able to decipher. He writes: "I will reveal to you part of the secret by hint: when you reach thirty-three you will know it." Nahmanides reveals the secret. Thirty-three verses later, the Torah commands: "They must no longer offer any of their sacrifices to the goat idols [se'irim] after whom they go astray" (Lev. 17:7).

Azazel, on this reading, is the name of a demon or hostile force, sometimes called Satan or Samael. The Israelites were categorically forbidden to worship such a force. Indeed, the belief that there are powers at work in the universe distinct from, or even hostile to, God is incompatible with Judaic monotheism. Nonetheless, some sages did believe that there were negative forces that were part of the heavenly retinue, like Satan, who brought accusations against humans or tempted them into sin. The goat sent into the wilderness to Azazel was a way of conciliating or propitiating such forces so that the prayers of Israel could rise to heaven without, as it were, any dissenting voices. This way of understanding the rite is similar to the saying on the part of the sages that we blow shofar in a double cycle on Rosh HaShana "to confuse Satan."[1]

The third interpretation, and the simplest, is that Azazel is a compound noun meaning "the goat [ez] that was sent away [azal]." This led to the addition of a new word to the English language. In 1530, William Tyndale produced the first English translation of the Hebrew Bible, an act then illegal and for which he paid with his life. Seeking to translate Azazel into English, he called it "the escapegoat," i.e., the goat that was sent away and released. In the course of time, the first letter was dropped, and the word "scapegoat" was born.

The real question, though, is: What was the ritual actually about? It was unique. Sin and guilt offerings are familiar features of the Torah

---

1.   Rosh HaShana 16b.

and a normal part of the service of the Temple. The service of Yom Kippur was different in one salient respect. In every other case, the sin was confessed over the animal that was sacrificed. On Yom Kippur, the High Priest confessed the sins of the people over the animal that was *not* sacrificed, the scapegoat that was sent away, "carrying on it all their iniquities" (Lev. 16:21–22).

The simplest and most compelling answer was given by Maimonides in *The Guide for the Perplexed*:

> There is no doubt that sins cannot be carried like a burden, and taken off the shoulder of one being to be laid on that of another being. But these ceremonies are of a symbolic character, and serve to impress people with a certain idea, and to induce them to repent – as if to say, we have freed ourselves of our previous deeds, have cast them behind our backs, and removed them from us as far as possible.[2]

Expiation demands a ritual, some dramatic representation of the removal of sin and the wiping clean of the past. That is clear. Yet Maimonides does not explain why Yom Kippur demanded a rite not used on other days of the year when sin or guilt offerings were brought. Why was the first goat, the one of which the lot "To the Lord" fell and which was offered as a sin offering (Lev. 16:9) not sufficient?

The answer lies in the dual character of the day. The Torah states:

> This shall be an eternal law for you: On the tenth day of the seventh month you must fast and not do any work.... This is because on this day you shall have all your sins atoned [*yekhaper*], so that you will be cleansed [*letaher*]. Before God, you will be cleansed of all your sins. (Lev. 16:29–30)

Two quite distinct processes were involved on Yom Kippur. First there was *kappara*, atonement. This is the normal function of a sin offering. Second, there was *tahara*, purification, something normally done in a

---

2. Maimonides, *The Guide for the Perplexed*, III:46.

different context altogether, namely the removal of *tuma*, ritual defilement, which could arise from a number of different causes, among them contact with a dead body, skin disease, or nocturnal discharge. Atonement has to do with guilt. Purification has to do with contamination or pollution. These are usually[3] two separate worlds. On Yom Kippur they were brought together. Why?

We owe to anthropologists like Ruth Benedict the distinction between shame cultures and guilt cultures.[4] Shame is a social phenomenon. It is what we feel when our wrongdoing is exposed to others. It may even be something we feel when we merely imagine other people knowing or seeing what we have done. Shame is the feeling of being found out, and our first instinct is to hide. That is what Adam and Eve did in the Garden of Eden after they had eaten the forbidden fruit. They were ashamed of their nakedness and they hid.

Guilt is a personal phenomenon. It has nothing to do with what others might say if they knew what we have done, and everything to do with what we say to ourselves. Guilt is the voice of conscience, and it is inescapable. You may be able to avoid shame by hiding or not being found out, but you cannot avoid guilt. Guilt is self-knowledge.

There is another difference, which explains why Judaism is overwhelmingly a guilt rather than a shame culture. Shame attaches to the person. Guilt attaches to the act. It is almost impossible to remove shame once you have been publicly disgraced. It is like an indelible stain on your skin. Shakespeare has Macbeth say, after his crime, "Will these hands ne'er be clean?" In shame cultures, wrongdoers tend either to go into exile, where no one knows their past, or to commit suicide. Playwrights have them die.

Guilt makes a clear distinction between the act of wrongdoing and the person of the wrongdoer. The act was wrong, but the agent remains, in principle, intact. That is why guilt can be removed, "atoned for," by

3. There were exceptions. A leper – or more precisely, someone suffering from the skin disease known in the Torah as *tzaraat* – had to bring a guilt offering [*asham*] in addition to undergoing rites of purification (Lev. 14:12–20).
4. Ruth Benedict, *The Chrysanthemum and the Sword* (London: Secker & Warburg, 1947).

confession, remorse, and restitution. "Hate not the sinner but the sin," is the basic axiom of a guilt culture.

Normally, sin and guilt offerings, as their names imply, are about guilt. They atone. But Yom Kippur deals not only with our sins as individuals. It also confronts our sins as a community bound by mutual responsibility. It deals, in other words, with the social as well as the personal dimension of wrongdoing. Yom Kippur is about shame as well as guilt. Hence there has to be purification (the removal of the stain) as well as atonement.

The psychology of shame is quite different to that of guilt. We can discharge guilt by achieving forgiveness – and forgiveness can only be granted by the object of our wrongdoing, which is why Yom Kippur only atones for sins against God. Even God cannot – logically, cannot – forgive sins committed against our fellow humans until they themselves have forgiven us.

Shame cannot be removed by forgiveness. The victim of our crime may have forgiven us, but we still feel defiled by the knowledge that our name has been disgraced, our reputation harmed, our standing damaged. We still feel the stigma, the dishonour, the degradation. That is why an immensely powerful and dramatic ceremony had to take place during which people could feel and symbolically see their sins carried away to the desert, to no-man's-land. A similar ceremony took place when a leper was cleansed. The priest took two birds, killed one, and released the other to fly away across the open fields (Lev. 14:4–7). Again, the act was one of *cleansing*, not *atoning*, and had to do with shame, not guilt.

Judaism is a religion of hope, and its great rituals of repentance and atonement are part of that hope. We are not condemned to live endlessly with the mistakes and errors of our past. That is the great difference between a guilt culture and a shame culture. But Judaism also acknowledges the existence of shame. Hence the elaborate ritual of the scapegoat that seemed to carry away the *tuma*, the defilement that is the mark of shame. It could only be done on Yom Kippur because that was the one day of the year in which everyone shared, at least vicariously, in the process of confession, repentance, atonement, and purification. When a whole society confesses its guilt, individuals can be redeemed from shame.

The Scapegoat: Perversion of an Idea

One of the great ironies of history is to be found in the shift of meaning attached to the word "scapegoat." As we noted in the previous essay, the word was born in 1530 when William Tyndale translated the Hebrew Bible into English for the first time. Seeking a word for the goat that was sent away into the desert on Yom Kippur, he called it "the (e)scapegoat." Since then "scapegoat" has come to mean something superficially similar but in fact utterly different, indeed opposite in meaning.

We owe to the French scholar René Girard one of the most compelling accounts in modern times of the connection between religion and violence. Girard's thesis is that violence is at the heart of religious ritual. The primary ritual is sacrifice, and the most fundamental form of sacrifice is the scapegoat.

Sacrifice, he argues, is born in the attempt to escape from the deadly circle of retaliation in societies that lack a judicial system and the impartial process of the law:

> Vengeance professes to be an act of reprisal, and every reprisal calls for another reprisal.... Vengeance, then, is an interminable, infinitely repetitive process. Every time it turns up in some part

of the community, it threatens to involve the whole social body. There is the risk that the act of vengeance will initiate a chain reaction whose consequences will quickly prove fatal to any society of modest size. The multiplication of reprisals instantaneously puts the very existence of the society in jeopardy, and that is why it is universally proscribed.[1]

This is a phenomenon we know from literature. It is a standard plot of tragedy, from the Montagues and Capulets in *Romeo and Juliet,* to the Jets and Sharks in *West Side Story,* to the Corleones and Tattaglias in *The Godfather.* A member of family (group, tribe) x kills a member of family y – intentionally or accidentally, it makes no difference. A member of family y then takes revenge. Next a member of family x retaliates, and so it goes. There is no natural closure to the sequence until massacre wipes out one or other of the tribes, or both.

The solution arrived at in certain societies, says Girard, was to deflect the internal violence of both sides by directing it outward against a victim – a third party who is not a member of either group but whose death brings the violence to an end, someone who is relatively unprotected and can therefore be killed without fear of reprisal. In ancient Athens, for example, there was the institution of the *pharmakos,* a cripple, beggar, or criminal who was kept alive so that he could be cast out of the city to die if disaster threatened.

This, according to Girard, is what a scapegoat is: an innocent victim, an outsider, killed in order to call a halt to the cycle of vengeance between warring tribes. His death is charged with an aura of sanctity. There is awe and exaltation at this ritual murder of an innocent human being. The warring tribes know that something profound has taken place. They stop fighting one another. The violent emotions of both sides are purged. Catharsis takes place. Peace returns. Order is restored. The victim has been made the scapegoat:

> The death of the individual has something of the quality of tribute levied for the continued existence of the collectivity. A human

1. Girard, op. cit., 14–15.

being dies, and the solidarity of the survivors is enhanced by his death. The surrendered victim dies so that the entire community, threatened by the same fate, can be reborn in a new or renewed cultural order.[2]

This, of course, calls for myth. Some story has to be told in which the outsider – ritually sacrificed – is held to be responsible for all the evils that have befallen the group.

> Ultimately, the persecutors always convince themselves that a small number of people, or even a single individual, despite his relative weakness, is extremely harmful to the whole of society.... There is only one person responsible for everything, one who is absolutely responsible, and he will be responsible for the cure because he is already responsible for the sickness.[3]

Tragically, of course, Jews have often been cast in this role, whether in early Christianity in its struggle with Rome, medieval Christianity in its struggle with Islam, nineteenth-century Europe with its political and industrial revolutions, twentieth-century Germany after its humiliation in World War I, or the Middle East today.

In a series of fascinating studies,[4] University of Virginia psychiatrist Vamik Volkan has added a psychological dimension to this phenomenon. He argues that at the root of ethnic and religious conflict is the incomplete work – whether by individuals or entire groups – of personal integration. As children, we idealise the figure of the good mother, and of ourselves. Eventually we are able to internalise a nuanced self-image in which we and others are seen to be a mix of good and evil, virtues and failings. But there are some in whom the integration never successfully

2. Ibid., 255.
3. Ibid., 15, 43.
4. Vamik Volkan, *The Need to Have Enemies and Allies* (Northvale, NJ: Jason Aronson, 1988). A number of Volkan's essays are available online at www.vamikvolkan.com. See especially: "The Need to Have Enemies and Allies: A Developmental Approach" (1985), "Suicide Bombers" (2000), and "Chosen Trauma, the Political Ideology of Entitlement and Violence" (2004).

takes place. They cannot acknowledge the evil within themselves or the complexity of the human personality. They develop a dualistic world-view: there is our side, the children of light, who are good, and there are the others, the children of darkness, who are bad, evil, and a threat to us and to those we love.

In order to see yourself and your group as all good, you have to project the evil you are unable to acknowledge in yourself onto an external entity: some other group, the ones not like us. The stronger the cognitive dissonance, the more intense will be the projection. The other becomes the embodiment of evil. This then gives rise to the pathology of victimhood and is the ultimate source of scapegoating: "It wasn't us, it was them." From this flowed rivers of blood of human sacrifice throughout the ages. They still do today.

If this is so, we can begin to understand some of the most funda-mental dimensions of Judaism. Almost at the outset of the human story, we are confronted with the phenomenon of human violence. The first religious offerings, those of Cain and Abel, lead to the first murder, the first fratricide. From there, says the Torah, it was only a short distance to the generation of the Flood, when "the earth was filled with violence." Immediately after the Flood, God makes a covenant with humanity whose central principle is the prohibition of murder: "He who sheds the blood of man shall by man have his blood shed, for in the image of God, God created man" (Gen. 9:6). Murder becomes not just the ulti-mate crime but also the ultimate sin.

Girard himself notes that the real solution to the cycle of retalia-tion and vengeance is not the scapegoat, but rather the rule of law. For now it is no longer the Montagues versus the Capulets, but both under the impartial reign of justice. We now understand the significance of the fact that Judaism is a religion of law. Only the rule of law and the primacy of justice can rescue a society from the ever-present threat of intergroup violence. That is why, at almost the very outset of the Jewish story, God defines Abraham's role as the grandfather of faith in these words: "I have chosen him so that he will instruct his children and his household after him that they may keep the way of the law by doing what is right and just" (Gen. 18:19). Only law-governed justice can ultimately redeem a society from violence.

We now understand how fundamental it was for the Torah to legislate, in the very verse that commands us to "Love your neighbour as yourself," the two negative commands, "Do not seek revenge or bear a grudge against anyone among your people" (Lev. 19:18). Equally, we see why it was so fundamental to the Torah's values that towns be set aside in the land of Israel as cities of refuge, to protect people found guilty of manslaughter, i.e., unintentional killing, from "the redeemer of blood," that is, a member of the victim's family who felt the need, even the duty, to kill the killer even though the death was an accident. The Torah here is telling us how deep is the instinct of revenge within the human heart, even when the legal process has been gone through and the accused has been found innocent of murder. Hence the need for this unique double protection.

More than this, we can now see that the institution of the scapegoat in biblical Israel was itself a protest against human sacrifice, widespread in the ancient world. Two features of the High Priest's ritual were crucial: (1) that the sacrifice was an animal, not a person, and (2) that it was not an occasion for denying responsibility by blaming the victim, but to the contrary, an acceptance of responsibility in the context of repentance and atonement.

The irony is that the ritual designed to eliminate scapegoating in the modern sense has become, in the Western imagination, the source of the idea of the scapegoat itself. That is an error. The biblical scapegoat was precisely not a scapegoat in Girard's sense. Projecting violence within the group onto an innocent outsider, who is held guilty and killed to preserve the group itself, is one of the most vicious ideas ever to disfigure the human mind. It survives today in the form of conspiracy theories, terror, suicide bombings, and ethnic conflict. Against this, Judaism held forth the alternative – a penitential culture in which we are able to accept responsibility for our own failings because of divine forgiveness and the human capacity to change.

Faced with problems that it cannot solve, all too often a group ensures its psychic survival by projecting its inner conflicts onto an external cause, held to be responsible for the plight of the community. Hence the demonisation that has time and again led to pogroms, massacres, and attempted genocides. Societies find it easier to blame a scapegoat than to face their own problems honestly and openly. "Scapegoating," as we use the word today, means blaming someone else for our troubles. The scapegoat of Yom Kippur existed so that this kind of blame would never find a home in Jewish life. We do not blame others for our fate. We accept responsibility. We say "Because of *our* sins," not "Because of *your* sins."

Those who blame others, defining themselves as victims, are destined to remain victims. Those who accept responsibility transform the world because they have learned to transform themselves.

Thinking Fast and Slow

If we put together recent discoveries in neuroscience with midrashic tradition we may be able to shed new light on the meaning of the central mystery of Yom Kippur: the two goats, identical in appearance, over which the High Priest cast lots, sacrificing one as a sin offering and sending the other, the scapegoat, into the wilderness to die.

In previous essays, we have looked at the scapegoat as it figures in Jewish tradition and, in a very different way, in other cultures. But there are other dimensions of the rite that cry out for explanation. We argued that there were two goats because Yom Kippur represents a dual process of *kappara*, atonement, and *tahara*, purification, directed respectively at guilt and shame. But this does not explain why the two animals were required to be as similar as possible to one another, nor does it account for the role of casting lots (*goralot*). Presumably, these elements were designed to inspire feelings of awe and penitence on the part of the crowds that thronged the Temple on the holiest day of the year, but how and in what way?

Over the centuries, the sages sought to decipher the mystery. Two animals, alike in appearance but different in fate, suggests the idea of twins. This and other clues led the Midrash, the Zohar, and classic commentators such as Nahmanides and Abrabanel to the conclusion that in some sense, the two goats symbolised the most famous of the Torah's twins: Jacob and Esau.

There are other clues. The word *se'ir*, "goat," is associated in the Torah with Esau. He and his descendants lived in the land of Seir. The word *se'ir* is related to *sei'ar*, "hairy," which is how Esau was born: "his whole body was like a hairy garment" (Gen. 25:25). When Rebecca urged Jacob to pretend to be Esau in order to take Isaac's blessing, Jacob said, "My brother Esau is a hairy [*sa'ir*] man while I have smooth skin" (Gen. 27:11). According to the Mishna, a red thread was tied to the scapegoat, and "red" (Edom) was Esau's other name. So there was a tradition that the scapegoat in some way symbolised Esau. Azazel, the mysterious place or entity for which the goat was intended, was Samael, Esau's guardian angel.

In particular, the phrase "two kids of the goats," *shnei se'irei izim*, mentioned in the High Priest's rites, reminds us of the very similar expression, "two kids of the goats," *shnei gedi'ei izim*, mentioned in Genesis 27, the scene of Jacob's deception. Isaac had asked Esau to catch him some wild game and prepare him a meal so that he could bless him. Rebecca tells Jacob to "Go out to the flock and bring me *two choice kids of the goats*, so I can prepare some tasty food for your father, the way he likes it. Then take it to your father to eat, so that he may give you his blessing before he dies." Such verbal parallels are not coincidental in the Torah. They are part of its sustained intertextuality, its finely woven prose in which one verse sheds light on another.

So the two goats of the High Priest's service evoke in multiple ways the figures of Jacob and Esau, and specifically the scene in which Jacob pretended to be Esau, dressing in his clothes so that he would feel and smell like his brother. It was then that, answering his father's question, "Who are you, my son?" Jacob said the words, "I am your firstborn Esau," leading Isaac to say, "The voice is the voice of Jacob, but the hands are the hands of Esau" (Gen. 27:22).

Who then were Esau and Jacob? What did they represent and how is this relevant to Yom Kippur and atonement? Midrashic tradition tends to portray Jacob as perfect and Esau as an evildoer. However, the

Torah itself is far more nuanced. Esau is not a figure of evil. His father loved him and sought to bless him. The sages say that in one respect – honouring his father – he was a supreme role model.[1] God insisted that no attempt be made by the Israelites to conquer the land of Esau's descendants: "You are about to pass through the territory of your relatives, the descendants of Esau, who live in Seir. They will be afraid of you, but be very careful. Do not provoke them to war, for I will not give you any of their land, not even enough to put your foot on. I have given Esau the hill country of Seir as his own" (Deut. 2:4–5). Moses commands, "Do not despise an Edomite [i.e., a descendant of Esau], because he is your brother" (Deut. 23:8).

Esau in the Torah is not the epitome of evil. Rather, he is the man of impulse. We see this in the scene in which he sells his birthright to Jacob. Coming in one day exhausted by the hunt, he sees Jacob making lentil broth:

> He said to Jacob, "Quick, let me have some of that red stew! I'm famished!"… Jacob replied, "First sell me your birthright." "Look, I am about to die," Esau said. "What good is the birthright to me?" But Jacob said, "Swear to me first." So he swore an oath to him, selling his birthright to Jacob. Then Jacob gave Esau some bread and some lentil stew. He ate and drank, and then got up and left. So Esau despised his birthright. (Gen. 25:30–34)

This vignette of Esau's impetuosity – selling part of his heritage for the sake of a bowl of soup – is reinforced by the unique description of the action in the staccato form of five consecutive verbs (literally, "he ate, he drank, he rose, he left, he despised"). Every time we see Esau we have the impression of an impulsive figure always driven by the emotion of the moment, be it hunger, filial devotion, a desire for revenge or, at last, generosity of spirit.

Jacob is the opposite. He does not give way to his feelings. He acts and thinks long-term. That is what he does when he seizes the opportunity to buy Esau's birthright, when he works for seven years for Rachel

---

1. See Exodus Rabba 46:4, Numbers Rabba 1:15.

(a period that "seemed to him but a few days"), and when he fixes terms with Laban for payment for his labour. Rebuking his son Joseph for the seeming presumptuousness of his dreams, the Torah tells us that the brothers were jealous of Joseph "but his father kept the matter in mind." Jacob never acts impulsively. He thinks long and hard before deciding.

Not only is impetuosity alien to him, he is also critical of it when he sees it in his children. On his death bed, he curses his three eldest sons in these words:

> Reuben, you are my firstborn.... Unstable as water, you will not excel.... Simeon and Levi are brothers. Their swords are weapons of violence...they have killed men in their anger and hamstrung oxen as they pleased. Cursed be their anger, so fierce, and their fury, so cruel!" (Gen. 49:3–7)

Acting on the basis of anger is for him the sign of an unworthy personality with which he does not wish to be associated.

What does all this have to do with sin, transgression, atonement, and two goats?

Recent years have seen a revolution in our understanding of the human brain, and with it, the human mind. One key text was Antonio Damasio's book *Descartes' Error*.[2] Damasio discovered something unusual about patients who had suffered brain damage to the ventromedial prefrontal cortex. Their ability to *think* remained unchanged, but their ability to *feel* dropped to almost zero. The result was that they found it impossible to make decisions. They would reason endlessly but fail to make their mind up on one course of action rather than another.

Much subsequent work has shown that Descartes and Kant were wrong in their assertion that we are, first and foremost, rational animals. Hume was right in his view that we are primarily emotional beings who make decisions on the basis of feelings, desires, and drives of which we may be barely conscious. We justify our choices, but brain

---

2. Antonio R. Damasio, *Descartes' Error: Emotion, Reason, and the Human Brain* (New York: Putnam, 1994).

scans show that we may have made those choices before being aware that we had done so.

We are more driven by emotion and less by reason than Enlightenment thinkers believed. This discovery has led to new fields of study like behavioural economics (what people actually do rather than what theory says they do), emotional intelligence, and interdisciplinary studies linking neuroscience to morality and politics.

We have, in fact, a dual-system or twin-track brain. This is what Daniel Kahneman is referring to in the title of his famous book *Thinking, Fast and Slow*.[3] One track is rapid, instinctive, emotional, and subconscious. The other is slower, conscious, deliberative, and calculating. The former allows us to react quickly to situations of immediate potential danger. Without it, we and our ancestors would not have survived. Many of our instinctive reactions are benign. It is natural to have empathy, and with it the tendency to feel other people's pain and come to their aid. We develop a strong sense of attachment that leads us to defend members of our family or community. But not all instincts are benign. Anger, envy, jealousy, fear, hate, and the desire for revenge may once have been functional, but they are often deeply destructive in social situations. That is why the ability to "think slow," to pause and reflect, matters so much. All animals have desires. Only human beings are capable of passing judgement on desires – of asking, should I or should I not satisfy this desire?

These recent discoveries in neuroscience and related fields do not tell us something new. Rather, they have vindicated an ancient insight that was often obscured by Enlightenment rationalism. We cannot live, choose, or love without emotion. But one of the fundamental themes of Genesis is that not all emotion is benign. Instinctive, impulsive behaviour can lead to violence. What is needed to be a carrier of God's covenant is the ability to "think slow" and act deliberatively. That is the contrast between Isaac and Ishmael (of whom it was said, "He will be a wild donkey of a man; his hand will be against everyone and everyone's hand against him," Gen. 16:12). Even more so, it is the contrast between Jacob and Esau.

---

3. Daniel Kahneman, *Thinking, Fast and Slow* (New York: Farrar, Straus and Giroux, 2011).

Which brings us to Genesis 27 and the moment when Jacob dressed up in Esau's clothes and said to his father, "I am Esau your firstborn." The two goats of the High Priest's service and the two goats prepared by Rebecca symbolise the duality within each of us: "The hands are the hands of Esau but the voice is the voice of Jacob." *We each have an Esau and Jacob within us,* the impulsive, emotional brain and the reflective, deliberative one. We can think fast or slow. Our fate, our *goral,* our life-script, will be determined by which we choose. Will our life be lived "to the Lord" or "to Azazel," to the random vicissitudes of chance?

This is the moral drama symbolised by the two goats, one dedicated "to the Lord," the other "to Azazel" and released into the wilderness. The power of ritual is that it does not speak in abstractions – reason versus emotion, instinctual deferral rather than gratification. It is gripping, visceral, all the more so when it evokes, consciously or otherwise, the memory of the twins, Jacob and Esau, together at birth yet utterly divergent in their character and fate.

Who am I? That is the question Yom Kippur forces us to ask. To be Jacob, we have to release and relinquish the Esau within us, the impulsiveness that can lead us to sell our birthright for a bowl of soup, losing eternity in the pursuit of desire.

Surviving Catastrophe

Parashat Aḥarei Mot deals with the service of the High Priest on the Day of Atonement. I want in this essay to look at what happened when this ritual was no longer possible and the High Priest's service came to an end.

The events of the first century CE precipitated the worst crisis in Jewish history until modern times. The various groups in Jewish life responded differently. Some – the Sadducees and Essenes for example – simply disappeared. Their worldviews could not survive a catastrophe of that order. One response, however, was fateful: that of the sages and rabbinic tradition. In this story, one name stands out as a giant of the rabbinic imagination – R. Akiva, the person who turned tragedy into hope.

So long as the Temple stood, once a year there was a national ceremony of atonement. It took place on the holiest day, Yom Kippur, at the holiest place, the Holy of Holies within the Temple in Jerusalem, and it was performed by the holiest person, the High Priest. It was a rite of intense drama. In an ascending series of declarations, the High Priest atoned, first for himself, then for his family, then for the whole nation. Two animals were brought, one to be offered as a sacrifice, the other, the "scapegoat," sent into the wilderness to die, symbolically carrying with it the sins of the people.

When the Second Temple was destroyed, this entire constellation was lost. There was now no Sanctuary, no sacrifices, no functioning priesthood. A psalm famously records the crisis felt when the First Temple was destroyed. "By the waters of Babylon we sat and wept as we remembered Zion.... How can we sing the Lord's song in a strange land?" (Ps. 137:1, 4). But the loss of the First Temple was accompanied by hope. The people would return. The Sanctuary would be rebuilt. Jeremiah said so. So did Ezekiel. They were right. Within two generations, the people *did* return.

By the late Second Temple period there was no longer such optimism. Israel was deeply divided. The Romans were stronger and less vulnerable than the Babylonians. Besides which, there were no prophets – or perhaps there were too many. The first Christians, though they were not yet known by that name, were only one group among several – the Dead Sea sectarians were another – expecting the apocalypse, the "end of history," and the beginning of a new era in the affairs of mankind.

We get the impression, from many sources from that time, of a widespread sense that a catastrophe was about to occur. It did. It was precipitated by the Great Rebellion against Rome in 66 CE. For seven years the battle raged. It was a hopeless task. The Romans were highly disciplined. They could call on the vast resources of an empire. The Jews had indomitable courage, but they were divided. They lacked a single vision, an effective leadership structure, and national cohesion. As Maimonides was later to write in his *Letter to the Sages of Marseilles*, they "neglected the arts of martial defence and government."

The rabbinic sages of Mishnaic times spoke of *sinat ḥinam*, "baseless [internal] hatred." The picture that emerges from both rabbinic sources and Josephus is of a fatally fragmented people, at times more intent on fighting one another than the enemy outside. In 70, Jerusalem fell and the Temple was destroyed. In 73, the last outpost of resistance at Masada committed collective suicide rather than hand themselves over to the Romans. It was a terrible defeat.

The crisis was not just military and political. It was also, and ultimately, spiritual. Atonement was a central part of Judaism. How could it be otherwise? The very life of the nation depended on its relationship with God. If an individual cannot avoid occasional failures – sins – how much less can a people as a whole? And if these failures could not be rectified or discharged, what then could lift the burden of accumulated and accumulating sin?

Without the ability to restore its integrity before God, there was no hope. And with the loss of Temple, priesthood, and sacrifices, the institutional base of atonement no longer existed. The service of Yom Kippur as prescribed in this *parasha* was impossible. How then could the people, individually and collectively, restore their relationship with God? How could they live without an overwhelming sense of guilt? Perhaps we in this guilt-free age find this hard to understand, but then (and even now if we have not yet lost the voice of conscience) it was a crisis without parallel and went to the very roots of life in the conscious presence of God.

It is from that period that a remarkable statement appears in the Mishna:

> R. Akiva said: Happy are you, Israel. Who is it before whom you are purified and who purifies you? Your Father in heaven. As it is said: *And I will sprinkle clean water upon you and you shall be clean.* And it further says: *You hope of Israel, the Lord.* Just as a fountain purifies the impure, so does the Holy One, Blessed Be He, purify Israel.[1]

This statement is one of the most transformative insights in the history of the Jewish people.

First, note the radical midrashic reading of the text. The words *mikve Yisrael Hashem* mean, "God is the *hope* of Israel." However, the root *k-v-h* has two meanings. One is "hope." The other is "a collection or gathering," hence "a gathering of water," and thus *mikve*, a ritual bath, a place you go to be purified. R. Akiva uses this *double entendre* or ambiguity to read the phrase as "God is the ritual bath of Israel," thus generating a daringly mystical vision. In his reading, God is the ritual

---

1. Mishna Yoma 8:9.

bath into which we plunge ourselves in order to be cleansed. Not only does God enter us. We, according to R. Akiva, enter God. We immerse ourselves in Him and emerge pure, our sins dissolved.

Second and more significantly, R. Akiva had turned one of the most tragic events in the history of Israel into a stunning disclosure of new spiritual possibility. According to him, when the Temple stood, the people of Israel atoned vicariously, through the service of the High Priest, who acted as representative of the people, the intermediary between them and God. Now that there was no Temple and no High Priest, no intermediary was necessary. God and the people were linked directly. Heaven had suddenly come closer. By atoning on Yom Kippur, every Jew became a High Priest. Every place where Jews gathered to pray became a Temple. Prayer took the place of sacrifice. Confession and remorse took the place of the scapegoat. Instead of being connected to God through the words and deeds of the High Priest, each individual Jew now stood directly in the Divine Presence. Atonement was democratised, and hope was saved.

Here, in dry legal prose, is how Maimonides puts it:

> At the present time, when the Temple no longer exists and we have no altar for atonement, nothing is left but repentance. Repentance atones for all transgressions. Even if a person was wicked all the days of his life, and repented at the end, nothing of his wickedness is recalled to him, as it is said, "As for the wickedness of the wicked, he shall not stumble thereby in the day that he turns from his wickedness." The Day of Atonement itself atones for the penitent, as it is said, "For on this day shall atonement be made for you."[2]

It is sometimes hard to understand in retrospect a revolution of thought. For us, centuries or millennia later, it has become part of our common sense, taken-for-granted interpretation of reality. We no longer believe that the earth is flat, or that it stands at the centre of the universe, and that the sun revolves around it. Yet there was a time when people believed

2. Maimonides, *Mishneh Torah, Hilkhot Teshuva* 1:3.

these things, and the suggestion that truth might be otherwise was radical and disturbing. Hence the battle between the Vatican and Galileo. The revolution implicit in R. Akiva's idea was no less dramatic, despite the fact that it did not generate controversy.

To understand what he was doing, we have first to realise that during the biblical era there were two quite different understandings of how people might find their way back to God after they had sinned. One, set out in great detail in the book of *Vayikra*, was essentially priestly. It involved sacrifices and a ritual. It took place in the Temple, at specified times and according to a precisely structured set of procedures. It used key terms like confession, atonement, and purification.

The other was prophetic and it used the verb "to return." We hear this many times in the prophetic literature:

> Return, O Israel, to the Lord your God. Your sins have been your downfall. Take words with you and return to the Lord. Say to Him: Forgive all our sins and receive us graciously, that we may offer our lips instead of sacrifices of bulls. (Hos. 14:1–2)

> Therefore this is what the Lord says: if you repent, I will restore you, that you may serve Me. (Jer. 15:19)

> I have swept away your offences like a cloud, your sins like the morning mist. Return to Me, for I have redeemed you. (Is. 44:22)

> "Do I take any pleasure in the death of the wicked?" declares the Sovereign Lord. "Rather, am I not pleased when they turn from their ways and live?" (Ezek. 18:23)

Prophetic repentance was not about ritual and sacrifice. It was about the change of heart – "return" – that changes lives. It involves remorse and the recognition that we have lost our way. It is spontaneous and internal. It represents a profound transformation in the lives of individuals and the nation that only emerges from a sense of crisis. It is central to the drama of covenant as it plays itself out in the course of history. It involves the recognition that bad things happen to us because we have done bad things. We will only recover our poise, our stability, if we return to the path from which we have drifted: the path of decency and righteousness, caring for others and for God.

The rabbinic concept of *teshuva* was an almost miraculous coming together of priestly and prophetic traditions. Like the ritual of the High Priest, it had its specific time, the Day of Atonement. It had prescribed words, a liturgy of confession. However, as for the prophets, atonement was less a matter of external deeds than internal rededication: a psychological process of remorse, repentance, and the determination to change. The emergence of a concept of *teshuva* that combined both priestly and prophetic elements was like the discovery that light is both a series of particles and a set of waves.

In a real sense, of course, this convergence of the two traditions was implicit at the outset. As the sages say, "Whatever new interpretation an experienced disciple will offer in the future was already given to Moses at Sinai."[3] Nonetheless, it took the most profound historical crisis to bring it to the surface. It is not too much to say that the concept of *teshuva* – atonement without sacrifice or High Priest – saved the Jewish people after the destruction of the Second Temple. It did more than save it. It invested ultimate spiritual dignity in the individual as such. No longer did he need someone else to atone on his behalf. At the very moment that redemption seemed distant, God had become very close.

We know several things about R. Akiva. He was known by his saying that "Whatever the Almighty does, He does for the good."[4] In a famous Talmudic scene, we see him comforting his contemporaries as they look down from Mount Scopus and see the Temple in ruins, a fox walking where once the Holy of Holies stood.[5]

He was not an optimist; he was a man of hope. This is not a simple achievement. It needs a combination of faith, imagination, and trust. It means what in contemporary psychology is called the ability to reframe. However deep the distress, there is a path from here to hope, but it sometimes takes a giant of the spirit to discern it. That is what R. Akiva

3. Y. Pe'ah 2:4.
4. Berakhot 60b.
5. Makkot 24b.

did and was. He was the man who saw through the veil of despair and witnessed beneath it a momentous possibility, that instead of a hierarchy of priests and people, Jews could become, in the words spoken by God immediately prior to the revelation at Mount Sinai, a "kingdom of priests," every one of whose members was holy.

Atonement was now not a sacrificial rite, but a turning – a *returning* – of the soul to God. This was always implicit in Judaism, but it took R. Akiva to see it and make it explicit. This is what he discovered: that all it takes for God to return to us is for us to return to God.

Why Judaism Needs a Land

In this *parasha*, Nahmanides raises a fundamental question about the religious significance of the land of Israel. What is our relation to it? Is it merely historical: it just happens to be the land to which Abraham travelled in response to the divine call and to which Moses led his people from slavery to freedom? Or is it more than that?

In *The Theme of the Pentateuch*,[1] D. J. Clines argues convincingly that the central narrative of the Torah is the promise of and journey to the land of Israel. Why though is this so? Why did the people of the covenant need their own land? Why was Judaism not, on the one hand, a religion that could be practised by individuals wherever they happen to be, or on the other, a religion like Christianity or Islam, whose ultimate purpose is to convert or conquer the world so that everyone can practise the one true faith?

Nahmanides arrives at an answer from an unexpected starting point. Leviticus 18 sets out a long list of forbidden sexual relationships. It then says:

---

1. David J. A. Clines, *The Theme of the Pentateuch* (Sheffield, Eng.: Department of Biblical Studies, University of Sheffield, 1978).

> Do not defile yourselves in any of these ways, because this is
> how the nations that I am going to drive out before you became
> defiled. The land was defiled; so I punished it for its sin, and the
> land vomited out its inhabitants. But you must keep My decrees
> and My laws.... If you defile the land, it will vomit you out as it
> vomited out the nations that were before you. (Lev. 18:24–28)

There is an obvious problem here. Reward and punishment in the Torah
are based on the principle of *midda keneged midda*, measure for measure.
The punishment must fit the sin or crime. It makes sense to say that if the
Israelites neglected or broke *mitzvot hateluyot baaretz*, the commands relating to the land of Israel, the punishment would be exile from the land of
Israel. So the Torah says in the curses in *Parashat Beḥukkotai*: "All the time
that it lies desolate, the land will have the rest it did not have during the sabbaths you lived in it" (Lev. 26:35), meaning: this will be the punishment for
not observing the laws of *Shemitta*, the sabbatical year. *Shemitta* is a command relating to the land. Therefore the punishment for its non-observance
is exile from the land. But sexual offences have nothing to do with the land.
They are *mitzvot hateluyot baguf*, commands relating to person, not place.
        Nahmanides' answer is fundamental:

> This is the meaning of the saying of the rabbis: "Whoever lives
> outside the land [of Israel] is as if he had no God".... When you
> are not in the land of Canaan, I am not your God, if it were pos-
> sible to say such a thing.... *For the main [fulfilment] of the com-
> mandments is when dwelling in the land of God.* Therefore the rabbis
> have said in Sifre: "'And you shall possess it and dwell therein,
> and you shall observe to do all these statutes'... this teaches that
> dwelling in the land of Israel is equal in importance to all the
> commandments of the Torah."[2]

All the commands, says Nahmanides, are fundamentally directed to the
land of Israel. To be sure, not all of them are conditional on it. But it
is there that they receive their main fulfilment. Why so? Nahmanides'

---

2.   Nahmanides, Commentary to Leviticus 18:25.

answer is mystical. Outside Israel, he says, it is impossible to encounter God directly. Over all other lands, God has set intermediaries (angels, stars, celestial powers). Only in Israel is His providence direct and unmediated. That is what gives the land its sanctity. Hence the land does not "tolerate the worshippers of idols or those who practise immorality."

That is why the Canaanites were punished for their idolatry and sexual licence while the Egyptians, who committed similar sins, were not – because the former, not the latter, lived in the holy land. That is also, according to Nahmanides, why Jacob felt able to marry two sisters, Leah and Rachel, while staying with Laban in Haran even though it is against Torah law (Lev. 18:18). The patriarchs kept the Torah before it was given, but *only when they were in the holy land* (which is why, suggests Nahmanides, Rachel died on the journey back to Canaan as they reached the border of the holy land). Hence the saying of the sages quoted by Nahmanides that "Whoever lives outside the land [of Israel] is as if he had no God."

In the course of making this case, Nahmanides quotes two remarkable midrashim. This is the first:

> "And you perish quickly from off the good land" – even though I banish you from the land to outside the land [says God], make yourselves distinctive by the commandments, so that when you return they shall not be new to you. This is like a husband who is angry with his wife and sends her back to her father's house, but tells her, "Continue to adorn yourself with ornaments so that when you come back, they will not be new to you."[3]

According to this midrash, the commands as we keep them outside Israel are a form of marking time until we return to the land, a mere rehearsal, not the real thing.

The second midrash is based on a verse from the book of Ezekiel:

> You say, "We want to be like the nations, like the peoples of the world, who serve wood and stone." But what you have in mind will never happen. (Ezek. 20:32)

3. Sifre, *Parashat Ekev*, 43.

According to the Talmud, the exiled Jews in Babylon came to the prophet Ezekiel and said, "Our master Ezekiel, if a servant is sold by his master, does the master still have any claim on him?"[4] What is going on in these strange passages?

The answer, ironically, was given by one of the great heretics of Judaism, Spinoza. Spinoza argued that all law – with the exception of the universal principles of ethics – is dependent on the existence of a political framework, a sovereign nation-state. That is precisely what the Torah was: Israel's constitution, its legal framework, as a body politic in its own land. It followed, according to Spinoza, that once Israel lost its land and sovereignty, it was no longer bound by the Torah. The covenant was at an end.[5] The people of Israel had ceased to be a nation under the sovereignty of God because they were no longer a sovereign nation at all. They were scattered, dispersed, under the rule of non-Jewish kings, and were not masters of their own destiny.

This, according to the sages, was the claim of the exiles at the time of the Babylonian conquest. The Temple lay in ruins. The land was no longer under Jewish rule. Many of the people had been taken as captives to a foreign country. A famous psalm conveys their sense of devastation: "By the rivers of Babylon we sat and wept as we remembered Zion…. How can we sing the songs of the Lord in a strange land?" The law is that if the owner of a slave sells him to someone else, he no longer has any claim to him. But surely, argued the exiles, that is our situation vis-à-vis God. He has sold us to the Babylonians. Are we then still His people, subject to His laws? Surely not.

The argument is unsustainable, for were it true, Judaism would have ended there and then.[6] What is astonishing is the extent to which the sages, and Nahmanides himself, recognise the force of the case. To be sure, God did not terminate His covenant with the Jewish people.

4. Sanhedrin 105a.
5. Baruch Spinoza, *Tractatus Theologico-Politicus*, part 1, chap. 3.
6. The reason the argument is unsustainable is the fact, unique in history, that the people of Israel received their laws *before* their entry into the land. Normally, first comes the land and only later, the laws. In the case of the Israelites, first came the laws and only afterwards, a generation later, the land. Therefore, even though they had lost the land, they still had the laws. The covenant was still in place.

Even "when you are in the land of your enemies" says God, I will not "break My covenant" with you (Lev. 26:44). In the marriage between God and His people, says Isaiah, there is no divorce (Is. 50:1). When Israel went into exile, say the sages, the *Shekhina*, the Divine Presence, went with them.[7]

Yet there was a deep fracture in the relationship. Outside Israel, Jews are subject to other powers. They are not under the direct, unmediated, rule of God. Hence they are *as if they had no God*. The commands continue in force. But they are no longer the laws of an independent people. They are like an ongoing rehearsal, century after century, for a state of affairs no longer real but nevertheless remembered from the past and awaited in the future, when Israel would once again come home and live as God's people in His land.

Nahmanides' account is mystical but Spinoza's insight allows us to understand it non-mystically by reflecting on the story the Torah tells about the human condition. Having sought a humanity that would freely choose to do the will of its creator, God suffered repeated disappointment. Adam and Eve sinned. Cain murdered his brother Abel. Within a short time, "the earth was filled with violence." God brought a flood and began again, this time with the righteous Noah, but again humans disappointed by building a tower on which they sought to reach heaven. God then chose another way of bringing humanity to recognise Him – this time not by universal rules (though these remained, namely the covenant with all humanity through Noah), but by a living example: Abraham, Sarah, and their children.

In Genesis 18, the Torah makes explicit what God sought from Abraham: that he would teach his children and his household after him "to keep the way of the Lord by doing what is right and just." We are social animals, and righteousness and justice are conditions of a good society. We know from the story of Noah and the ark that righteous individuals can save themselves but not the society in which they live, unless they transform the society in which they live.

Taken collectively, the commands of the Torah are a prescription *for the construction of a society* with the consciousness of God at its centre.

---

7. *Mekhilta DeRabbi Ishmael, Parashat Bo*, 14.

God asks the Jewish people to become a role model for humanity by the shape and texture of the society they build on the principles of justice and the rule of law, welfare and concern for the poor and vulnerable, a society in which all would have equal dignity under the sovereignty of God. Such a society would win the admiration, and eventually the emulation, of others:

> See, I have taught you decrees and laws ... so that you may follow them in the land you are entering to take possession of it. Observe them carefully, for this will be your wisdom and understanding to the nations, who will hear about all these decrees and say, "Surely this great nation is a wise and understanding people".... What other nation is so great as to have such righteous decrees and laws as this body of laws I am setting before you today? (Deut. 4:5–8)

A society needs a land, a home, a location in space where a nation can shape its own destiny in accord with its deepest aspirations and ideals. The Jewish people has had a long and varied history during the almost four thousand years since Abraham began his journey. During that time they have lived in every country on the face of the earth, under good conditions and bad, freedom and persecution. Yet in all that time, there was only one place where they formed a majority and exercised sovereignty: the land of Israel, a tiny country of difficult terrain and all too little rainfall, surrounded by enemies and empires.

Only in Israel is the fulfilment of the commands a society-building exercise, shaping the contours of a culture as a whole. Only in Israel can we fulfil the commands in a land, a landscape, and a language saturated with Jewish memories and hopes. Only in Israel does the calendar track the rhythms of the Jewish year. In Israel, Judaism is part of the public square, not just the private, sequestered space of synagogue, school, and home.

Judaism is more than a metaphysical faith, a private drama within the soul. It is more than a set of moral-spiritual principles that can be lived anywhere. It is the constitution of a holy nation in a holy land. The great principles of the Torah – freedom, justice, respect for human dignity, and a code of holiness governing all aspects of life from eating and drinking to marriage and sexual fidelity – are about the way we structure a society and its laws, and they require independent national existence.

That is the significance of the return to Zion in modern times. Emil Fackenheim called it the "Jewish return into history" but it is more than that. It is the Jewish return to the full terms of the covenant. Outside Israel, we strive to keep the commands as individuals and communities. Only in Israel are they part of the public domain, shaping its culture and character as a nation. Jews are the people of the covenant charged with bringing the Divine Presence down to earth in the shared spaces of our collective life. A holy people needs a holy land.

Kedoshim
קְדוֹשִׁים

With *Parashat Kedoshim*, the laws of holiness broaden out from the world of the Sanctuary and priests to that of the Israelites as a whole, commanding them to be holy because "I the Lord your God am holy." The opening chapter contains the famous "holiness code" with its commands to love the neighbour and the stranger, as well as other laws more ritual in character. The second half of the *parasha* deals with forbidden sexual relations and other prohibited pagan practices.

The first essay explores the idea of the democratisation of holiness in Judaism. Not only priests, but all members of the nation are expected to be holy. The second analyses the connection between the apparently unrelated laws of the holiness code, showing that they represent a unique moral vision, that of priestly consciousness, which is one of three different approaches to morality in the Torah and Judaism generally.

The third essay asks what it is to "be holy," over and above the specific demands of Jewish law. The fourth explores the centrality of love in Judaism, and the fifth looks at the prohibition against taking revenge.

From Priest to People

Something fundamental happens at the beginning of this *parasha* whose story is one of the greatest, if unacknowledged, contributions of Judaism to the world.

Until now *Vayikra* has been largely about sacrifices, purity, the Sanctuary, and the priesthood. It has been, in short, about a holy place, holy offerings, and the elite and holy people – Aaron and his descendants – who minister there. Suddenly, in chapter 19, the text opens up to embrace the whole of the people and the whole of life:

> The Lord said to Moses: "Speak to *the entire assembly of Israel* and say to them, 'Be holy because I the Lord your God am holy.'" (Lev. 19:1–2)

This is the first and only time in Leviticus that so inclusive an address is commanded. The sages say that it means that the contents of the chapter were proclaimed by Moses to a formal gathering of the entire nation (*hak'hel*). It is the people as a whole who are commanded to "be holy," not just an elite, the priests. It is life itself that is to be sanctified, as the chapter goes on to make clear. Holiness is to be made manifest in the way the nation makes its clothes and plants its fields, in the way justice is administered, workers are paid, and business conducted. The vulnerable – the deaf, the blind, the elderly, and the stranger – are to be afforded special protection. The whole society is to be governed by love, without resentments or revenge.

What we witness here, in other words, is the radical *democratisa-tion of holiness*. All ancient societies had priests. We have encountered four instances in the Torah thus far of non-Israelite priests: Malki-zedek, Abraham's contemporary, described as a priest of God Most High; Potiphera, Joseph's father-in-law; the Egyptian priests as a whole, whose land Joseph did not nationalise; and Yitro, Moses' father-in-law, a Midianite priest. The priesthood was not unique to Israel, and every-where it was an elite. Here for the first time, we find a code of holiness directed to the people as a whole. We are all called on to be holy.

In a strange way, though, this comes as no surprise. The idea, if not the details, had already been hinted at. The most explicit instance comes in the prelude to the great covenant-making ceremony at Mount Sinai when God tells Moses to say to the people, "Now if you obey Me fully and keep My covenant, then out of all nations you will be My trea-sured possession. Although the whole earth is Mine, you will be for Me *a kingdom of priests and a holy nation*" (Ex. 19:5–6), that is, a kingdom *all* of whose members are to be in some sense priests, and a nation that is in its entirety holy.

The first intimation is much earlier still, in the first chapter of Genesis, with its monumental assertion, "'Let us make mankind in Our image, in Our likeness'.... So God created mankind in His own image, in the image of God He created them; male and female He created them" (Gen. 1:26–27). What is revolutionary in this declaration is not that a human being could be in the image of God. That is precisely how kings of Mesopotamian city states and pharaohs of Egypt were regarded. They were seen as the representatives, the living images, of the gods. That is how they derived their authority. The Torah's revolution is the statement that not some, but *all*, humans share this dignity. Regardless of class, colour, culture, or creed, we are all in the image and likeness of God.

Thus was born the cluster of ideas that, though they took many millennia to be realised, led to the distinctive culture of the West: the non-negotiable dignity of the human person, the idea of human rights, and eventually, the political and economic expressions of these ideas: liberal democracy on the one hand, and the free market on the other.

The point is not that these ideas were fully formed in the minds of human beings during the period of biblical history. Manifestly, this is not so. The concept of human rights is a product of the seventeenth century. Democracy was not fully implemented until the twentieth. But already in Genesis 1 the seed was planted. That is what Jefferson meant in his famous words, "We hold these truths to be self-evident, that all men are created equal," and what John F. Kennedy alluded to in his Inaugural Address when he spoke of the "revolutionary belief" that "the rights of man come not from the generosity of the state, but from the hand of God."

The irony is that these three texts, Genesis 1, Exodus 19:6, and Leviticus 19, are all spoken in the priestly voice Judaism calls *Torat Kohanim*.[1] On the face of it, priests were not egalitarian. They all came from a single tribe, the Levites, and from a single family, that of Aaron, within the tribe. To be sure, the Torah tells us that this was not God's original intention. Initially, it was to have been the firstborn – those who were saved from the last of the plagues – who were charged with special holiness as the ministers of God. It was only after the sin of the Golden Calf, in which the tribe of Levi did not participate, that the change was made. Even so, the priesthood would have been an elite, a role reserved specifically for firstborn males. So deep is the concept of equality written into monotheism that it emerges precisely from the priestly voice, from which we would least expect it.

The reason is this: religion in the ancient world was, not accidentally but essentially, a defence of hierarchy. With the development, first of agriculture, then of cities, what emerged were highly stratified societies with a ruler on top, surrounded by a royal court, beneath which was an administrative elite, and at the bottom, an illiterate mass that was

---

1. There is, of course, a prophetic call to equality also. We hear, in all the prophets, a critique of the abuse of power and the exploitation of the poor and powerless. What made the priestly voice so significant is that it is the voice of law, and thus of the legal structures that alleviated poverty and set limits to slavery.

conscripted from time to time either as an army or as a corvée, a labour force used in the construction of monumental buildings.

What kept the structure in place was an elaborate doctrine of a heavenly hierarchy whose origins were told in myth, whose most familiar natural symbol was the sun, and whose architectural representation was the pyramid or ziggurat, a massive building broad at the base and narrow at the top. The gods had fought and established an order of dominance and submission. To rebel against the earthly hierarchy was to challenge reality itself. This belief was universal in the ancient world. Aristotle thought that some were born to rule, others to be ruled. Plato constructed a myth in his *The Republic*, in which class divisions existed because the gods had made some people with gold, some with silver, and others with bronze. This was the "noble lie" that had to be told if a society was to protect itself against dissent from within.

Monotheism removes the entire mythological basis of hierarchy. There is no order among the gods because there are no gods, there is only the One God, creator of all. Some form of hierarchy will always exist: armies need commanders, films need directors, and orchestras, conductors. But these are functional, not ontological. They are not a matter of birth. So it is all the more impressive to find the most egalitarian sentiments coming from the world of the priest, whose religious role *was* a matter of birth.

The concept of equality we find in the Torah specifically and Judaism generally is not an equality of wealth: Judaism is not communism. Nor is it an equality of power: Judaism is not anarchy. It is fundamentally an equality of dignity. We are all equal citizens in the nation whose sovereign is God. Hence the elaborate political and economic structure set out in Leviticus, organised around the number seven, the sign of the holy. Every seventh day is free time. Every seventh year, the produce of the field belongs to all, Israelite slaves are to be liberated, and debts released. Every fiftieth year, ancestral land was to return to its original owners. Thus the inequalities that are the inevitable result of freedom are mitigated. The logic of all these provisions is the priestly insight that God, creator of all, is the ultimate owner of all: "The land must not be sold permanently, because the land is Mine and you reside in My land as strangers and temporary residents" (Lev. 25:23). God therefore has the right, not just the power, to set limits to inequality. No one should be robbed of dignity by total poverty, endless servitude, or unrelieved indebtedness.

What is truly remarkable, however, is what happened *after* the biblical era and the destruction of the Second Temple. Faced with the loss of the entire infrastructure of the holy, the Temple, its priests, and sacrifices, Judaism translated the entire system of *avoda*, divine service, into the everyday life of ordinary Jews. In prayer, every Jew became a priest offering a sacrifice. In repentance, he became a High Priest, atoning for his sins and those of his people. Every synagogue, in Israel or elsewhere, became a fragment of the Temple in Jerusalem. Every table became an altar, every act of charity or hospitality, a kind of sacrifice.

Torah study, once the speciality of the priesthood, became the right and obligation of everyone. Not everyone could wear the crown of priesthood, but everyone could wear the crown of Torah. A *mamzer talmid ḥakham*, a Torah scholar of illegitimate birth, say the sages, is greater than an *am haaretz Kohen Gadol*, an ignorant High Priest. Out of the devastating tragedy of the loss of the Temple, the sages created a religious and social order that came closer to the ideal of the people as "a kingdom of priests and a holy nation" than had ever previously been realised. The seed had been planted long before, in the opening of Leviticus 19: "Speak to *the entire assembly of Israel* and say to them, 'Be holy because I the Lord your God am holy.'"

Holiness belongs to all of us when we turn our lives into the service of God, and society into a home for the Divine Presence.

The Priestly Moral Imagination

The structure of Leviticus 19, the so-called holiness code, is one of the most bewildering in the whole Torah. It contains the great moral commands. Love your neighbour as yourself. Love the stranger. Do not steal. Do not tell lies. Do not go about spreading gossip and slander. Do not take revenge or harbour a grudge. Do not hate your brother in your heart.

It contains the great social commands that between them structure a just and compassionate society. Leave portions of the harvest for the poor. Do not hold back the wages of a hired labourer. Use honest scales and honest weights. Do not attempt to interfere with the course of justice. Do not take advantage of other people's helplessness. Do not curse the deaf or put a stumbling block before the blind. Show respect in the presence of the elderly.

But then it also contains a whole series of seemingly ritual or irrational commands that look as if they belong in some other chapter altogether. Do not interbreed different kinds of animals. Do not wear clothing made of interwoven wool and linen. Do not plant your field with mixed seeds. Do not eat meat with the blood still in it. Do not cut the hair at the sides of your head.

What is the relationship between all these commands? Why are some of them about ethics but others not? What is the compositional principle structuring the chapter? What mindset sees these heterogeneous commands and prohibitions as part of the same code, the same vision of humanity and its place in the universe? Many have tried to discern a logic in this list and its order. Most have given up in despair. The answer, however, is given in almost the first sentence: "Be holy because I the Lord your God am holy." What we have in Leviticus 19 is a highly distinctive form of the moral imagination, one we have almost completely lost in the modern age. The rabbinic name for it was *Torat Kohanim*.

A fundamental truth was lost in the course of the Enlightenment, with its pursuit of simple answers to complex questions: the truth that there is not one single system that can do justice to the moral life. What we need is a combination of several. Attempt to reduce them to "one very simple principle," in John Stuart Mill's phrase, and you will fail to do justice to morality itself.

That is why in the Torah and in Judaism as a whole, we find not one but three basic moral voices, corresponding to the three kinds of leader in biblical Israel: the king, the prophet, and the priest. The rabbis called these "the three crowns." But the distinction is already present in the Torah. In *Parashat Shoftim* (Deut. 17–19) they are set out sequentially. They are spelled out also in a verse in Isaiah: "For the Lord is our *judge*, the Lord is our *lawgiver*, the Lord is our *king*" (Is. 33:22). *Judge* in biblical times was part of the role of the priest. *Lawgiver* was the role of the prophet, supremely Moses. The *king* was the political leader of the nation. Isaiah is saying that above all earthly powers is God, but note how he is careful to articulate the *separation* of powers between the three roles.

Jeremiah and Ezekiel both talk about the distinctive sensibilities of the three functions:

> For the teaching of the law [*Torah*] by the priest will not cease,
> nor will counsel [*etza*] from the wise [*ḥakham*],
> nor the word [*davar*] from the prophets. (Jer. 18:18)

They will go searching for a vision [*ḥazon*] from the prophet,
priestly instruction in the law [*Torah*] will cease,
the counsel [*etza*] of the elders will come to an end. (Ezek. 7:26)

Priests have Torah. Prophets have "the word" or "a vision." Elders and the wise have *etza*, good counsel, sound advice. These are three different approaches to the moral life.

One ethical system in Judaism is associated with *wisdom – ḥokhma, etza*, and their synonyms. Tanakh contains several books dedicated to wisdom, most conspicuously Proverbs and Ecclesiastes. Wisdom is a quality usually associated with kings, especially Solomon, and royal courts. It is the most universal form of knowledge in Judaism, and the wisdom literature is the closest the Hebrew Bible comes to other literatures of the ancient Near East, as well as the philosophers and sages of ancient Greece and Rome. Wisdom-based morality is practical, pragmatic, based on experience and observation. It is sensible, sound, judicious, and prudent. It is a prescription for a life that is balanced, moderate, and focused on the long run. Wisdom avoids excess and extremes. It is the virtue of kings who have to listen carefully to a multiplicity of voices, balance conflicting considerations, and act in the long-term interest of the nation as a whole. It is the voice of power combined with responsibility.

The prophetic voice, by contrast, is impassioned, vivid, radical in its critique of the abuse of power and the exploitative pursuit of wealth. The prophet speaks on behalf of the people, the poor, the downtrodden, the abused. He or she thinks of the moral life in terms of relationships: between God and humanity and between human beings themselves. The key terms for the prophet are *tzedek* (distributive justice), *mishpat* (retributive justice), *ḥesed* (loving-kindness), and *raḥamim* (mercy, compassion). The prophet has emotional intelligence, sympathy, and empathy, and feels the plight of the lonely and oppressed. Prophecy is never abstract. It does not think in terms of universals. It responds to the here and now of time and place. While the priest heeds the word of God for *all* time, the prophet hears the word of God for *this* time.

The third voice, and in the Torah itself, the dominant one, is that of the priest, and the most powerful of all priestly passages in the Torah is the opening chapter of Genesis, the story of creation. Fundamental to *Torat Kohanim*, priestly consciousness, is the idea of order. The priest represents Judaism's most profound protest against the view of the world, from ancient myth to social Darwinism, that sees conflict as the basic structure of reality. In Genesis 1, uniquely among all the creation accounts of the ancient world, there is no battle of the gods, no clash of the elements. God speaks and the universe comes into being. God creates order, and where there is order, there is *shalom* (the last word of the priestly blessing). *Shalom* means more than peace. It means completion, wholeness, the integration of the parts into a single interlocking system, ordered complexity, harmony.

Order, for the priest, is a matter of distinction and separation. A key priestly verb, appearing five times in Genesis 1, is *lehavdil*, to separate and divide. For the first three days, God separates the elements into distinct domains: day and night, upper and lower waters, sea and dry land. For the next three days, He fills the domains with their appropriate contents: sun and moon, birds and fish, animals and humankind. The result is the seventh day, Shabbat, the apotheosis of creation, harmony in the midst of time, the first thing in the Torah to be called holy, the key priestly word.

For the priest, creation is itself moral. That is what we find hard to understand. Seven times in Genesis 1 the word "good" appears, the last with the addition of the word "very," meaning that the universe is not just good in its individual elements but also in their complex interaction. For the priest, natural (or "scientific") law, moral law, and "religious" or "ritual" law are all part of the same phenomenon: the God-given, law-governed structure of reality. When this is honoured by human beings, there is order. When it is violated, there is chaos and violence.

The priest is the guardian of order in the life of the holy nation. He does this partly by acting as a judge, bringing legal order to contending parties, partly by making the necessary discriminations between holy and secular, pure and impure, partly by officiating at the Sanctuary, bringing the sacrifices that restore order to the relationship between the people and God, and partly by teaching the law to the people so that they too can honour the principle of order in their daily lives.

The priest's task is to protect order from the ever-present threat of chaos, the result not of some ultimate dimension of reality – the universe is essentially harmonious and fundamentally good – but of the continued wilfulness of human beings in seeking their own good rather than the good of society, humanity, and creation as a whole. This requires the maintenance of boundaries in both time and space. There are holy times and holy places, and each time and place has its own integrity, its own role in the total scheme of things. What the priest protests is the blurring of boundaries so common in pagan religions – between gods and humans, between life and death, between the sexes, and so on. A sin, for the priest, is an act in the wrong place, and its punishment is exile, being cast out of your rightful place. A good society, for the priest, is one in which everything has its place, and in which special sensitivity is shown to the stranger, the person who has no place of his or her own.

So the strange collection of commands in Leviticus 19 turns out not to be strange at all. *Torat Kohanim* sees love and justice as part of a total vision of an ordered universe in which each thing, person, and act has its proper place, and it is this order that is threatened when the boundary between different kinds of animals, grains, or fabrics is breached, when the human body is lacerated, when people eat blood, the sign of death, in order to feed life, and so on.

In the secular West we are familiar with the voice of wisdom. It is common ground between Proverbs and Ecclesiastes and the great sages from Aristotle to Marcus Aurelius to Montaigne. We are accustomed also to the prophetic voice and what Einstein called its "almost fanatical love of justice." We are far less familiar with the priestly voice and its message that just as there is a scientific order to nature, so there is a moral order, and it consists of keeping separate the things that are separate, and maintaining the boundaries that respect the integrity of the world God created and seven times pronounced good.

No one better expressed the priestly vision of a structured, precisely calibrated universe than Shakespeare in *Troilus and Cressida*:

> The heavens themselves, the planets and this centre
> Observe degree, priority and place,

> Insisture, course, proportion, season, form,
> Office and custom, in all line of order.

And no one better described what happens when this delicate order is broken, namely conflict resolved by violence:

> What discord follows! each thing meets
> In mere oppugnancy...
> Then every thing includes itself in power,
> Power into will, will into appetite;
> And appetite, an universal wolf,
> So doubly seconded with will and power,
> Must make perforce an universal prey,
> And last eat up himself.[1]

This – the world before the Flood – is what the priestly mind fears most of all: the chaos that ensues when we fail to respect the integrity of the universe and of life itself as we pursue our own desires by the use of force.

The priestly voice is not marginal to Judaism. It is central and pivotal. It is the voice of the Torah's first chapter. It is the voice that defined the Jewish vocation as "a kingdom of priests and a holy nation." It dominates *Vayikra*, the central book of the Torah. And whereas the prophetic spirit lives on in Aggada, the priestly voice prevails in Halakha. The very name *Torah* – from the verb *lehorot* – is a priestly word.

Perhaps the idea of *ecology*, one of the key discoveries of modern times, will allow us to understand better the priestly vision and its code of holiness, both of which see ethics not just as practical wisdom or prophetic justice but also as honouring the deep structure – the sacred ontology – of being. An ordered universe is a moral universe, a world at peace with its Creator and itself.

1.   William Shakespeare, *Troilus and Cressida*, Act 1, scene iii.

Being Holy

Be holy, for I the Lord your God am holy.
Leviticus 19:2

What does it mean to be holy? More pointedly, what does it mean to be holy *because God is holy*? Surely holiness is precisely what *separates* God from human beings. "For I am God, and not a man – the Holy One among you" says the prophet Hosea (11:9). *Kadosh*, "holy," means "distinct, set apart," above, beyond. Holiness is what makes God, God: transcendent, eternal, all-powerful, beyond image and imagination. How can we, mere mortals – this quintessence of dust, as Hamlet put it – be like God?

Yet that is the paradox stated bluntly at the outset of the great chapter 19 of Leviticus. God is not like us, but we are commanded to be like God. How are we to understand this idea?

The sages[1] understand the command to be holy to mean "be *perushim*" (from which the word Pharisee comes), that is, "be separate,

1. Sifra, *Parashat Kedoshim* 19:1.

practise abstinence, exercise self-restraint." Rashi in his commentary to the Torah understands this narrowly, applying it specifically to sexual conduct.[2] Nahmanides, as we will see below, disagrees and holds that it applies more generally to moderation and self-restraint in all matters. The sages also add that the phrase "for I the Lord your God am holy" means, "If you sanctify yourselves, I will account it to you as if you had sanctified Me."[3]

The idea is that by being distinctive in their behaviour, Jews testify to God. Just as God stands outside the natural universe though He acts within it, so the Children of Israel, though they live in the world, stand at a calibrated distance from it. They are called on to do so by setting an example of self-restraint. They should not give way to instinct or desire. They must practise self-control. They thereby show that Homo sapiens is not a mere biological phenomenon. Human beings are not simply "naked apes" or "a gene's way of making another gene." We can transcend the network of causality that sees human behaviour as genetically determined, a set of responses to stimuli. Animals have desires, but only humans can engage in "second-order evaluations,"[4] choosing which desires to satisfy and which not. That is the freedom God gave us by making us in His image. Being holy means showing that we have a soul as well as a body, that we have spiritual principles, not just physical appetites. Sigmund Freud held that the mark of civilisation was the ability to defer the gratification of instinct. That is precisely how the sages understand the idea of holiness in human behaviour.

Nahmanides takes the idea further in a powerful formulation:

> The meaning is as follows: the Torah has warned us against immorality and forbidden foods, but it permits sexual relations between man and wife, and the eating of certain kinds of meat

2. Rashi is influenced here by the fact that the command appears immediately after Leviticus 18, which details prohibited sexual practices and relationships. Chapter 20 also returns to this theme.
3. Sifra ad loc.
4. I borrow this way of putting it from Charles Taylor, *Sources of the Self* (Cambridge, UK: Cambridge University Press: 1992), 62–65.

and wine. Since this is so, a person could think that it is permitted to be passionately addicted to intercourse with his wife, or many wives, and be "among those who guzzle wine or glut themselves on meat" (Prov. 23:20) and speak freely of all profanities, since this is not explicitly forbidden. The result is that he will become a scoundrel within the permissible realm of Torah [*naval bireshut HaTorah*]. Therefore, after listing the specific conduct that is forbidden, the Torah continues with a general command that we practise moderation even in matters which are permitted.[5]

Nahmanides goes on to explain that this is a general feature of Jewish law: detailed examples followed by a general command. Thus in the case of ethics, the Torah explicitly forbids certain kinds of conduct, such as theft, robbery, and overcharging in business. But it also contains general rules such as, "You shall do that which is right and good" (Deut. 6:18) – which include going "beyond the strict requirements of the law" and a willingness, for the sake of equity, to forego the full extent of one's legal rights.

Maimonides arrives at a similar idea, though from a different source:

> For the Lord will establish you as His holy people, as He swore to you, if you keep the commandments of the Lord your God, *and walk in His ways.* (Deut. 28:9)

From this, he infers[6] that we are commanded to develop certain traits of character – to be gracious, merciful, and holy, as God is gracious, merciful, and holy. As his son, Rabbi Abraham, explains in one of his responsa,[7] Maimonides holds that in addition to prescribing or forbidding specific actions, Judaism requires us to develop certain virtues – what Alexis de Tocqueville called "habits of the heart." The Torah is concerned not only with behaviour but also with character; not just with *what we do* but also *the kind of person we become.*

5. Nahmanides, Commentary to Leviticus 19:2.
6. Maimonides, *Mishneh Torah, Hilkhot Deot* 1:5.
7. *Teshuvot Rabbi Avraham ben HaRambam*, 63.

The point is fundamental. To put it technically, Maimonides and Nahmanides oppose halakhic *reductivism* and *positivism*. The first, reductivism, is the idea that Halakha, Jewish law, is all there is to Judaism: the belief that if we have obeyed every law in the *Shulḥan Arukh*, we have done all that is required of us. There is nothing else. Judaism is a set of laws, a code of conduct, a choreography of behaviour and no more.

The second idea, halakhic positivism, is that Jewish law is a self-contained, self-sufficient system with no underlying logic other than obedience to the word of God. It has no further purposes, no ultimate aim, no rationale – at least none that can be known to us.

Maimonides and Nahmanides believe otherwise. They hold that there are matters of great religious significance which lie beyond the scope of precise legislation. They cannot be spelled out in terms of exact, exhaustive rules, because life does not obey exact, exhaustive rules.

You can keep all the laws of kashrut, implies Nahmanides, and still be a glutton. You can drink only kosher wine and still be a drunkard. You can be faithful to the laws of marriage and still be a sensualist. He calls such a person a *naval bireshut haTorah*, meaning, one who is coarse, crude, self-indulgent, but who justifies his conduct by claiming, perhaps sincerely, that he is a strict observer of the law. Likewise, Maimonides is concerned to refute the idea that you could be an observant Jew and at the same time arrogant, insensitive, tactless, prone to anger or pride. Both believe that such people profoundly fail to understand the nature of Judaism.

The law itself points to something beyond the law. Nahmanides locates this in the command, "You shall be holy." Maimonides finds it in the phrase, "and walk in His ways." Both, however, are convinced that there is a dimension of the moral and spiritual life that cannot be specified in the form of precise legislation. It has to do with self-restraint, moderation, gentleness, sensitivity, and the many other forms of moral literacy which you cannot learn from a book of rules, but only from experience and example.

The Talmud says that R. Akiva followed R. Yehoshua wherever he went, to see how he behaved.[8] One of the great Jewish mystics,

8. Berakhot 62a.

Rabbi Leib Saras, used to say that he travelled to Rabbi Dov Baer of Mezeritch, not to learn biblical interpretations but to see how the rabbi tied his shoelaces. The Talmud speaks of the "foolish" Jews of Babylon who "stand in the presence of a Torah scroll but not in the presence of a great human being."[9] A great sage *is* a living Torah scroll. There are textbooks and there are textpeople. We learn rules from books. But we learn virtue by finding virtuous people and observing how they behave.

Law is not the whole of Judaism. That is why the Torah contains not only law but also narrative, and why the rabbinic literature includes not only Halakha but also Aggada: stories, speculations, and ethical reflections. Along with commentaries and codes, medieval Jewry produced ethical treatises such as Bahya ibn Pekuda's *Duties of the Heart* (*Hovot HaLevavot*) and Rabbi Judah of Regensburg's great work of German-Jewish spirituality, *The Book of the Pious* (*Sefer Hasidim*). The tradition was continued in the eighteenth and nineteenth centuries by the hasidic movement in one direction, and Rabbi Israel Salanter's *Musar* movement in another.

To be holy, for Nahmanides, or to walk in God's ways for Maimonides, is to undergo an extended process in character formation and moral growth. In this sense, ethics is like art. There are rules for constructing a sonnet, but obeying them does not turn you into Shakespeare. The same applies to leadership. There are a few basic rules, but beyond that, leaders have little in common. The best way of learning about leadership is to study leaders (in life, or through their biographies) and see how they behave. Halakha defines the basic parameters of a Jewish life. It is *within* those parameters that the search for moral wisdom takes place. Halakha is a necessary but not sufficient condition of a life lived in pursuit of the ideal. That is why we have such works as Mishna Avot (*Ethics of the Fathers*) and why Maimonides composed his *Laws of Ethical Character* (*Hilkhot Deot*).

Wittgenstein once wrote: "Amongst Jews 'genius' is found only in the holy man."[10] The command to be holy is God's call to us to become *a*

9. Makkot 22b.
10. Ludwig Wittgenstein, *Culture and Value* (Chicago: University of Chicago Press, 1980), 18e.

different sort of person from one who believes that the physical world is all there is, that there is no authority beyond mere power, and that there is no meaning to existence. It is not easy to define what makes people holy, but you recognise it by their demeanour, their way of relating to people, their gentleness, their gravitas, their humility. In their presence you feel a little better than you thought you were. In themselves, they radiate a presence beyond themselves. That, says Nahmanides, is the challenge of those simple words at the beginning of *Parashat Kedoshim*: "Be holy." Holiness is not just what we do but also the kind of person we become.

The Logic of Love

> *If love in the Western world has a founding text,*
> *that text is Hebrew.*
>
> Simon May, *Love: A History*

One text in the Torah is famous above all others, the phrase from this *parasha*: "You shall love your neighbour as yourself" (Lev. 19:18). This, said R. Avika, is "the great principle" of the Torah.[1] The rule of justice is common in moral codes. The first moral judgement a child tends to make is, "It's not fair." Justice as fairness is common. What is distinctly uncommon is the idea, born in Judaism and adopted by Christianity, that love is the central virtue of the moral life.

It is remarkable how rarely this simple truth has been acknowledged. For many centuries, Christians taught that the God of the Old Testament was a God of law and retribution while the God of the New Testament was a God of love and forgiveness, despite the fact that

---

1. Genesis Rabba 24:7.

Christians believed Him to be the same God. Whenever "Love your neighbour" is mentioned in the New Testament, it is always explicitly as a quotation from the Torah. Yet to this day, if you look up or encounter the quote, "Love your neighbour as yourself," more often than not, you will find it attributed to the New Testament.

More perversely still, there was often criticism of "priestly legalism" despite the fact that the command to love your neighbour appears in the most quintessentially priestly text of all, Leviticus 19. It is precisely *Torat Kohanim* that tells us to love our neighbour. Indeed priestly consciousness is suffused with love. *Vayikra*, the Hebrew name of the book of Leviticus, means, as we pointed out in the introduction, "to call, beckon, or summon in love." Whenever God is mentioned in the context of sacrifice, the supreme priestly act, He is always described with the four-letter name, *Hashem*, that signals *middat rahamim*, love and compassion.

Simon May is therefore accurate when he writes:

> The widespread belief that the Hebrew Bible is all about vengeance and an eye for an eye, while the Gospels supposedly invent love as an unconditional and universal value, must therefore count as one of the most extraordinary misunderstandings in all of Western history. For the Hebrew Bible is the source not just of the two love commandments but of a larger moral vision inspired by wonder for love's power.[2]

Indeed, Leviticus 19 teaches us a third love also, in addition to that of God and our neighbour: "If a stranger dwells with you in your land, you shall not mistreat him. The stranger who dwells among you shall be to you as one born among you, and you shall love him as yourself; for you were strangers in the land of Egypt: I am the Lord your God" (Lev. 19:33–34). It is easy to love your neighbour as yourself because throughout most of history, your neighbours were often like yourself, in culture, class, nationality, and ethnicity. The challenge is to love the stranger, the one who is not like you.

2. Simon May, *Love: A History* (New Haven: Yale University Press, 2011), 19.

But the Torah's approach to love goes deeper than this, as we can see if we look not just at the famous phrase but at the context in which it is set:

> Do not hate your brother in your heart.
> You must admonish your neighbour,
> And not bear sin because of him.
> Do not take revenge
> nor bear a grudge against the children of your people.
> You must love your neighbour as yourself.
> I am the Lord. (Lev. 19:17–18)

The Torah does not begin with the command to love. Instead it starts with the hard case: what to do with a neighbour, or brother, whom you dislike, even hate? He may have harmed you, offended you, insulted you. He may have acted in a way that you deeply believe is wrong. Your hatred, let us say, is not irrational. What to do in such a case? To command blandly that you must stifle your feelings is naïve. It is also unlikely to be effective in the long run. Freud coined the phrase "the return of the repressed," to signal that feelings we consciously hide or deny have a way of returning in full and destructive force.

Hence phrase two: "You must admonish your neighbour." Instead of silencing your feelings, you have to verbalise them. You have to confront the person openly and honestly. Here is how Maimonides puts it in his law code:

> When one person sins against another, the latter should not hate him and remain silent. As it is said about the wicked: "And Absalom spoke to Amnon neither good nor evil, although Absalom hated Amnon." Rather, he is commanded to speak to him and to say to him, "Why did you do such-and-such to me? Why did you sin against me in such-and-such a matter?" As it is said, "You must surely admonish your neighbour." If he repents and requests forgiveness from him, he must forgive and not be cruel.[3]

3. Maimonides, *Mishneh Torah, Hilkhot Deot* 6:6.

And here in a similar vein is Nahmanides:

> It seems to me that the correct interpretation is that the expression "you shall surely remonstrate" is to be understood in the same way as [in the phrase], "And Abraham remonstrated with Abimelech." The verse is thus saying: "Do not hate your brother in your heart when he does something to you against your will, but instead you should remonstrate with him, saying, "Why did you do this to me?" and you will not bear sin because of him by covering up your hatred in your heart and not telling him, for when you remonstrate with him, he will justify himself before you [so that you will have no cause to hate him] or he will regret his action and admit his sin, and you will forgive him."[4]

Maimonides' example of why remonstration is necessary is the story (11 Sam. 13) of how Amnon, one of King David's children, raped his half-sister Tamar. When Absalom, Tamar's brother, hears about the episode, his reaction seems on the face of it irenic, serene:

> Her brother Absalom said to her, "Has that Amnon, your brother, been with you? Be quiet, now my sister; he is your brother. Don't take this thing to heart." And Tamar lived in her brother Absalom's house, a desolate woman. When King David heard all this, he was furious. Absalom never said a word to Amnon, neither good nor bad.

Appearances, however, deceive. Absalom was anything but forgiving. He waited for two years, then invited Amnon to a festive meal at sheep-shearing time. He gave instructions to his men: "Listen! When Amnon is in high spirits from drinking wine and I say to you, 'Strike Amnon down,' then kill him." And so it happened. Absalom's silence was not the silence of forgiveness but of hate – the hate of which Pierre de LaClos spoke in *Les Liaisons Dangereuses* when he wrote the famous line: "Revenge is a dish best served cold."

4. Nahmanides, Commentary to Leviticus 19:17.

Nahmanides gives the opposite example, of a case in which remonstration succeeded. Abraham had dug a well. The servants of Abimelech king of Gerar had seized possession of it. We then read: "Abraham rebuked Abimelech because of a well of water which Abimelech's servants had seized. And Abimelech said, 'I do not know who has done this thing; you did not tell me, nor had I *heard of it* until today'" (Gen. 21:25–26). The two men then made a covenant to avoid such events in the future.

The key example, though, is neither of these, but rather the story of Joseph and his brothers:

> Now Israel loved Joseph more than any of his other sons, because he had been born to him in his old age, and he made a richly ornamented robe for him. When his brothers saw that their father loved him more than any of them, they hated him and could not speak a kind word to him [*velo yakhlu dabro leshalom*, literally, "they could not speak with him to peace"]. (Gen. 37:3–4)

On this, Rabbi Jonathan Eybeschutz (c. 1690–1764) comments: "Had they been able to sit together as a group, they would have spoken to one another and remonstrated with each other, and would eventually have made their peace with one another."[5] The tragedy of conflict is that it prevents people from talking together and listening to one another. A failure to communicate is often the prelude to revenge.

The inner logic of the two verses in this *parasha* is therefore this: Love your neighbour as yourself. But not all neighbours are loveable. There are those who, out of envy or malice, have done you harm. I do not command you to live as if you were angels, without any of the emotions natural to human beings. I do, however, forbid you to hate. That is why, when someone does you wrong, you must confront the wrongdoer. You must tell him of your feelings of hurt and distress. It may be that you misunderstood him. Or it may be that he genuinely meant to do you harm, but now, faced with the reality of the injury he has done you, he may sincerely repent of what he did. If, however,

5. *Tiferet Yehonatan*, Commentary to Genesis 37:4.

you fail to talk it through, there is a real possibility that you will bear a grudge and in the fullness of time, come to take revenge – as did Absalom.

What is impressive about the Torah is that it *both* articulates the highest of ideals, *and* at the same time speaks to us as human beings. If we were angels it would be easy to love one another. But we are not. An ethic that commands us to love our enemies, without any hint as to how we are to achieve this, is unliveable. Instead, the Torah sets out a realistic programme. By being honest with one another, talking things through, we may be able to achieve reconciliation – not always, to be sure, but often. How much distress and even bloodshed might be spared if humanity heeded this simple command.

Do Not Take Revenge

One of the more tragic aspects of religious history has been the tendency of faiths to define themselves in relation to other faiths, which they must then negate to prove their own superiority. This is damaging and dangerous. The pages of history are stained with the blood of people killed in the name of God. This was surely not the intention of theologians, but it was the result.

One of the charges levelled by Christians against Jews and Judaism was that the "Old Testament" speaks of a God of vengeance while the New Testament speaks of a God of forgiveness and love.[1] It is a claim still made today.

---

1. Writing about America in the 1940s, Peter Novick says, "No lesson in comparative theology was as assiduously taught in Sunday schools across the United States as the contrast between the Old Testament God of vengeance and the New Testament God of love and forgiveness." Peter Novick, *The Holocaust in American Life* (Boston: Houghton Mifflin, 1999), 91.

Sadly, even Shakespeare could not avoid the calumny. In the very speech in *The Merchant of Venice* in which he almost humanises Shylock, he stops short at precisely this point. He has him say: "Hath not a Jew eyes? Hath not a Jew hands, organs, dimensions, senses, affections, passions? Fed with the same food, hurt with

It is important to know that it is not so. Tanakh, the Hebrew Bible, teaches forgiveness. Divine forgiveness is at the heart of the holiest day in the Jewish year, Yom Kippur (Lev. 16). In the great encounter between God and Moses after the sin of the Golden Calf, God defines Himself in these terms: "The Lord, the Lord, is a merciful and gracious God, long-suffering, and abounding in goodness and truth, keeping mercy for thousands, forgiving iniquity and transgression and sin" (Ex. 34:6–7). Ezekiel says in God's name, "'Do I desire the death of the wicked?' declares the Sovereign Lord. 'Rather, am I not pleased when they turn from their ways and live?'" (Ezek. 18:23).

God forgives. But so do human beings. Forgiveness is the point of the episode in which the book of Genesis reaches its climax and culmination. Joseph's brothers fear that he will take revenge for the fact that they sold him into slavery. He comforts them, saying, "Don't be afraid. Am I in the place of God? You intended to harm me, but God intended it for good, to accomplish what is now being done, the saving of many lives. So then, don't be afraid. I will provide for you and your children." Joseph "reassured them and spoke kindly to them" (Gen. 50:19–21). According to the philosopher David Konstan,[2] the concept of forgiveness was born in ancient Israel. Christianity derives its ethic of forgiveness directly from Judaism.

Far from being a religion of vengeance, Judaism forbids it in this *sedra*:

> *Do not take revenge* or bear a grudge against one of your people, but love your neighbour as yourself. I am the Lord. (Lev. 19:18)

What is the difference between taking revenge and bearing a grudge? The sages give the following homely example:

the same weapons, subject to the same diseases, healed by the same means, warmed and cooled by the same winter and summer as a Christian is? If you prick us, do we not bleed? If you tickle us, do we not laugh? If you poison us, do we not die? And if you wrong us, shall we not revenge?"

2. David Konstan, *Before Forgiveness: The Origins of a Moral Idea* (Cambridge, UK: Cambridge University Press, 2010).

"You shall not take revenge" – What is the scope of vengeance? [An example is] if x says to y, "Lend me your sickle," and y refuses to lend it. The next day y says to x, "Lend me your axe," and x replies, "I will not lend you an axe, because you refused to lend me a sickle." That is what is forbidden by the law, "You shall not take revenge."[3]

Maimonides explains: "[Being vengeful] is an exceedingly bad trait of character. Instead, a person should be forgiving in all his dealings since, for those who have understanding, everything [that happens to them in worldly matters] is insignificant and unimportant and not a proper cause for seeking revenge."[4] Maimonides gives this account to answer an obvious question. Why should the Torah legislate against a perfectly natural emotional reaction as in the case cited by the sages? You are not obliged to lend me your sickle, just as I am not obliged to lend you my axe. Why should I not reciprocate your lack of goodwill? Maimonides' answer is that while my response may be justified, in harming you I am ultimately harming myself by becoming a lesser person than I should strive to become.

We should, suggests Maimonides, cultivate forbearance. That is strength of character. Revenge is reactive, forgiveness proactive. One who seeks revenge is allowing himself to be governed by someone else's behaviour, to be dragged down to his level. That is something we should never do, however natural it may be to want to do so. When someone is rude to us we instinctively feel like being rude in return. But holiness – and the chapter in which the prohibition of revenge appears has the heading "Be holy" – is the ability to stand above instinct and not allow our actions to become reactions. Our task is to act graciously to others even if they act ungraciously to us. This is difficult but necessary. The alternative is revenge, and revenge is forbidden.

The prohibition against bearing a grudge is even more demanding, according to the sages:

What is the scope of bearing a grudge? [An example is] if x says to y, "Lend me your axe," and y refuses to lend it. The next day

---

3. Sifra, *Parashat Kedoshim* 2:4 (10).
4. Maimonides, *Mishneh Torah, Hilkhot Deot* 7:7.

Y says to X, "Lend me your sickle," and X replies, "Take it. I am not like you who would not lend me an axe." That is what is forbidden by the law, "You shall not bear a grudge."[5]

This is a remarkable passage. On the face of it, the second person has acted correctly, even generously. He has *not* taken revenge. To the contrary, he has repaid wrong (a refusal to lend) with right (he *does* lend). All that is wrong is his manner. Why is this a sin? The question is all the stronger when we remember that the Torah is for the most part concerned with acts, not motives, deeds, not thoughts. "Bearing a grudge" as the sages understand it seems to be all about motive.

Again it is Maimonides who provides the explanation. He writes: "One should wipe [the offence someone has committed against him] from his heart and not continue to bear a grudge, because for as long as he continues to bear a grudge and remembers [the wrong done to him], he may come to take revenge."[6] Animosity is not a safe emotion. It can explode into action at any time. The prohibition against bearing a grudge, implies Maimonides, is a kind of "fence," a protective barrier, around the command not to take revenge. Not only is revenge forbidden, but so too is anything that might lead to it.

Yet we cannot end the subject there. The Hebrew Bible *does* contain several references to revenge, if not on our part, then on the part of God: "It is Mine to avenge; I will repay," says God (Deut. 32:35). "The Lord is a God who avenges. O God who avenges, shine forth" (Ps. 94:1). "For the Lord has a day of vengeance," says Isaiah (Is. 34:8). Besides which, vengeance is surely an aspect of justice. What is justice if not the principle that, as we act towards others, so will others act towards us? If we do right, we are rewarded. If we do wrong, we are punished. What is the difference between retributive justice and revenge?

This is an important and much misunderstood subject. In the human domain there is a fundamental difference between justice and revenge. Revenge is personal, justice impersonal. Revenge involves taking the law into your own hands. Justice is the opposite. It means handing

5. Sifra, *Parashat Kedoshim* 2:4 (11).
6. Maimonides, *Mishneh Torah, Hilkhot Deot* 7:8.

over your cause to an impartial tribunal to examine the evidence and apply the law. The move from revenge to justice is the most fundamental any society can make. When courts and the legal process take the place of retaliation, it is no longer the Montagues against the Capulets but both under the impartial rule of law. Justice is not revenge.[7] It is the only sane alternative to it.

What then does Tanakh mean when it speaks of the vengeance of God? The answer is this: vengeance only exists under conditions of lawlessness. In giving the Torah to Israel, God wants His people to be role models of the opposite: lawfulness. That is the only way violence can be eliminated from society. Not only are His people to keep the law. They are to study it day and night, and teach it to their children "when they sit at home and when they walk on the way, when they lie down and when they rise up." God wants the law to be engraved on His people's hearts. Only thus can justice and freedom coexist.

Almost invariably, when we hear of vengeance on the part of God, it is in the context of international politics, where violence, aggression, and war, rather than peace and justice, rule the affairs of humankind. God's promise that He will execute vengeance is an assurance to His people that there is justice in the world because there is a Judge. Judaism is a religion of justice and love, because without love, justice is harsh and inhuman, but without justice, love is partial and selective. That is one of the themes of Genesis. Love is beautiful but it is also divisive. It leads to family conflict and sibling rivalry, between Cain and Abel, Isaac and Ishmael, Jacob and Esau, Joseph and his brothers. There must be justice as well as love if humanity is to survive.

Justice is fundamental to Judaism, and in its name even God Himself can be held to account. That is the meaning of Abraham's challenge, "Shall the Judge of all the earth do justice?" But while the Torah is a scheme for justice *within* society it cannot in and of itself be a code for justice *between* societies until all nations acknowledge the sovereignty of God; in other words, until the Messianic Age. The question before the

7. This was the point often emphasised by Simon Wiesenthal. See his *Justice, Not Vengeance* (New York: Grove Weidenfeld, 1989).

End of Days is therefore this: How is a nation to respond to the injustices committed against it by other nations?

To this, the Torah gives a radical answer: it must leave this to God. *If a nation seeks to right the injustices committed against it by other nations, it will find itself held prisoner by its past, unable to build the future, and it will be caught in a cycle of retaliation that will lead to war without end.* That is what happened at the Treaty of Versailles of 1919. The victors of the First World War sought to execute retribution against Germany and it led eventually to World War II.

What the prophets mean when they say in the name of God that "vengeance is Mine," is that there are forms of justice that only God can execute, not human beings. Only for the God of justice are revenge and retribution the same thing. When the psalmist prays, "O God who avenges, shine forth," he means: God, let there be justice in this world. But You must do it, not us. We can judge individuals in courts of law, but we cannot judge nations. We do not know who is innocent and who is guilty. We can wage war to defend ourselves and our children, but we cannot wage war to execute justice: You alone are the Judge of all the earth. *The call for divine vengeance is a renunciation of human vengeance while keeping faith in the ultimate rule of justice in the affairs of humankind.*

The Christian theologian who has seen this most clearly in our time is Miroslav Volf, who makes the powerful point that "Most people who insist on God's 'nonviolence' cannot resist using violence themselves (or tacitly sanctioning its use by others)." In fact, he says, "in a world of violence it would not be worthy of God *not to wield* the sword; if God were *not angry* at injustice and deception and *did not* make the final end to violence, God would not be worthy of our worship."[8]

It is no coincidence that Volf knows whereof he speaks. He is a native Croatian who writes out of personal experience of the ethnic warfare that ravaged the former Yugoslavia after its breakup in the early 1990s. His words are worth quoting at length:

My thesis that the practice of non-violence requires belief in divine vengeance will be unpopular with many Christians,

---

8.   Miroslav Volf, *Exclusion and Embrace* (Nashville, Tenn.: Abingdon Press, 1996), 303.

especially theologians in the West. To the person who is inclined to dismiss it, I suggest imagining that you are delivering a lecture in a war zone.... Among your listeners are people whose cities and villages have been first plundered, then burned and levelled to the ground, whose daughters and sisters have been raped, whose fathers and brothers have had their throats slit. The topic of the lecture: a Christian attitude towards violence. The thesis: that we should not retaliate since God is perfect noncoercive love. Soon you would discover that it takes the quiet of a suburban home for the birth of the thesis that human nonviolence corresponds to God's refusal to judge. In a scorched land, soaked in the blood of the innocent, it will invariably die. And as one watches it die, one would do well to reflect about many other pleasant captivities of the liberal mind.[9]

Vengeance is one of the most profoundly dangerous of human instincts, and Judaism (and Christianity) are a prolonged battle against it. Wrongs must be righted through the due process of law, reactive emotion must be conquered by a discipline of the mind, and larger questions of ultimate justice belong to God. There are times when violence must be met with violence: hence the concept of a justified war of self-defence (*milḥemet mitzva*). But to commit violence in the name of God is to forget the difference between God and humankind. There are some things, and vengeance is one, that belong to heaven, not to fallible creatures of earth.

9. Ibid., 304.

Emor
אמור

Parashat Emor deals with two kinds of holiness: that of person and of time. Chapter 21 relates to holy people: priests, and above them, the High Priest. Their close contact with the Sanctuary means that they must live with certain restrictions: on contact with the dead and whom they may marry. Chapter 22 recaps similar laws relating to ordinary Israelites when they seek to enter the Sanctuary, as well as defects in animals that bar them from being offered as sacrifices. Chapter 23 is about holy time, the festivals of the year. Chapter 24 speaks about the Menora, lit daily, and the show bread, renewed weekly, and ends with a story – one of the only two narratives in Leviticus – about the fate of a man who blasphemed in the course of a fight.

The first of the essays that follow is about the laws, whose source is in this *parasha*, of sanctifying and not desecrating God's name. The next four are about the list of festivals in chapter 23: what makes it different from the Torah's other lists, why Shabbat is described here differently from anywhere else, the great controversy about what the Torah means when it says that the Omer should be offered on "the day after the Sabbath," and why Sukkot is different from all other festivals. The last essay is about the story of the blasphemer: what is it about and why is it here?

Sanctifying the Name

Two of the most fundamental principles of Jewish law make their appearance in *Parashat Emor*:

> Do not desecrate My holy name, that I may be sanctified among the Children of Israel. I am the Lord who sanctifies you. (Lev. 22:32)

From this verse come the twin commands of *ḥillul Hashem* and *kiddush Hashem*, the prohibition against desecrating God's name, and the command to sanctify it. These are ultimate values in Judaism, one negative, the other positive. *Ḥillul Hashem* is the only transgression for which there is no atonement during a person's lifetime.[1] *Kiddush Hashem* is the supreme act of faith, even to the point of laying down one's life for it. The meaning of these terms has a fascinating history, unfolding over time.

In the first instance, a plain reading of the verse as given by Ibn Ezra suggests that it be understood in the context of the chapter in which it appears. It has been speaking about the special duties that attach to the

---

1. Maimonides, *Mishneh Torah, Hilkhot Teshuva* 1:4.

priesthood and the extreme care the priests must take in serving God within the Sanctuary. All Israel is holy, but the priests are a holy elite within the nation. It was their task to preserve the purity and glory of the Sanctuary as God's symbolic home in the midst of the nation. So the commands are a special charge to the priests to take exemplary care as guardians of the holy. It was their failure to do so at a later age that led to Malachi's stinging charge in the name of God: "From the rising of the sun to where it sets, My name is great among the nations.... But you profane it" (Mal. 1:11–12). The slovenliness of the priests in bringing injured and ailing animals as sacrifices, says Malachi, is a kind of *lèse-majesté*, a contempt for the honour of God, that no other nation would show. That is a desecration.

The next level of meaning appears in the prophets, Amos and Jeremiah, for whom it is a description of immoral conduct that brings dishonour to God's law as a code of justice and compassion. Amos (2:7) speaks of people who "trample on the heads of the poor as on the dust of the ground, and deny justice to the oppressed...and so profane My holy name." Jeremiah uses the notion of *ḥillul Hashem* to describe those who circumvent the law by emancipating their slaves only to recapture and enslave them again (Jer. 34:16). The sages[2] suggest that Abraham was invoking this same idea when he challenged God on His plan to destroy Sodom and Gomorrah, if this meant punishing the righteous as well as the wicked: "Far be it from You [*ḥalila lekha*] to do such a thing." God and the people of God must be associated with justice. Failure to do so constitutes a *ḥillul Hashem*.

A third level of meaning appears in the book of Ezekiel. The Jewish people, or at least a significant part of it, have been forced into exile in Babylon. The nation has suffered defeat and the Temple lies in ruins. For the exiles, the result was a human tragedy. They had lost their home, freedom, and independence. It was a spiritual tragedy: "How can we sing the Lord's song in a strange land?"[3] But Ezekiel, in a devastating series of prophecies, sees it as a tragedy for God also:

> Son of man, when the people of Israel were living in their own land,
> they defiled it by their conduct and their actions.... I dispersed

2. Genesis Rabba 49:9.
3. Psalms 137:4.

them among the nations, and they were scattered through the
countries; I judged them according to their conduct and their
actions. And *wherever they went among the nations they profaned My
holy name,* for it was said of them, "These are the Lord's people,
and yet they had to leave His land." (Ezek. 36:17–20)

The very fact of exile constitutes a desecration of God's name because the
fact that He had punished His people by letting them be conquered was
interpreted by the nations as His inability to protect them. This recalls
Moses' prayer after the Golden Calf:

"Lord," he said, "why should Your anger burn against Your people,
whom You brought out of Egypt with great power and a mighty
hand? Why should the Egyptians say, 'It was with evil intent
that He brought them out, to kill them in the mountains and to
wipe them off the face of the earth'? Turn from Your fierce anger;
relent and do not bring disaster on Your people." (Ex. 32:11–12)

This is part of the divine pathos. Having chosen to identify His name
with the people of Israel, God is, as it were, caught between the demands
of justice on the one hand, and public perception on the other. What
looks like retribution to the Israelites looks like weakness to the world.
In the eyes of the nations, for whom national gods were identified with
power, the exile of Israel could not but be interpreted as the powerless-
ness of Israel's God. That, says Ezekiel, is a *ḥillul Hashem,* a desecration
of God's name.

The fourth sense emerged in the late Second Temple period. Israel
had returned to its land and rebuilt the Temple, but they came under
attack first from the Seleucid Greeks in the reign of Antiochus IV, then
from the Romans, both of whom attempted to outlaw Jewish practice.
The assault was more than military and political: it was religious and
cultural. For the first time, martyrdom became a significant feature of
Jewish life. The question arose: Under what circumstances were Jews to
sacrifice their lives rather than transgress Jewish law?

The question was real and deep. During the great revolt against
Rome, in the years 66–73, there were several tragic cases in which Jews

committed collective suicide rather than be taken captive. Similar events took place in Northern Europe during the age of the Crusades. On the one hand, Judaism has a strong bias towards life. The sages understand the verse, "You shall keep My decrees and laws which a person shall keep and live by them" (Lev. 18:5), to mean "and not die by them."[4] Saving life takes precedence over most of the commands. But there are three exceptions: the prohibitions against murder, forbidden sexual relations, and idolatry, where the sages rule that it is necessary to die rather than transgress. Even so, they also say that "at a time of persecution" one should resist at the cost of death even a demand "to change one's shoe-laces," that is, performing any act that could be construed as going over to the enemy, betraying and demoralising those who remained true to the faith. It was at this time that the phrase *kiddush Hashem* began to mean the willingness to die as a martyr.

One of the most poignant of all collective decisions on the part of the Jewish people was to categorise all the victims of the Holocaust as "those who died *al kiddush Hashem,*" that is, for the sake of sanctifying God's name. This was far from inevitable. Martyrdom means choosing to die for the sake of God. That is what happened in previous persecutions of Jews. Faced with a choice between life and abandonment of the faith, or death and fidelity to it, many chose death. One of the demonic aspects of the Nazi genocide was that Jews were not given the choice. By calling them martyrs in retrospect, Jews gave the victims the dignity in death of which they were so brutally robbed in life.

There is a fifth dimension. This is how Maimonides sums it up:

> There are other deeds which are also included in the desecration of God's name. When a person of great Torah stature, renowned for his piety, does deeds which, although they are not transgres-sions, cause people to speak disparagingly of him, this is also a desecration of God's name. For example, a person who makes a purchase and does not pay for it immediately, although he has the money to do so…or someone who jests immoderately, or eats and drinks among the common people, or whose conduct

4. Yoma 85b.

with other people is not gentle, nor does he receive them with affably, but is quarrelsome and prone to anger, and so on. All this depends on the stature of the sage.[5]

The converse, adds Maimonides, is also true. If a sage "speaks pleasantly to others, is affable and gracious, receives people pleasantly, never humiliates others even though they humiliate him and honours others even though they disrespect him... with the result that all praise him, love him, and approve of his deeds – such a person sanctifies God's name. Of him, Scripture (Is. 49:3) says: "And He said to me: Israel, you are My servant, in whom I will be glorified."

On this view, *kiddush Hashem* and *ḥillul Hashem* are not specific commands, but rather the result of a life taken as a whole, especially on the part of people who are or should be role models for others. If they act and bear themselves in such a way as to earn the respect of others, it is as if the honour of God were raised, and vice versa. If people "of great Torah stature" behave in a way that incurs the disdain of others, it is as if God's honour were diminished.

So we can trace a progression from *ḥillul Hashem* meaning carelessness on the part of a priest, to immoral behaviour, to the exile of a nation, and *kiddush Hashem* from priestly vigilance, to exemplary conduct, to the ultimate sacrifice of life itself in the name and for the sake of God. The common factor in all these cases is the concept of "name." In many languages, "name" is a metonym for reputation. A "good name" means being admired for integrity, honour, and high principle.

The drama behind the idea of *kiddush* and *ḥillul Hashem* is that by linking His presence in history to the Israelites, God, as it were, has taken an immense risk. If Jews bring disgrace on themselves, it is as if they had done so to God. God has placed His reputation in our hands. That is why *ḥillul Hashem* is the gravest of sins – it brings disgrace not just to the sinner, or even the Jewish people as a whole, but as it were, to God Himself.

Isaiah said: "'You are My witnesses,' declares the Lord, 'that I am God'" (Is. 43:12). On this there is an extraordinary midrash that

5. Maimonides, *Mishneh Torah, Hilkhot Yesodei HaTorah* 5:11.

adds: "And if you are not My witnesses, it is as if I were not God."[6] God is God whatever we do or fail to do. But God, having set His image on every human being, took the risk of identifying His presence in history with one small people with whom He made a covenant in a lonely desert long ago, and that fact has charged Jewish existence with immense responsibility ever since. We are God's witnesses. How the people of God behave affects how God Himself is perceived.

6. *Pesikta DeRav Kahana*, 12; *Midrash Tehillim* 123:1.

The Calendar

In five places, the Torah lists the festivals of the Jewish year. Two of these, Exodus 23:14–17 and 34:18–26, are brief. Three, in Leviticus, Numbers 28–29, and Deuteronomy 16:1–17, are set out at length, and they are very different from one another. The list in Numbers sets out the precise specification of the sacrifices to be offered on each of the holy days. The account in Deuteronomy looks at the social impact of the festivals when Israel became a nation in its own land. It emphasises the importance of these days for collective celebration: "You, your sons and daughters, your male and female servants, and the Levites, the foreigners, the fatherless, and the widows who live in your towns."

The accounts in Numbers and Deuteronomy each have a clearly defined focus. This is harder to see when it comes to the list in this *parasha*. It mentions some of the offerings but not others. It lacks a social dimension. It gives some details we do not find elsewhere, such as the commands to live in booths and take the "four kinds" on Sukkot. It goes into greater detail about the counting of days and weeks from the offering of the Omer to the festival of Shavuot. But it seems to lack a clear theme. The sages say that it comes to tell us the "order" (*sidran*) of the festivals,[1] but so, in a way, do the other accounts. They list the days in sequence and give their dates. Evidently the sages mean something deeper by "order," but what is it?

In one respect in particular, the Leviticus account is quite strange – in its treatment of Shabbat. Here is how the chapter begins:

> The Lord said to Moses, "Speak to the Israelites and say to them: 'These are the appointed festivals [*mo'adei*] of the Lord, which you are to proclaim [*tikre'u*] as sacred assemblies [*mikra'ei kodesh*]: these are My appointed festivals. Six days shall work be done, but the seventh day is a day of sabbath rest, a day of sacred assembly. You shall do no work; wherever you live, it is a sabbath to the Lord. These are the appointed festivals of the Lord, the sacred assemblies you are to proclaim at their appointed times.'"
> (Lev. 23:1–4)

It then continues with the details of the festivals. The problem is glaring and was noted by the commentators. Two terms are used here in connection with Shabbat that are not used elsewhere: *mo'ed*, "appointed festival," and *mikra kodesh*, "sacred assembly." But neither fits Shabbat. It is not a *mo'ed* in the sense of a day with a date on the calendar.[2] The Hebrew calendar is both lunar and solar, lunar in respect of months, solar in relation to the seasons of the year. Shabbat is neither. It creates its own unique rhythm, the seven-day week, which did not exist in any other ancient system of counting time. The very institution of the seven-day week, now a global phenomenon, has its origin in the Hebrew Bible. So Shabbat is not a fixed date on the calendar. It is not a *mo'ed*.

Nor is it a *mikra kodesh*. The commentators give two explanations of this phrase. One is "sacred assembly," meaning a time when the nation gathered in a central sanctuary (Nahmanides). But this does not apply to Shabbat. It was celebrated locally, not centrally. The other is "a day proclaimed holy" (Rashi, Rashbam), referring to the fact that the calendar depended on the proclamation of the *Beit Din* as to which day

1. Sifre, *Parashat Re'eh*, 127.
2. See Sifra and Rashi to Leviticus 23:2.

or days were announced as Rosh Ḥodesh, the start of the new month. It is precisely in this respect that Shabbat differs from the festivals. It is *not* dependent on any human proclamation. Shabbat is holy because God Himself sanctified it on the seventh day of creation.

So Shabbat does not belong in a list of the festivals. The text seems to be aware of this because after the introduction, "These are the appointed festivals of the Lord," and the one-line account of Shabbat, it goes on to *repeat* the introduction, in almost the same words, and then lists the festivals themselves. Near the end of the chapter, there is another indication that Shabbat does not fully fit. The text states: "These are the Lord's appointed festivals, which you are to proclaim as sacred assemblies for bringing food offerings to the Lord … *in addition to* those for the Lord's Sabbaths." So what is Shabbat doing here? It seems both to belong and not to belong.

The problem is made more acute because of a phrase to be found three times in this chapter *and nowhere else in the whole of Tanakh*: "which you are to proclaim [*tikre'u*]." It was this phrase with its three-fold emphasis that led the sages to conclude that the holiness of the holy days depends entirely on the determination of the *Beit Din*.[3] In relation to the calendar, the verdict of the court is constitutive, not regulative. When a court declares a man guilty, it may be right or it may be wrong. But when it declares a certain day Rosh Ḥodesh, the day of the new moon, it cannot be wrong because its declaration makes it so. So it is all the more strange that Shabbat makes an appearance in this chapter, because the court has no role whatsoever to play in the determination of Shabbat. No ruling of any court can turn a weekday into Shabbat or Shabbat into a weekday.

These are problems that cannot be solved fully by focusing on the subject at hand, namely the calendar. We have before us a classic instance where the meaning of a text is to be found by stepping back and seeing its place in the biblical narrative as a whole.

The subject of the second half of the book of Leviticus is *holiness*. This is a concept we readily understand in connection with God. It means that God is radically distinct from anything in the physical universe.

3. See Mishna Rosh HaShana 2:9.

He is not bounded by time or space. He cannot be represented by any icon. To make an image of God is to take the first step to idolatry. God is not a force of nature but the creator of nature itself. That was the real revolution of monotheism: not reducing the number of gods from many to one, but rather understanding that God transcends the universe. He is One, unique, alone. That is what holiness means: radical difference from anything within the human world.

That is what makes the command in Leviticus 19:2 so paradoxical: "You shall be holy, for I the Lord your God am holy." How can human beings be holy, if holiness is precisely what makes God utterly different from us? There are two answers to this question, one before and one after the sin of the Golden Calf.

The first answer is contained in a verse that appears immediately before the revelation at Mount Sinai and the giving of the Ten Commandments. God tells Moses to say to the Israelites: "You yourselves have seen what I did to Egypt, and how I carried you on eagles' wings and brought you to Myself. Now if you obey Me fully and keep My covenant, then out of all nations you will be My treasured possession. Although the whole earth is Mine, you will be for Me a kingdom of priests and a holy nation." The emphasis here is on covenant. The Israelites will be unique because they will have God as their king, their sovereign, their lawmaker. They will serve Him and He will protect them. They will be God's people. They will be a holy nation in the sense of being the nation of the holy God. This is *holiness by association*. God is holy. We are His. Therefore we are holy.

After the sin of the Golden Calf, however, the arc of Israel's destiny changes. A new tone enters the narrative. We sense it immediately with the construction of the Sanctuary in the last third of the book of Exodus. It dominates the entire book of Leviticus. Now the emphasis is less on God, the worker of wonders, the ruler, the sovereign, the hand that changes history, and the voice that shakes the world. Instead, the focus is on the Israelites and the space they create for God to become a permanent presence in their midst. The focus shifts from what God does to what we do.

Holiness has suddenly come close, and the centre of action has shifted from heaven to earth. The Israelites are no longer to be holy merely by association as the "treasured possession" of God. Holiness in the sense of an encounter with God is to become a regular feature of their lives. The rabbis beautifully expressed this new dimension in the blessing they attributed to Moses when the people completed the Sanctuary: "May it be God's will that His presence rests in the work of your hands." That is *holiness by action*: living in such a way that God's presence lives in what we do.

The pattern is set by the Sanctuary itself. As we noted elsewhere,[4] the language the Torah uses at the end of Exodus as the work reaches completion deliberately evokes the language the Torah uses of God on the seventh day of creation in Genesis 2:1–3. The Sanctuary is, in other words, a microcosmos, a universe in miniature, made by human beings at God's request so that they can create as He creates – while remembering that He is our creator. *The Sanctuary represents the order we create to mirror the order God creates*, thus becoming, in the rabbinic phrase, "God's partner in the work of creation."

What Leviticus 23 is telling us is that what the Sanctuary was in relation to place, the calendar is in relation to time: *it is the holy time we create to mirror the holy time God creates*. The holy time God creates is Shabbat. This is the first thing God declares holy (Gen. 2:3), the only time the word "holy" appears in the book of Genesis. That is why the list of festivals in Leviticus begins with Shabbat, just as the construction of the Tabernacle begins with Shabbat (Ex. 35:2–3). It is to remind us that our creation must mirror and serve as a permanent reminder of God's creation.

How do the festivals mirror Shabbat? The answer lies in the single most distinctive feature of the list in Leviticus: the number seven. There are seven holy days enumerated in Leviticus 23: Pesaḥ (14 Nisan), Ḥag HaMatzot, Shavuot, Rosh HaShana, Yom Kippur, Sukkot, and Shemini Atzeret. There are seven days on which "regular work" (*melekhet avoda*) is forbidden.[5] The two extended festivals, Ḥag HaMatzot and Sukkot, are both seven days long. Shavuot is celebrated seven weeks of seven days

---

4. *Covenant and Conversation: Exodus – The Book of Redemption*, 329–337.
5. Subtracting Pesaḥ (14 Nisan) from the previous list, because it is not a day on which work is forbidden by the Torah, and adding the seventh day of Ḥag HaMatzot.

after the offering of the Omer. The largest cluster of festivals is in the seventh month. The passage as a whole contains seven paragraphs. There are seven instances of words that appear only in this chapter and not elsewhere in the Torah (*tikre'u*, three times and *mo'adei* or *mo'adai*, four times). And what we find in Leviticus 23 in relation to days, weeks, and months, we find in Leviticus 25 in relation to years: an entire structure of social legislation built around the number seven in the form of the sabbatical and Jubilee years.

Seven is the number of holiness, because God Himself declared the seventh day holy. It is also holy because the seven-day week corresponds to nothing in nature. It is the day that points to the One who transcends nature and created nature. So Leviticus 23 is revolutionary in two ways. First, it takes the number associated with non-natural time and transposes it into natural time: the calendar of lunar months and solar years. Second, it emphasises the human contribution to the sanctification of time by insisting three times that these are sacred days "which *you* are to proclaim." It takes the principle of Leviticus 19:2 – "You shall be holy because I the Lord your God am holy" – and applies it to time. You shall make time holy because I make time holy, says God. Thus the calendar does for time what the Sanctuary did for place.[6] It allowed the Israelites to create a mirror of what God had created when He made the universe.

There is a word that connects the festivals and the Sanctuary: *mo'ed*. It describes the festivals and it is also used – in the very first verse of Leviticus – of the *Ohel Mo'ed*, the "Tent of Meeting" within the Sanctuary. Thus *mo'ed* in Leviticus means not just "an appointed time" but also any time or place designated as a meeting point between man and God. Only in this sense is Shabbat, like the festivals, a *mo'ed*. Holy times are times when, setting aside our daily devices and desires, we have a tryst, a lover's meeting, with God, whether at His initiative or ours.

No sooner have we made the connection between the word *mo'ed* in our chapter and in the opening line of the book than we sense another stroke of intertextuality: the word *Vayikra* itself. This, the opening word

6. Abraham Joshua Heschel famously spoke of the Sabbath as a sanctuary in time. My argument is that this is not the right analogy. It is the festivals that are the sanctuary in time because they, like the Sanctuary, are brought into being by human acts.

of the book, is echoed in our chapter fifteen times in the phrases *mikra kodesh,* "a sacred assembly," and *asher tikre'u otam,* "which you shall proclaim." Leviticus opens by God calling to man. It reaches its culmination here by man calling to God.

Leviticus 23 can only be understood in terms of the larger drama set in motion by the sin of the Golden Calf. It became clear at that point that if the Israelites were to grow to maturity, they had to become more than the passive beneficiaries of God's goodness. They had to become, under His direction, active creators of spaces that would become filled by His presence. Whether in place or time, in social structures or private lives, from the way they ate to the way they conducted their most intimate relations, they had to introduce that which is beyond nature into a life lived within the realities of nature. That is holiness by human action, making space for God.

Leviticus 23 takes this idea and applies it to time. On Shabbat, God issues the invitation. On the festivals, we do. Both are forms of *mo'ed* in the sense of meeting. The calendar is where *Vayikra,* the call of God, meets *tikre'u,* the call of man.

Three Versions of Shabbat

I n the previous essay we saw that there was something unique about the way *Parashat Emor* speaks about Shabbat. It calls it a *mo'ed* and a *mikra kodesh* when, in the conventional sense of these words, it is neither. *Mo'ed* means an appointed time with a fixed date on the calendar. *Mikra kodesh* means either a sacred assembly, a time at which the nation gathered at the central Sanctuary, or a day made holy by proclamation, that is, through the human court's determination of the calendar. Shabbat is none of these things. It has no fixed date on the calendar. It is not a time of national assembly. And it is not a day made holy by the proclamation of the human court. Shabbat was the day made holy by God Himself at the beginning of time.

The explanation lies in the context in which the passage containing these terms appears, the chapters of the Torah whose primary theme is holiness (Lev. 18–27). The radical claim made in these chapters is that holiness, a term normally reserved for God, can be acquired by human beings when they act like God. The festivals stand to Shabbat the way the Sanctuary stands to the universe. Both are humanly created domains of holiness constructed on the model of divine creation and sanctification as they appear at the beginning of Genesis. By inviting human beings to create a sanctuary and determine the monthly and yearly calendar, God invests us with the dignity of a holiness we have not just received passively as a gift but acquired actively as co-creators with God.

Mikra kodesh and *mo'ed* as they appear in Leviticus have an extra sense that they do not bear elsewhere because they evoke the opening verse of the book: "He called [*Vayikra*] to Moses, and the Lord spoke to him in the Tent of Meeting [*Ohel Mo'ed*], saying..." (Lev. 1:1). The focus is on *mikra* as "call" and *mo'ed* as "meeting." When the Torah uses these words uniquely in this chapter to apply to Shabbat as well as the festivals, it is focusing on the encounter between God and humanity in the arena of time. Whether it is God's call to us or ours to Him, whether God initiates the meeting or we do, holy time becomes a lovers' rendezvous, a still point in the turning world when lover and beloved, Creator and creation, "make time" for one another and know one another in the special form of knowledge we call love.

If this is so, what does *Parashat Emor* tell us about Shabbat that we do not learn elsewhere? The answer becomes clear when we look at two other passages, the two versions of the Decalogue, the Ten Commandments, as they appear in Exodus and Deuteronomy. Famously, the wording of the two versions is different. The Exodus account begins with the word *Zakhor*, remember. The Deuteronomy account begins with *Shamor*, "keep, guard, protect." But they differ more profoundly in their very understanding of the nature and significance of the day. Here is the Exodus text:

> Remember the Sabbath day by keeping it holy. Six days you shall labour and do all your work, but the seventh day is a sabbath to the Lord your God. On it you shall not do any work.... *For in six days the Lord made the heavens and the earth, the sea, and all that is in them, but He rested on the seventh day.* Therefore the Lord blessed the Sabbath day and made it holy. (Ex. 20:7–9)

According to this, Shabbat is a *reminder of creation.* The Deuteronomy text gives a very different account:

> Observe the Sabbath day by keeping it holy, as the Lord your God has commanded you. Six days you shall labour and do all

your work, but the seventh day is a sabbath to the Lord your God. On it you shall not do any work, neither you, nor your son or daughter, nor your male or female servant, nor your ox, your donkey, or any of your animals, nor any foreigner residing in your towns, so that your male and female servants may rest, as you do. *Remember that you were slaves in Egypt and that the Lord your God brought you out of there with a mighty hand and an outstretched arm.* Therefore the Lord your God has commanded you to observe the Sabbath day. (Deut. 5:11–14)

Here there is no reference to creation. Instead the Torah speaks about a historical event: the Exodus. We keep Shabbat not because God rested on the seventh day but because He took our ancestors out of Egypt, from slavery to freedom. Therefore, Shabbat is a day of freedom even for servants, and even for domestic animals. One day in seven, no one is a slave.

Of course, both are true, and we integrate both accounts into the text of the Kiddush we make on Friday night. We call Shabbat a remembrance of creation (*zikaron lemaaseh bereishit*) as well as a reminder of the Exodus (*zekher liyetziat Mitzrayim*). However, once we set the Leviticus account in the context of these other two, a richer pattern emerges.

I have argued throughout these studies that we can hear three primary voices in the Torah: those of kingship, priesthood, and prophecy. These are the three fundamental leadership roles and they have distinctive modes of knowledge. So we find in the book of Jeremiah that "the teaching of the law [*Torah*] by the priest will not cease, nor will counsel from the wise, nor the word from the prophets" (Jer. 18:18). Ezekiel says that a time will come when "They will go searching for a vision from the prophet, priestly instruction in the law will cease, the counsel of the elders will come to an end" (Ezek. 7:26).

Priests, prophets, and the governing elite (the wise, the elders, kings and their courts) each have their own ways of thinking and speaking. Kings and courts use the language of *ḥokhma*, "wisdom." Priests teach Torah, the word of God for all time. Prophets have visions. They have "the word" of God not for *all* time but for *this* time. Prophecy is about history as the interaction between God and humanity.

Is it merely accidental that there happen to be three voices, when there could have been four, or two, or one? The answer is no. There are three voices because, axiomatic to Jewish faith is the belief that God is encountered in three ways: in creation, revelation, and redemption.[1]

Wisdom is the ability to see God in creation, in the intricate complexity of the natural universe and the human mind. In contemporary terms, *ḥokhma* is a combination of the sciences and humanities: all that allows us to see the universe as the work of God and human beings as the image of God. It is summed up in a verse from Psalms (104:24), "How many are Your works, O Lord; You have made them all in wisdom."

Revelation, Torah, the speciality of the priest, is the ability to hear God in the form of the commanding voice, most characteristically in the form of law: "And God said," "And God spoke," "And God commanded." Revelation is a matter not of seeing but of listening, in the deep sense of hearing and heeding, attending and responding. Wisdom tells us how things are. Revelation tells us how we should live.

Prophetic consciousness is always focused on redemption, the long and winding road towards a society based on justice and compassion, love and forgiveness, peace and human dignity. The prophet knows where we came from and where we are going to, what stage we have reached in the journey and what dangers lie ahead. The prophetic word is always related to history, to the present in relation to the past and the future: not history as a mere succession of events, but as an approach to or digression from the good society, the Promised Land, and the Messianic Age.

Creation, revelation, and redemption represent the three basic relationships within which Judaism and human life are set. Creation is God's relationship to the world. Revelation is God's relationship with us. When we apply revelation to creation, the result is redemption: the world in which God's will and ours coincide.

---

1. Rabbi Shimon ben Tzemaḥ Duran (1366–1441) argued that all of Maimonides' Thirteen Principles of Faith could be reduced to these three. See Menachem Kellner, *Dogma in Medieval Jewish Thought* (Oxford: Littman Library Of Jewish Civilization; New Ed edition, July 22, 2004). In the modern era, this idea is primarily associated with Franz Rosenzweig.

We now understand why the Torah contains three distinct accounts of Shabbat. The account in the first version of the Ten Commandments, "For in six days the Lord made the heavens and the earth," is the Shabbat of creation. The account in the second version, "Remember that you were slaves in Egypt and that the Lord your God brought you out," is the Shabbat of redemption. The *Parashat Emor* account, spoken in the priestly voice, is the Shabbat of revelation.

In revelation, God calls to man. That is why the middle book of the Torah that more than any other represents *Torat Kohanim*, "the law of the priests," begins with the word *Vayikra*, "and He called." It is also why Shabbat is, uniquely here, included in the days "which you shall proclaim (*tikre'u*) as sacred convocations (*mikra'ei kodesh*)," with the double emphasis on the verb *k-r-a*, "to call, proclaim, convoke." Shabbat is the day in which, in the stasis of rest and the silence of the soul, we hear the *Vayikra* of God.

Hence too, the word *mo'ed*, which in general means "appointed times," but here means "meeting." Judah Halevi, the eleventh-century poet and philosopher, said that on Shabbat, it is as if God had personally invited us to be dinner guests at His table.[2] The Shabbat of revelation does not look back to the birth of the universe or forwards to the future redemption. It celebrates the present moment as our private time with God. It represents "the power of now."

Not only is this threefold structure set out in the Torah, it is embodied in the prayers of Shabbat itself. Shabbat is the only day of the year in which the evening, morning, and afternoon prayers are different from one another. In the Friday night *Amida*, we refer to the Shabbat of creation: "You sanctified the seventh day for Your name's sake as the culmination of the creation of heaven and earth." On Shabbat morning we speak about the supreme moment of revelation: "Moses rejoiced at the gift of his portion.... A crown of glory You placed on his head when he stood before You on Mount Sinai. He brought down in his hands two tablets of stone on which was engraved the observance of the Sabbath." On Shabbat afternoon we look forwards to the ultimate redemption,

---

2. Judah Halevi, *The Kuzari*, II:50.

when all humanity will acknowledge that "You are One, Your name is One, and who is like Your people Israel, a nation one on earth."[3]

Creation, revelation, and redemption form the basic triad of Jewish faith. They are also the most fundamental structuring principle of Jewish prayer. Nowhere is this clearer than in the way the Torah understands Shabbat: one day with three dimensions, experienced successively in the experiences of evening, morning, and afternoon. What is fragmented in secular culture into science, religion, and political ideology is here united in the transforming experience of God who created the universe, whose presence fills our homes with light, and who will one day lead us to a world of freedom, justice, and peace.

3. The phrase *goy eḥad baaretz*, which appears three times in Tanakh, has two meanings: "a nation unique on earth" (II Sam. 7:23, I Chr. 17:21), and "a nation reunited" after its internal divisions (Ezek. 37:22). It bears both meanings here.

New Light on an Old Controversy

Asingle phrase in *Parashat Emor* led to one of the great controversies in Jewish history. It occurs in the context of the Omer and the count it initiated to the next festival, Shavuot. Here is the law as stated in this *parasha*:

> When you enter the land that I am giving to you, and you reap its harvest, you shall bring the first sheaf [Omer] of your harvest to the priest. He shall wave it before the Lord for acceptance on your behalf; the priest shall make this wave offering on *the day after the Sabbath*.... And from the day on which you bring the Omer as a wave offering – *the day after the Sabbath* – you shall count seven complete weeks. You must count until the day after the seventh week, fifty days; then you shall bring an offering of new grain to the Lord. (Lev. 23:10–11, 15–17, 22)

The phrase that generated the controversy was, "the day after the Sabbath." What does this mean? The plain sense is Sunday. But which Sunday? And why? And did it really mean Sunday here? There are, after all, two cycles of time in the Jewish year. There is weekly time, determined by the cycle of seven days culminating in Shabbat, set by God Himself in the act of creation. And there is monthly time, entrusted by God in His first command to the Israelites themselves (Ex. 12:2), to determine the calendar in a complex synthesis between the sun that gives rise to seasons and the moon that gives rise to months. So the reference to Shabbat in the context of Passover and Shavuot seems discordant, a confusion of two time modes – God's time (Shabbat) and Israel's time (the festivals).

The ambiguity was accentuated by deep schisms in Jewish life in the late Second Temple period between Pharisees and other groups like the Boethusians, Sadducees, Samaritans, and the Qumran sect of the Dead Sea Scrolls. Later in the age of the *Geonim*, from the eighth century onward, a similar controversy arose between the followers of the rabbis and the Karaites. The Pharisees and the rabbis held, as we do, that there is an Oral Tradition, the *Torah Shebe'al Peh*, of equal authority with the Torah's written text, the *Torah Shebikhtav*.[1] That tradition said that "the day after the Sabbath" meant "the day after the first day of the festival," which, being a day of rest, could also be called Shabbat.[2]

The other groups, lacking an oral tradition, held that the word Shabbat was to be construed literally. For them the Omer was offered on a Sunday, and Shavuot fell on Sunday seven weeks later. The Boethusians, Sadducees, and Karaites understood the phrase to mean "the day after the Shabbat during Passover." The Qumran sect understood it to refer to the Shabbat *after* Passover. The Jews of Ethiopia held a fourth view, understanding it to mean the last day of the festival, so for them Shavuot fell six days later than for the Pharisees and rabbis.

1. See in the present context, Judah Halevi, *The Kuzari*, III:41.
2. Another view was that the first day of Passover was called Shabbat because of the command to "remove" (*tashbitu*, from the same verb as "Shabbat") all leaven from the home (Ex. 12:15). My own view is that the Torah here uses the word Shabbat to mean "first day of the festival" because of a unique ambiguity in the preceding passage. The Torah specifies not one day but two, Pesaḥ (14 Nisan) and Ḥag HaMatzot (a seven-day festival beginning on 15 Nisan). Any term like *ḥag, mikra kodesh,* or *mo'ed* would be ambiguous in this context. The one difference between Pesaḥ and the first day of Ḥag HaMatzot is that on the latter, but not the former, work was forbidden. Hence, relative to Pesaḥ (14 Nisan), the first day of Ḥag HaMatzot is Shabbat, that is, a non-working day.

The result was chaos: different groups celebrating a major festi-val on different days. Jewish life still bears the scar of that dispute in the form of the second day of the festival outside Israel. During the Sec-ond Temple period, there was no need for a second day even in Baby-lon because the decision of the court as to the start of the month was instantly conveyed by the lighting of a series of bonfires that stretched from Israel to Babylon. During the Omer/Shavuot controversy however, the Boethusians sabotaged the bonfires and so the news had to be con-veyed by messengers instead.[3] That is a lingering irony of monotheism. Serving one God does not always create unity.

Those who understood "the day after the Sabbath" literally as Sunday had strong arguments in their favour. First, that is what the phrase would normally be taken to mean. If the Torah meant "the day after the first day of the festival," why did it not say so? Besides which, only by starting the count on the first day of the week does a count of forty-nine days yield "seven complete weeks" in the usual sense, namely a seven-day period beginning on Sunday and ending on Shabbat. One Boethusian reported in the Talmud[4] offered a third and endearingly human consideration. Moses, he said, was "a lover of Israel." Realising that after seven exhausting weeks in the field, farmers would be tired, Moses (or rather, God) had compassion on them and gave them a long weekend!

However, the Boethusians may have had another reason, not mentioned in the Talmudic sources but a connection crying out to be made. The word "omer" appears three times in this *parasha*. But it appears six times in Exodus 16, the only place it has been mentioned before. *It was the measure of the manna that fell for the Israelites when they finished the unleavened bread they had brought with them from Egypt.* The Torah (Ex. 16:1–18) tells us that the food ran out, the people were starv-ing, they complained to Moses, and God sent them the manna, one of whose miraculous properties was that however much people collected, they always found that they had an omer's quantity.

The Boethusians and other sectarians may thus have had a specific historical understanding of what the Omer offering represented. It was a

---

3. Mishna Rosh HaShana 2:2.
4. Menaḥot 65a.

way of remembering the manna itself. This is not absurd: still today we observe the custom of having two loaves of bread on Shabbat to recall the double portion of manna that fell on Friday in honour of Shabbat. If so, then the Boethusians would have had a powerful argument to deploy in their debate with the Pharisees: *the manna first fell on a Sunday!* On this even the Talmud, the classic text of rabbinic Judaism, agrees.[5] That, the Boethusians might have argued, is why the Omer is always offered on Sunday since it recalls the manna that first fell on Sunday. On this interpretation, the symbolism of the Omer becomes clear. By recalling the manna, *it represents the bread of freedom they ate in the wilderness once the unleavened bread of affliction had been finished.* It was the first taste of liberty.

The manna, however, brings us to the simplest argument against the Boethusians, given by Maimonides.[6] He refers to the passage in the book of Joshua that we read as the *haftara* for the first day of Passover:

> On the evening of the fourteenth day of the month, while camped at Gilgal on the plains of Jericho, the Israelites celebrated the Passover. *The day after Passover,* that very day, they ate some of the produce of the land: unleavened bread and roasted grain. The manna stopped on that next day when they ate the produce of the land; there was no longer any manna for the Israelites; that year they ate the produce of Canaan. (Josh. 5:10–12)

Here we see the Israelites eating from the new produce "the day after Passover [*mimahorat HaPesah*]," not "the day after the Sabbath." New produce may only be eaten after the Omer has been brought. Clearly then, the Omer was brought on the day after the festival, rather than on a Sunday. The proof is compelling. But Maimonides is implicitly telling us something more. *The offering of the Omer recalls not the beginning but the end of the manna.* If this is so, the implications are immense.

---

5. Shabbat 87b; Rashi, Commentary to Exodus 16:1.
6. Maimonides, *Mishneh Torah, Hilkhot Temidin UMusafin,* 7:11. Note however the objection to this explanation given by Ibn Ezra, Commentary to Leviticus 23:11.

The differences between the manna and the new produce of the land, the food Joshua and his contemporaries were the first to eat, were these:

1. The manna came from the wilderness; the new grain came from the land of Israel.
2. The manna was in many respects miraculous; the new grain was not.
3. The manna was the gift of God; the new grain involved the work of humans, farmers.
4. The manna is described in the Torah as "bread from heaven" (Ex. 16:4); the new grain is "bread from the earth" (Ps. 104:14).
5. The manna was, according to R. Akiva, "bread that the angels eat" (Yoma 75b). The Omer, brought from barley, was coarse food, sometimes the feed of animals.

The manna was special. The Israelites did not have to work for it. There was no ploughing and planting and tending and reaping. It was God's gift. It fell from the sky. New manna appeared every day. All they had to do was collect it. Entering the land must have seemed in one sense a disappointment, an entry into the prosaic quotidian world of labour in the fields and waiting anxiously to see whether the harvest would be a good one or whether it would be ruined by drought, as often happened in the land of Israel.

The mainstream of Judaism, though, has historically taken a different view of the world of work. It contains a polemic against the idea of a leisured class, and a strong sense of the dignity of labour. God Himself, in Genesis 2, plants a garden and fashions the first human from the earth. The first man is himself charged with serving and protecting the garden. "Sweet is the sleep of a labouring man," says Ecclesiastes (5:11). "When you eat from the labour of your hands, you will be happy and it will be well for you," says Psalms (128:2). Flay carcasses rather than be dependent on others, says the third-century Rav.[7] Someone who does not engage in *yishuv haolam*, constructive work, is invalid as a witness in

7.   Y. Berakhot 9:2.

Jewish law.[8] Work is a source of dignity and self-respect. Jewish mysticism coined the phrase *nahama dekisufa*, "the bread of shame," for food you receive from others without having to work for it.

Work is dignity. Work without cease, however, is slavery. *Parekh*, the term used to characterise the labour the Egyptians imposed on the Israelites, probably means work without rest and without an end in sight.[9] That is why Shabbat is central to the project of constructing a world that is not Egypt. Keep Shabbat, said Moses in the second iteration of the Ten Commandments, so that "Your male and female slaves will be able to rest as you do. Remember that you were slaves in Egypt…. It is for this reason that God your Lord has commanded you to keep the Sabbath" (Deut. 5:13–14). Freedom does not mean not working. It means the ability to stop working. Shabbat is the first taste of freedom. *That is why the first day of Passover is described in the Torah as Shabbat.*

What then, for the Pharisees, was the significance of the phrase *maḥorat HaShabbat*, "the day after the Sabbath"? To understand this, we have to go back to the story of creation itself. In six days God created the world, and on the seventh He rested. As the sages read the text, dovetailing the two accounts in Genesis 1 and 2–3, God created the first humans on the sixth day. That same day they sinned and were sentenced to exile from the garden. God granted them one complete day in paradise, Shabbat itself. Immediately after Shabbat they left Eden for the darkness of the world. God however made them "garments of skin" (interpreted in the school of R. Meir of the Mishna as "garments of light")[10] and, according to rabbinic tradition, taught them how to make fire, which is why we make a blessing over light in Havdala, the service to mark the end of Shabbat. If so, the symbolism becomes clear: *On Shabbat we celebrate the world God creates. The day after Shabbat is when we celebrate the world we create.* The phrase *maḥorat HaShabbat* is a metaphor for human endeavour and achievement – the space God makes for us.

The argument between the Boethusians and the Pharisees now takes on a completely new dimension. It is generally argued by scholars

---

8. Sanhedrin 24b.
9. Exodus 1:13–14, normally translated as "with rigour"; Sifra, *Parashat Behar* 25:6.
10. Genesis 3:21; Genesis Rabba 20:21.

that the Sadducees and Boethusians were an elite. They were either priests in the Temple or officials or landowners, as close as Judaism came to a leisured class. The sectarians at Qumran were an elite community who had turned their backs on society as a whole. The Pharisees were largely made up of the working class. The image we have of figures like Hillel, R. Akiva, R. Yehoshua, and others is that they were poor but refused to live on charity. It is to them that we owe many of the key rabbinic statements about the importance of independence and working for a living.

We can now hypothesise that for the Boethusians, Sadducees, and sectarians, the event we would wish to memorialise is the first falling of the manna. This was holy, miraculous, spiritual, the gift of God, bread from heaven that fell through no earthly labour. This, the bread that first fell on Sunday, is what we recall when we offer the Omer, whose dimensions (one-tenth of an ephah) are precisely those of the manna itself. It was the first taste of freedom marking the end of the bread of affliction.

For the Pharisees, the opposite was the case. As long as the Israelites were completely dependent on God they were querulous, ungrateful, rebellious, and immature. That is what dependence does. It arrests the growth of character. The first time the Israelites achieved their real dignity was when they laboured together to build the Tabernacle. They worked. They gave of their time and skills and possessions. There was harmony. They gave so much that Moses had to say to stop. That was their true apprenticeship in liberty.

The supreme moment of religious achievement came when, no longer homeless nomads, they entered the land God had promised Abraham. The first moment they ate of its produce was the first taste of that long-delayed fulfilment. Each year that event was recaptured in a single symbolic moment: the first produce of the grain harvest. This was the dream finally made real: a holy people working the land God had called holy – as His partners in the work of creation. The land was His, the labour was theirs. The rain was His, the grain was theirs. They had sown in tears, now they were reaping in joy.

Though the grain was coarse – barley – and though it was entirely non-miraculous and came from earth, not heaven, it was precious in their eyes because it was precious in God's eyes. It was the humble symbol of the day after Shabbat, the first day of human creation after the seven days of God's creation. They had received so much from God. Now God had given them the greatest gift of all – the ability to give Him a gift. What mattered was not that it was refined like the finest wheat flour (that came later, in the two loaves of Shavuot), but that it was the work of their hands.

Now we can understand in a new light the significance of *counting the days*.[11] Genesis 1 describes divine creation. God said, "Let there be light," and there was light. For God there is no delay between conception and execution, the idea and the fact. For humans, however, there is a delay. *It is the ability to endure delay that makes all human creative achievement possible.* It takes time to become a farmer, to learn how to plough and plant and tend. It takes time to become anything worth becoming.

A slave never learns this. He or she lives in the moment. The master commands, the slave does. The slave does not have to worry about long-term risks and consequences. For the Pharisees, the manna the Israelites ate in the wilderness was not yet the bread of freedom, for it involved no time consciousness. It fell each day, it had to be eaten each day, and except on Friday, it could not be kept for the morrow. The Israelites ate it the way slaves eat their daily subsistence diet. It had the taste of holiness but not yet the taste of freedom.

A free human being has to learn the art of time that goes with risk-taking and creation. He or she has to acquire skill and wisdom, patience, and the ability to persist through many failures without giving way to despair. The fundamental lesson of the wilderness years, as Maimonides emphasises in *The Guide for the Perplexed* (III:32), is the time it takes for erstwhile slaves to acquire the mental and emotional habits of free and responsible human beings. In the case of the Israelites, it took a generation.

The mark of a free human being is the ability to count time, to endure a lengthy delay between the start of a journey and its completion. "Teach us to number our days," says Psalms, "that we may get a heart of wisdom" (Ps. 90:12). Counting the days, without impatience or

11. The traditional explanations are that it represented counting the days to the revelation at Sinai (Maimonides), or counting the days of purification after the defilement of Egypt (Zohar).

attempting shortcuts, is the precondition of all creative endeavour – and at the heart of the Pharisees' and rabbis' creed is the belief that the God of creation wants us to be creative rather than dependent on the creativity of others. There were some who believed otherwise: the wealthy Sadducees, the apocalyptic desert dwellers of Qumran, mystics like R. Shimon bar Yohai, who at one stage apparently believed that the words, "you shall gather in your corn, your wine, and your oil" were not a blessing but a curse, and who viewed with contempt people who ploughed fields.[12] But these were voices at the margins. The mainstream held otherwise.

The Omer is the immensely powerful symbol of an offering from the first fruits of the humanly planted and reaped grain, brought on the anniversary of the day the "bread from heaven" ceased and "bread from the land" of Israel began, coarse, unsophisticated, yet the combined work of land and rain from God and labour from man – partners in the work of creation. The journey to freedom begins on Passover with "Shabbat," the first taste of freedom, which is knowing that you do not have to work without cease. But immediately, on the second day, it passes to "the day after Shabbat," the world of human work, the day on which Adam and Eve left paradise to make their way in the world, a world full of difficulties and threats, yet one in which they are robed, in R. Meir's lovely phrase, in "garments of light." You do not have to live in Eden to be bathed in divine light. Work that is creative is not the work of slaves. But it requires one discipline: the art of counting time or as Freud put it, the ability to defer the gratification of instinct. Much of Jewish law is a form of training in the art of deferring the gratification of instinct.[13]

So the argument about the Omer and its significance was a deep one and not just about the authority of the Oral Law. It was about the nature of the religious life. Does God want us to be involved with society, contributing to it and being creative within it, or is that for others, not for us? It is fair to say that the argument has not yet ceased. This side of the End of Days, perhaps it never will.

12. Berakhot 35b; Shabbat 33b.
13. This is the argument of Maimonides in *The Guide for the Perplexed*, III:33.

Sukkot: The Dual Festival

In each of the three major passages of the Torah where the festivals are set out in detail, there is something unusual about Sukkot. Consider first the list in Deuteronomy 16, where the emphasis is on the civic dimension of the festivals as occasions of social inclusion, when not only "you, your sons, and daughters," celebrate but also "your male and female servants, and the Levites, the foreigners, the fatherless, and the widows who live in your towns."

One of the keywords of Deuteronomy as a whole is s-m-ḥ, collective celebration. It occurs only once in the book of Exodus, once in Leviticus (specifically in the context of Sukkot), and once in the book of Numbers. It appears twelve times in Deuteronomy. And in the passage dealing with the festivals, it occurs not once but twice in connection with Sukkot:

> Be joyful [vesamaḥta] at your festival .... For seven days celebrate the festival to the Lord your God at the place the Lord will choose. For the Lord your God will bless you in all your harvest and in all the work of your hands, and your joy will be complete [vehayita akh same'aḥ]. (Deut. 16:14–15)

Deuteronomy makes no mention of joy in connection with Passover. It mentions it once in relation to Shavuot. In the context of Sukkot, it refers to it twice. Doubtless it was this that led to the traditional description of Sukkot as *zeman simḥatenu*, "the season of our joy." But why a double joy?

The second strange feature appears in this *parasha*, the only place in the Torah to specify the two special practices of Sukkot. This is the first:

> Beginning with the fifteenth day of the seventh month, after you have gathered the crops of the land, celebrate the festival to the Lord for seven days…. On the first day you are to take choice fruit from the trees, and palm fronds, leafy branches, and willows of the brook, and rejoice before the Lord your God for seven days. (Lev. 23:39–40)

This is a reference to the *arba minim*, the "four kinds" – palm branch, citron, myrtle, and willow leaves – taken and waved on Sukkot. The second command is quite different:

> Live in booths for seven days: All native-born Israelites are to live in booths, so your descendants will know that I made the Israelites live in booths when I brought them out of Egypt. I am the Lord your God. (Lev. 23:42–43)

This is the command to leave our houses and live in the temporary dwelling that gives Sukkot its name: the festival of "booths, huts, tabernacles," an annual reminder of the temporary and portable homes in which the Israelites lived during their journey through the wilderness.

No other festival has this dual symbolism. Not only are the "four kinds" and the tabernacle different in character: they are even seemingly *opposed* to one another. The "four kinds" and the rituals associated with them are about *rain*. They were, says Maimonides,[1] the most readily available products of the land of Israel, reminders of the fertility of the land. By contrast, the command to live for seven days in booths, with

1. Maimonides, *The Guide for the Perplexed*, III:43.

only leaves for a roof, presupposes the *absence* of rain. If it rains on Sukkot we are exempt from the command (for as long as the rain lasts, and providing it is sufficiently strong to spoil food on the table).

The difference goes deeper still. On the one hand, Sukkot is the most *universalistic* of all festivals. The prophet Zechariah foresees the day when it will be celebrated by all humanity:

> The Lord will be king over the whole earth. On that day the Lord will be One, and His name the only name…. Then the survivors from all the nations that have attacked Jerusalem will go up year after year to worship the King, the Lord Almighty, and to celebrate the Feast of Tabernacles. If any of the peoples of the earth do not go up to Jerusalem to worship the King, the Lord Almighty, they will have no rain. If the Egyptian people do not go up and take part, they will have no rain. (Zech. 14:9, 16–17)

Hence the interpretation given by the sages about the list of the festivals in the book of Numbers. On Sukkot, seventy bulls were sacrificed in the course of the festival (Num. 29:12–34). The sages say they correspond to the seventy nations (the traditional number of civilisations; see Gen. 10). Following the cues in Zechariah, they said that "On the festival [of Sukkot], the world is judged in the matter of rain."[2] There is nothing distinctively Jewish about the need for rain. All countries, especially in the Middle East, needed it.

At the same time, though, it is also the most *particularist* of festivals. When we sit in the sukka we recall Jewish history – not just the forty years of wandering in the wilderness, but also the entire experience of exile. The sukka is defined as a "temporary dwelling" (*dirat arai*). It is the most powerful symbol of Jewish history. No other nation could see its home not as a castle, a fortress, or a triumphal arch, but as a fragile tabernacle. No other nation was born, not in its land, but in the desert. Far from being universalistic, Sukkot is intensely particularistic, the festival of a people like no other, whose only protection was its faith in the sheltering wings of the Divine Presence.

2. Mishna Rosh HaShana 1:2.

It is almost as if Sukkot were two festivals, not one.

It is, and therein lies its unique character. Although all the festivals are listed together, they in fact represent two quite different cycles. The first is the cycle of Passover, Shavuot, and Sukkot. These tell the particularistic story of Jewish identity and history: the Exodus (Passover), the revelation at Mount Sinai (Shavuot), and the journey through the wilderness (Sukkot). Celebrating them, we re-enact the key moments of Jewish memory. We celebrate what it is to be a Jew.

There is, however, a second cycle: the festivals of the seventh month: Rosh HaShana, Yom Kippur, and Sukkot. Rosh HaShana and Yom Kippur are not only about Jews and Judaism. They are about God and humanity as a whole. The language of the prayers is different. We say: "Instil Your awe upon *all* Your works, and fear of You on *all* that You have created." The liturgy is strikingly universalistic. The Days of Awe are about the sovereignty of God over all humankind. On them, we reflect on the *human*, not just the Jewish, condition.

The two cycles reflect the dual aspect of God: as *creator* and as *redeemer*. As creator, God is universal. We are all in God's image, formed in His likeness. We share a covenant of human solidarity, the Noahide covenant. We are fellow citizens of the world God made and entrusted to our care. As redeemer, however, God is particular. Whatever His relationship to other nations (and He *has* a relationship with other nations – so Amos and Isaiah insist), Jews know Him through His saving acts in Israel's history: Exodus, revelation, and the journey to the Promised Land.

No sooner have we identified the two cycles than we see what makes Sukkot unique. It is the only festival belonging to both. It is part of the cycle of Jewish history (Passover-Shavuot-Sukkot), and part of the sequence of the seventh month (Rosh HaShana-Yom Kippur-Sukkot). Hence the double joy.

The "four kinds" represent the universality of the festival. They symbolise nature, rain, the cycle of the seasons – things common to all humanity. However, the sukka itself, the tabernacle, represents the singular character of Jewish history with its repeated experiences of exile and homecoming and its long journey across the wilderness of time.

In a way not shared by any other festival, Sukkot celebrates the dual nature of Jewish faith: the *universality of God* and the *particularity of Jewish existence*. We all need rain. We are all part of nature. We are all dependent on the complex ecology of the created world. Hence the "four kinds." But each nation, civilisation, religion is different. As Jews, we are heirs to a history unlike that of any other people: small, vulnerable, suffering exile after exile, yet surviving. Hence the sukka.

Humanity is formed out of our commonalities and differences. Our differences give us our identity. Our commonalities give us our humanity. *If we were completely different, we could not communicate. If we were completely alike, we would have nothing to say.* Sukkot brings both together: our uniqueness as a people and our participation in the universal fate of humankind.

The Blasphemer

arashat Emor, which deals with the holiness of priests, the Sanctuary, and time, ends with an episode that has long puzzled commentators. Leviticus, a book of law rather than narrative, is suddenly interrupted by a tragic and disturbing story:

> Now the son of an Israelite mother and an Egyptian father went out among the Israelites, and a fight broke out in the camp between him and an Israelite. The son of the Israelite woman blasphemed the Name with a curse; so they brought him to Moses. (His mother's name was Shelomith, the daughter of Dibri the Danite.) They put him in custody until the will of the Lord would be made clear to them. (Lev. 24:10–12)

Two men start fighting. The text does not tell us why. Evidently, the details of their quarrel are irrelevant to the subject at hand. One of the men, in the course of the struggle, blasphemes. He curses God, or possibly, uses the sacred Name to curse his opponent. Everyone present knew that something serious had happened: that is why they put him in custody immediately. Taking God's name in vain had already been forbidden in the Ten Commandments (Ex. 20:6). Just a few chapters earlier, a law had been given: "Anyone who curses his father or mother is to be put to death" (Ex. 21:17, Lev. 20:9). If cursing your parents is a capital sin, how much more so is cursing God.

What the people were unsure of is whether the law applies to someone of mixed parentage. That much is clear from the answer God eventually gave: "Say to the Israelites: Anyone who curses his God will be held responsible; anyone who blasphemes the name of the Lord shall be put to death…. Whether foreigner or native-born" (Lev. 24:15–16). So their doubt is resolved. But in the course of the revelation, the people learn something else: "Take the blasphemer outside the camp. All those who heard him are to lay their hands on his head," prior to carrying out the punishment. This, as Maimonides notes in his law code, is unique. In no other case of the death sentence do people, in this case the witnesses, lay their hands on the condemned man.[1]

The episode raises many questions. What is the story doing here? Leviticus is not a book of narrative. It contains only one other story, about the death of two of Aaron's sons, Nadav and Avihu, on the day the Sanctuary was consecrated. But that story belonged to the subject at hand, namely the inauguration of the Sanctuary. The story of the blasphemer, by contrast, seems to have no relevance to the subject at hand. It is preceded by laws about the Menora and the show bread. It is followed by the social legislation of Leviticus 25. The Torah deals with curses elsewhere. So why is it here?

Even stranger is the fact that the revelation in which God tells Moses the punishment for the offender does not end there. It passes immediately to another topic, one about which Moses had not asked:

> Whoever takes a human life is to be put to death. One who takes the life of an animal must make restitution – life for life. One who injures his neighbour, as he has done so shall it be done to him: fracture for fracture, eye for eye, tooth for tooth. One who has inflicted an injury must suffer the same injury. One who kills an

---

1. Maimonides, *Mishneh Torah, Hilkhot Avodat Kokhavim*, 2:10.

animal must make restitution, but one who kills a human being is to be put to death. (Lev. 24:17–21)

This is the famous and much misunderstood *lex talionis*, the law of retribution. As the sages make clear, the principle of "an eye for an eye" was never meant literally.[2] A world based on a literal practice of an eye for an eye would eventually go blind. Other than in the case of murder, it meant monetary compensation. The principle is simply that the punishment must fit the crime. It was meant restrictively, to forbid either excessive leniency or excessive harshness.

The question here, though, is this: What are these laws doing here, in the middle of the story of the blasphemer? Seemingly, they have nothing to do with one another. The blasphemer has committed a sin against God. The laws that follow are about crimes against people or property. One is spiritual, the others are physical. Yet they are presented seamlessly as part of a single narrative, as God's answer to Moses' question. But Moses did not ask about injury. He asked about blasphemy. Besides which, he and the people already knew the laws about injury and murder. They appear in the book of Exodus (21:24–25). There seems to be no connection between them whatsoever.

It may be that the story of the blasphemer is brought here because Leviticus has been about the sanctity of time, person, and place. The Torah now turns to sanctity of speech. Just as special care must be taken in entering the house of God, so must the same care be taken about using the name of God. The priests had already been warned: "Do not profane My holy name, that I may be sanctified in the midst of the Children of Israel. I am the Lord who sanctify you" (Lev. 22:32). The story of the blasphemer tells us that the same applies to ordinary Israelites, "whether foreigner or native-born." The reason the law is told by way of a story may simply be because that is how it happened. Moses and the Israelites learned the law because of an incident that occurred.

Holiness, Leviticus tells from chapter 19 onward, is not only the special preserve of an elite, the priests. It belongs to the people as a whole, for they are "a kingdom of priests and a holy nation." Not only are there

2. Bava Kamma 84a.

holy times and holy places that must be honoured and not abused. So there are holy words. Language itself can sometimes be sacred.

The story may be conveying no more than this. But there is another possibility. Recall that the story of the blasphemer occurs at the end of chapter 24 in Leviticus. The next chapter begins with the words, "The Lord said to Moses at Mount Sinai." According to most commentators, the remaining chapters (25–27) were actually recorded earlier, *before* the construction of the Sanctuary. The first twenty-four chapters of Leviticus are set several months later, *after* the construction. So the episode of the blasphemer represents the end of the long sequence of laws which began forty chapters earlier (Ex. 25:1), about the Sanctuary, sacrifices, the priesthood, purity, and the entire code of holiness as it applied to the people as a whole. Why end this literary unit, which stands at the very centre of the Torah, with so negative a note?

The end of the book of Exodus gives us a clue. As we have noted,[3] Exodus ends the way Genesis begins: with an act of creation. In Genesis it was God's creation of the universe. In Exodus it was the Israelites' creation of the Sanctuary, the microcosmos, the universe in miniature. The connection is deliberate. In the beginning, God created order. Then He gave humans free will and they proceeded to create chaos. Only with the completion of the Sanctuary do we find humans creating order, symbolised in the holy place they have made for God. Perhaps the Torah wants us to make the same connection in the case of Leviticus also. To understand the end we must revisit the beginning.

The Torah begins with a swift set of narratives telling us in a highly schematic way about humanity's decline and fall. First comes the story of Adam and Eve, then Cain and Abel, followed by the generation of the Flood. These are not three independent stories. They are three chapters in a single story. It begins with what seems to be a minor offence. Adam and Eve eat forbidden fruit. They do not harm anyone. There is no physical injury. All they do is transgress a boundary between permitted and forbidden. But small acts have large consequences. A generation later, their eldest son commits murder. Within a few generations, "God saw the world, and it was corrupted. All flesh had perverted its way on the

---

3. *Covenant and Conversation: Exodus – The Book of Redemption*, 329–337.

earth." Violence had become pervasive. Humanity had reached a dead end. What begins as a seemingly minor offence, a crossing of boundaries, never ends there. An offence against God eventually leads to assaults against humans. Spiritual sins lead to physical crimes. Once boundaries are disrespected, a process has begun that leads, not immediately but ultimately, to civilisational breakdown.

That is one of the defining insights of *Torat Kohanim*, priestly consciousness. We can summarise it in a single sentence: *sacred order leads to social order*. The two are inextricably intertwined. When people lose their fear of God, eventually they lose their other inhibitions. They become creatures of impulse and desire, and the end of this long road is violence. The priest is the guardian of this truth. It is an unpopular one. The serpent is always waiting in the wings, saying to us as he said to Eve: "What harm is there in eating one forbidden fruit?" Yet the result is paradise lost. A world God created and pronounced good can all too easily be destroyed if we forget the concept of boundaries and the habits of self-restraint.

This story, told in the first six chapters of Genesis, is told again near the end of Leviticus in the single story of the blasphemer. It begins with the crossing of a boundary. The man is "the son of an Israelite mother and an Egyptian father." Recall that the story is set about a year after the Exodus and the man is already mature. So we are dealing with a woman who, in Egypt itself, had physical relations with a member of the nation that was oppressing her people.[4] A line had been crossed.

The next fact we are told is that "a fight broke out in the camp between him and an Israelite." There is physical violence. Immediately thereafter we read: "The son of the Israelite woman blasphemed the Name with a curse." There is a desecration of God's holy name. What follows, as we have seen, is that God not only answers the question put to Him – what is the punishment for blasphemy? – but goes on to repeat the laws about murder and injury. Sacred and secular, spiritual and physical, offences against God and crimes against human beings are indissolubly connected. Sacred order and social order go together.

---

4. There are many midrashic traditions, some of which say that the Egyptian was the man Moses saw beating an Israelite slave.

Lose one and you will eventually lose the other. That is the message with which the book of Leviticus draws to a close.

The question to which the story of the blasphemer is the answer is this: Why is there a book of the Torah – indeed the central book – entirely dedicated to the subject of the holy? What difference does it make to have God at the heart of a society, symbolised by the Sanctuary and its service?

The fundamental issue addressed by the Torah is violence and the misuse of power. That has remained the greatest threat to the future of humankind from the dawn of history to today. There is more than one way of thinking about violence. There is the way of wisdom: Judaism's insights into philosophy and the social sciences. There is the way of prophecy, focusing on emotion and the moral sense. And there is the way of priesthood, whose central insight is the connection between sacred order and social order. When human beings lose respect for God, they eventually lose respect for humanity. Therefore, the way to defend humanity is to make sure people never lose their respect for God.

Does blasphemy injure God? No. The very idea is blasphemous. God cannot be injured, but humanity can. Blasphemy injures society by desecrating the sacred. That is why, uniquely in this case, the witnesses are to lay their hands on the sinner, to indicate that they understand that this affects all of them. Language has been debased. Something sacred has been abused. A word – God's name – that signals peace has been used like a weapon in a fight.

The message of Leviticus throughout is that life itself is holy. Everything to do with the Sanctuary had to be cleansed of connections with death and mortality. People, not just priests, are holy, as is the whole of life, not just edited parts of it. So we have to be holy in the way we eat, the way we conduct our most intimate sexual relationships, and the way we use language. We must not curse even the deaf, let alone our parents, let alone God Himself, because verbal abuse leads to physical abuse. A sense of the sacred is what lifts us above instinct and protects us from our dysfunctional drives. What begins with dishonouring God ends by desecrating humanity.

Behar
בהר

Parashat Behar consists of a single chapter that, despite its brevity, had a transformative impact on the social structure of ancient Israel and provided a unique solution to the otherwise intractable conflict between two fundamental ideals: freedom and equality. Much of human history has illustrated the fact that you can have freedom without equality (laissez-faire economics), or equality without freedom (communism, socialism), but not both. The powerful insight of the Torah is that you can have both, but not at the same time. Therefore time itself has to become part of the solution, in the form of the seventh year and, after seven sabbatical cycles, the Jubilee. These become periodic corrections to the distortions of the free market that allow some to become rich while others suffer the loss of land, home, and even freedom. Through the periodic liberation of slaves, release of debts, and restoration of ancestral lands, the Torah provides a still-inspiring alternative to individualism on the one hand, collectivism on the other.

The first of the essays that follow is about the principle that underlies the social legislation here and elsewhere in the Torah, the legal principle known as eminent domain. This sheds fascinating light on the connection in Judaism between creation, redemption, and law. The second is about the difference between the politics of revolution and those of evolution and why the Torah prefers the latter. The third is about a key term in Judaism, "redemption," and explains why it is a concept of both history and law.

The fourth is about what I call the chronological imagination – a way of thinking about truth as something that unfolds through the medium of time, as opposed to the logical imagination of the Greeks that sees truth as essentially timeless. The fifth is about the Torah's solution to the conflict between freedom and equality, and the sixth about its pioneering statement of minority rights.

Eminent Domain

The vision of a just society, set out in *Parashat Behar*, brings to the fore with exceptional clarity two instances of a fundamental principle of Judaism. Once we understand it, we will see the Torah and Judaism itself differently. It will shed new light on the creation narrative in Genesis 1. It will help us understand one of the most beautiful of Jewish laws, that of making a blessing over the things we enjoy: over food, drink, beautiful sights, and so on. And it will suggest a surprising answer to the question: What difference does religious belief make to the moral life?

The principle is simply this: *God is the ultimate owner of the universe.* What we possess, we do not own, we merely hold in trust, and there are conditions to that trust, most fundamental of which is that we must show concern for the good of all. We find this principle set out twice in Leviticus 25, in different contexts.

The first has to do with the land. The context is the Jubilee, the fiftieth year in which land that people were forced to sell because of poverty returns to its original owners. This raises the obvious question: How can a valid sale be revoked at some later stage? The Torah gives the following answer:

The land may not be sold permanently, because *the land is Mine.*
You are strangers and temporary residents as far as I am concerned. Therefore, there shall be a time of redemption for all your
hereditary lands. (Lev. 25:23–24)

Because the land of Israel belongs to God, there can be no permanent
freehold. God grants the Israelites possession of it on certain conditions,
one of which is that the original owner can buy it back for a fair price at
any time he has the money and wishes to do so. The other is that in any
case, it returns to the original owner in the Jubilee year.

The second example has to do with the treatment of Israelites
forced to sell themselves into servitude. They are not to be treated as
slaves, but rather as hired workers or temporary hands. Nor should they
be treated ruthlessly in a way that breaks their spirit. And they must go
free in the Jubilee year. Explaining why, the Torah twice invokes the
principle that Israelites are, first and foremost, God's servants. Therefore
no Israelite may enslave a fellow Israelite:

Because *the Israelites are My servants*, whom I brought out of
Egypt, they must not be sold as slaves. (Lev. 25:42)

For *the Israelites belong to Me as servants.* They are My servants, whom I brought out of Egypt. I am the Lord your God.
(Lev. 25:55)

On what are these two statements – God's ownership of the land, and
His prior claim to the service of the Israelites – based? The answer to the
second is that God *redeemed* the Israelites from slavery in Egypt. *Geula,*
redemption, is a legal as well as religious term. It means "to buy back."
Thus God, redeeming the Israelites, became in legal terms their owner.

That is the meaning of one of the phrases in the song the Israelites
sang at the Red Sea: "until Your people pass by, Lord, until the people
You acquired [*kanita*] pass by" (Ex. 15:16). The passage of the Israelites
through the sea is construed here as *a legal act of acquisition* on the part
of God. The people pass from Egypt, the domain of Pharaoh, to the
desert and thus into the domain of God.

On what specific legal basis does God own the land of Israel? To answer this, we must turn back to Genesis 1, the biblical account of creation. This has been understood throughout the ages as one of three things. Some read it as a historical narrative, an answer to the question: "What happened?" Others read it as a kind of early proto-scientific account, an answer to the question: "How did it happen? How did the universe come into being?" Yet others have understood it as a philosophical statement about the relationship of God to the universe. He is the first cause, the prime mover, the necessity that underlies our contingency, the eternity that frames our existence in time. We are because He is.

However, these are all *mis*readings of the creation narrative. We know this because of the name of the book. Torah means not history or science or philosophy but *law* in the widest sense of the word. The Torah is primarily a legal and moral text. It is an answer to the question: How shall we live? Genesis 1 is first and foremost a foundational statement about law itself. It is a jurisprudential text: that is, it sets out the basis of divine authority, God's right to issue the laws and commands that are the principled bases of human existence. It is there to provide an answer to the fundamental question of any legal system: By what authority does a legislator legislate? What is the source and justification of sovereignty? By what right does x rule over y?

There is a principle in Jewish law that states that a craftsman acquires title to a work he has created[1] – the same principle that, for example, underlies the idea of intellectual copyright. We own what we create. That is the point of Genesis 1. God created the world. Therefore He owns the world.[2] Therefore He can lay down conditions under which He allows others to live there.

This is not a historical, scientific, or philosophical point but a legal one, and it applies generally, not just in the case of God or Judaism. It arises, for example, in the context of the rule attributed in the Talmud

---

1. See Kiddushin 48b.
2. This is the meaning of the description of God in Genesis 14:19, 22, as "owner of heaven and earth" (*koneh shamayim vaaretz*). There are those who argue that the word *koneh* in other ancient Semitic languages also means "creator" as well as owner, but that is just the point. Legally, the creator of something is its owner.

to the third-century sage Shmuel, known as *dina demalkhuta dina,* "the law of the land is law."[3] As exiles in lands not their own, under a legal and political order they did not initiate, Jews nonetheless accept the authority of the law of the land. The Talmud states this as a rule, and in the Middle Ages the commentators asked: What was its basis?

Several suggestions were offered. The most fundamental, argued by the Rosh (Rabbenu Asher) and cited by Rabbenu Nissim in the name of the Tosafists, is that the king is the ultimate owner of the land within his jurisdiction. He is therefore legally entitled to specify the conditions under which he allows others to live there. This is called the principle of eminent domain, whereby the head of state or the state itself holds a prior title to the land within its borders, and can thus, for reasons of state, order the compulsory purchase of land even against the will of its owners.

The Torah opens with a creation narrative *to establish the principle of eminent domain as the legal relationship between God and the universe.* This is remarkable. What it tells us is that God rules by right, not might. Even though God is the force of forces, who turns the sea into dry land, sends bread from heaven and water from a rock, He rules not as a tyrant by virtue of power[4] but as a constitutional monarch answerable to the claims of righteousness and justice ("the ways of the Lord," Gen. 18:19). That is both a revelation and a revolution. It represents the first and most systematic attempt in the history of human thought to ethicise the universe and all that is therein.

The Torah lives with the fact that in its time – and in ours – this is not how politics is normally constructed or societies shaped. They are usually the result of the distribution of power, political, military, or economic. Hence the decision of God, after the Flood and the Tower of Babel, to reveal His sovereignty through one people – a people who completely lacked any political, military, and economic power of their own, namely the Israelites. What Leviticus 25 makes clear is that God's sovereignty over Israel, the people and the land, is rooted in the principle of eminent domain. God's ultimate ownership of both is the basis of the biblical vision of the just society.

3. Nedarim 28a; Gittin 10b; Bava Kamma 113a.
4. Avoda Zara 3a.

Ideally, people should care for one another because of benevolence, empathy, sympathy, and compassion, the "better angels of our nature." Leviticus 19 sets out just such a code based on the love of neighbour and stranger. Ideally too, people should see society as an extended family and thus help one another out of a sense of kinship and fraternity. That is why Leviticus 25 repeatedly uses the word *aḥikha*, "your brother," when it actually means "your fellow Israelite." But such feelings are too fragile a basis for a gracious social order. Kinship and neighbourliness are for relatives and friends. We rarely extend them to complete strangers, especially when our own interests are at stake. Therefore Leviticus 25 grounds its vision of social justice on a fundamental legal principle: the ownership of God.

According to the sages, it is this principle we reiterate every time we make a blessing over something we enjoy. The Talmud points to the apparent contradiction between two verses in Psalms.[5] On the one hand, "The earth is the Lord's and the fullness thereof" (Ps. 24:1). On the other, "The heavens belong to the Lord, but the earth He has given to the children of men" (Ps. 115:16). The Talmud resolves the contradiction by saying that the first applies before we have made a blessing, the second after we have made a blessing. In other words, every time we say a blessing over food or drink, we are doing more than thanking God. We are acknowledging the *ownership* of God. The food we eat and the wine we drink are His. We "redeem" them, that is, buy them back for secular use, by means of the benediction.

This extraordinary integrated vision, extending from the creation of the universe to the laws of land ownership and employment law in biblical Israel, to the blessings we say over bread and wine, derives from and constantly rehearses the law of eminent domain. God is the ultimate owner of all and we are mere strangers and temporary residents on earth. That is a vision more likely in the long run to produce societal beatitude than any secular political ideology in the history of human thought.

---

5.   Berakhot 35a.

Evolution or Revolution?

There are, it is sometimes said, no controlled experiments in history. Every society, every age, and every set of circumstances is unique. So there is no science of history. There are no universal rules to guide the destiny of nations. Yet this is not quite true. The history of the past four centuries does offer us something close to a controlled experiment, and the conclusion to be drawn is surprising.

The modern world was shaped by four revolutions: the English (1642–1651), the American (1776), the French (1789), and the Russian (1917). Their outcomes were radically different. In England and America, revolution brought war, but led to a gradual growth of civil liberties, human rights, representative government, and eventually, democracy. On the other hand, the French revolution gave rise to the "Reign of Terror" between September 5, 1793, and July 28, 1794, in which more than forty thousand enemies of the revolution were summarily executed by the guillotine. The Russian revolution led to one of the most repressive totalitarianism regimes in history. As many as twenty million people are estimated to have died unnatural deaths under Stalin between 1924 and 1953. In revolutionary France and the Soviet Union, the dream of utopia ended in a nightmare of hell.

What was the salient difference between them? There are multiple explanations. History is complex and it is wrong to simplify, but one in particular stands out. The English and American revolutions were inspired by the Hebrew Bible as read and interpreted by the Puritans. This happened because of the convergence of a number of factors in the sixteenth and seventeenth centuries: the Reformation, the invention of printing, the rise of literacy and the spread of books, and the availability of the Hebrew Bible in vernacular translations. For the first time, people could read the Bible for themselves, and what they discovered when they read the prophets and stories of civil disobedience like that of Shifrah and Puah, the Hebrew midwives, was that it is permitted, even sometimes necessary, to resist tyrants in the name of God. The political philosophy of the English revolutionaries and the Puritans who set sail for America in the 1620s and 1630s was dominated by the work of the Christian Hebraists who based their thought on the history of ancient Israel.[1]

The French and Russian revolutions, by contrast, were hostile to religion and were inspired instead by philosophy: that of Jean-Jacques Rousseau in the case of France, and of Karl Marx in the case of Russia. There are obvious differences between Torah and philosophy. The most well-known is that one is based on revelation, the other on reason. Yet I suspect it was not this that made the difference to the course of revolutionary politics. Rather, it lay in their respective understandings of time.

Parashat Behar sets out a revolutionary template for a society of justice, freedom, and human dignity. At its core is the idea of the Jubilee, whose words ("Proclaim liberty throughout all the land unto all the inhabitants thereof") are engraved on one of the great symbols of freedom, the Liberty Bell in Philadelphia. One of its provisions is the release of slaves:

> If your brother becomes impoverished and is sold to you, do not work him like a slave. He shall be with you like an employee or a resident. He shall serve you only until the Jubilee year and then he and his children shall be free to leave you and return to their

1. See Eric Nelson, *The Hebrew Republic: Jewish Sources and the Transformation of European Political Thought* (Cambridge, Mass.: Harvard University Press, 2010).

family and to the hereditary land of their ancestors. For they are My servants whom I brought out of the land of Egypt; they shall not be sold as slaves. Do not subjugate them through hard labour – you shall fear your God…. For the Children of Israel are servants to Me: they are My servants whom I brought out of the land of Egypt – I am the Lord your God. (Lev. 25:39–42)

The terms of the passage are clear. Slavery is wrong. It is an assault on the human condition. To be "in the image of God" means to be summoned to a life of freedom. The very idea of the sovereignty of God means that He alone has claim to the service of mankind. Those who are God's servants may not be slaves to anyone else. As Judah Halevi put it, "The servants of time are servants of servants. Only God's servant alone is free."[2]

At this distance of time it is hard to recapture the radicalism of this idea, overturning as it did the very foundations of religion in ancient times. The early civilisations – Mesopotamia, Egypt – were based on hierarchies of power which were seen to inhere in the very nature of the cosmos. Just as there were (so it was believed) ranks and gradations among the heavenly bodies, so there were on earth. The great religious rituals and monuments were designed to mirror and endorse these hierarchies. In this respect, Karl Marx was right. Religion in antiquity was the opium of the people. It was the robe of sanctity concealing the naked brutality of power. It canonised the status quo.

At the heart of Israel was an idea almost unthinkable to the ancient mind: that God intervenes in history to liberate slaves – that the supreme Power is on the side of the powerless. It is no accident that Israel was born as a nation under conditions of slavery. It has carried throughout history the memory of those years – the bread of affliction and the bitter herbs of servitude – because the people of Israel serves as an eternal reminder to itself and the world of the moral necessity of liberty and the vigilance needed to protect it. The free God desires the free worship of free human beings.

2. *Ninety-Two Poems and Hymns of Judah Halevi*, trans. Thomas Kovach, Eva Jospe, and Gilya Gerda Schmidt (Albany, NY: State University of New York Press, 2000), 124.

Yet the Torah does not abolish slavery. That is the paradox at the heart of *Parashat Behar*. To be sure, it was limited and humanised. Every seventh day, slaves were granted rest and a taste of freedom. In the seventh year, Israelite slaves were set free. If they chose otherwise they were released in the Jubilee year. During their years of service they were to be treated like employees. They were not to be subjected to back-breaking or spirit-crushing labour. Everything dehumanising about slavery was forbidden. Yet slavery itself was not banned. Why not? If it was wrong, it should have been annulled. Why did the Torah allow a fundamentally flawed institution to continue?

It is Moses Maimonides in *The Guide for the Perplexed* who explains the need for *time* in social transformation. All processes in nature, he argues, are gradual. The foetus develops slowly in the womb. Stage by stage, a child becomes mature. And what applies to individuals applies to nations and civilisations:

> It is impossible to go suddenly from one extreme to the other. It is therefore, according to the nature of man, impossible for him suddenly to discontinue everything to which he has been accustomed.[3]

So God did not ask of the Israelites that they suddenly abandon everything they had become used to in Egypt. "God refrained from prescribing what the people by their natural disposition would be incapable of obeying." But surely God can do anything, including changing human nature. Why then did He not simply transform the Israelites, making them capable immediately of the highest virtue? Maimonides' answer is simple:

> I do not say this because I believe that it is difficult for God to change the nature of every individual person. On the contrary, it is possible and it is in His power... but it has never been His will to do it, and it never will be. If it were part of His will to change the nature of any person, the mission of the prophets and the giving of the Torah would have been superfluous.[4]

3. Maimonides, *The Guide for the Perplexed*, III:32.
4. Ibid.

In miracles, God changes physical nature but never *human* nature. Were He to do so, the entire project of the Torah – the free worship of free human beings – would have been rendered null and void. There is no greatness in programming a million computers to obey instructions. God's greatness lay in taking the risk of creating a being, Homo sapiens, capable of choice and responsibility and thus of freely obeying God.

God wanted mankind to abolish slavery, but *by its own choice, in its own time.* Ancient economies were dependent on slavery. The particular form dealt with in *Parashat Behar* (slavery through poverty) was the functional equivalent of what is today called "workfare," i.e., welfare benefit in return for work. Slavery as such was not abolished in Britain and America until the nineteenth century, and in America, not without a civil war. The challenge to which Torah legislation was an answer is: how can one create a social structure in which, of their own accord, people will eventually come to see slavery as wrong and freely choose to abandon it?

The answer lay in a single deft stroke: to change slavery from an *ontological condition* to a *temporary circumstance*: from what I am to a situation in which I find myself, now but not forever. No Israelite was allowed to be treated or to see himself as a slave. He might be reduced to slavery for a period of time, but this was a passing plight, not an identity. Compare the account given by Aristotle:

> By analogy, [the difference between animals and human beings] must necessarily apply to mankind as a whole. Therefore all men who differ from one another by as much as the soul differs from the body or man from a wild beast...these people are slaves by nature, and it is better for them to be subject to this kind of control, as it is better for the other creatures I have mentioned [i.e., domesticated animals]. For a man who is able to belong to another person is by nature a slave.[5]

For Aristotle, slavery is an ontological condition, a fact of birth. Some are born to rule, others to be ruled. This is precisely the worldview to which the Torah is opposed. The entire complex of biblical legislation

5.   Aristotle, *Politics* I:5.

is designed to ensure that neither the slave nor his owner should ever see slavery as a permanent condition. A slave should be treated "like an employee or a resident," in other words, with the same respect as is due a free human being. In this way the Torah ensured that, although slavery could not be abolished overnight, it would eventually be. And so it happened.

There are profound differences between philosophy and Judaism, and one lies in their respective understandings of time. For Plato and his heirs, philosophy is about the truth that is *timeless*. For Hegel and Marx, it is about "historical inevitability," the change that comes, regardless of the conscious decisions of human beings. Judaism is about ideals like human freedom that are realised *in and through time, by the free decisions of free persons.*

That is why we are commanded to hand on the story of the Exodus to our children every Passover, so that they too taste the unleavened bread of affliction and the bitter herbs of slavery. It is why we are instructed to ensure that every seventh day, all those who work for us are able to rest and breathe the expansive air of freedom. It is why, even when there were Israelite slaves, they had to be released in the seventh year, or failing that, in the Jubilee year. This is the way of evolution, not revolution, gradually educating every member of Israelite society that it is wrong to enslave others so that eventually the entire institution will be abolished, not by divine fiat but by human consent. The end result is a freedom that is secure, as opposed to the freedom of the philosophers that is all too often another form of tyranny. Chillingly, Rousseau once wrote that if citizens did not agree with the "general will," they would have to be "forced to be free." That is not liberty but slavery.

In his *Essays in the History of Liberty*, Lord Acton argued that it was in ancient Israel, not the Athens of antiquity, that freedom was born:

> Thus the example of the Hebrew nation laid down the parallel lines on which all freedom has been won – the doctrine of national tradition and the doctrine of the higher law; the principle that a constitution grows from a root, by process of development, and not of essential change; and the principle that all political

authorities must be tested and reformed according to a code which was not made by man.[6]

The Torah is based, as its narratives make clear, on history, a realistic view of human character, and a respect for freedom and choice. Philosophy is often detached from history and a concrete sense of humanity. Philosophy sees truth as *system*. The Torah tells truth as *story*, and a story is a sequence of events extended through time. Revolutions based on philosophical systems fail because change in human affairs takes time, and philosophy has rarely given an adequate account of the human dimension of time.

Revolutions based on Tanakh succeed, because they go with the grain of human nature, recognising that it takes time for people to change. The Torah did not abolish slavery, but it set in motion a process that would lead people to come of their own accord to the conclusion that it was wrong. That it did so, albeit slowly, is one of the wonders of history.

6. Lord Acton, *Essays in the History of Liberty* (Indianapolis: Liberty Classics, 1985), 8.

The Concept of Redemption

Oce idea central to Judaism but difficult to explain in terms of Western thought is the close interlinking between law, ethics, and nature. For the ancient Greeks there was a conflict between *nomos*, law, and *physis*, nature. Law represented order, nature meant chaos, and there was a constant struggle between them. Apollo, god of order, found himself having to fight snakes, dragons, and sea monsters, symbols of the wild, untameable forces at work in the universe. As for ethics, these were hardly the interest of the gods at all. The word "ethics" comes from the Greek *ethos*, meaning the character of an individual or a community. It also meant custom, established practice. That is what ethics were: not divinely mandated edicts, but rather man-made customs that varied from place to place.

In Judaism, these concepts – law, ethics, and nature – are part of a single, coherent, integrated vision of the universe and our place within it. There is a direct connection between scientific law[1] and moral law.

---

1. This, of course, is an anachronistic way of putting it. The word "science" is a relatively recent coinage, and scientific method in the modern sense dates from the seventeenth century. The regularity of nature was, however, well known to the ancients

Both are part of the fabric of the universe, made by a loving Creator. The one difference is that the moral law, handed over to humans endowed with free will, can be broken. God creates natural order in the universe and asks us to create order in the social universe, and in the same way: through law.

There is also a deep connection in Judaism – equally strange to the Western mind insofar as it was influenced by Greece – between *law* and *narrative*.[2] In the West, there are narratives (mythic, historical, or fictional) and there are laws, legislated by parliaments and collected in codes. But the two literatures are utterly distinct. We know that constitutional monarchy emerged after the invention of printing and the spread of literacy, that democracy grew under the impact of the industrial revolution, and that the enfranchisement of women emerged as old social systems crumbled in the wake of the First World War. So there may be a connection between law and history, but they remain two different literatures with very little in common.

Not so in the case of Judaism. The Torah contains both and weaves them together in deep and subtle ways. Law generates history and history generates law. The history of Israel as seen through the eyes of Tanakh is the story of how Israel kept or broke the laws it received from God. And the laws themselves had their logic in the history of the people: "Do not oppress a stranger; you yourselves know how it feels to be a stranger, because you were strangers in Egypt" (Ex. 23:9). It was precisely because of their historical experience, regularly recalled and re-enacted, that the Israelites were expected to understand the law.

So the Torah weaves law, ethics, and narrative together using an extraordinary array of literary techniques. I want in this essay to show how it does so in the form of a single word, *g-a-l*, meaning "to redeem."

The last three chapters of Leviticus, 25–27, the *parashot* of *Behar* and *Beḥukkotai*, form a single literary unit.[3] They seem to be about completely different subjects. Chapter 25 is about the social structure

and the Mesopotamians and Egyptians achieved astonishingly accurate predictions of, for example, the movements of the planets and the regularity of the seasons.

2.   See Robert Cover's famous article, "Nomos and Narrative," *Harvard Law Review* (1983).

3.   This is one reason why they are often read together.

to be implemented in the land of Israel. It deals with issues relating to land, slavery, and debt. Chapter 26 is about the blessings and curses that will be Israel's fate in the land, depending on whether they are faithful or disobedient to the covenant they made with God at Mount Sinai. Chapter 27 reads like an appendix to the book as a whole, and deals with donations to the Sanctuary.

On the face of it there is no connection between them, but actually they are very tightly integrated. First, note how they are joined together. Chapters 25 and 27 are about law, while chapter 26 is about history. This is a literary device we find elsewhere. A central chapter is framed by being placed between two passages that seem to belong together. So the "holiness code" of Leviticus 19 is framed by chapters 18 and 20, which belong together because both are about sexual offences. The story of the Golden Calf (Ex. 32–34) is framed by being placed between two sections (Ex. 25–31 and Ex. 35–40) that belong to one another because they are both about the construction of the Sanctuary. The priestly imagination works through the device of chiasmus – a literary unit of the form ABCBA, in which the climax is in the centre. So it uses framing devices (AB and BA) to draw attention to the central term as the axis on which all else turns.

What unites Leviticus 25 and 27 is a shared keyword: the verb *g-a-l*, "to redeem," which features in chapter 25 nineteen times and in chapter 27, twelve times. Significantly, though it does not appear at all in chapter 26, another word that sounds almost identical – *g-'-l* (with the guttural *ayin* in place of the *aleph*) – does appear five times. This is fascinating because the two words, despite their similarity in sound, are almost opposite in meaning. The first means "to redeem, buy back, restore to its proper place," while the second means "to despise, cast away, reject." As I noted in an earlier essay,[4] the beginning and end of Leviticus are linked by a similar play on two words that sound almost the same but have opposite meanings, *k-r-a*, meaning "a call," and *k-r-h*, meaning "a chance event."

Turning to the word *g-a-l* itself, the basic idea of redemption is that the law provides for the possibility of reclaiming land, property, or

4. "Between Destiny and Chance," above.

even liberty itself if one has the means to do so. Leviticus 25 discusses three cases in which an individual finds himself forced, through poverty, to sell something valuable. It may be land, or a house, or selling himself as a slave. In each case, provision is made for a relative of the seller, or the seller himself should he suddenly find himself with the means to do so, to buy it back by providing the buyer with appropriate compensation. If neither of these is possible then redemption will automatically take place in the Jubilee year (with the exception of a house in a walled city).

At stake in these laws are two deep ethical principles. First is that when it comes to certain goods essential to human dignity – land, a house, and freedom of employment – a distinction must be made between temporary poverty and permanent deprivation. The market economy functions on the basis of binding exchange. If I sell something to a purchaser at a price both of us accept as fair, I cannot change my mind tomorrow and say, "I have decided not to sell it after all. Give it back and I will return your money." If the purchaser does not want to do so, I cannot force him. But there are certain things, says the Torah, that should not be left entirely to the vagaries of the market because they are too fundamental to self-respect and human flourishing. In such cases, while respecting the integrity of the market – the redeemer must pay the proper market value of what he redeems – a basic law of justice takes priority. No one should be permanently disadvantaged because of temporary misfortune.

The second, no less fundamental, is the role of the family within society. Leviticus 25 uses familial language (what the French revolutionaries called "fraternity") throughout: "If *your brother* becomes poor." But there is a difference between this metaphorical use of the term to describe society as an extended family, and the literal use to signal the duty of close relatives to come to the aid of an impoverished member of the family. Set out here for the first time is the idea later articulated by Edmund Burke: "We begin our public affections in our families."[5] By caring for those closest to us we learn to care for our fellow citizens

---

5. Edmund Burke, *Reflections on the French Revolution*, The Harvard Classics, vol. XXIV, part 3, paragraph 331 (New York: P.F. Collier & Son, 1909–14), www.bartleby.com/24/3/.

as a whole. The family is "the first link in the series by which we proceed towards a love to our country, and to mankind."[6] Evolutionary psychologists have recently reminded us that sacrifice for the sake of kin is a fundamental principle of human nature. The Torah embodies this idea in the laws of redemption. Tanakh later gives it moving narrative expression in the book of Ruth, in Boaz's willingness to come to the aid of his impoverished relative Naomi and her widowed, childless daughter-in-law Ruth. *Geula* is a keyword of that narrative also, appearing more than twenty times in the course of the book.

But redemption is more than a legal idea. It is the way the Torah describes God's intervention in history to liberate the Israelites from slavery in Egypt. God tells Moses, "I am the Lord, and I will bring you out from under the yoke of the Egyptians. I will free you from being slaves to them, and *I will redeem you* with an outstretched arm and with mighty acts of judgement. I will take you as My own people, and I will be your God" (Ex. 6:6–7). At the Red Sea the Israelites sang, "In Your unfailing love, You led the people You *redeemed*" (Ex. 15:13).

Only now, retrospectively, given the laws of Leviticus 25, do we understand the significance of the first words God commands Moses to say to Pharaoh: "This is what God says: Israel is My son, My firstborn" (Ex. 4:22). God is doing more than rescuing people from oppression or liberating slaves. He is engaged in an *act of redemption*, that is to say, exercising the right and responsibility of a close relative, in this case a father. The fusion here between law, ethics, and narrative, and between God's interventions in history and our duties within society, is complete.[7] In the Exodus, God was engaged in more than miracles. He was teaching us how we too ought to behave when people close to us fall into destitution.

To be sure, the Torah does more than leave redemption to the willingness of family members to do their duty. The Jubilee provided equal redemption for all, even for those who did not have willing and

6. Ibid., IV, 50.
7. For an extended study of the connection between law, narrative, and theology in relation to the idea of redemption, see David Daube, *Studies in Biblical Law* (Cambridge, UK: Cambridge University Press, 1947), 39–62.

wealthy relatives to come to their rescue before then. What I have tried to show here, though, is how law and theology are intrinsically linked in the Torah. One word, *geula*, redemption, figures in both, and in the same sense: restoring something, be it land, a house, or a person, to its proper place after it had been forfeited because of misfortune.

This becomes an essential element of a world of hope, not in the trivial sense of wishing or wanting things to be better, but in the grounded confidence that things will become better, because we are part of a society in which people know they have a duty to help out family members in distress, and part of a nation whose founding memory is of just such an act performed by God Himself.

The Chronological Imagination

S ometimes a modern discovery so changes our ways of looking at things that it allows us to revisit ancient truths that had become deeply obscured and see them with pristine clarity as if for the first time. That is surely the case with quantum physics. What it allows us to do is to understand afresh a biblical way of thinking about truth that is profoundly different from the way we have been accustomed to think in the West. I call the Greek approach the *logical* imagination, and the Jewish approach, the *chronological* imagination.

Niels Bohr famously said about quantum mechanics that if it hasn't profoundly shocked you, you haven't understood it yet. Without entering the details of this tangled territory, the most profoundly shocking thing about the subatomic reality it exposed is that it does not fit our standard logical categories. Is light a wave or a particle? Do subatomic particles have position or momentum? Is Schrödinger's cat alive or dead?[1]

---

1. Schrödinger's cat is the name given to the thought experiment proposed by the Austrian physicist Erwin Schrödinger in 1935 to dramatise the paradoxical nature of quantum physics. It involves thinking about a cat in a sealed box whose fate

The answer to each of these questions reminds us of the story about the rabbi who listens to a husband's account of an unhappy marriage and says, "You're right." He then listens to the wife's conflicting account and says, "You're right." His disciple, who has been present at both meetings, says to the rabbi, "But they can't both be right," to which the rabbi replies, "You're also right."

There are phenomena, from subatomic particles to domestic disputes, to which the standard rules of Aristotelian logic do not apply. Chief of these is the principle of contradiction that states that a proposition and its negation cannot both be true. Two contradictory statements cannot be true at the same time. Bohr's complementarity theory, Heisenberg's uncertainty principle, and other counterintuitive ideas challenge this head-on. Light is both a wave and a particle. Schrödinger's cat is both alive and dead. There are phenomena that bear contradictory characteristics until we, the observer, enter the scene, at which point the contradiction is resolved retroactively.

Bohr tells the story of how he came to his theory. It happened after his son had stolen something from the local store. He found himself thinking about this, first as a judge, then as a father, and found that he couldn't think both thoughts at the same time. As a judge he had to think impartially. As a father he could not but have compassion for his son. One way of thinking leads to justice, the other to mercy, but these are conflicting perspectives and involve different kinds of relationships.

The same is true about the well-known drawing that can be seen as a duck or as a rabbit, but not both at the same time. The multidimensionality of reality may simply be too complex for us to grasp it all at one time. But what we cannot think simultaneously we can often think sequentially. That is what I mean by the chronological imagination.

We owe our concepts of logic to the ancient Greeks. The Greeks thought of knowledge as a special kind of seeing. We still, in Western languages, preserve this visual metaphor. We speak of foresight and

depends on an earlier random event involving subatomic particles. According to the Copenhagen interpretation of quantum theory, the particles exist only in a state of probability until they are measured. It follows that the cat is only alive or dead once the box is opened. Until then it is equally true to say that it is alive and that it is dead.

insight, of people of vision, and of making an observation. When we understand something we say, "I see." For Plato, knowledge was deep insight into a world beyond the senses, where you see not the physical embodiments but the true form of things. The guiding metaphor for Greek epistemology, buried deep in the culture, was the image of Zeus, chief of the gods, looking down on the affairs of human beings from his lofty perch on Mount Olympus.

The worldview of the Torah was quite different. True knowledge is acquired less through seeing (God is not visible, and throughout the Hebrew Bible appearances deceive[2]) than through listening. The key-word is *shema*, meaning, "listen, hear, understand, respond." Knowledge, *daat*, is not detached observation but intimate personal engagement: "And Adam knew his wife and she conceived." God in the Torah is not a detached observer of the affairs of humankind, but an active partici-pant. In Judaism, words are not just pictures of reality, the "forms" of things. They affect relationships. Words can injure or inspire. Words can bless or curse. Words can create new moral facts, such as when we make a promise. Words shape the reality they describe. This is more like Heisenberg's uncertainty principle, in which the observer affects the reality he observes, than like Greek-inspired theories of knowledge in which a sentence can be true or false but not both.

The psychotherapist Viktor Frankl pointed out that what can be a contradiction in two-dimensional space need not be when we add a third dimension. So a square cannot be a circle, and a circle cannot be a square. But they can both be shadows cast by a single object, a canister, lit first from the side, then from above. Add the third dimension and the contradiction disappears. Nor is this a mere mathematical curiosity. As Niels Bohr, one of the masters of quantum physics put it, "The opposite of a trivial truth is a falsehood, but the opposite of a profound truth may well be another profound truth."

This is absolutely fundamental to Judaism. There is more than one valid way of looking at the universe. Minimally, there is the point of view of God and there is the point of view of man, and they are radically

2. Think of Joseph, seen by his brothers but not recognised, or the spies sent by Moses who saw the land but misinterpreted what they saw.

distinct. The only time in the whole of Tanakh in which a human being is invited to see the world from the vantage point of God occurs in the last four chapters of the book of Job, when Job finally understands that the universe is not anthropocentric. Not everything exists for the benefit of humankind. God is at the centre, not us.

No less significantly, though the Torah has a single author, it does not speak in a single voice. I have argued throughout these studies that there are at least three discernible voices, a wisdom voice, a priestly voice, and a prophetic voice, corresponding to the three modes in which God discloses Himself: through creation, revelation, and redemption. Each captures something of reality but none, on its own, portrays it all. That is why the Torah is such a complex interplay of different genres and tones of voice. The book of Numbers, for example, is structured as a fugue between law and narrative. There is no other book in the whole of literature that is quite like it. In it we see the interplay between prophetic and priestly sensibilities, and we begin to understand how law – the "ought-ness" of things – grows out of, and in turn influences, history, the "is- or was-ness" of things.

How then do you represent the three-dimensional nature of reality with its conflicting perspectives and multifaceted truths? One way in which the Torah does it is through what I call the *dialogical imagination*. We are shown a situation from two radically opposed viewpoints at the same time. Two powerful examples occur in Genesis 21 and 27. In Genesis 21, first we see Sarah and her joy as at last she holds her long-awaited son, then we see the pathos of Hagar and Ishmael, dismissed from the household and on the brink of death under the heartless desert sky. In Genesis 27, first we see Rebecca arrange for her beloved Jacob to be blessed, then we see Isaac and Esau, bound together in shock and dismay as they realise what has happened.

These narratives subvert any simplistic tendency to moralise, to divide reality into black and white. They force us to see the world from more than one point of view. The only way of bridging these perspectives is though conversation. Hence the idea of truth as dialogue. In Genesis, when speech breaks down, violence – the attempt to impose my version of the truth on you by force – is often waiting in the wings.

The other way is through the *chronological imagination*. Conflicting propositions may both be valid – the opposite of a profound truth may be another profound truth – but not at the same time. A classic example of this is the interpretation by Rabbi Joseph Soloveitchik in *The Lonely Man of Faith* of the two creation accounts in Genesis 1, and in chapters 2–3. In the first, man is created in the image of God and given dominion over all other life forms. In the second, man is formed from the dust of the earth, and told to "serve and conserve" the garden. In the first, man and woman are created simultaneously, side by side. In the second, woman is created in the wake of the loneliness of man, and they exist face to face.

Rabbi Soloveitchik argued that the first describes the "majestic" man, the second, the "covenantal" man, and we are both. The result, he argued, was that to be human is to be conflicted, torn between the two facets of our being. In fact, though, the Torah resolves the contradiction in the simplest and most elegant way: through time. "Six days you shall labour and do all your work, but the seventh day is a sabbath to the Lord your God." For six days we are majestic; on the seventh we are covenantal.

The chronological imagination – what Bohr meant when he said he could see his son through the eyes of a judge and a parent, but not both at the same time – was one of the great gifts of *Torat Kohanim*. The priest guards the border between sacred and secular, eternity and mortality, the physical and spiritual, the infinite and finite. He knows these are two different orders of reality and is all too conscious of the danger that awaits any blurring of the boundary. At one level of reality, all that exists is God. At another, all that exists is human beings and their devices and desires. The separation between heaven and earth is what makes the universe and human life possible. But their connection is what makes human life meaningful.

The priest resolves the contradiction between sacred and secular by seeing both as true and valid, but we can only experience them at different times. The times and places at which we focus on our human, mortal condition are called ḥol, secular. Those in which we focus on God, the infinite eternal, we call *kodesh*. They are integrated in the form of a precisely calibrated rhythm of time: six units (days, months, years) of *ḥol* followed by a seventh that is holy, with the occasional addition of a fiftieth (day, year) after a sequence of seven sevens.

Biblical texts using the priestly voice are conspicuous for their mathematical precision. So, as Umberto Cassuto pointed out,[3] the creation account is not only divided into seven days. It also contains the word "good" seven times, "God" thirty-five times, and "earth" twenty-one times. The first verse contains seven words, the second fourteen, and the description of the seventh day, thirty-five. The whole passage is 469 (7 x 67) words. Likewise Leviticus 23, 25, and 26 are all structured around the repeated words "seven" and "Shabbat." Mathematical precision is essential to the priestly understanding of reality, just as we now know it is to the universe, almost unimaginably finely tuned for the emergence of conscious life. Had any of the mathematical constants that govern the shape of the universe been even slightly different, the chemical elements necessary for life would simply not have formed.[4]

But the precision of the priest is different from that of the scientist. The division of time in the priestly calendar is a way of living out sequentially different and conflicting truths. We have already seen one in our study of Sukkot. Judaism embraces both the universal and the particular, the universality of our humanity, given religious force in the Noahide covenant, and the particularity of our people's relationship with God, epitomised in the covenant at Mount Sinai. The Jewish calendar gives weight to both. There is the cycle of the three pilgrimage festivals, Passover, Shavuot, and Sukkot, representing the particularity of Jewish history – the Exodus, the giving of the Torah, and the years of wandering in the desert. And there is the cycle of festivals of the seventh month, Rosh HaShana, Yom Kippur, and Sukkot, representing the universals of the human condition: creation, divine sovereignty, justice, judgement, life, death, rain, and the renewal of nature.

One of the most beautiful consequences of the chronological imagination – seen clearly in *Parashat Behar* – is its ability to reconcile the

3. Umberto Cassuto, *Commentary on Genesis*, vol. 1 (Jerusalem: Magnes Press, 1961), 12–15.
4. One classic account is Martin Rees, *Just Six Numbers* (London: Weidenfeld & Nicolson, 1999).

real with the ideal. History is full of ideal worlds. We call them utopias, a word that means "no place," because no utopia has ever happened. *Torat Kohanim* has a different, indeed unique, approach to ideal worlds. We live them, periodically, in the here-and-now of real time. On Shabbat we engage in a full dress rehearsal for the Messianic Age when no one will exercise power, political or economic, over anyone else. Something similar is true of the two great institutions in this *parasha*: *Shemitta* and the Jubilee year, the seventh and fiftieth years. By cancelling debts, releasing slaves, leaving the produce of the land to be enjoyed by everyone equally, and restoring ancestral property to its original owners, we inhabit a world in which the inequities of the market economy have been redressed and for a year, sometimes two, we suspend the world of competition and live in a world of co-operation and the fellowship of equals.

There is no other system quite like this, and it gives truth – not the truth we think or discover, but the truths we live and to which we owe loyalty – a three-dimensional character it does not have in the either/or world of Aristotelian logic.[5] That is the power of dialogical and chronological thought, and it comes from the depth reality acquires when we add to the two-dimensional nature of humanity the third dimension that is God.

---

5. Not that Aristotle was narrowly Aristotelian. He was one of the first philosophers to realise that different intellectual disciplines had different criteria of truth and different internal logics.

Freedom and Equality

In his book *Moral Tribes*, Joshua Green asks us to imagine four very different groups of people, each living at a different edge of a giant forest.[1] They have limited contact with one another and each has its own way of running its affairs.

To the north of the forest is a tribe where each family has its own plot of land, surrounded by a fence. The plots vary greatly in size and productivity, partly because some families are wiser and more industrious than others and have thus been able to buy land from their less prosperous neighbours. Some families are poor because they have worked less hard or less wisely, others because of plain bad luck. There are vast differences in wealth. The council of elders of the tribe ensures that people keep their promises and respect one another's property, but beyond that they do little. The result is that some members of the tribe die each winter for lack of food or warmth. But the tribe as a whole prospers.

To the south, there is a tribe where people share their land and animals, as well as the fruits of their labours. The council of elders manages the fields and flocks and is kept very busy. There are frequent

---

1. Joshua Green, *Moral Tribes* (London: Atlantic Books, 2014), 1–3.

complaints that various members of the tribe are lazy or careless and do not carry their fair share of the common load. Most, however, work hard, moved by community spirit or by fear of their neighbours' criticism. The tribe is, as a whole, less prosperous than their counterparts in the north, but they survive, and no one has ever died for lack of food or warmth.

These are, of course, two extreme ways of structuring a society (the two others in Green's fable are intermediate options), and they are deeply incompatible with one another. As Isaiah Berlin pointed out,[2] the great ideals are not necessarily capable of being realised simultaneously. We value freedom and cherish equality, but it does not follow that we can have both. Green's parable of the tribes shows us schematically how they work out. The northerners have much freedom but little equality. The southerners have much equality but little freedom. That is the classic choice between a free market economy and a communist or socialist state.

I argued in the previous essay, though, that *Torat Kohanim*, the priestly voice that dominates the book of Leviticus, has a novel way of dealing with contradiction. Freedom and equality are both fundamental values. The fact that they cannot be realised simultaneously does not mean that they cannot be realised sequentially. This is precisely what the social legislation of *Parashat Behar* does. It sets out a programme that combines liberty with equality by introducing periodic corrections to the market every seventh and fiftieth year.

Leviticus 25 creates a mechanism whose aim is to correct the tendency towards radical and ever-increasing inequality that result from the unfettered play of free market economics. There is the sabbatical year in which debts are released, Hebrew slaves set free, the land lies fallow, and its produce, not to be harvested, belongs to everyone. There is the Jubilee year in which, with some exceptions, ancestral land returns to its original owners. There is the command to help the needy: "If any of your fellow Israelites become poor and are unable to support themselves among you, help them as you would a foreigner and stranger, so they can

2. Isaiah Berlin, "Two Concepts of Liberty," in *Four Essays on Liberty* (New York: Oxford University Press, 1969).

continue to live among you" (Lev. 25:35). And there is the obligation to treat slaves not slavishly but as "hired workers or temporary residents" (Lev. 25:40).

As Heinrich Heine pointed out, "Moses did not want to abolish ownership of property; he wished, on the contrary, that everyone should possess something, so that no man might, because of poverty, be a slave with a slavish mind. Liberty was forever the ultimate thought of this great emancipator, and it still breathes and flames in all his laws which concern pauperism."[3]

Despite the sheer antiquity of these laws, time and again they have inspired those wrestling with issues of liberty, equity, and justice. The verse about the Jubilee year, "Proclaim liberty throughout all the land unto all the inhabitants thereof" (Lev. 25:10) is inscribed on the Liberty Bell in Philadelphia. The international movement that began in the late 1990s, involving more than forty nations in a campaign for cancellation of Third World debt, was called Jubilee 2000 and was directly inspired by this *parasha*.

The approach of the Torah to economic policy is unusual. Clearly we can make no direct inference from laws given more than three thousand years ago, in an agricultural age and to a society consciously under the sovereignty of God, to the circumstances of the twenty-first century with its global economy and international corporations. Between ancient texts and contemporary application comes the whole careful process of tradition and interpretation that we call *Torah Shebe'al Peh*, the Oral Law in its broadest sense.

Nonetheless, there are some important parameters. Work – making a living, earning your daily bread – has dignity. A psalm (128:2) states: "When you eat of the labour of your hands, you are happy and it shall be well with you." We say this every Saturday night at the start of the working week. Unlike aristocratic cultures such as that of ancient Greece, Judaism was never dismissive of work or the productive economy. It did not favour the creation of a leisured class. "Torah study without an occupation will in the end fail and lead to sin" (Mishna Avot 2:2).

3. Israel Tabak, *Judaic Lore in Heine* (1948; reprint, Baltimore: Johns Hopkins University Press, 1979), 32.

Another principle is that unless there are compelling reasons otherwise, one has a right to the fruits of one's labours. Judaism distrusts large government as an infringement of liberty. That is the core of the prophet Samuel's warning about monarchy: A king, he says, "will take the best of your fields and vineyards and olive groves and give them to his attendants.... He will take a tenth of your flocks, and you yourselves will become his slaves" (1 Sam. 8).

Judaism is the religion of a people born in slavery and longing for redemption, and the great assault of slavery against human dignity is that it deprives me of the ownership of the wealth I create. At the heart of the Hebrew Bible is the God who seeks the free worship of free human beings, and one of the most powerful defences of freedom is private property as the basis of economic independence. The ideal society envisaged by the prophets is one in which each person is able to sit "underneath his own vine and fig tree" (Mic. 4:4).

The free economy uses the fuel of competition to sustain the fire of invention. Long before Adam Smith, Judaism had accepted the proposition that the greatest advances are often brought about through quite unspiritual drives. "I saw," says the author of Ecclesiastes, "that all labour and all achievement spring from man's envy of his neighbour." Or as the Talmudic sages put it, "Were it not for the evil inclination, no one would build a house, marry a wife, have children, or engage in business." The rabbis even favour the free market in their own sphere of Jewish education. An established teacher, they say, cannot object to a rival setting up in competition. The reason they give is simply: "Jealousy among scholars increases wisdom."

The market economy is the best system we know for alleviating poverty through economic growth. In a single generation, its adoption lifted 100 million Indians and 400 million Chinese from poverty. The sages see poverty as a moral issue, not just an economic one. It is, they believe, incompatible with human dignity. Poverty is not a blessed or divinely ordained condition. It is, the rabbis say, "a kind of death" and "worse than fifty plagues." They say, "Nothing is harder to bear than poverty, because he who is crushed by poverty is like one to whom all the troubles of the world cling and upon whom all the curses of Deuteronomy have descended. If all other troubles were placed on one side and poverty on the other, poverty would outweigh them all."[4]

However, the market economy is better at producing wealth than at distributing it equitably. The concentration of wealth in a few hands gives disproportionate power to some at the cost of others. Today in Britain, it is not unusual for top CEOs to earn at least four hundred times as much as their employees. As I write, inequalities have increased dramatically in most market economies in the past decade. At such times we need to be acutely aware of the responsibilities wealth brings to alleviate the condition of the poor. That flows directly from the principle of eminent domain,[5] that what we possess we do not own. We merely hold it in trust from God, and one of the conditions of that trust is that those who have more than they need should share their blessings with those who have significantly less. That is why *tzedaka* in Judaism means justice, not just charity.

The legislation in *Parashat Behar* represents the architectonics of a just society. It tells us that an economic system must exist within a moral framework. It need not aim at economic equality but it must respect human dignity. No one should become permanently imprisoned in the chains of debt. No one should be deprived of a stake in the commonwealth, which in biblical times meant a share in the land. No one should be a slave to his or her employer. Everyone has the right – one day in seven, one year in seven – to respite from the endless pressures of work. None of this means dismantling the market economy, but it may involve periodic redistribution.

At the heart of these laws is a profoundly humane vision of society. "No man is an island." We are responsible for one another and implicated in one another's fate. That is fundamental to the ethics and politics of covenant. We are bound by a common fate. We are jointly responsible to God for social conditions. We are, as *Parashat Behar* reminds us five times, "brothers" (and sisters) to one another. Covenant

4. On the subjects of this chapter, see Jonathan Sacks, *The Dignity of Difference* (London: Continuum, 2002) and "Wealth and Poverty: A Jewish Analysis," in *Tradition in an Untraditional Age* (London: Vallentine Mitchell, 1990), 183–202.

5. See "Eminent Domain," above.

sees society as an extended family. The welfare of all is the concern of each. That is what was to make biblical Israel different from its neighbours. They were greater in terms of size, population, power, and wealth. But in Israel, everyone mattered. All were to be equal citizens under the sovereignty of God.

Jeremiah put the connection between religion and society bluntly in his assessment of two kings, Josiah and his son Yehoahaz. The son pursued personal wealth at the cost of social justice. Jeremiah said of him: "Woe to him who builds his palace by unrighteousness, his upper rooms by injustice, making his own people work for nothing, not paying them for their labour" (Jer. 22:13). He was about to be punished, said the prophet, by being led into captivity where he would die an ignominious death.

About the father, Josiah, Jeremiah said: "He defended the cause of the poor and needy, and so all went well. Is that not what it means to know Me? declares the Lord" (Jer. 22:16). This is a stunning sentence. To know God, says Jeremiah, is not a matter of abstract theology or conspicuous piety. It is to defend the cause of the poor and needy, to work for social and economic justice and a fair society.

In an age of vast inequalities within and between nations – in which a billion people lack adequate food and shelter, clean water, and medical facilities, and thirty thousand children die each day from preventable diseases – the vision of *Parashat Behar* still challenges us with its ideals. Wealth and power are not privileges but responsibilities, and we are summoned to become God's partners in building a world less random and capricious, more equitable and humane. The Torah shows us one way of combining freedom with equality. There may be others. But the overarching principle remains. Mankind was not created to serve markets. Markets were made to serve the image of God that is mankind.

Minority Rights

I argued in the two previous essays that Judaism found a way of embracing both sides of a contradiction, turning an either/or into a both/and. Nowhere is this more strikingly in evidence than in the concept, set out in *Parashat Behar*, of the *ger toshav*, the "resident alien," the "stranger within your gates."

Christianity borrowed two of Judaism's great commands of love: "You shall love the Lord your God with all your heart and with all your soul and with all your might" (Deut. 6:5) and "You shall love your neighbour as yourself" (Lev. 19:18). It gave far less emphasis to the third command, love of the stranger:

> When a stranger lives with you in your land, you shall not do him wrong. You shall treat the stranger who lives with you as the native among you, and you shall love him as yourself, for you were strangers in the land of Egypt: I am the Lord your God. (Lev. 19:33–34)

> For the Lord your God is God of gods and Lord of lords, the great God, mighty and awesome, who shows no partiality and accepts

no bribes. He defends the cause of the fatherless and the widow, and loves the stranger residing among you, giving them food and clothing. You are to love those who are strangers, for you yourselves were strangers in Egypt. (Deut. 10:17–19)

The sages say that the Torah commands us in only one place to love our neighbour but in thirty-six places to love the stranger.[1] This was one of the fundamental lessons of history translated into law. "You yourselves *know what it feels like* to be a stranger," says the Torah (Ex. 23:9), meaning that a sense of our people's past should prompt our conscience when the "mystic chords of memory," in Lincoln's words, are touched by "the better angels of our nature."

Why does this matter so much that the Torah should have to repeat it so often? The answer is simple. Two phenomena have gone hand in hand throughout history: ethnocentrism and xenophobia. They are the two sides of the coin called community. Every act that binds a group through a sense of shared identity, an "us," differentiates the group from others, from "them," the ones not like us. The more strongly we feel bound to the people like us, the more likely we are to fear and thus dislike the people who are different.

Nor is this unique to humans. It used to be thought that Homo sapiens was the only life form that deliberately killed members of its own species. We now know this is not so. Jane Goodall spent decades studying chimpanzees at Gombe Stream National Park in Tanzania. A member of her team, Richard Wrangham, tells the story of what happened when a feud between two alpha males led to a split in the population into two subgroups. Within a few years they had marked out their respective territories. Borders were patrolled by hunting parties. If they came across an isolated individual, they would attack. Soon they were mounting raids into one another's territory, and within three years one group had annihilated all the other group's males. Wrangham estimated that around thirty per cent of adult male chimpanzees had died as the result of violence by another member

1. Bava Metzia 59b.

of their own species.[2] We are, it seems, genetically predisposed to mistreat the stranger.[3]

A number of recent scholars have suggested that the answer lies in the abandonment of the ethics of identity altogether in favour of cosmo-politanism, a world without community.[4] But no cosmopolitan society is as tolerant as it seems. In antiquity, both the Greeks and Romans attempted at one time or another to eliminate the practice of Judaism. Europe of the Enlightenment did not end anti-Semitism: it gave rise to a new and violent strain of it. Nor has any cosmopolitan society lasted for long. As the great fourteenth-century Islamic historian Ibn Khaldun pointed out, societies that lack *asabiyah*, social solidarity, soon decline and fall.

So the Torah's project of an ethic that combines love of neighbour (ethnocentrism) with love of the stranger (xenophilia) is almost unique in moral history. Its theological basis is already set out in the first chapter of Genesis in the proposition that every human being, regardless of colour, class, or culture, is created in the image and likeness of God: the single most revolutionary statement of human dignity. What, though, does the Torah mean by *ger*, "the stranger"?

Clearly the reference is to one who is not Jewish by birth. It could mean one of the original inhabitants of the land of Canaan. It could mean one of the "mixed multitude" who left Egypt with the Israelites. It might mean a foreigner who has entered the land seeking safety or a livelihood.

Whatever the case, immense significance is attached to the way the Israelites treat the stranger. This was what they were meant to have learned from their own experience of exile and suffering in Egypt. They were strangers. They were oppressed. Therefore they knew what it feels like to be a member of a minority, an alien, an outsider, and they were to learn from this experience not to inflict on others what was once inflicted on them.

---

2. Richard Wrangham, *Demonic Males* (Boston: Houghton Mifflin, 1996).
3. For an impressive recent study, see Avi Tuschman, *Our Political Nature: The Evolu-tionary Origins of What Divides Us* (New York: Prometheus, 2013).
4. See among others, Amartya Sen, *Identity and Violence* (London: Penguin, 2007); Anthony Appiah, *The Ethics of Identity* (Princeton, NJ: Princeton University Press, 2005) and *Cosmopolitanism: Ethics in a World of Strangers* (London: Allen Lane, 2006); Joshua Green, *Moral Tribes*.

The sages hold that the word *ger* might mean one of two things. One was a *ger tzedek*, a convert to Judaism who had accepted all its commands and obligations. The other was the *ger toshav*, the "resident alien," who had not adopted the religion of Israel but who lived in the land of Israel. *Parashat Behar* spells out the rights of such a person. Specifically:

> If any of your fellow Israelites become poor and are unable to support themselves among you, help them as you would a resident alien, so they can continue to live among you. (Lev. 25:35)

There is, in other words, an obligation to support and sustain a resident alien. Not only does he have the right to live in the holy land, but he has the right to share in its welfare provisions. Recall that this is a very ancient law indeed, long before the sages formulated such principles as *darkhei shalom*, "the ways of peace,"[5] obligating Jews to extend charity and care to non-Jews as well as Jews.

What then is a *ger toshav*? There are three views in the Talmud. According to R. Meir, it is anyone who takes it upon himself not to worship idols. According to the sages, it is anyone who commits himself to keep the seven Noahide commands. A third view, more stringent, holds that it is someone who undertakes to keep all the commands of the Torah except one, the prohibition of meat not ritually slaughtered.[6] The law follows the sages. A *ger toshav* is thus a non-Jew living in Israel who accepts the Noahide laws binding on everyone.

Ger toshav legislation is thus one of the earliest extant forms of minority rights. According to Maimonides, there is an obligation on Jews in Israel to establish courts of law for resident aliens to allow them to settle their own disputes – or disputes they have with Jews – according to the provisions of Noahide law. Maimonides adds: "One should act towards resident aliens with the same respect and loving-kindness as one would to a fellow Jew."[7]

5. Gittin 59a–61a.
6. Avoda Zara 64b.
7. Maimonides, *Mishneh Torah, Hilkhot Melakhim* 10:12.

The difference between this and later "ways of peace" legislation is that the ways of peace apply to non-Jews without regard to their beliefs or religious practice. They date from a time when Jews were a minority in a predominantly non-Jewish, non-monotheistic environment. "Ways of peace" are essentially pragmatic rules of what today we would call good community relations and active citizenship in a multi-ethnic and multicultural society. *Ger toshav* legislation cuts deeper. It is based not on pragmatism but religious principle. According to the Torah, you do not have to be Jewish in a Jewish society and land to have many of the rights of citizenship. You simply have to be moral.

One biblical vignette portrays this with enormous power. King David has fallen in love and has an adulterous relationship with Batsheva, wife of a *ger toshav*, Uriah the Hittite. She becomes pregnant. Uriah meanwhile has been away from home as a soldier in Israel's army. David, afraid that Uriah will come home, see that his wife is pregnant, realise that she has committed adultery, and come to discover that the king is the guilty party, has Uriah brought home. His pretext is that he wants to know how the battle is going. He then tells Uriah to go home and sleep with his wife before returning, so that he will later assume that he himself is the father of the child. The plan fails. This is what happens:

So David sent this word to Joab: "Send me Uriah the Hittite." And Joab sent him to David. When Uriah came to him, David asked him how Joab was, how the soldiers were, and how the war was going. Then David said to Uriah, "Go down to your house and wash your feet." So Uriah left the palace, and a gift from the king was sent after him. But Uriah slept at the entrance to the palace with all his master's servants and did not go down to his house.

David was told, "Uriah did not go home." So he asked Uriah, "Haven't you just come from a military campaign? Why didn't you go home?"

Uriah said to David, "The Ark and Israel and Judah are staying in tents, and my commander Joab and my lord's men are camped in the open country. How could I go to my house to eat and drink and make love to my wife? As surely as you live, I will not do such a thing!" (II Sam. 11:6–11)

Uriah's utter loyalty to the Jewish people, despite the fact that he is not himself Jewish, is contrasted with King David, who has stayed in Jerusalem, not been with the army, and instead had a relationship with another man's wife. The fact that Tanakh can tell such a story in which a resident alien is the moral hero, and David, Israel's greatest king, the wrongdoer, tells us much about the morality of Judaism.

It takes more than democracy to create a free society. As Alexis de Tocqueville and John Stuart Mill pointed out in the nineteenth century, democracy can lead to the "tyranny of the majority" and the loss of minority rights. Lord Acton was therefore surely right when he wrote, "The most certain test by which we judge whether a country is really free is the amount of security enjoyed by minorities."[8]

Since the days of Moses, minority rights have been central to the vision of the kind of society God wants us to create in the land of Israel. A strong sense of group identity can co-exist with love of, and care for, the people who belong to other groups or to none. That is part of *Torat Kohanim*, ethics in the priestly mode. Our common humanity precedes our religious differences. This remains one of the towering insights of Judaic ethics.

8.   Lord Acton, *Essays in the History of Liberty*, 7.

Beḥukkotai
בחוקותי

Parashat Beḥukkotai is dominated by the passage in which God speaks of the blessings that will be experienced by the Israelites if they are faithful to the covenant and the curses they will encounter if they are not. The essays that follow examine various aspects of this passage.

The first argues that it is divine involvement in history that forms the basis for the Jewish principle of hope. It was this that made it so different from the tragic culture of ancient Greece. The second looks at recent empirical evidence that a belief in divine justice helps create the social virtue of trust. The third makes the case that it is the perennial choice between blessing and curse that lies at the heart of Judaism as an ethic of responsibility – the opposite of a victim culture.

The fourth asks why the sages take an unlikely passage from the curses as the prooftext for the principle that "all Israel are responsible for one another." The fifth is about the Christian argument against Judaism, that God had rejected the "old" covenant in favour of a new one. The remarkable statement at the end of the curses explicitly rules this out. It says in effect that whatever happens, God will not reject His people.

The Birth of Hope

*In reality, hope is the worst of all evils because it
prolongs the torments of man.*
                    Nietzsche, *Human, All Too Human*

*In tragedy nothing is in doubt and everyone's
destiny is known. That makes for tranquillity.
There is a sort of fellow feeling among characters
in a tragedy: he who kills is as innocent as he who
gets killed: it's all a matter of what part you are
playing. Tragedy is restful; and the reason is that
hope, that foul, deceitful thing, has no part in it.*
                    Anouilh, *Antigone*

*Were it not for my faith that I would see God's
goodness in the land of the living! Hope in God.
Be strong and He will give you courage. And hope
in God.*
                    Psalms 27:13–14

At the end of the *Tokheḥa*, the terrifying curses warning of what would happen to Israel if it betrayed its divine mission, there is a sudden change of key. We have been reading a prophecy of history gone wrong. If Israel loses its way spiritually, say the curses, it will lose it physically, economically, and politically also. The nation will experience defeat and disaster. It will forfeit its freedom and its land. The people will go into exile and suffer persecution. Customarily we read this passage in the synagogue *sotto voce*, in an undertone, so fearful is it. It is hard to imagine any nation undergoing such catastrophe and living to tell the tale. Yet the passage does not end there. In an abrupt transition, we hear one of the great consolations in the Bible:

> *Yet in spite of this*, when they are in the land of their enemies, I will not cast them away, neither will I abhor them, to destroy them utterly and to break My covenant with them: for I am the Lord their God. But I will for their sakes remember the covenant of their ancestors, whom I brought forth out of Egypt in the sight of the heathen, that I might be their God: I am the Lord. (Lev. 26:44–45)

This is a turning point in the history of the human spirit. It is *the birth of hope*: not hope as a dream, a wish, a desire, but as the very shape of history itself, "the arc of the moral universe," as Martin Luther King put it. God is just. He may punish. He may hide His face. But He will not break His word. He will fulfil His promise. He will redeem His children. He will bring them home.

Hope is one of the very greatest Jewish contributions to Western civilisation, so much so that I have called Judaism "the voice of hope in the conversation of humankind."[1] In the ancient world, there were tragic cultures in which people believed that the gods were at best indifferent to our existence, at worst actively malevolent. The best humans can do is avoid their attention or appease their wrath. In the end, though, it is all in vain. We are destined to see our dreams wrecked on the rocks of

1. Jonathan Sacks, *Future Tense: A Vision for Jews and Judaism in the Global Culture* (London: Hodder & Stoughton, 2011), 231–252.

reality. The great tragedians were Greek. Judaism produced no Sophocles or Aeschylus, no Oedipus or Antigone. Biblical Hebrew did not even contain a word that meant "tragedy" in the Greek sense. Modern Hebrew had to borrow the word: hence, *tragedia*.

Then there are secular cultures like that of the contemporary West in which the very existence of the universe, of human life and consciousness, is seen as the result of a series of meaningless accidents intended by no one and with no redeeming purpose. All we know for certain is that we are born, we live, we will die, and it will be as if we had never been. Hope is not unknown in such cultures, but it is what Aristotle defined as "a waking dream," a private wish that things might be otherwise. As seen through the eyes of ancient Greece or contemporary science, there is nothing in the texture of reality or the direction of history to justify belief that the human condition could be other and better than it is.

Judaism is not without an expression of this mood. We find it in the opening chapters of the book of Ecclesiastes. For its author, time is cyclical. What has been, will be. History is a set of eternal recurrences. Nothing ever really changes:

> What has been will be again,
> what has been done will be done again;
> there is nothing new under the sun. (Eccl. 1:9)

Ecclesiastes, though, is a rare voice within Tanakh. For the most part, the Hebrew Bible expresses a quite different view: that there *can* be change in the affairs of humankind. We are summoned to the long journey at whose end is redemption and the Messianic Age. *Judaism is the principled rejection of tragedy in the name of hope.*

The sociologist Peter Berger calls hope a "signal of transcendence," a point at which something *beyond* penetrates into the human situation. There is nothing inevitable or even rational about hope. It cannot be inferred from any facts about the past or present. As the quotations from Nietzsche and Anouilh that head this chapter show, those with a tragic sense of life hold that hope is an illusion, a childish fantasy, and that a mature response to our place in the universe is to accept its fundamental meaninglessness and cultivate the stoic virtue of acceptance. Judaism insists otherwise: that the reality that underlies the universe is *not* deaf to our prayers, blind to our aspirations, indifferent to our existence. We are not wrong to strive to perfect the world, refusing to accept the inevitability of suffering and injustice.

We hear this note at key points in the Torah. It occurs twice at the end of Genesis when first Jacob then Joseph assure the other members of the covenantal family that their stay in Egypt will not be endless. God will honour His promise and bring them back to the Promised Land. We hear it again, magnificently, as Moses tells the people that even after the worst suffering that can befall a nation, Israel will not be lost or rejected:

> Then the Lord your God will restore your fortunes and have compassion on you and gather you again from all the nations where He scattered you. Even if you have been banished to the most distant land under the heavens, from there the Lord your God will gather you and bring you back. (Deut. 30:3–4)

But the key text is here at the end of the curses of Leviticus. This is where God promises that even if Israel sins, it may suffer, but it will never die. It may experience exile, but eventually it will return. It may undergo the most terrible suffering, but it will never have reason to despair. Israel may betray the covenant but God never will. This is one of the most fateful of all biblical assertions. It tells us that no fate is so bleak as to murder hope itself. No defeat is final, no exile endless, no tragedy the story's last word.

Subsequent to Moses, all the prophets delivered this message, each in his own way. Hosea told the people that though they may act like a faithless wife, God remains a loving husband. Amos assured them that God would rebuild even the most devastated ruins. Jeremiah bought a field in Anatot to assure the people that they would return from Babylon. Isaiah became the poet laureate of hope in visions of a world at peace that have never been surpassed.

Of all the prophecies of hope inspired by Leviticus 26, none is as haunting as the vision in which Ezekiel saw the people of the covenant as a valley of dry bones. Gradually they came together, took on flesh, and lived again:

> Then He said to me: Son of man, these bones are the whole house of Israel. They say, "Our bones are dried up and *our hope is lost* [*avda tikvatenu*]; we are cut off." Therefore prophesy and say to them, "This is what the Sovereign Lord says: 'O My people, I am going to open your graves and bring you up from them; I will bring you back to the land of Israel.'" (Ezek. 37:11–14)

No text in all of literature is so evocative of the fate of the Jewish people after the Holocaust, before the rebirth in 1948 of the State of Israel. Almost prophetically, Naftali Herz Imber alluded to this text in his words for the song that eventually became Israel's national anthem. He wrote: *od lo avda tikvatenu*, "our hope is *not yet* lost." Not by accident is Israel's anthem called *HaTikva*, "The Hope."

Where does hope come from? Berger sees it as a constitutive part of our humanity:

> Human existence is always oriented towards the future. Man exists by constantly extending his being into the future, both in his consciousness and in his activity.... An essential dimension of this "futurity" of man is hope. It is through hope that men overcome the difficulties of any given here and now. And it is through hope that men find meaning in the face of extreme suffering.[2]

Only hope empowers us to take risks, engage in long-term projects, marry and have children, and refuse to capitulate in the face of despair:

> There seems to be a death-refusing hope at the very core of our *humanitas*. While empirical reason indicates that this hope is an illusion, there is something in us that, however shamefacedly in an age of triumphant rationality, goes on saying "no!" and even says

2. Berger, op. cit., 68–69.

"no!" to the ever so plausible explanations of empirical reason. In a world where man is surrounded by death on all sides, he continues to be a being who says "no!" to death – and through this "no!" is brought to faith in another world, the reality of which would validate his hope as something other than illusion.[3]

I am less sure than Berger that hope is universal. It emerged as part of the spiritual landscape of Western civilisation through a quite specific set of beliefs: that God exists, that He cares about us, that He has made a covenant with humanity and a further covenant with the people He chose to be a living example of faith. That covenant transforms our understanding of history. God has given His word, and He will never break it, however much we may break our side of the promise. Without these beliefs, we would have no reason to hope at all.

History as conceived in this *parasha* is not utopian. Faith does not blind us to the apparent randomness of circumstance, the cruelty of fortune, or the seeming injustices of fate. No one reading Leviticus 26 can be an optimist. Yet no one sensitive to its message can abandon hope. Without this, Jews and Judaism would not have survived. Without belief in the covenant and its insistence, "Yet in spite of this," there might have been no Jewish people after the destruction of one or other of the Temples, or the Holocaust itself. It is not too much to say that Jews kept hope alive, and hope kept the Jewish people alive.

3. Ibid., 72.

When Curses Are a Blessing

> Society cannot exist, unless a controlling power
> upon will and appetite be placed somewhere; and
> the less of it there is within, the more there must be
> without. It is ordained in the eternal constitution
> of things, that men of intemperate minds cannot
> be free. Their passions forge their fetters.
>
> Edmund Burke, *Letter to a Member of the*
> *National Assembly of France* (1791)

> Let us with caution indulge the supposition that
> morality can be maintained without religion.
> Whatever may be conceded to the influence of
> refined education on minds of peculiar structure,
> reason and experience both forbid us to expect
> that national morality can prevail in exclusion of
> religious principle.
>
> George Washington, *Farewell Address* (1796)

Beḥukkotai

The blessings of *Parashat Beḥukkotai* are brief and serene. When Israel lives in harmony with the will of God it will live in harmony with the land. The rain will fall in its due time, the soil will be fruitful, there will be food to eat and there will be peace. Your enemies will fail in their attacks upon you. And you will have children. Children and a land: the promise God gave to the patriarchs. God will establish His presence, His Tabernacle, among you, and you will be free. "I have broken the bars of your yoke and made you walk upright" (Lev. 26:3–13).

The curses, by contrast, are long and terrifying. First nature will turn against you: "I will break down your stubborn pride and make the sky above you like iron and the ground beneath you like bronze." Then will come the wild animals, then your enemies. You will be defeated, humiliated, forced into exile. The land you did not allow to rest in the seventh year will lie fallow because there will be no one left to cultivate it. Your spirit will be utterly broken: "As for those of you who survive, I will send faintness into their hearts in the lands of their enemies. The sound of a driven leaf shall put them to flight, and they shall flee as one flees from the sword, and they shall fall though no one is pursuing them" (Lev. 26:14–41). It is the starkest of all possible choices.

Passages like these have often been criticised by non-Jews for portraying God as jealous, vengeful, and vindictive. How are we to reconcile this dark scenario of the curses, here and in Deuteronomy, with the God of love and forgiveness and the Thirteen Attributes of Mercy, the God who, said Hosea, loves the people like a husband who continues to love his wife even though she has repeatedly been unfaithful to him, the God who said through Isaiah, "Though the mountains be shaken and the hills be moved, yet My steadfast love for you will not be shaken nor My covenant of peace removed" (Is. 54:10)?

Recent research has provided a surprising answer. Before we turn to it, let us first recall the context of the Mosaic covenant, the problem to which it is the solution. The central question to which the Torah is the answer is: *How can we secure co-operation between two or more individuals with conflicting desires and wills, without the use of violence or power, political or economic?* How can the two fundamental values of Genesis 1 coexist: freedom and order?

410

The early history of humankind as portrayed in the opening chapters of Genesis can be summed up in three sentences: First God creates order. Then He gives man freedom. Then man creates chaos. There can be freedom without order: that is the world before the Flood, the Torah's description of Hobbes' state of nature, the war of every man against every man in which life is "solitary, poor, nasty, brutish, and short."[1] And there can be order without freedom. That is the world of Egypt, Pharaoh, and slavery.

The question is: Can there be, at one and the same time, *both* order and freedom? Can there be a society of law-governed liberty, in which the rule of law prevails without the use of force, in which the rich honour their responsibilities to the poor, justice is impartial, and the principles of welfare are such that extremes of poverty are eliminated and no one is a permanent slave to debt or landlessness: all this without an intrusive, oppressive government, a police force, and a hierarchy of privilege and power?

This was and remains a unique experiment: a nation in which the only ultimate sovereign is God Himself, in which even a king has no legislative power, and where the people as a whole is collectively responsible, each for the conduct of all. Such is the vision behind the covenant society inaugurated at Mount Sinai.

All ancient covenants had treaty stipulations including specification of reward for obedience (usually the protection of the weaker party by the stronger) and punishment in case of non-compliance. Most covenants, though, were between rulers of states. Unique to the Sinai covenant were the two parties. Never before had an entire nation been party to a covenant on the one hand, and never before had God bound Himself to one nation.[2] It was essential therefore that the promise of reward and the threat of punishment be sufficiently powerful to have an impact on the people as a whole, for it was they who bore responsibility for the fate of the nation. They had to secure the rule of law without relying on a liberty-restricting government to do it for them. Hence the devastating, terrifying rhetoric of the curses.

1. Thomas Hobbes, *Leviathan*, XIII:9.
2. The two previous covenants had been with all humanity, through Noah (Gen. 9), and one family, Abraham and his descendants (Gen. 17).

Now let us turn to recent research. One of the ironies of twenty-first-century thought is that Darwinian biology has been taken as a master discipline to explain not only the evolution of life but also of culture, while at the same time it has become the substitute faith of some of the most famous critics of religion. Darwin, wrote one of them, "made it possible to be an intellectually fulfilled atheist."[3]

The irony is that religion, Abrahamic monotheism in particular, has proved to be the most robust of all cultural adaptations. It has survived all the attacks on it throughout the centuries. It has spread to include, today, half of the seven billion people on the face of the earth. By the test of adaptive fitness – transmission to future generations – it is measurably more successful than secularism on the one criterion Darwinians recognise, namely the ability to pass on one's genes. Contemporary demographic studies show, virtually without exception, that religious families, groups, and nations have higher birthrates than their secular counterparts.[4] As an argument against religion, Darwinism fails. Instead, it proves the opposite. Religion survives because it enables religious people to survive, whether individually or as groups.[5]

How so? The most recent and detailed study is Ara Norenzayan's *Big Gods: How Religion Transformed Cooperation and Conflict.*[6] Clearly the way a Darwinian understands religion is not the way a believer understands faith. But Norenzayan's findings, all of them on the basis of empirical research, are nonetheless fascinating. The first is: Watched people are nice people. The belief that you are being observed measurably changes people's behaviour for the better.[7] The second is: Trust people who trust in God. Throughout the world, in survey after survey, people

---

3. Richard Dawkins, *The Blind Watchmaker* (New York: Norton, 1986), 6–7.
4. Eric Kauffmann, *Shall the Religious Inherit the Earth? Demography and Politics in the Twenty-First Century* (London: Profile, 2010).
5. Whether natural selection operates at group level is a topic of heated debate among Darwinians. See E. O. Wilson, *The Social Conquest of Earth* (New York: Liveright Publishing Corporation, 2012).
6. Ara Norenzayan, *Big Gods: How Religion Transformed Cooperation and Conflict* (Princeton, NJ: Princeton University Press, 2013).
7. Ibid., 13–32.

indicate that they trust individuals with strong religious convictions, even if they belong to a different faith. Even atheists are somewhat inclined to say so. Atheists are trusted less.[8]

Norenzayan's view is that the belief that God sees our actions, rewards the righteous, and punishes wrongdoers is what allowed large-scale human associations to come into existence in the first place. Hunter-gatherer and tribal societies in which people lived in smaller groups with more regular face-to-face contact did not tend to think in such terms. As biologists have learned through computer simulations of the prisoner's dilemma, two individuals will arrive at co-operative behaviour if they meet often enough and learn through experience the high cost of self-interest when pursued to the detriment of others. But large societies depend on trust between strangers. What will motivate me to act well towards someone I may never meet again? Shared belief that God rules our destinies, rewarding us for the good we do and penalising us for the bad, is the most effective source of society-wide trust. This is an entirely secular view of religion, but it remains interesting that contemporary social-psychological research, like the Torah itself though from a vastly different vantage point, sees religious faith as the solution to the coexistence of freedom and order.

One of the most striking of Norenzayan's findings is that the more people believe that God punishes wrongdoers, the less likely they are to cheat their fellow human beings when no one else is looking. Experiments were made among religious believers, some of whom held strong beliefs about divine retribution, others of whom held equally strong beliefs about divine forgiveness. They were later invited to take part in a seemingly unrelated study in which they were given a number of anagrams to solve and told they should pay themselves $1 for every solution they reached. Unbeknown to them, only five of the ten anagrams actually had solutions. They were being given the opportunity to cheat. Those who were strong in their beliefs about divine punishment cheated less than those who believed in divine mercy.

The effects went further in powerful and surprising ways. When given the opportunity to punish someone violating a social norm,

8. Ibid., 55–75.

believers in a punitive God were *less* likely to do so than others. In other words, *belief that God will punish offenders makes people more forgiving.* They leave punishment to God. That frees them to be forgiving. Belief in divine punishment also makes people kinder neighbours, and it reduces crime rates. International research shows a consistent pattern: the more retributive people's concept of God is, the more law-abiding they become. Why then do some religions emphasise the opposite, namely, divine forgiveness? One of the researchers suggests this hypothesis: "If you're looking to gain converts, it's much easier to sell a religion that promises a divine paradise after death than one that threatens believers with fire and brimstone."

These are remarkable findings, and they allow us to see the curses in *Parashat Beḥukkotai* in a completely new light. If contemporary research is correct, the very vehemence of the curses would have been likely to make the Israelites more law-abiding and the nation itself stronger in interpersonal trust than would otherwise have been the case. It would also have made people less likely to take the law into their own hands by punishing antisocial behaviour. They would have become more forbearing. Exactly as we noted in an earlier chapter on revenge, belief that this is a matter for God has the effect of making people less vengeful.

The paradoxical conclusion is that the harsher God seems to be, the less harsh human beings become. This is what Abraham seems to have meant when he said to Abimelech king of Gerar, "I said to myself, 'There is surely no fear of God in this place, and they will kill me because of my wife'" (Gen. 20:11).[9] When people fear God, they act less fearfully towards their fellow humans. This is also why so many serious minds, among them Edmund Burke and George Washington in the quotes that head this chapter, held that religious belief ("the fear of God") was essential to civil society.

The more we internalise the idea that we are accountable to Heaven for what we do, and that God sees our acts even when no one else is watching, the less likely we are to give way to temptation by cheating or bending the rules in our favour. Secular societies that have lost

9. See in particular the comments of Malbim ad loc. on the limits of secular ethics in the presence of strong temptation.

the belief that God sees what we do are forced to resort to all kinds of surveillance devices from CCTVs to electronic monitoring to make sure that *someone is watching* after all, with the massive invasion of privacy this involves. The more we believe in God and divine providence, the more trustworthy we become. The more social institutions can rely on trust, the less they have to rely on laws, police, regulations, surveillance, and punishment as deterrence.

So in a strange way, belief in curses creates blessings. It gives people the strongest possible motive for self-restraint, creates law-abiding citizens, promotes trust in society, and secures order while minimising external constraints on freedom. That is what Maimonides calls "the perfection of society," which, though a lesser value than perfection of the soul, is essential to it. Fear of God helps create respect for our fellow humans. Fear of punishment from heaven helps create liberty on earth.

The Politics of Responsibility

The twenty-sixth chapter of *Vayikra* sets out with stunning clarity the terms of Jewish life under the covenant. On the one hand, there is an idyllic picture of the blessing of divine favour. If Israel follows God's decrees and keeps His commands, there will be rain, the earth will yield its fruit, there will be peace, the people will flourish, they will have children, and the Divine Presence will be in their midst. God will make them free. "I broke the bars of your yoke and enabled you to walk with heads held high."

The other side of the equation, though, is terrifying: the curses that will befall the nation should the Israelites fail to honour their mission as a holy nation:

> But if you will not listen to Me and carry out all these commands.... I will bring upon you sudden terror, wasting diseases, and fever that will destroy your sight and drain away your life. You will plant seed in vain, because your enemies will eat it.... If after all this you will not listen to Me, I will punish you for your sins seven times over. I will break down your stubborn pride and make the sky above you like iron and the ground beneath you

like bronze.... I will turn your cities into ruins and lay waste your sanctuaries, and I will take no delight in the pleasing aroma of your offerings. I will lay waste the land, so that your enemies who live there will be appalled.... As for those of you who survive, I will send faintness into their hearts in the lands of their enemies. The sound of a driven leaf shall put them to flight, and they shall flee as one flees from the sword, and they shall fall though no one is pursuing them. (Lev. 26:14–36)

Read in its entirety, this passage is more like Holocaust literature than anything else. The repeated phrases – "If after all this.... If despite this.... If despite everything" – come like hammer-blows of fate. It is a passage shattering in its impact, all the more so since so much of it came true at various times in Jewish history. Yet the curses end with the most profound promise of ultimate consolation. Despite everything, God will not break His covenant with the Jewish people. Collectively they will be eternal. They may suffer, but they will never be destroyed. They will undergo exile but eventually they will return.

Stated with the utmost drama, this is the logic of covenant. Unlike other conceptions of history or politics, covenant sees nothing inevitable or even natural about the fate of a people. Israel will not follow the usual laws of the rise and fall of civilisations. The Jewish people were not to see their national existence in terms of cosmology, written into the structure of the universe, immutable and fixed for all time, as did the ancient Mesopotamians and Egyptians. Nor were they to see their history as cyclical, a matter of growth and decline. Instead, it would be utterly dependent on moral considerations. If Israel stayed true to its mission, it would flourish. If it drifted from its vocation, it would suffer defeat after defeat.

Only one other nation in history has consistently seen its fate in similar terms, namely the United States. The influence of the Hebrew Bible on American history – carried by the Pilgrim Fathers and reiterated in presidential rhetoric ever since – was decisive. Here is how one writer described the faith of Abraham Lincoln:

We are a nation formed by a covenant, by dedication to a set of principles and by an exchange of promises to uphold and advance certain commitments among ourselves and throughout the world. Those principles and commitments are the core of American identity, the soul of the body politic. They make the American nation unique, and uniquely valuable, among and to the other nations. But the other side of the conception contains a warning very like the warnings spoken by the prophets to Israel: If we fail in our promises to each other, and lose the principles of the covenant, then we lose everything, for they are we.[1]

Covenantal politics is moral politics, driving an elemental connection between the fate of a nation and its vocation. This is statehood as a matter not of power but of ethical responsibility.

One might have thought that this kind of politics robbed a nation of its freedom. Spinoza argued just that. "This, then, was the object of the ceremonial law," he wrote, "that men should do nothing of their own free will, but should always act under external authority, and should continually confess by their actions and thoughts that they were not their own masters."[2] However, in this respect, Spinoza was wrong. Covenant theology is emphatically a politics of liberty.

What is happening in *Vayikra* 26 is an application to a nation as a whole of the proposition God spelled out to individuals at the beginning of human history:

> Then the Lord said to Cain, "Why are you angry? Why is your face downcast? If you do what is right, will you not be accepted? But if you do not do what is right, sin is crouching at your door; it desires to have you, but you must master it." (Gen. 4:6–7)

The choice – God is saying – is in your hands. You are free to do what you choose. But actions have consequences. You cannot overeat and take no exercise, and at the same time stay healthy. You cannot act selfishly and win the respect of other people. You cannot allow injustices to

---

1. John Schaar, *Legitimacy and the Modern State* (Piscataway Township, NJ: Transaction Publishers, 1981), 291.
2. Baruch Spinoza, *Tractatus Theologico-Politicus*, part I, chap. 5.

prevail and sustain a cohesive society. You cannot let rulers use power for their own ends without destroying the basis of a free and gracious social order. There is nothing mystical about these ideas. They are eminently intelligible. But they are also, and inescapably, moral.

I brought you from slavery to freedom – says God – and I empower you to be free. But I cannot and will not abandon you. I will not intervene in your choices, but I will instruct you on what choices you ought to make. I will teach you the constitution of liberty.

The first and most important principle is this: A nation cannot worship itself and survive. Sooner or later, power will corrupt those who wield it. If fortune favours it and it grows rich, it will become self-indulgent and eventually decadent. Its citizens will no longer have the courage to fight for their liberty, and it will fall to another, more Spartan, power.

If there are gross inequalities, the people will lack a sense of the common good. If government is high-handed and non-accountable, it will fail to command the loyalty of the people. None of this takes away your freedom. It is simply the landscape within which freedom is to be exercised. You may choose this way or that, but not all paths lead to the same destination.

To stay free, a nation must worship something greater than itself, nothing less than God, together with the belief that all human beings are created in His image. Self-worship on a national scale leads to totalitarianism and the extinction of liberty. It took the loss of more than 100 million lives in the twentieth century to remind us of this truth.

In the face of suffering and loss, there are two fundamentally different questions an individual or nation can ask, and they lead to quite different outcomes. The first is, "What did I, or we, do wrong?" The second is, "Who did this to us?" It is not an exaggeration to say that this is the fundamental choice governing the destinies of people.

The latter leads inescapably to what is today known as the *victim culture*. It locates the source of evil outside oneself. Someone else is to blame. It is not I or we who are at fault, but some external cause. The attraction of this logic can be overpowering. It generates sympathy. It calls for, and often evokes, compassion. It is, however, deeply destructive. It leads people to see themselves as objects, not subjects. They are done to, not doers; passive, not active. The results are anger, resentment, rage, and a burning sense of injustice. None of these, however, ever leads to freedom, since by its very logic this mindset abdicates responsibility for the current circumstances in which one finds oneself. Blaming others is the suicide of liberty.

Blaming oneself, by contrast, is difficult. It means living with constant self-criticism. It is not a route to peace of mind. Yet it is profoundly empowering. It implies that, precisely because we accept responsibility for the bad things that have happened, we also have the ability to chart a different course in the future. Within the terms set by covenant, the outcome depends on us. That is the logical geography of hope, and it rests on the choice Moses was later to define in these words:

> This day I call heaven and earth as witnesses against you that I have set before you life and death, blessings and curses. Now choose life, so that you and your children may live. (Deut. 30:19)

One of the most profound contributions Torah made to the civilisation of the West is this: that the destiny of nations lies not in the externalities of wealth or power, fate or circumstance, but in moral responsibility: the responsibility for creating and sustaining a society that honours the image of God within each of its citizens, rich and poor, powerful or powerless alike.

The politics of responsibility is not easy. The curses of *Vayikra* 26 are the very reverse of comforting. Yet the profound consolations with which they end are not accidental, nor are they wishful thinking. They are testimony to the power of the human spirit when summoned to the highest vocation. A nation that sees itself as responsible for the evils that befall it is also a nation that has an inextinguishable power of recovery and return.

All Israel Are Responsible for One Another

The book of *Vayikra* reaches a climax with an account of the blessings and curses attendant on Israel's obedience, or lack of it, to the terms of the covenant. The blessings are relatively brief. By contrast, the curses – the *Tokheḥa* – are set out at length and with elemental, terrifying power. This is the dark side of covenant. It may be a privilege to be chosen by God, but it is also an awesome responsibility. As the prophet Amos says, in a verse at once paradoxical yet definitive of the Jewish destiny: "You only have I known of all the families of the earth: therefore I will punish you for all your iniquities" (Amos 3:2).

One verse in the *Tokheḥa* however, gave rise to one of the great doctrines of Judaism:

> "They shall stumble over one another" – one because of another. This teaches that all Israel are responsible (literally, "sureties") for one another.[1]

---

1.   Sifra, *Parashat Beḥukkotai* 2:7; Sanhedrin 27b; Shevuot 39a.

The rule of *kol Yisrael arevin zeh bazeh* – that the Jewish people is collectively, not just individually, responsible before God – is one of the great principles of rabbinic Judaism. Explaining it, the sages give a number of striking metaphors:

> R. Shimon bar Yoḥai taught: It can be compared to people on a boat. One took out an awl and began boring a hole in the boat beneath his seat. The others said to him, "What are you doing?" He replied, "Is that any concern of yours? [I am not boring a hole beneath your seat] but only under mine." They said, "But you will sink the whole ship, and we will all drown."[2]

Hence the idea that "we are all in the same boat." My actions do not affect me alone. They have consequences for the whole of society. Elsewhere the rabbis focus on the positive: the strength that comes from community:

> It is the way of the world that if a person takes a bundle [*aguda*] of reeds and tries to break them together he cannot. If, however, the sticks are taken one by one, even a child can break them. So too with Israel: they are redeemed only when they form one band [*aguda aḥat*].[3]

The *Mekhilta DeRabbi Shimon bar Yoḥai* sees collective responsibility implicit in the very idea that by the covenant, Jews are called on to be a "holy nation":

> "A [holy] nation" – this teaches that they [the Jewish people] are like one body with one soul [the midrash identifies *goy*, nation, with the word *geviya*, body], and thus it says, "Who is like Your people Israel, a nation one on earth." When one sins, all are punished, as it says, "Did not Akhan ben Zeraḥ sin in the matter of devoted things, and wrath fell upon all the congregation of Israel,

2. Leviticus Rabba, *Parashat Vayikra* 4, s.v. *Tani Ḥizkiya*.
3. *Midrash Tanḥuma* (Buber), *Parashat Nitzavim* 4.

and he did not perish alone for his iniquity?" (Josh. 22:20). When one is injured, all feel the pain.[4]

The idea of collective destiny and responsibility is more than a metaphor. It is constitutive of Jewish identity. The covenant at Mount Sinai was made not with individuals alone, but with a people – an entire people, righteous and not-yet-righteous alike. This principle has many halakhic ramifications. Among them, for example, is the rule that one person can recite a commandment blessing of behalf of another even though he has already fulfilled the mitzva. As Ritva explains,[5] this is based on the idea that I am responsible for your fulfilment of the commands. Therefore even though I have already fulfilled my personal duty, I can make a blessing over yours and exempt you thereby, because your duty is, in a sense, mine as well.

To be a Jew is to be part of a people, sharing its joys, participating in its griefs, recalling its history, making its hopes my own. That is why our most basic prayers, even our confessions, are in the first-person plural. Our aspiration is not to become a "lonely man of faith," but rather to be part of the *community* of faith. In Judaism, the fundamental encounter is not I-Thou, but rather *We*-Thou.

There is, though, one remarkable feature of this idea as it appears in the rabbinic literature. Let us remind ourselves of the prooftext the rabbis took for the principle of collective responsibility:

> As for those of you who survive, I will send faintness into their hearts in the lands of their enemies. The sound of a driven leaf shall put them to flight, and they shall flee as one flees from the sword, and they shall fall though no one is pursuing them. *They shall stumble over one another,* as if to escape the sword, though no one pursues; and you shall have no power to stand against your enemies. (Lev. 26:36–37)

This is an extraordinary source on which to base the idea. First, it is not the plain sense of the verse. "Stumbling over one another" is not

4. *Mekhilta DeRabbi Shimon bar Yoḥai* to Exodus 19:6.
5. *Ḥiddushei HaRitva,* Rosh HaShana 29a.

425

a description of a nation bound by a sense of shared duty. To the contrary, it is a description of panic, as people fall over one another in their efforts to escape. Second, the passage is not speaking of strength in unity but about weakness and fear. The third difficulty, though, is the most fundamental.

It should not be necessary to search for a prooftext for the idea that the Jewish people flourishes and suffers together. The whole of the Torah from Exodus onward is dedicated to this principle. It is basic to Moses' vision and to the people's experience. They suffered slavery together. They experienced liberation together. If a text were needed, the second paragraph of the *Shema* would do as well as any: "If you are careful to heed My commandments … I will give the rain for your land in its season … and you will eat and be satisfied …. Be careful that your heart not be tempted to go astray …. The land will not give forth its crops, and you will rapidly vanish from the good land that God is giving you" (Deut. 11:13–17). The nation will prosper together or suffer together. Why then search for so recherché a source when the whole Torah testifies to this idea?

The answer, I believe, is fundamental. It is not too much to say that the whole of Jewish history subsequent to the fall of the Second Temple depended on it. The idea that "all Israel are responsible for one another" is not, in and of itself, unusual. It is part of the normal experience of any people living in the same land, under the same political system and sovereign power. When the rain falls, it falls on the righteous and wicked alike. When there is drought, all farmers suffer, whatever their virtue or lack of it. When a nation is at peace, and its economy strong, most people benefit. When government breaks down and anarchy takes its place, the suffering is general and widespread. Within a societal or national context, fate *is* shared. Though some are rich and some poor, some healthy and others stricken by disease, there is a sense in which the general conditions of life affect all. Many things made biblical Israel unique when it was a nation in its own land, but not this.

The concept of collective responsibility was not problematic in biblical times. It became so after the devastating tragedy of defeat at the hands of the Romans – first, when the Temple was destroyed, then, some sixty years later, with the suppression of the Bar Kokhba revolt and the subsequent Hadrianic persecutions. The Jewish people lost its most basic institutions, its autonomy, and its national life. There were no more kings or prophets. There was no Temple, no sacrifices, no central site of collective worship. Little by little, Israel ceased to be the home of most Jews. The intellectual centre moved to Babylon. There were significant Jewish communities elsewhere: in Egypt and many parts of Europe. Israel was no longer a nation in the conventional sense: a people living in a single territory under the same government. It was in exile, but a more profound, scattered exile than Jews had ever known before.

It was then that the question arose in all its force and potential tragedy: *Is Israel still a nation?* If so, how? In what respect? By virtue of what characteristic? Yes, to be sure, Jews shared memories, dreams, prayers. But within two or three generations, memories fade, dreams falter, and prayers, unanswered, slowly lapse into silence. It was the deepest crisis in Jewish history. And it was then that from the very heart of tragedy, the sages rescued a vestige of hope. The covenant of Sinai was still in force. The Jewish people were still bound by its terms. They were therefore still a nation – constituted by the responsibility they had undertaken together, first at Sinai, then on the banks of the Jordan at the end of Moses' life, then again in the last days of Joshua, and subsequently during the period of Israel's kings and in the days of Ezra.

That remained when all else was lost. Since the covenant was still in force, they were bound to God, and being bound to God, they were bound to one another. That is what Saadia Gaon meant when he made his famous remark that "Our people is a people only in virtue of its Torah."[6] No other nation ever constituted itself in such a way. Lacking all the normal prerequisites of nationhood – territory, proximity, sovereignty – Jews remained *even in exile* a people, the world's first global people, the first-ever virtual community, a community not in space but in the mind, held together solely by the invisible filaments of collective belonging, shared fate, and mutual responsibility.

It is now dazzlingly clear why the sages choose their prooftext from this most poignant of all biblical passages, the curses of *Parashat Beḥukkotai*. All other Mosaic texts refer to Israel's fate as a nation in, or journeying towards, its own land. This passage alone spoke of exile and

---

6. Saadia Gaon, *Sefer Emunot VeDeot*, 3.

the "hiding of the face" of God. "*They shall stumble over one another* – one because of another. This teaches that all Israel are responsible for one another" – even in dispersion and defeat, even when they are no longer a nation in any conventional sense.

This strange and apparently unintelligible act of exegesis is one of the most majestic of all leaps of the rabbinic imagination in discerning the deep underlying meaning of Torah. Though they may be scattered across the world, divided by space, language, culture, and outward fortune, Jews remain a people, inextricably bound to one another in and through their covenant with God. Though they are parted physically, they remain united spiritually, and that unity will one day give them the strength to return to God and to the land He gave their ancestors. And so it happened. For almost two thousand years, Jews were sustained as a nation by faith alone. They preserved it, and it preserved them. Thus was a curse turned into a blessing, and a description of weakness turned into a source of indomitable strength.

The Rejection of Rejection

For one reason more than any other, Jewish-Christian relations have been scarred by tragedy: the doctrine known as Supersessionist or Replacement theology, which maintains that Christianity represents God's rejection of the Jewish people, the "old Israel."

It says that God once had a covenant with the people of Israel, but no longer. Hence the Christian name for the Hebrew Bible: "The Old Testament." "Old" here means the testament or covenant once in force but no more. On this view, God no longer wants us to serve Him the Jewish way, through the 613 commandments, but a new way, through a New Testament. His old chosen people were the physical descendants of Abraham. His new chosen people are the spiritual descendants of Abraham, that is, not Jews but Christians.

The results of this doctrine were devastating. They were chronicled after the Holocaust by the French historian and Holocaust survivor Jules Isaac. Subsequently they were set out in works like Rosemary Ruether's *Faith and Fratricide*, and James Carroll's *Constantine's Sword*.[1]

---

1. Rosemary Ruether, *Faith and Fratricide: The Theological Roots of Anti-Semitism* (New York: Seabury Press, 1979); James Carroll, *Constantine's Sword: The Church and the Jews* (Boston: Houghton Mifflin, 2001).

The story they tell is of a doctrine that led to centuries of persecution and to Jews being treated as a pariah people. Reading Jules Isaac's work led to a profound *metanoia* or change of heart on the part of Pope John XXIII, which led ultimately to the Second Vatican Council (1962–65) and the declaration *Nostra Aetate*, which transformed relations between the Catholic Church and the Jews.

I tell the story only because, as we will see, it has been transformed in our time into a narrative of hope. It belongs here because one of the key sources of the untenability of the doctrine appears in this *parasha*, in perhaps the darkest passage of the entire Torah, the curses of *Parashat Beḥukkotai*. Here in the starkest possible terms are set out the consequences of the choices the people Israel must make throughout history. If they stay faithful to God they will be blessed. But if they are faithless the result will be defeat, devastation, destruction, and despair. The rhetoric is relentless, the warning unmistakable, the vision terrifying. Yet at the end come these utterly unexpected lines:

> Yes in spite of this, when they be in the land of their enemies, I will not cast them away, neither will I abhor them, to destroy them utterly, and to break My covenant with them: for I am the Lord their God. But I will for their sakes remember the covenant of their ancestors, whom I brought forth out of the land of Egypt in the sight of the heathen, that I might be their God: I am the Lord. (Lev. 26:44–45)

This is an absolutely fundamental statement. It is the foundation on which Judaism rests. It says that though the people may be faithless to God, God will never be faithless to the people. He may punish them but He will not abandon them. He may judge them harshly but He will not forget their ancestors who followed Him, nor will He break the covenant He made with our ancestors. God does not break His promises even if we break ours. "I the Lord do not change. So you, the descendants of Jacob, are not destroyed" (Mal. 3:6).

There were moments of crisis when Jews feared that all was lost. The Talmud describes a conversation between the Jewish exiles in Babylon and a prophet:

Samuel said: Ten men came and sat down before the prophet. He told them, "Return and repent." They replied, "If a master sells his slave, or a husband divorces his wife, has one a claim upon the other?" Then the Holy One, Blessed Be He, said to the prophet, "Go and say to them: Thus says the Lord, 'Where is your mother's certificate of divorce with which I sent her away? Or to which of My creditors did I sell you? Because of your sins you were sold; because of your transgressions your mother was sent away.'"[2]

The Talmud places in the mouths of the exiles an argument that would later be repeated by Spinoza,[3] that the very fact of exile terminated the covenant between God and the Jewish people. God had rescued them from Egypt and thereby become their only sovereign, their king. But now, having allowed them to suffer exile, He had abandoned them. The result was that they were under the rule of another king, the ruler of Babylon. It was as if He had sold them to another master, or as if Israel were a wife God had divorced. Having sold or divorced them, God could have no further claim on them.

It is precisely this that the verse in Isaiah – "Where is your mother's certificate of divorce with which I sent her away? Or to which of My creditors did I sell you?" – denies. God has not divorced, sold, or abandoned His people. That too is the meaning of the great prophecy in Jeremiah:

This is what the Lord says, he who appoints the sun to shine by day, who decrees the moon and stars to shine by night, who stirs up the sea so that its waves roar – the Lord Almighty is His name: "Only if these decrees vanish from My sight," declares the Lord, "will Israel ever cease to be a nation before Me." This is what the Lord says: "Only if the heavens above can be measured and the foundations of the earth below be searched out will I reject all the descendants of Israel because of all they have done," declares the Lord. (Jer. 31:34–36)

2. Isaiah 50:1; Sanhedrin 105a.
3. Baruch Spinoza, *Tractatus Theologico-Politicus*, part 1, chap. 3.

Isaiah's and Jeremiah's prophecies are in turn based on the promise at the end of the curses of *Parashat Beḥukkotai*: "Yet in spite of this, when they be in the land of their enemies, *I will not cast them away... nor break My covenant with them*: for I am the Lord their God." God may send His people into exile but they remain His people, and He will bring them back.

This is not an isolated verse. A careful examination of the Torah as a whole reveals an underlying principle, namely *the rejection of rejection*. At first, God rejects humanity, saving only Noah, when He sees the world full of violence. Yet after the Flood He vows: "Never again will I curse the ground because of humans, even though every inclination of the human heart is evil from childhood. And never again will I destroy all living creatures, as I have done" (Gen. 8:21). That is the first rejection of rejection.

Then come a series of sibling rivalries. The covenant passes through Isaac not Ishmael, Jacob not Esau. But God sees Hagar and Ishmael's tears. Evidently He hears Esau's also, for He later commands, "Do not despise an Edomite [i.e., a descendant of Esau] because he is your brother" (Deut. 23:8). Finally God brings it about that Levi, one of the children Jacob curses on his deathbed – "Cursed be their anger, so fierce, and their fury, so cruel" (Gen. 49:6) – becomes the father of Israel's spiritual leaders, Moses, Aaron, and Miriam. From now on, all Israel are chosen. That is the second rejection of rejection.

Even when Israel suffer exile and find themselves "in the land of their enemies," they will remain the children of God's covenant, which He will not break because God does not abandon His people. They may be faithless to Him. He will not be faithless to them. That is the third rejection of rejection, stated in this *parasha*, reiterated by Isaiah, Jeremiah, and Ezekiel. The God of Abraham keeps His promises.

Thus the claim on which Replacement or Supersessionist theology is based – that God rejects His people because they rejected Him – is unthinkable in terms of Abrahamic monotheism. God keeps His word even if others break theirs. God does not, will not, abandon His people. The covenant with Abraham, given content at Mount Sinai, and renewed at every critical juncture in Israel's history since, is still in force, undiminished, unqualified, unbreakable.

I have told this story because of what has happened to the Catholic Church after Pope John XIII met Jules Isaac and realised the historic depth and tragic consequences of the *Adversus Judaeos* ("Against the Jews") tradition within the early church. Having set in motion the historic change in the Church's relationship with the Jews, codified in the *Nostra Aetate* declaration (1965), his precedent was followed by Pope John Paul II and his successor Benedict XVI. On September 12, 2013, Pope Francis took the reconsideration further still. In an open letter to the editor of an Italian newspaper, *La Repubblica*, he wrote: "God's fidelity to the close covenant with Israel never failed, and … through the terrible trials of these centuries, the Jews have kept their faith in God. And for this we shall never be sufficiently grateful to them as a Church but also as humanity."

In November 2013, in the course of the declaration *Evangelii Gaudium*, he wrote that "the friendship that has grown" between Jews and Christians "makes us bitterly and sincerely regret the terrible persecutions which they have endured and continue to endure, especially those that have involved Christians." The Catholic Church, he added, holds "the Jewish people in special regard because their covenant with God has never been revoked."

That truth, denied by many within the Church over the course of centuries, has now been firmly acknowledged by Pope Francis in one of the great transformations in religious history. God's promise through Moses and the prophets that His covenant with the Jewish people would never be revoked remains true and is now seen to be so not only by Jews but also by the head of the Catholic Church. The Old Testament is not old. God's relationship with the Jewish people is still alive, still strong. Acknowledgement of this fact has changed the relationship between Christians and Jews and helped begin to wipe away many centuries of tears.

About the Author

A global religious leader, philosopher, author and moral voice for our time, Rabbi Lord Jonathan Sacks served as chief rabbi of the United Hebrew Congregations of the Commonwealth between September 1991 and September 2013.

Described by HRH The Prince of Wales as "a light unto this nation" and by former British Prime Minister Tony Blair as "an intellectual giant," Rabbi Sacks is a frequent academic lecturer and contributor to radio, television, and the press in Britain and around the world. He holds sixteen honorary degrees, including a Doctor of Divinity conferred to mark his first ten years in office as chief rabbi, by the then Archbishop of Canterbury, Lord Carey.

In recognition of his work, Rabbi Sacks has won several international awards, including the Jerusalem Prize in 1995 for his contribution to Diaspora Jewish life, The Ladislaus Laszt Ecumenical and Social Concern Award from Ben-Gurion University in Israel in 2011, the Guardian of Zion Award from the Ingeborg Rennert Center for Jerusalem Studies at Bar-Ilan University, and The Katz Award in recognition of his contribution to the practical analysis and application of Halakha in modern life in Israel in 2014. He was knighted by Her Majesty The

Queen in 2005 and made a Life Peer, taking his seat in the House of Lords in October 2009.

The author of twenty-five books, Rabbi Sacks has published a new English translation and commentary for the *Koren Sacks Siddur*, the first new Orthodox siddur in a generation, as well as powerful commentaries for the *Rosh HaShana, Yom Kippur*, and *Pesaḥ Maḥzorim*. A number of his books have won literary awards, including the Grawemeyer Prize for Religion in 2004 for *The Dignity of Difference*, and National Jewish Book Awards for *A Letter in the Scroll* in 2000, *Covenant & Conversation: Genesis* in 2009, and the *Koren Sacks Pesaḥ Maḥzor* in 2013. His Covenant & Conversation commentaries on the weekly Torah portion are read in Jewish communities around the world.

After achieving first-class honours in philosophy at Gonville and Caius College, Cambridge, he pursued post-graduate studies in Oxford and London, gaining his doctorate in 1981, and receiving rabbinic ordination from Jews' College and Yeshivat Etz Chaim. He served as the rabbi for Golders Green Synagogue and Marble Arch Synagogue in London, before becoming principal of Jews' College.

Born in 1948 in London, he has been married to Elaine since 1970. They have three children and several grandchildren.

www.rabbisacks.org / @RabbiSacks

The fonts used in this book are from the Arno family

The Covenant & Conversation Series:

Genesis: The Book of Beginnings
Exodus: The Book of Redemption
Leviticus: The Book of Holiness
Numbers: The Wilderness Years
Deuteronomy: Renewal of the Sinai Covenant

Ceremony and Celebration
Lessons in Leadership
Essays on Ethics

Maggid Books
The best of contemporary Jewish thought from
Koren Publishers Jerusalem Ltd.